THE POLITICAL THEORY
OF JOHN TAYLOR
OF CAROLINE

John Taylor of Caroline County, Virginia.
(By permission of the Virginia State Library.)

THE POLITICAL THEORY OF JOHN TAYLOR OF CAROLINE

C. William Hill, Jr.

RUTHERFORD • MADISON • TEANECK
FAIRLEIGH DICKINSON UNIVERSITY PRESS
LONDON: ASSOCIATED UNIVERSITY PRESSES

Associated University Presses, Inc.
Cranbury, New Jersey 08512

Associated University Presses
Magdalen House
136-148 Tooley Street
London SE1 2TT, England

Library of Congress Cataloging in Publication Data

Hill, Charles William, 1940-
The political theory of John Taylor of Caroline.

Originally presented as the author's thesis, American
University, 1969.
Bibliography: p.
Includes index.
1. Separation of powers—United States. 2. Federal
government—United States. 3. Taylor, John, 1753-1824.
I. Title.
JK305.H54 1977   320.5′092′4   75-39115
ISBN 0-8386-1902-9

To Jean H. Wheeler (1927–1969), with grateful appreciation
and fond memory

PRINTED IN THE UNITED STATES OF AMERICA

CONTENTS

ACKNOWLEDGMENTS

The author gratefully acknowledges the wise and ruthless advice of Robert E. Goostree, who read this manuscript in the form of a dissertation. The American University School of Government and Public Administration is owed a debt not easily incurred these days: it was willing to recognize that political science is still an eclectic discipline and that theoretical research has its place. The expert, patient, and cheerful assistance provided by the manuscripts sections of the Alderman Library of the University of Virginia, Duke University Library, Library of Congress, Massachusetts Historical Society, New York Historical Society, Virginia Historical Society, and Virginia State Library made much of the primary research for this book possible. Thanks are extended to the editors of *Publius: the Journal of Federalism* for permission to quote from an article that appeared in that publication. The encouragement and financial support of Jean H. Wheeler's "Founders' Project" allowed the author to pursue his interest in Taylor. The sacrifices made by Mary Lou, Billy, and Stewart can only be acknowledged in this weak fashion. Most of all, John Taylor of Caroline needs to be congratulated for daring to be an anchronism. What was out of place in his time may come to rest in ours.

Roanoke College   C. William Hill
Salem, Va.

INTRODUCTION

Among specialists in the field of American intellectual history and political thought there has been wide agreement for at least fifty years that John Taylor of Caroline County, Virginia, deserves the status of a major thinker. Since these commentators have included some of the most prolific and influential writers active in the study of American thought, one is justified in wondering whether Taylor has not already achieved the status of a recognized major writer. It is the thesis of this book that he may have, but for the wrong reasons. The concepts Taylor considered most important have not always been the ones for which he is remembered.

Assuming that Taylor has not received his just recognition as a thinker whose writings possess applicability for a wide range of political issues of contemporary significance, a partial explanation for the lack of appreciation may lie in the sharp disagreement that has existed among Taylor's commentators. Although they have often agreed that Taylor was important, they have seldom agreed why.

One recent writer has said "the truth is that his reputation has suffered very nearly as much at the hands of his friends as those of his detractors."[1] The same writer thought that Taylor's reputation for being linked with states' rights and farming interests has also injured the objective evaluation of his thought. Although the controversy over Taylor has diminished in recent years, this has occurred at the expense of a knowledge of some of his writings, without suggesting what, if anything, can be learned from him that is of importance to the study of politics.

One early group of commentators emphasized Taylor's connection to agrarianism and an economic theory of politics.

Notes for this chapter begin on p. 22.

9

Charles Beard led the way by the effusive praise that he heaped upon Taylor and the extended discussion he gave to Taylor's works in the *Economic Origins of Jeffersonian Democracy* (1915).[2] Beard thought Taylor's *Inquiry* deserved to be ranked with the top two or three political works ever produced in the United States because it attempted to put egalitarian political democracy on sound economic foundations. Beard enlisted Taylor in a personal struggle against the domination of American life by unresponsible economic interests. He agreed with Jefferson's judgment that Taylor's *Inquiry* was the "textbook of agrarian political science, conceived in opposition to capitalism and dedicated to a republic of small farmers."[3] His discussions of Taylor concentrated on the latter's attacks upon economic elites and consisted largely of quotations from Taylor. Beard was especially delighted with the list of the members of Congress who belonged to the pecuniary aristocracy in 1793, which he thought Taylor had authored. Such a list was a form of analysis that Beard himself had used in his *Economic Interpretation of the Constitution of the United States* (1913). Although Beard considered Taylor an agrarian democrat, he made little attempt to discuss his agrarian writings.[4]

Beard's deficiency in this respect was corrected by Avery Craven and William Grampp.[5] Craven discussed Taylor's techniques of cultivation from the viewpoint of an agricultural historian, while Grampp discussed Taylor's contributions to economic theory. Both considered Taylor a significant thinker, but ultimately deficient in his grasp of technical details. Craven found that Taylor's theory of manures and enclosing simply did not work for anyone but Taylor, who had overrated the fertility of soil as a factor in agricultural production. Grampp awarded Taylor high marks for his understanding that increases in currency through bank loans increased the level of prices, affecting a redistribution of income much like taxation; and that the rate of return on banking investments diverted the capital investment that would have gone to agriculture. Grampp thought, however, that much of Taylor's attack upon funding was based on a misreading of Adam Smith, a mistrust of Hamilton, and an inadequate understanding of the purpose of public debt. Both Craven and Grampp neglected to push their criticism of Taylor beyond their own areas of technical expertise in order to determine *why* he fell short.[6]

The controversy that has raged over the Beard thesis has

affected subsequent interpretations of Taylor. An inversion of roles has occurred in the choosing of sides, however. Some of Beard's critics, such as Forrest McDonald, have attempted to refute him by using the methods of economic analysis that Beard popularized. Others, such as Arthur Schlesinger, Jr., have attempted to defend Beard by using more conventional politico-historical studies, which leave the authors free to defend the impact of ideas and individuals upon events.[7]

The group of writers who agreed with Beard's interpretation of Taylor as an anti-aristocratic defender of the disadvantaged against irresponsible elites have seldom used Beard's economic analyses to defend their position. Nor did Beard analyze Taylor economically. For example, Vernon Parrington's treatment of Taylor in *Main Currents in American Thought* very closely paralleled Beard's and even quoted from Beard in summarizing Taylor's contribution.[8] Charles Wiltse considered Taylor's work the economic expression of Jeffersonian aristocratic individualism, a point of view similar to Beard's.[9] Richard Current considered Taylor, like Calhoun, to have been interested in class war, but thought Taylor's conception of the struggle to have been more forward-looking and ecumenical, including all productive interests.[10] Benjamin F. Wright's discussion of Taylor avoided, in general, the economic arguments and emphasized Taylor's ideas on the division of powers in order to achieve self-government, political equality, popular sovereignty, and freedom of thought.[11] Arthur Schlesinger, Jr., was sympathetic to Taylor's fears of industrialism, and did not find fault with his critique of the Federalist Party, but pointed out that "events passed on, hardly pausing to refute him."[12] Taylor's friends, then, seem to have advanced the knowledge of his work little beyond the point that Beard reached, and in reaching that point were able to preserve Taylor's reputation as a democrat only by agreeing that he was an anachronism.

Critics of Beard's evaluation of Taylor have used Beard's method to point out that Taylor was a wealthy man, thereby casting suspicion on him as a possible apologist for the large planter class. After Beard, much significant research on Taylor took this approach. Bernard Drell dug into the social and economic background of Caroline County and decided that Taylor was the defender of a conservative social order that may have been dominant in Caroline County but that was out of touch with the rest of the country.[13] Manning Dauer and Hans

Hammond followed Drell's lead by arguing that Taylor was consistently the advocate of measures that would have helped only large landowners.[14] He was not, in their view, as much of a friend of popular government as Jefferson and Madison were. George Dangerfield should also be considered with critics because he suggested that Taylor was curiously blind to aristocracies in his own backyard and that industrialization made his ideas irrelevant.[15]

The most extensive previous study on Taylor was written by Eugene Mudge (1939).[16] Mudge's book however, was neither an economic analysis nor a historical study, but an elaboration of Taylor's writings with a heavy emphasis on the *Inquiry*. Mudge's conclusions were compatible with the anti-Beard group just discussed: Taylor was the apologist for the tidewater landed gentry. Dauer and Hammond, who did not disagree with Mudge's assessment of Taylor as an ideologist, said that Mudge's *Social Philosophy of John Taylor of Caroline* was "competent and useful as a compilation," but "not satisfactory in terms of putting Taylor in his setting in the field of political theory."[17] Stephen Kurtz said that "Mudge has paraphrased his works and added about one hundred letters to the result."[18] Mudge included few comparisons of Taylor with other Jeffersonians, particularly the states' rights school, and compared him with few European theorists. Mudge's conception of Taylor was a static one that allowed little possibility for change in position as Taylor responded to changing circumstances. For all these reasons, Mudge's work is not very useful for the development of hypotheses, although it is a quick introduction to Taylor's major works.

While the Beardites and the anti-Beardites were quarreling over the proper economic interpretation of Taylor, a third group was preoccupied with the view that the heart of his thought amounted to a states' rights defense of the Constitution. In this opinion they followed the lead of Gaillard Hunt, who was impressed with the fact that Federalist politicians had given Taylor just cause to doubt their commitment to the Union.[19] This view was endorsed by William Dodd, who termed Taylor the "prophet of secession." [20] Charles Wiltse's interpretation of Taylor was not limited to his theory of states' rights, but it does credit him with formulating the doctrine that the Constitution was a compact between the states and with convincing Jefferson of the advisability of using the Virginia Resolutions to dramatize this doctrine.[21] Various surveys of American or Southern thought have also focused on Taylor's theory of states' rights, including Jesse Carpenter's, which linked Taylor with Spencer Roane; Alan Grimes's, which also discussed Taylor's theory of aristocracy; Alpheus Mason and Richard Leach's, which said that "Taylor carried the states' rights doctrine to the very brink of secession";[22] and Saul Padover's, which said that Taylor was a "states' righter par excellence" who "disliked government altogether."[23] August Spain's study of Calhoun offers Taylor as a predecessor of the theory of the concurrent majority through his advocacy of a mutual state-federal veto; and through his equivocation on whether states possessed sovereignty, whether it had been divided between the states and the federal government, or whether sovereignty existed at all.[24] In summary, the interpretation of Taylor as an advocate of states' rights, nullification, or secession is one that continues. Yet, these interpretations suffer because of the monolithic unity they seemed to see in states' rights theories. None of these critics, for example, has actually defined what Taylor meant by the term *states' rights*. The assumption seems to have been that the twentieth-century understanding of the term is applicable to Taylor's conception. The fact is that Taylor seldom used the term.

John Taylor was reviewed by yet another group of commentators. The members of this group did not share a common approach or set of biases, and their treatment of Taylor is more evenhanded and balanced than that of the first three groups.

Louis Hartz, for example, has resolved the dispute over the Beard thesis by taking both sides. He pointed out that the bitter argument between Taylor and Alexander Hamilton was really a falling-out of capitalists, because the feudal system of agriculture never had taken root in the United States. Taylor himself firmly rejected the inheritance laws that gave feudal institutions a secure basis. For Hartz, Taylor stood at the head of a long line of agrarian protestors who denounced capitalism while practicing it; who preached the common interests of labor while looking fearfully over their shoulders for the mob.[25] Yehoshua Arieli added to this discussion by pointing out the similarity between Taylor's conception of economic groups and that of Destutt de Tracy, whose idea of the unity of all economic processes may have allowed Taylor to connect the American Revolution's ideals of the pursuit of happiness with the self-regulating mechanisms of the marketplace.[26] Such a view was hardly compatible with class warfare. Arieli maintained that Jeffersonianism must be distinguished from socialist thought, not just because of its disinterest in class war, but because of the primacy it gave to political institutions in discussions of economic exploitation. In summary, the debate over Taylor's role as either the defender of a privileged class or the proponent of class struggle remains unresolved. On the one hand, his rhetoric could be borrowed by the disadvantaged, as Beard argued; but on the other hand, he may only have intended to defend an aristocratic society as Drell, Dauer and Hammond, and Dangerfield have stated.

Grant McConnell has written the most sympathetic recent account of Taylor's ideas and defended him against the charges of irrelevance leveled by Schlesinger and Dangerfield.[27] It does not matter, McConnell argued, that Taylor's solution to the problems of his time was not accepted and that time passed him by. Where does one go to find a thinker who has not been similarly treated? Instead, it should be recognized that Taylor was generally democratic in his orientation, if he is allowed the following major assumptions: that the cause of political conflict can be almost wholly explained by economic cleavages; that the vast majority of the population continue to be farmers; and that an abundant supply of land continues to exist. One paid penalties for such a form of democracy, McConnell thought, because it denied the "value of diversity in democratic life."[28] In spite of the fact that the United States has not known the kind of socially homogenous democracy envisioned by Taylor, that ideal allowed him to write warnings about the dangers of factions, which McConnell offered as having highest current relevance.

Two other recent commentators on Taylor have tended to disagree with each other. On the one hand, Loren Baritz maintained that Taylor was a golden-age philosopher who, almost alone among nineteenth-century American thinkers, had a vision of a time when the United States had been better. [29] In many ways Baritz's discussion of Taylor's ideas on political structure is the best yet, for it recognizes the primacy Taylor gave federalism over separation of powers. Taylor remained a tragic figure for Baritz, however, for the Virginian had devoted his talents to the defense of a way of life that was drawing to an end. Thus, Baritz returned the argument to its stage before McConnell, but without accepting the position of Schlesinger et al. that Taylor was irrelevant. Without specifically mentioning whom he had in mind, Baritz observed that many Southerners had fallen under Taylor's influence and "his tenacity became a sectional mood, a mood which itself was no small contribution to the disaster he had feared."[30] Thus, in the short run Taylor helped convince the entire South to adopt values that were doomed in the long run. Taylor was anything but irrelevant in Baritz's view, and therein lay the tragedy.

A different view was taken by Keith Bailor, who emphasized Taylor's views on slavery more than any previous commentator.[31] Bailor emphasized the sense of personal danger that slaveholders shared after the uprising in Santo Domingo and after the 1820 Gabriel Conspiracy. Taylor's agrarian writings were, in his view, a response to this danger and an attempt to turn the moral liability of slavery into an economic asset for his native state, then in the throes of depression. In the process, an evolutionary settlement could be devised that would allow the gradual separation of slaves from white civilization, and their colonization in some appropriately remote place (but not Africa, which Taylor considered no secure home for freedmen who could be sold into slavery again). Bailor's attitude toward Taylor considered his impact as moderately progressive in the short run but a failure in the long run, since the South did not accept his solution. Instead, the South combined the causes of slavery and states' rights, a connection Taylor did not make. In so doing, the South was being less progressive in its socioeconomic theories than Taylor, who wanted to ease the parting of the races. Viewed in this light, Taylor was not an anachronistic Jeremiah of a golden-age civilization as Baritz and Schlesinger seemed to imply, but a responsible and moderate planter who was attempting to apply his best talents to a grievous social problem while keeping an eye on his own self-interest.

All of the previous commentators have added to our knowledge about Taylor. Most of them have used his writings as a tool for understanding the historical events of his time. This is certainly a justifiable and useful practice, but it may lead to an inadequate understanding of the totality of what a thinker intended. The problem is not that everything that has been written about Taylor is wrong. It is simply that previous studies have not emphasized some of the concepts that Taylor considered crucial. This study attempts to determine whether

Taylor's writings were more than a collection of pieces and had the internal consistency and explanatory power sufficient to warrant considering him a major thinker in his own right.

To evaluate Taylor's thought as a whole it will be helpful to examine a central doctrine that is discussed throughout his writings. Without such a unifying principle it is doubtful that a thinker could develop a theoretical framework of any important proportions. The concept of *the division of power* seems to have been the doctrine that Taylor considered central.

The hypotheses used in this study either define the meaning of division of power or relate it to the other concepts used by Taylor. *The division of power* was a term used by Taylor to refer to the fragmentation of governmental authority in order to ensure its electoral responsibility and the guaranteeing of its existence through physical force. This doctrine differed from the simple belief that liberty was the inverse of centralized power. Taylor's view of division included both a fear of centralized power, and a desire to provide a method by which government could he held accountable to the will of the people. He strongly felt that fragmentation alone was not the answer, and never accepted the thesis that the organized clash of groups through governmental processes was any insurance against tyranny. Moreover, he was keenly aware of the extent to which governmental agencies could become the captives of organized groups. Taylor's belief in the division of power could have been derived naturally from the intellectual influences of his background. It led him to examine the subversive designs of organized minorities, such as political parties and aristocracies. He argued that the increase in man's knowledge that had made such aristocratic elites unnecessary had also popularized the principles of the division of power. In response to this popular understanding, American governmental practices had rejected certain age-old constitutional devices as insufficient guards for liberty. The division of power was necessary for the limitation of governmental power, and, once division was secure, such constitutional devices as election, rotation, bicameralism, and separated powers could be retained or altered as circumstances required. Division of power also was important for the effects it had upon the morals of the governors and governed alike. When division of power was working properly, it both freed men to study the laws of nature in order to apply them for the good of society, and prevented government from undertaking activities that would violate the laws of nature. Division encouraged the best qualities in human nature, rather than exciting the worst, as happened under separated, checked, and balanced powers.

Thomas Jenkin has offered a conceptual framework that contains parts that are relevant to this attempt to evaluate Taylor's thought.[32] Jenkin has divided normative thinkers into ideologists, theorists, and philosophers. Ideologists are apologists for a social, political, or economic status quo. As such, they are highly responsive to events happening around them, and select from their experiences to justify their ideological positions. The ideas offered by ideologists therefore, have ulterior motives behind them. Philosophers, in contrast, are concerned with the totality of human experience and consequently speculate on both current events and abstract ultimate questions such as the nature of truth, the meaning of history, the limits of human will, how persons know, and the nature of any supernatural forces. Philosophers, like ideologists, may have axes to grind, but their biases often are more rooted in a protective regard for their intellectual system rather than merely in their positions as members of a class. One must admit, however, that the social positions even of philosophers may color their motives (e.g., Hegel and the Prussian state, Plato and Dion, Aristotle and Alexander, Cicero as thinker and Cicero as statesman, Hobbes and any convenient sovereign). Somewhere between ideologists and philosophers are theorists who respond to current political events, but who also offer generalizations that are not necessarily limited to their own cultural situation. These generalizations stop short, however, of the cosmic speculations that are the specialty of the philosopher.

A few examples might help distinguish these three types of thinkers. Ideologists who have defended a status quo with little apparent regard for advancing human knowledge about politics could include: James the First; Robert Filmer; Walter Scott; Robert Fenno, the Federalist editor; Philip Freneau, the Republican editor; and possibly Alexander Hamilton, who also might qualify as a theorist. Theorists include many of the names listed in the tables of contents of political theory texts: Machiavelli, Harrington, Montesquieu, Burke, John Adams, or Madison and Thomas Paine, who might also qualify as ideologists. Philosophers include familiar names such as Plato, Aristotle,

Hobbes, Rousseau, Hume, Hegel—and Locke, assuming that his doctrines of natural rights and human perception do not require him to be considered both as a theorist and as a philosopher.

It should be apparent from this listing that the boundaries are hazy between these groups, and that individuals may fall into several, according to what is being written and why. The difficulty with John Taylor is that too often he has been considered merely as an ideologist. Most of Taylor's previous commentators seem to have had a restricted view of his ideas, leading them to typify him as primarily an agrarian, a Jeffersonian democrat, a tidewater ideologist, or a states' righter. Such abbreviated designations are sometimes helpful, but are seldom precise enough to do justice to the full scope of what Taylor advocated. Taylor was both an ideologist *and* a theorist, and even his ideological writings, such as *A Defence of the Measures of the Administration of Thomas Jefferson,* were generally consistent with those writings in which he consciously avoided defending a social order, as in his *Tyranny Unmasked.*

To have any pretensions of qualifying as a theorist according to the Jenkin classification, a writer must concern himself with a fairly wide range of issues. Which issues are discussed depend on the theorist, but the politics of his time, the role of leadership in society, the structure and processes of government, and certain aspects of moral philosophy that provide the basis for discrimination in political choices probably cannot be ignored. Happily for the purposes of this study, John Taylor devoted major portions of his writings to each of these topics.

Each of these topics will be discussed in a separate chapter after an attempt has been made to determine Taylor's intellectual influences. This sequence of discussion corresponds roughly to the order in which Taylor addressed these issues. Thus, his first writings were on political parties, his middle writings on aristocracy and governmental structure, and his later writings on federalism and dangers to the Union. His writings on agrarianism were spread throughout his career, but are studied to their best advantage after a survey of Taylor's governmental system, when one is aware of the political responsibilities for which Taylor was attempting to free the planter.

It must be noted, however, that Taylor was more of a circular theorist than a linear one; that is, there was very little evolution in his basic ideas from their first statement to the last. Although he sometimes switched the topic being discussed, he did not change his fundamental assumptions. There was very little linear development in his thought, which was not true of some of his contemporaries, such as Calhoun, Jefferson, Madison, or Randolph of Roanoke, who each underwent significant evolution in his thought as he reacted to contemporary events or simply changed his mind. Taylor changed the topics of his discussion, but it will be demonstrated that he changed his basic point of view very little.

The methodology used here consisted primarily of a textual analysis of Taylor's writings. Although his consistency has been overrated, it is true that he was a fairly static philosopher who applied basically the same theoretical framework to any political problem.[33] Since consistency is an important quality in a theorist who proposed wide-ranging but integrated political conceptualizations, several procedures were used to test Taylor's. One was the chronological tracing of important concepts through all of Taylor's writings in order to see if any changes occurred. A second procedure was the comparing of Taylor's public and private writings to see if he advocated the same things to both friends and strangers. Moreover, Taylor's actual activities as both a public official and private citizen have been compared to his doctrines for the same reason. Finally, the position of the *Inquiry* in Taylor's works deserves special consideration. Since it was written over a twenty-year period, it can provide a check for his *Arator* essays and his private letters written during the same period.[34]

Taylor's writings are considered below as consisting of three strata. There were the writings he prepared for a general audience in order to criticize political problems threatening the Jeffersonian Republican Party. Next were his letters to friends and acquaintances. Third were his works of serious political theory, which he prepared at a more leisurely pace and in which he discussed topics in greater detail and more dispassionately than in the other two groups of writings.

In the first group of sources fall Taylor's shorter writings, such as his *Definition of Parties* (1794), *An Enquiry into the Principles and Tendencies of Certain Public Measures* (1794), *An Argument Respecting the Constitutionality of the Carriage Tax* (1795), and *A Defence of the Measures of the Administration of Thomas Jefferson* (1804). In this group also belong such disputed writings as *Cautionary Hints to Congress* (1795) and two Caroline County broadsides that Taylor may have written.[35] Legislative debates and court cases have also been considered as a part of this group because of their emphasis upon political issues current at the time. All of these writings share certain characteristics. They addressed political issues which were relevant to the time, and none of them was very long. Even more important is the fact that they were written fairly early in Taylor's career, when he still may have harbored political ambitions. In these writings, much more than his later ones, he was willing to rely on the authority of others as a source of information and argumentation.

Taylor's letters, the second group of sources, are rich in political commentary, owing to his generation's habit of using letters as a vehicle for expressing political views. Among his correspondents, Wilson Cary Nicholas, Henry Tazewell, James Monroe, and Thomas Ritchie most often received letters containing capsule summaries of political theory. Nicholas was Taylor's ear to the Jefferson administration, and Taylor often complained to Nicholas, who owed him money, rather than bother Jefferson or Madison. Tazewell was a trusted confidant and Taylor was very candid in letters to him. In them Taylor attacked the Adams administration and laid out his plan for implementing the Virginia Resolutions—a plan that he did not share even with Jefferson. James Monroe was Taylor's young Alexander, and Taylor carefully coached his protégé, attempting to refine his views and protect his reputation so the doctrines of "Old Republicanism" could be carried to the highest councils.[36] Thomas Ritchie, on the other hand, suffered the full blast of Taylor's wrath when they clashed over the presidential election of 1808. In his replies to Ritchie's letters published in the Richmond *Enquirer* (Ritchie's newspaper and the organ of Madisonian Republicanism in the Upper South at the time), Taylor began to define what he meant by a *division of powers* and why James Madison's contributions to the *Federalist* had made him unworthy of support. Although Taylor's letters to Jefferson were deferential in tone and dealt usually with personal and agricultural matters, the one dated June 25, 1798, was the most concise summary of Taylor's early thought and waxed eloquent on the nature of man and the kinds of governmental devices necessary to preserve liberty.[37]

The third group contains Taylor's major works: *Arator* (four editions, the last dated 1818), *An Inquiry into the Principles of the Government of the United States* (finished November 17, 1811, but published in 1814), *Construction Construed* (1820), *Tyranny*

Unmasked (1822), and *New Views of the Constitution* (1823).[38] Taylor regarded the first two of these as the twin pillars of his theoretical system, describing in detail his thoughts on the economic and political life of a republic. Although *Arator* takes the form of a series of essays, they are linked conceptually and Taylor considered them a unit. The last three books were attempts by Taylor to apply his system to challenges facing the development of republican institutions. *Construction Construed* was a detailed exegesis of Marshall's decision in *McCulloch v. Maryland*, and as such was an extended discussion of the relative powers of states and the federal government. *Tyranny Unmasked* was an attack upon a congressional committee's report on manufacturing, dated January 15, 1821. *Tyranny Unmasked* is organized as a point-by-point refutation of the committee's thesis that protective tariffs were beneficial. *New Views* was Taylor's attempt to explain and defend what he considered to be the true intentions of the framers of the United States Constitution, who had been defamed by the authors of the *Federalist*. Taylor drew upon the recently published journal of the 1787 Framing Convention and Yates's notes as sources for *New Views*.

There are some generalizations that apply to all three groups of Taylor's writings. First of all, he was hardly a child prodigy. His first pamphlet was published when he was forty, after he had had nearly a dozen years experience in state and national governmental service. He was not a closet philosopher, and the claim sometimes advanced that he owed the consistency of this theories to his lack of practical experience is untenable. A third observation is that Taylor often allowed the arguments of others to frame the sequence and even the substance of his writings. The *Inquiry* was manifestly an attack upon John Adams, but its approach was duplicated in most of Taylor's works. Only the passages in *Arator* dealing with agricultural experiments are relatively free of the open or implied influence of an unseen antagonist. This manner of argumentation probably came from Taylor's training as a lawyer. It had several effects upon his works and their influence. It made them difficult to read, for Taylor's reluctance to acknowledge the intellectual debts he had outstanding made it difficult to tell who was being criticized in particular contexts. Taylor's crusading zest for intellectual refutations also caused him to become known as an abstract philosopher removed from practicalities: he was respected for his intellect, but dismissed by his enemies and patronized by his friends (such as Randolph of Roanoke, who called him "Tris-megistus" after the ancient diety of occult sciences). Finally, Taylor's defensive tone thoughout all his writings kept him from specifying completely the governmental program that he favored. As with many writers, he was surer of what he did not like than of what he wanted.[39]

A final generalization that can be made about all of Taylor's writings is that his working habits seem to have been sporadic. Within a space of one year (1794-95) he may have written and published four important short pamphlets. Then he lapsed into a silence that lasted until his somewhat half-hearted defense of Jefferson in 1804. He leisurely took twenty years to complete his critique of John Adams's *Defence*, but completed three major books within three years (1820-1823) while in his seventies. Without any explanation from Taylor, it is difficult to evaluate the significance of these peculiarities, but partial explanations may be that his early works were clearly partisan, his *Inquiry* a 650-page labor of love that would have taken a sizable portion of anyone's life to write (and still does to read), and his last three books a final desperate attempt to save the country from itself. The drive to complete the final three books may have come from the convictions that nothing but political action could save agriculture; that anyone as old as he could scarcely be attacked for a selfish interest in the theories defended in his last three books; and that his political idol James Monroe had proved to be as much of a disappointment in office as Jefferson and Madison.

Notes to Introduction

1. McConnell, "John Taylor and the Democratic Tradition," *Western Political Quarterly* 4 (March 1951): 19.

2. Charles A. Beard, *Economic Origins of Jeffersonian Democracy* (New York: The Free Press, 1965).

3. Ibid., p. 322.

4. Ibid., p. 322. Beard assumed along with most scholars, that Taylor had authored the list of bank stockholders; see n. 35 below.

5. Avery O. Craven, *Soil Exhaustion as a Factor in the Agricultural History of Virginia and Maryland, 1606–1860* (Urbana Ill.: University of Illinois Press, 1926); and William D. Grampp, "John Taylor: Economist of Southern Agrarians," *Southern Economic Journal* 11 (January 1944): 255–68.

6. Craven, *Soil Exhaustion*, pp. 14–16, 81; Grampp, "John Taylor", pp. 262–63.

7. Forrest McDonald, *We the People* (Chicago: University of Chicago Press, 1958); Arthur M. Schlesinger, Jr., *The Age of Jackson* (Boston: Little, Brown and Company, 1946).

8. Vernon L. Parrington, *Main Currents in American Thought,* (New York: Harcourt, Brace and Company, 1930), 2: 15.

9. Charles M. Wiltse, *The Jeffersonian Tradition in American Democracy* (New York: Hill and Wang, Inc., 1960), p. 217.

10. Richard N. Current, "John C. Calhoun, Philosopher of Reaction," *Antioch Review 3* (June 1943): 223–34.

11. Benjamin F. Wright, "The Philosopher of Jeffersonian Democracy," *American Political Science Review* 22 (November 1928): 870–92.

12. Schlesinger, *Age of Jackson,* p. 25.

13. Bernard Drell, "John Taylor and the Preservation of an Old Social Order," *Virginia Magazine of History and Biography* 46 (1938): 286, 292–3.

14. Manning Dauer and Hans Hammond, "John Taylor: Democrat or Aristocrat?", *Journal of Politics* 6 (November 1944): 391, 402–3.

15. George Dangerfield, *The Era of Good Feelings* (New York: Harcourt, Brace and World, Inc., 1963), pp. 190–96. Dangerfield eloquently concluded that Taylor was an anachronism in his own time: "Was he not a forerunner who succeeded the Messiah, a prophet who foretold the past?" (p. 193).

16. Eugene Mudge, *The Social Philosophy of John Taylor of Caroline* (New York: Columbia University Press, 1939).

17. Dauer and Hammond, p. 382.

18. Stephen G. Kurtz, *The Presidency of John Adams: The Collapse of Federalism, 1795–1800* (New York: A. S. Barnes and Company, Inc., 1957), p. 436.

19. Gaillard Hunt, *Dsiunion Sentiment in Congress in 1794* (Washington, D. C.: W. H. Lowdermilk and Company, 1905).

20. William E. Dodd, "John Taylor of Caroline, Prophet of Secession," *The John P. Branch Historical Papers of Randolph-Macon College* 2 (June 1908): 214.

21. Wiltse, pp. 218–21.

22. Alpheus Thomas Mason and Richard H. Leach, *In Quest of Freedom* (Englewood Cliffs, New Jersey: Prentice-Hall, Inc. 1959), p. 223. Also see Jesse Thomas Carpenter, *The South as a Conscious Minority, 1789–1861* (New York: New York University Press, 1930), pp. 72, 202; Alan P. Grimes, *American Political Thought* (New York: Henry Holt and Company, 1955), p. 167.

23. Saul K. Padover, *The Genius of America* (New York: McGraw-Hill Book Company, Inc., 1960) p. 116.

24. August O. Spain, *The Political Theory of John C. Calhoun* (New York: Bookman Associates, 1951), pp. 54, 170–71.

25. Louis Hartz, *The Liberal Tradition in America* (New York: Harcourt, Brace and World, Inc., 1955), pp. 124–25.

26. Yehoshua Arieli, *Individualism and Nationalism in American Ideology* (Cambridge, Mass.: Harvard University Press, 1964), p. 177.

27. McConnell, pp. 30–31.

28. Ibid.

29. Loren Baritz, *City on a Hill* (New York: John Wiley and Sons, Inc., 1964).

30. Ibid., pp. 202–3.

31. Keith M. Bailor, "John Taylor of Caroline: Continuity, Change, and Discontinuity in Virginia's Sentiments toward Slavery, 1790–1820," *Virginia Magazine of History and Biography* 75 (July 1967): 302–4.

32. Thomas P. Jenkin, *The Study of Political Theory* (Garden City, N. Y.: Doubleday and Company, Inc., 1955).

33. Among those emphasizing Taylor's consistency have been Beard, *Economic Origins,* p. 322; Dauer and Hammond, p. 402; Hunt, p. 5; McConnell, p. 23; Spain p. 51; Wiltse, p. 218; Benjamin F. Wright, "Jeffersonian Democracy", p. 889.

34. Letter from John Taylor to Wilson Cary Nicholas, 16 September 1802, Wilson Cary Nicholas Papers, Library of Congress, Washington, D. C.

35. After the first full citations, all of Taylor's works will be referred to by these short titles: *Definition of Parties* (Philadelphia: Francis Bailey, 1794), as *Definition; An Enquiry into the Principles and Tendencies of Certain Public Measures* (Philadelphia: Thomas Dobson, 1794), as *Enquiry; An Argument Respecting the Constitutionality of the Carriage Tax* (Richmond, Va.: Augustine Davis, 1795), as *Argument; A Defence of the Measures of the Administration of Thomas Jefferson* (Washington, D. C.: Samuel H. Smith, 1804), as *Defence; Cautionary Hints to Congress* (Philadelphia: William H. Woodward, 1795), as "Columbus"; "To the Freeholders of Essex, Caroline, King and Queen, and King William" (Fredericksburg, Va.: n.p., 1803), as "Pocion," with a second broadside with the same title by "We the People" (Fredericksburg, Va.: n.p., 1803), as "We the People." The case for Taylor's authorship of the latter three documents is anything but firm. The University of Virginia library lists him as one of three possible authors of *Cautionary Hints to Congress,* the other two being James Madison and Governor James Wood. The Library of Congress Union Catalogue entry for this work bears the penciled notation that St. George Tucker (1752–1827) probably was the author of this and two other pamphlets from the period written by "Columbus." C. L. Riley, the notation continues, was writing a thesis at Duke University on the subject at the time (1935–36.). Subsequent correspondence has failed to turn up such a thesis at Duke. The University of Virginia gives no authors for "Pocion" and "We the People" other than Taylor. If Taylor did not actually write these three works, they are certainly compatible with his positions. Nevertheless, assertions in the following pages that are based on these disputed works are made with care. Charles Beard assumed that Taylor had written *An Examination of the Late Proceedings in Congress Respecting the Official Conduct of the Secretary of the Treasury* (Richmond, Va.: n.p., 1793), as had most authorities until the article by Edmund and Dorothy Smith Berkely, "The Piece Left Behind," *Virginia Magazine of History and Biography* 75 (January 1967): 174–80.

36. Taylor's letters to Nicholas are contained largely in the Edgehill-Randolph collection in the library of the University of Virginia, Charlottesville; the Tazewell correspondence in the Tazewell Papers in the Virginia State Library, Richmond; and most of the Monroe correspondence included in the collection, "John Taylor Correspondence," William E. Dodd, *The John P. Branch Historical Papers of Randolph-Macon College,* 2 (June 1908): 253–353, hereafter referred to as "Correspondence."

37. The letters to Ritchie are in the collection of Taylor letters edited by E. C. Stanard, *A Pamphlet Containing a Series of Letters Written by Colonel John Taylor, of Caroline, to Thomas Ritchie, Editor of the "Enquirer" . . . Richmond in Consequence of an Unwarrantable Attack Made by that Editor upon Colonel Taylor* (Richmond, Va.: E. C. Stanard, 1809), hereafter referred to as *Pamphlet.*

38. John Taylor, *Arator* (Petersburg, Va.: John M. Carter, 1818). The 1818 edition was used for this study. *An Inquiry into the Principles and Policy of the Government of the United States* (Fredericksburg, Virginia: Green and Cady, 1814), hereafter as *Inquiry; Construction Construed and Constitutions Vindicated* (Richmond, Va.: Shepherd and Pollard, 1820), hereafter as *Construction; Tyranny Unmasked* (Washington, D.C.: Davis and Force, 1822), hereafter as *Tyranny; New Views of the Constitution of the United States* (Washington, D.C.: Way and Gideon, 1823), hereafter as *New Views.* Photocopies of all of these works, as well

as the *Enquiry,* are available from University Microfilms and were the documents used in this study. The *Inquiry* has been reprinted twice. The Yale University Press edition, 1950, is now out of print. Loren Baritz has recently edited an edition (Bobbs-Merrill, 1969). Both the Yale and Baritz editions have paginations that run behind the first edition. In the text below one should be careful to distinguish the *Enquiry* (1794) from the *Inquiry* (1814).

39. See letters of John Randolph to James Mercer Garnett, January 3, 1820, and April 26, 1824, Letters of John Randolph of Roanoke to James Mercer Garnett, in Transcripts, Library of Congress, Washington, D.C.

THE POLITICAL THEORY
OF JOHN TAYLOR
OF CAROLINE

1
THE INTELLECTUAL AND SOCIAL BACKGROUND

ALTHOUGH most persons would agree that a study of the background of a theorist is helpful to an understanding of his writings, the contributions of this background often depend on which theorist is under study. In the case of John Taylor the reasons for studying his background result from the probable influence of it on his own ideas, the biases attributed to him by others, and the importance he gave to it himself.

It is difficult for anyone to stand apart from the historical and intellectual forces that produced and sustain him. Persons who share the same historical tradition and similar problems are often impressed with the cogency of each other's ideas. On the other hand, as Camus has observed, even in rebellion one acknowledges and dignifies by his protest the condition opposed. An examination of the intellectual forces that affected Taylor's life provides some insight into why he took certain intellectual positions.

The background of John Taylor is also important because of what some have put into his foreground. Most of Taylor's commentators have agreed that his status as a member of the tidewater landed gentry was an important influence upon his ideas. While some have considered him an apologist for tidewater culture, and others an agrarian reformer attacking special privileges, both groups agree that his milieu was important. More than any of his contemporaries, perhaps, Taylor is

Notes for this chapter begin on p. 54.

considered by modern commentators to be the ideologist of an
economic class. Since a theorist's influence includes both what he
said and what most have come to accept as his meaning, a study
of John Taylor is forced to deal with biographical influences.

Finally, a study of Taylor's background is important because
he said it was. He implied its importance when he advocated the
benefits of local economic and political institutions. He demonstrated its importance when he frequently drew upon examples from personal experience or Virginia governing practices to illustrate points. He flaunted its importance when he
issued warnings to his readers that his views might be colored
by his biases, and that appropriate caution must be taken. Any
study of Taylor, then, begins with biographical influences
because they seem to have had an impact, some have claimed
they did, and Taylor admitted that they did. This is revealed in a
study of the intellectual influences on Taylor, his social class
status, and his occupational activities.

Taylor's position as a child of the American Enlightenment
presents difficulties for a biographical survey. On the one hand,
the hallmark of the Enlightenment was the free play of human
reason.[1] The permeating expectation was that each individual
could use his mental facilities to govern his own life and could
improve his judgment by testing it against the judgments of
others collectively expressed through organizations. Even in
organizations each man was to decide for himself. Appeals to
authority and recognition of nonrational and irrational
influences were scarce. This was especially true for Taylor, who
was in conscious rebellion against the use of borrowed theories
as a form of argument.[2] This reluctance to borrow may account
for the rich diversity among the opinions of Enlightenment
theorists who started from similar assumptions about the
rationality of humanity. The modern commentator is left with
the problem of measuring the crucially important variable of
personal history in the writings of a generation that was
reluctant to admit that such an irrational factor could have much
importance.

A. Taylor's Intellectual Heritage

In spite of the difficulties of attributing causality to the
influence of intellectual and other biographical influences on

Taylor's thought, there can be no excuse for ignoring the problem completely. The possibility of the connection justifies the venture.

In the case of intellectual influences Taylor fell heir to a rich heritage. Whether or not Caroline County was a veritable new Athens, as one zealous county historian has claimed, is an issue that will not be resolved here. It is sufficient to note that there was a legacy of political and spiritual freedom on which Taylor could draw. Moreover, it is interesting that members of his family were usually in the thick of whatever experiments in freedom were being attempted.

Political liberalism in Caroline County dated from some of its earliest settlers, and the county retained a frontier style in its thought and manners long after it has passed through that stage of development.[3] One of the early delegates to the Virginia House of Burgesses from the area was William Byrd (called "the frontiersman" to distinguish him from his more learned kinsman, William Byrd of "Westover"), who insisted on representing his constituency. His attempts were sufficient to brand him as a radical. Byrd pressed his political opinions to the point where he was found guilty of sedition for refusing to take an oath of allegience to Queen Anne.[4]

Another political liberal, and the most important author to live in Caroline before Taylor, was Robert Beverly of "Beverly Park." Author of one of the first histories of Virginia, his *History and Present State of Virginia* (1705) attacked both the British colonial officials and their planter supporters, charging them with malfeasance.[5] Although this book was partially responsible for the appointment of the reform Governor, Alexander Spotswood, it did nothing to endear its author to those of his fellow planters whom he had excoriated. Forced into retirement on his property in the Caroline area, Beverly began to implement the principles he had advocated in his *History and Present State*. He foreshadowed Taylor in illustrating the virtues of the simple life, although he was more interested than Taylor in manufacturing. Beverly's vast land holdings in Augusta County were sold cheaply to settlers, and he arranged time payments for men without cash. His enlightenment stretched to religious and racial tolerance.[6]

Shortly after Beverly's death in 1722 Caroline County was formed. It was the twenty-ninth Virginia county, and its local political institutions knew the influence of only two kingly administrations. As a political unit, Caroline County never gave monarchy much of a chance to prove itself.[7]

Difficulties for royal administrators soon began and were ended only by independence. Crown candidates were defeated at the polls by Whigs. Although colonial officials took steps to dry up the sources of revenue sustaining the dissent, the institution of the jury took on new significance. Juries were drawn predominantly from the disenfranchised middle and lower classes, and their decisions at times seemed tinged with class prejudices. For example, when Caroline's magistrates once tried to purify juries of Whig prejudices, a whispering campaign was begun against one of the magistrates that drove him from office.[8]

As independence approached, the jealousy of Caroline residents for their rights increased even more. Francis Coleman, for example, the son of a well-to-do tavern keeper, became a follower of Patrick Henry. He ran for a seat in Burgesses against Edmund Pendleton and Walker Taliaferro (a member of one of Caroline's elite families) and defeated the latter. Although Coleman died soon afterward, he was remembered for his dedication to Whig principles. During his tenure as jailkeeper he sometimes would indoctrinate his prisoners with the principles of Patrick Henry, and then arrange their release.[9]

Taylor's own father-in-law and first cousin, John Penn, was a dynamic lawyer whose sympathies were decidedly Whiggish. Penn expressed his convictions with such force and frequency that he finally was indicted for treasonable remarks before a County Court on which his relatives Edmund Pendleton and James Taylor II were sitting. Penn's local reputation may have been damaged by this scrape, because he soon moved to North Carolina (1774). Taylor gave Penn's reason for moving as simply a wish to follow members of his family who had already moved to North Carolina. During the revolution, Penn was a member of the board of war for the prosecution of the war effort in North Carolina, and as such was invested with near-dictatorial powers.[10] Penn's mishap had little effect on some of the ardent Whigs in Caroline. Soon after the Penn trial Taylor's aunt, Amy Taylor, and a half-dozen others stood trial for disloyal opinions. Independence and patriotism, thus, were values insisted upon by many of John Taylor's neighbors, and especially by his own relatives and future in-laws.[11]

Penn was one person whose influence John Taylor did not

hesitate to acknowledge. In urging others to emulate Penn, Taylor even offered a general theory of hero worship. In his opinion it was far better to copy someone of modest talents who made the most of them, such as Penn, rather than national heroes whose very accomplishments made them arrogant. Taylor thought that the example of men such as John Penn taught individuals to take courage and make their competence equal to their virtue. It was error to assume that exceptional talents were the exclusive possessions of an aristocratic few.[12]

Religious liberalism was also characteristic of Caroline County. Although Taylor's personal convictions on theological issues can only be inferred, as a practical politician he actively supported the disestablishment of the Anglican Church. His own congregational membership could have reinforced this attitude. Caroline County was divided into three parishes. Drysdale Parish was the one in which the Pendletons, and John Taylor for the twenty-eight years he lived with his uncle Edmund Pendleton, held membership. Drysdale Parish had a reputation for being secularly minded, possibly owing to Beverly's influence. For example, Drysdale imposed no fines for lax church attendance as was the legal requirement and common practice. Although Taylor's relatives, John Taylor and James Taylor, had served as church wardens, there was no change in Drysdale's erring ways until Edmund Pendleton ascended to the governing body.

In spite of the fact that Drysdale Parish had a history of secularism, it was internally divided on the issue of extending toleration to dissenters. Taylor's relatives maintained their Anglican ties, but were reluctant to join the persecution of dissenters. For example, during a controversy involving John Craig, an irrepressible Baptist preacher, Sheriff James Taylor did not have the heart to discipline Craig and was forced to give the prosecution over to an assistant. In the 1770s a similar confrontation occurred, which resulted in such a violent Anglican response that even Edmund Pendleton, pious defender of the Anglican establishment, joined to unfrock an over zealous rector.[13]

Other denominations pressed religious liberalism further than the Anglican congregations. Dissenting ministers had begun to settle in the county at least by the early 1700s, and their activities eventually broadened the religious horizons of Caroline. A commentator in 1830 remarked on the large number of Baptist and other dissenting congregations in the county. Enthusiastic evangelists seemed to have gravitated toward Drysdale Parish, possibly both for its center location and the likelihood that its parishioners would be less disturbed by their presence. By 1739 a Quaker meeting had been established in Caroline. Its members' attitudes toward slavery were a constant source of difficulty: in 1746 the denomination as such formally declared against slavery, although individual Quakers continued to hire the slaves of others on a temporary basis. By 1773 the Caroline meeting was opposing even this. Religious liberalization in Caroline continued through Taylor's time. During the 1830s it was carried further, especially by the growth in popularity of the rationalistic Disciples of Christ denomination, whose early leader, Andrew Broadus, headed a congregation in the county. This denomination has been interpreted as one of the truest religious expressions of the frontier spirit, because of its rejection of reason-offending formal creeds.[14]

The influence of this religious dissent on Taylor is difficult to determine. Although he criticized in *Arator* the views of Quakers on slavery, he also defended the harmony prevailing among various sects in Virginia: "Our religious sects mingle and worship in harmony, and the State abounds with Christian ministers, whose religion is not banished."[15]

If a writer is influenced by men, ideas, or situations, he may react positively toward them through imitation, or negatively by attempting to wipe them out. The intellectual background of John Taylor provided him with both kinds of examples.

One negative influence may have been Johnathan Boucher, who from 1764 to 1772 was pastor of the parish immediately north of Drysdale. Boucher was an ardent Royalist in political sympathies, being reduced in the latter part of his Caroline ministry to carrying cocked pistols into the pulpit with him in order to ensure his survival until the benediction. Boucher was a Royalist of complex convictions, however, for on some matters he was more advanced in his thinking than his congregation. He felt an obligation toward the religious growth of the parish's slaves, and baptized them into his faith.[16]

Thus, Boucher's cumulative influence on his congregation and neighbors probably was negative. His unapologetic Royalism may have encouraged Whig gains, while his relatively tolerant racial views may have caused slaveowners to become confirmed in their attitudes toward Negroes as property.

Boucher's writings, produced in safety after he had returned to good English soil shortly before the American Revolution, provided an even wider audience for his variety of Royalism. When he published *A View of the Causes and Consequences of the American Revolution* in 1797, most of its contents were not new to the residents of Caroline County. It contained thirteen sermons that Boucher had preached between 1764 and 1775, most of which time he had been pastor in Caroline. Even though the book bore a dedication to George Washington (whom Boucher numbered among his friends when the political climate was appropriate), it argued unequivocally for the connection between Anglicanism and allegiance to the King.[17]

These political views were even more pro-English than those of Daniel Leonard or Samuel Seabury, the New England Royalists. These two had deduced political obligation from the nature of the British Constitution and from the necessity of supporting both the Parliament and the King, instead of only the latter, as Boucher had done. As others have pointed out, the views of Leonard and Seabury were in a way more progressive than those of the rebellious colonists, who insisted upon allegiance to the King alone. Boucher, however, deduced political obligation from the nature of man. True liberty was only the freedom to do what was *right,* not whatever one wished. Judging what was right was a job for the church; and therefore, the authority of government was rooted in a Divine commission and was channeled to man through such leaders as George III. After Boucher's book was published the entire country had available a statement of outrageous Toryism previously known only to the residents of Caroline. Vernon Parrington later thought that this book accomplished the direct opposite of that which Boucher intended. "In laying bare the heart of Toryism, he unwittingly gave aid and comfort to the detested cause of liberalism."[18] Although Taylor never mentioned Boucher, it is possible that the *Inquiry's* attack on the use of priestcraft to condition popular acceptance of tyranny derived from the activities of the fire-eating Royalist.

It is difficult to determine whether Taylor's family was, on balance, more of a positive than a negative influence. It seems safe to say only that it was an influence. Some of this ambiguity may result from the nature of tidewater aristocratic families. In a modern setting the opinions of a relative often might be expected to be a dominant force on the thinking of a member of his family. Tidewater Virginia families, however, were so intermarried and large that the numbers of relatives one possessed could defy enumeration. With such a surplus of kin, it may be possible that the primacy that normally would have been given to the opinions of a relative was weakened. To disagree with anyone in Virginia at that time usually meant disagreeing with a relative!

Taylor often disagreed with his relatives on political issues. In his case the freedom to disagree may have come from the very abundance of distant relatives who surrounded him and the absence of direct parental influence. The Taylors, Pendletons, and Pollards were intermarried to a great extent, and Taylor had many aunts, uncles, and cousins in Caroline and Orange Counties.[19] On the other hand, Taylor and his younger sister lost their father during the French and Indian Wars. They were adopted by Edmund and Sarah Pendleton, who were each related to the Taylors by blood. Edmund Pendleton, Taylor's uncle and cousin, thus became the only father Taylor probably remembered. At the same time, John Taylor shared his status as adopted son with several others whom the hospitable Pendletons took in from time to time.[20]

The influence of the various members of the Pendleton family on Taylor differed. John Penn was one of the young men to whom Pendleton opened his heart and law library, and Penn's importance for Taylor has already been noted. On the other hand, none of the women of the family seems to have had any intellectual influence on Taylor. There were no Abigail Adamses there, although the girls of the family received secondary educations along with the boys.[21]

James Taylor, John's great-uncle, was a surveyor, magistrate, sheriff, member of the House of Burgesses, Chairman of the Caroline County Committee of Safety, member of the re-volutionary conventions of 1775 and 1776, delegate to the state ratifying convention in 1788, and state Senator. In spite of James's accomplishments, John did not hesitate to disagree with him over the desirability of the U.S. Constitution. Only the respect he bore his uncle James kept John from opposing him in the election for delegates to the 1788 ratifying convention. The influence of James Taylor could only have been a mixed one.[22]

The most important single influence upon John Taylor was undoubtedly offered by Edmund Pendleton. Pendleton started from humble origins and steadily applied considerable talents to hard work, profitable marriages, and influential acquaintances. He held at various times his state's highest offices in all three branches of its government. Pendleton's political activities began with county offices but soon led to state office: from 1752 to 1774 he was a member of the House of Burgesses; a member of the committee of correspondence in 1773; a member of the Continental Congress in 1774 and 1775; the President of the State Committee of Safety in 1775 (and as such de facto governor of the nascent state during 1774-1776); a member of the House of Delegates and its first Speaker in 1776-77; a judge of the General Court and the Court of Chancery in 1777; the presiding judge of the Court of Appeals in 1779; and member and president of the Virginia ratifying convention in 1788. In this last position Pendleton provided important support for James Madison, who may have known few equals in knowledge of political and legal history, but whose slight voice, balding head, and financial dependence hardly commanded respect when matched against the eloquent anti-federalists George Mason and Patrick Henry.[23]

It was Taylor's fortune to fall heir to the chain of influence that Pendleton had constructed over a lifetime, without having to make any of the psychological, moral, and legal compromises that Pendleton unquestionably had made. At the same time, Taylor was acquiring his own fortune. He could have, therefore, the freedom of conscience to disagree with Pendleton whenever he chose without any feelings that he was biting the hand.[24] He exercised that freedom regularly. Indeed, on many of the most important political questions of the day, Taylor and Pendleton found themselves on opposite sides. It would be presumptuous to claim that Taylor's political attitudes were formed in rebellious opposition to his guardian's, but they did often disagree.

For example, Taylor's first important expression of political awareness came when he sided with Patrick Henry. Henry had become a bitter political enemy of Pendleton's when the latter favored one of Henry's subordinates instead of Henry with a military appointment. Moreover, Henry was associated with Coleman, the zealous jailer who had challenged Pendleton for election to Burgesses in Caroline. Pendleton also seems to have been more of an admirer of Washington than was Taylor, who only reluctantly came around to supporting the General. Taylor's abhorrence of paper money could not have disposed him very kindly toward his uncle's involvement in the Robinson affair, the scandal that rocked Virginia on the death of John

Robinson, Speaker of the House of Delegates, who had been misusing his public trust as chief financial officer to favor his friends with loans of "old" paper money that should have been burned. As mentioned before, Taylor was on the opposite side from Pendleton and James Taylor on the issue of whether the draft Constitution should be ratified. Taylor was also instrumental in the attack upon the established church, while Pendleton was known for his reverance for that organization. Similarly, Taylor approved of abolition of medieval land ownership laws of descent, entail, and primogeniture, while Pendleton fought a last-ditch defense of these laws. Taylor's support of Jefferson may have been discomfiting to Pendleton, who, as Mays has pointed out, was more of a separationist than an actual revolutionary. For Pendleton independence was an end in itself, but for Jefferson and his followers, in the early years at least, it represented only the preliminaries for root-and-branch change. When the opinions of Pendleton and Taylor began to become more compatible, as they did toward the last few years of Pendleton's life, it may be a commentary on the two men involved that it was Pendleton who adopted the stand of Taylor by supporting Jefferson in the election of 1800.[25]

Taylor must have owed much of his intellectual awareness to his education. Yet, his education did not present him with a single ideology. Taylor was educated in a manner customary for the time. He was enrolled in February of 1726 at a fine private boarding school about fifteen miles from Pendleton's estate in adjoining King and Queen County. Donald Robertson was the schoolmaster, and the curriculum centered upon languages. Yet, neither Taylor's later contacts with the French volunteers during the American Revolution, nor his writings, evidence any familiarity with modern languages. On the contrary, his liking for Latin maxims and obscure classical allusions probably indicates a study of the classics. Robertson's school library included 100 volumes, featuring such Enlightenment theorists as Dryden, Hume, Milton, Montaigne, Montesquieu, and Pope. Both John Penn and James Madison attended the Robertson School, the latter at the same time as Taylor. Even so, there are no boyhood reminiscences in Taylor and Madison's correspondence; in fact, at times they sounded as though they were barely acquainted and regretted that familiarity.[26]

Taylor's college experiences presented him with both Whig and Tory views. As Simms pointed out, while Taylor was attending William and Mary, at least three of the faculty were decided Anglophiles: Rev. John Camm, President, and advocate of an Anglican bishopric in America; the Rev. Samuel Henly, professor of moral and intellectual philosophy; and the Rev. Thomas Gwatkins, professor of mathematics. During and after Taylor's stay at the college a schism opened between these ardent Tories and the other professors, most of whom possessed Whig sympathies. Finally, the two loyalist professors returned to England in 1770, and President Camm was removed from office in 1777.[27]

None of the statesmen whose ideas and activities were to occupy so much of Taylor's attention in later life were college classmates of his. Madison went to Princeton, Jefferson graduated from William and Mary before Taylor, Monroe did not attend the latter until 1776, and John Marshall had a fleeting six-week exposure to the lectures of George Wythe in 1780.[28] Taylor returned from college to study law at Pendleton's home and finally began his law practice in 1774. Throughout his education Taylor was presented with a succession of influences that would have reinforced Whig attitudes, but that also would have given him the opportunity to dabble in Toryism if he had wished. There was no single teacher who dominated Taylor's development as Wythe had Jefferson's, unless it was Pendleton. Pendleton, for his part, found nothing remarkable about Taylor's education.[29]

Taylor shared the common eighteenth-century "belief in the unity and immutability of reason" discerned by Cassirer. In this acceptance of reason he seems closest to the "political hedonism" described by Leo Strauss, because his view of man was intensely individualistic and apolitical, if not "a-social." Of the three "generations" of the Enlightenment discussed by Peter Gay, Taylor seems closest to the first, which was dominant before 1750. Taylor's ethical and epistemological views changed little over the course of his life and probably reflected his education. Not an originator in basic philosophy, Taylor seems to have been content to apply the doctrines of the early Enlightenment. He avoided, thus, the anticlericism of Gay's second generation and the materialist ontology of the third generation.[30]

Taylor's reluctance to use appeals based on authority makes it difficult, but not impossible, to trace most of his philosophic and literary interests. He insisted that the context had to be nearly identical to make the quotation of an authority applicable.

Among those used as sources by Taylor are, in rough order of frequently, John Adams, the *Federalist,* popular historians, English economists, English political theorists, and literary sources.

Taylor's refutation of John Adams's *Defence* will be explored at length in the chapters to follow. Taylor resented the use of the *Federalist* as a commentary on the principles of the United States Constitution. Although he agreed with much in the *Federalist*, he was the first commentator to distinquish Hamilton's contribution from Madison's. Taylor also thought that the theories of each were dangerous for different reasons, and, thus, deserved different attacks. He considered Hamilton a constitutional monarchist and Madison a republican centralist. Both men, however, had sometimes used genuine federal principles. Taylor's philosophic break with Madison began in 1806 after a close examination of the *Federalist*, and he thereafter often invidiously compared Madison and Hamilton, stating, tongue-in-cheek, that Hamilton was more republican. Taylor always admired Madison's Virginia Resolutions, regardless of what defects existed in the *Federalist*.[31]

Taylor seems to have accepted the interpretations of historians more readily than the opinions of theorists probably considering them more empirical. He was especially fond of William Russell and used his rationalist popular *History of Modern Europe* (1779-1784) for information throughout the *Inquiry*. For American history Taylor used David Ramsay's *History of the American Revolution* (1789), a rationalistic defense of the American view of that struggle. Other historians sometimes referred to included John Marshall and G. T. Raynal.[32]

Taylor's economic theories seem to have been influenced by Adam Smith, with whose writings he seemed to be thoroughly acquainted. Yet he quoted Smith more often in criticism than praise and especially disapproved of his use of the term *tax* to refer to levies on revenue. Taylor wanted *tax* to cover land and people so that he could declare the carriage tax tantamount to a tax on land and, therefore, unconstitutional. In attacking Smith, Taylor approvingly referred to the Physiocrats (the only time he ever mentioned them) as being better able than Smith to appreciate the value of land. Taylor also approvingly quoted Sir James Steuart, whom Taylor incorrectly considered a more recent writer than Smith, and, therefore, more informed on the United States. In fact, Steuart's *Inquiry into the Principles of*

Political Economy, to which Taylor referred, was published in 1767. Taylor also mentioned Malthus, whose pessimism he found as distasteful as Godwin's optimism. Yet, he agreed with Malthus, and through him with Smith, that the fertility of land and the pursuit of self-interest was the secret of prosperity. Taylor was also acquainted with the economist Thomas Tooke, a member with Malthus and Ricardo of the London Political Economy Club. A critic of Ricardo. Arthur Young, was compared to Newton by Taylor for his experimental approach to agricultural problems.[33]

Taylor occasionally mentioned the great Whig theorists Locke and Harrington, but said little about them. He agreed with Locke's doctrine of popular sovereignty, and with Harrington's dominion-following-property rule; but he considered political utopias appropriate only for amusement.[34]

The two fiction writers most often mentioned by Taylor were Jonathan Swift and Miguel Cervantes. His attention to Swift, whom he acknowledged to have been a Tory, was partially forced by Adams's reliance upon him. Yet Taylor disagreed with Adams that Swift was the foe of popular sovereignty. The references to Cervantes' *Don Quixote* were scattered throughout Taylor's works to illustrate the futility of agriculture's situation and the capacity for self-delusion possessed by capitalists.[35]

The frequency and approval with which Taylor used the terms *Republican* and *Republican principles* suggest that he was familiar with the English Republican tradition that has been seen recently as influential in the thinking of the American revolutionary generation. Writers of the Republican tradition included James Harrington in the seventeenth century, but it was the eighteenth-century critics of the Robert Walpole administration who earned the greatest approval from their American imitators. The British group included: John Trenchard, Thomas Gordon, Bishop Hoadly, Robert Viscount Molesworth, Bolingbroke, and, later, Richard Baron, James Burgh, Richard Price, Joseph Priestly, John Cartwright, and, of course, John Wilkes. The American revolutionists were fond of seeing themselves as the defenders of the same English liberties as those defended by their counterparts in the Walpole era and later. The English radicals considered themselves to be engaged in a moral crusade to preserve virtue and uproot immorality by preserving an ancient constitution rooted in man's moral sense and the practices of Saxon Britain. In brief, this was the same political platform adopted later by the American revolutionists, who added popular sovereignty and the need to separate from the corrupt mother country as contributions of their own. It is reasonable to assume that Taylor accepted these ideas as did most other intellectuals of the independence movement. Unlike some of them, however, these concerns always remained central for him.[36]

The intellectual influences upon John Taylor, in summary, tended to reinforce a Whig outlook on politics. His home county's aristocrats were in the forefront of developing a rationale for political change, and his own family was important in achieving this change. Yet, he was exposed to the ideas of Toryism, and could have chosen that persuasion had it appealed to him. There seems to have been no single thinker who was a predominating influence on him, although his closeness to Pendleton provided him with an immediate, influential audience for his ideas. On important issues he often went his own way, regardless of the opinions of relatives and associates whose judgment he otherwise respected. A study of the sources used in his writings reveals a greater tendency to argue with authors than to adopt the positions of any particular individual or school. However, these appearances of intellectual independence do not justify the conclusion that Taylor was an autonomous thinker, unaffected by background influences. The point is that independence and individualism were valued by Enlightenment theorists in general and by the resident of Caroline County in particular. When Taylor acted and wrote as an individualist he was conforming to a traditional pattern of behavior, given his intellectual antecedents.

B. The Influence of Class

Some authorities have given great weight to Taylor's position as a member of a privileged class of planters. Taylor himself freely admitted to having the biases of a farmer. A contradiction can exist, however, between these two conditions. His social class status resulted from his possessions as a planter; but his frame of mind was that of a farmer, an occupation of value to all men. A defense of either position could have been expected from someone of Taylor's interests. The extent to which Taylor was a member of a privileged class is examined below; considerations qualifying his status as an aristocratic planter are in the next section.[37]

Among the many characteristics distinguishing the possessions of a tidewater planter from individuals lower in the social hierarchy were the number of slaves and the amount of land. Although other measures of planter status might be devised, such as clothes, diet, conveniences, libraries, or architectural tastes, data on these are incomplete for Taylor. Moreover, many of these factors are unreliable measures for the period of time under study (1790-1824), because a more frontier style of living characterized many plantations in their early years.[38] Land and slaves were the economic basis on which the South grew, and comparing planters on that basis will include the men who achieved the economic status of planters before they had time to consolidate their positions socially. This method is particularly appropriate for Taylor, but for a different reason. Since he seems to have maintained a relatively austere style of living, a study of his household's amenities alone might give the impression that he was less wealthy than he really was.

The tradition of interpreting tidewater Virginia planters as a self-interested aristocracy who had economic reasons for supporting liberal causes when they supported them is a hoary one, dating at least from John Fiske. Bernard Drell was especially impressed by the fact that Caroline County was fairly old (created in 1727, but settled long before), and that its population was very stable (gaining but 271 persons from 1790 to 1830). In addition, the number of slaves was very high (fifty percent of all persons in 1810), and the county was among the most highly taxed in the state in the decade between 1790 and 1800. These facts combine to illumine Taylor's opinions on out-migration, the burdens borne by agriculture, and slavery. The last is particularly relevant to this discussion.[39]

Caroline ranked second in total number of slaves among all Virginia counties in 1790. There were roughly thirty families in the county in 1810 owning large numbers of slaves (forty or more). In comparing the number of slaves owned by these large slaveholders to the total number of slaves, however, one finds that only about one slave in four was owned by a large slaveholder. Three-fourths of the slaves in Caroline were scattered throughout the county's white families in small-to-moderate sized holdings. Thus, slavery was a widespread practice in Taylor's home county.[40]

The Taylors and Pendletons were among the thirty or so largest slaveholding families in Caroline. The Pendletons owned 171 slaves, while the Taylors owned 292, so that both families together owned 463 slaves, or nearly half of all owned by families with forty or more slaves.[41] John Taylor was the second largest slaveholder in Caroline. He had accumulated slaves at a very rapid rate during his rise to wealth after the American Revolution. Both his lucrative law practice and his wife's wealth were responsible for this increase in property. In 1783 Taylor owned nine slaves; by 1787 he owned forty-seven; in 1798, more than sixty-two; and by 1810 he owned 145. Unlike John Randolph of Roanoke, Taylor did not inherit a white man's burden; he expended considerable energy in achieving it, and became one of the largest slaveholders in the South for the time.[42]

Recent research has rasied questions as to how much can be inferred from the presence and number of slaves in the tidewater.[43] A study of the characteristics of this area during the prerevolutionary period, likely to be the most intellectually formative time for Taylor, suggested that slaveowning was not the source of class or sectional conflict in Virginia that one might expect. Slavery was actually becoming more and more widespread at the time. Slaves constituted a large portion of personal property in Virginia and were owned by all classes except the poorest. As has been mentioned, this still seems to have been the case in Caroline in 1810. Furthermore, slave counties were not limited to the tidewater, and the greatest density of slaves was in a strip bounded by the James and Rappahannock Rivers, which extended from the ocean almost to the mountains. The rate of growth in slaveowning was actually highest in the piedmont from 1750 to 1778 "so the issue was not one of slaveowning tidewater versus non-slaveowning piedmont."[44] Thus, even if one accepts Mudge's statement that Taylor's ideas reached beyond a strict construction of the Constitution to "a defense of the tidewater landed gentry and a plea for the security of the individual freeholder,"[45] it is still difficult to discern rigid class differences caused by slavery that could have influenced Taylor. This does not mean that slavery itself did not affect him. It profoundly did, as will be seen in a later chapter, but he discussed it in other than class terms. Of course, even if slaveowning was an unlikely basis for the nurturing of class tensions, it must be admitted that an individual's class consciousness does not have to be rooted in actual economic status, or that persons always perceive their economic positions correctly. All that can be said is that Taylor did not express himself as a defender of an elite either in his private correspondence or his published writings.

Land was the other chief criterion of wealth in a planter's values. Just as Taylor's human possessions had been assembled quickly and in impressive numbers, his accumulation of land proceeded apace.

Returning from the army in 1779, Taylor faced distressing personal economic circumstances. He turned immediately to the practice of law, probably receiving a boost from the fact that Pendleton had given up his practice the previous year when he was appointed as a judge. Simms described in detail the rapid rise in Taylor's fortunes during the thirteen years in which he practiced law full-time. Simms notes that Taylor's skill as an attorney must have achieved a wide reputation, for he represented the Preston family of Montgomery County, near the far southwestern corner of the state. Taylor also tried tax collecting, but could not find the records necessary to make a success of the venture.[46]

Taylor's income in these years reached $10,000 a year, "which he invested in lands always paying cash,"[47] according to his grandson. He soon was able to buy and stock two plantations, "Hayfield" and "Mill Hill." In 1787 he owned 1,123 acres of land, and by 1798 he had nearly doubled that. His holdings were valued at $6,701.18 when he moved into the "Hazelwood" estate in the spring of 1798. A visitor estimated in 1814 that Taylor had 1,400 acres under cultivation on "Hazelwood."[48]

Measured in land, Taylor was undoubtedly a rich man, but he still may have ranked well back in the pack of the richest twenty percent of all landholders. This generalization is based on Leonard Woods Labaree's estimate that in 1704 the section of Virginia below the Rappahannock included at least twenty-five individuals who each owned 5,000 or more acres. A few estates were three to five times bigger, and the largest estates had not yet been assembled. By the time of Taylor's birth, the average estate was around 750 acres, but some owned thirty to one hundred thousand acres. Eighty percent of the landholders owned less than 1,000 acres. Among the estates of his own time, John

Taylor's was substantial, but not huge. His three Caroline estates together did not surpass the Pendleton estate, "Edmundsbury," which eventually covered six square miles, or 3,840 acres. At the time of the Constitution's ratification, James Taylor II owned 2,070 acres. Compared to some of their contemporaries, the Taylor-Pendleton holdings do not seem large: in 1788 Patrick Henry owned 8,534 acres, James Monroe owned 5,333 acres (including Kentucky land for war service), and George Mason owned 75,000 acres. Clement Eaton has estimated the middle-sized plantation as usually 1,000 to 1,500 acres in size, which was no larger than the walking distance in an hour from the slave quarters. By this standard, Hazelwood would have been a middle-sized plantation. Taylor's additional land holdings in Caroline and elsewhere would have qualified him as a wealthy man, but not the wealthiest tidewater Virginia had ever seen by a wide mark. The Virginia aristocracy covered a wide range and the planters of Port Royal were of middling means.[49]

As with the possession of slaves, it is not a question of how much land Taylor had, but how he felt about it and whether this affected his writings.

Taylor's lands were the key to his wealth, coming before his acquisition of slaves, and he did things to obtain land that he afterward was quick to criticize in others. After the Revolution he had presented separate land claims to the state for himself and a relative whose health had been broken by military service. Records indicate that some 5,000 acres were given Taylor in the Ohio territory, although he never seems to have mentioned them later. He may have refused the offer. After becoming a member of the legislature, however, he was able to use his position successfully to protect land claims he and Pendleton had in a part of North Carolina that had been considered a part of Virginia in 1765 when the Crown granted the claim to Pendleton. Squatters had settled on the 3,000-acre tract in question and the State of North Carolina seemed ready in the summer of 1781 to recognize the squatters' claims. The two distressed speculators drafted a petition to the Virginia legislature, whose members by that time were on the run from the British. The petition was assigned to a committee on which John Taylor sat. The committee and the full legislature reacted favorably to the petition and memorialized the North Carolina Legislature to observe the superior title of land grants from the Crown. Taylor went to North Carolina when the issue came before the legislature and, after minor procedural difficulties, obtained North Carolina's agreement to his claims. All of this is a measure of the extent to which Taylor was willing to use governmental privilege when his property was at stake.[50]

These actions were in flagrant violation of some of Taylor's later ideas on the proper use of government. Pendleton, first, may have been debasing his official position when the claims were granted. Second, during a desperate struggle for national survival, Taylor did not hesitate to use his position in the legislature to importune the state for a personal favor. Third, his petition called upon North Carolina in the name of a principle of "general citizenship," the existence of which Taylor always denied in later years. Fourth, the logic of the claim required that the authority of a state be subjugated to that of the Crown, an unusual doctrine for a Revolutionary patriot. Finally, Taylor was John Penn's cousin, and Penn was one of the top three officials in North Carolina at the time. Despite Taylor's later fulminations on the abuse of governmentally bestowed privilege and the primacy of state governments, when the chips were down he kept his eye on his own self-interest.[51] Sale of the lands brought income for Taylor and Pendleton for years. In an 1811 letter Taylor discussed a complicated financial transaction that resulted from his accepting horses in payment for Western lands that were being sold so that the payments could be used to purchase lands in Virginia. Thus the personal fortune of one of the greatest critics of governmentally bestowed privileges was built in the beginning on that basis.[52]

Land ownership undoubtedly had an effect on what Taylor *did*. There seems to be no evidence, however, that Taylor's activities in securing land had any influence on what he *thought*. He never attempted to justify his action in acquiring the North Carolina lands. The inconsistency of what he had done with what he later wrote seems never to have occurred to him. His theoretical position, therefore, remained intact but tattered because he did not apply it to his own behavior.

In summary, an examination of Taylor's status as a planter finds that in slaves and land he was without question a wealthy man. Compared to other planters, the number of slaves he owned was probably more impressive than the number of acres. This may have been the result of the intensive cultivation and heavy labor requirements that his experimental farming methods needed. Although his status as a planter cannot be disputed, it is important to remember that, measured in slaves, this status may not have been a source of class conflict in the formative years of Taylor's life; and, measured in land, Taylor's holdings were comparable to other tidewater patriots less often associated than he with a defense of planter aristocracy.[53]

C. The Influence of Farming

Throughout the preceding section the necessity of determining a writer's actual perceptions was stressed. It is not necessarily the actual economic station of an individual that is translated into his views, but his perceptions of that status, and what use he chooses to make of his perceptions. Even though it may be true that a cultural milieu imposes limitations on the very nature of what one can perceive, an individual's impressions are what ultimately counts. They may be a distorted picture of reality, but they are decisive.

Taylor saw things as a working farmer and as an agricultural experimenter. He was deeply affected by any circumstances that hindered his ability to produce profitable harvests. Such circumstances threatened almost constantly from the time he retired from law practice until his death. Taylor always escaped economic disaster, but he often wrote as though tottering on the abyss. Moreover, his passionate concern for the agricultural decline throughout Virginia was a constant concern, regardless of his personal fortunes. His orientation throughout his writings, therefore, is not one of a defender of a class. Instead, it is that of a professional farmer who was worried about the problems of agriculture in general, whose experimental methods limited his knowledge but not his concern for the agricultural problems of regions other than his own, and who was feeling the pinch a little himself. A better view of the purposes of his theories will be provided by an appreciation for first, the economic conditions experienced by Taylor; second, the fluctuations in his personal wealth; and third, by his ideas on the difficulties faced by agriculture in general.

Taylor's personal fortune had been accumulated quickly in the years 1779-1792. While Taylor was prospering, so was his section. Even though the Revolution had devastated parts of the Upper South, especially in Virginia, this had been confined largely to the winter of 1780-81. Before that time rising prices and inflation due to the demand for food by towns had created good times for farmers. After the Revolution, Southern farmers prospered for a time in spite of the fact that most merchants had come to demand payment of debts in specie, and they controlled almost the complete supply of it. The price of tobacco in the Virginia tidewater during 1784 had increased nearly twenty percent, and this was from the very region that had been raided by Cornwallis and Arnold. Farmers poured into the southern back country and tobacco growing spread throughout Kentucky, Tennessee, and Georgia. By 1792 American tobacco exports were one-third more than they had been in 1770. But this prosperity was short-lived: by 1793 tobacco exports fell to slightly less than half that of 1792, and not until 1851 did the quantity shipped exceed 1792's record. The year 1792, it will be recalled, is when Taylor retired from full-time legal practice in order to pass a quiet retirement engaged in the improvement of agricultural science.[54]

Taylor retired only to witness the agricultural degeneration of the Upper South. Several major forces were responsible for this economic decline. One explanation that has been offered for this decline was that aristocratic waste caused a misue of capital and land. This view held that the cavalier settlers of the tidewater refused to surrender their genteel but profligate life-style to the exigencies of scarce resources. The economic crisis that eventually followed was one of expectations as well as of actual economic scarcity. A cavalier expected not just to live, but to live well.[55]

A second view agreed that waste occurred, but emphasized the frontier nature of the South and the exploitative nature of its settlement. Not only had the planter been freed from the anti-materialistic inhibitions of the puritans, but he fell heir to the ideology of capitalism, which made no apologies for the productive exploitation of men, land, and resources.[56]

Caroline County's growth during the first half of Taylor's life seemed to support the second of these views. The population of the county grew from 6,796 in 1732 to 15,667 in 1789. Thirty-six of these years paralleled the first half of Taylor's life. It may be true, as Bernard Drell has pointed out, that during the active period of Taylor's writing the population of Caroline was stable, but it was also true that the formative years of his life had been spent during a period of rapid expansion and settlement.[57]

In addition to whatever deficiencies in Southern agriculture were caused by waste, the very Southern climate that at first had brought crops in profusion, gradually began to deplete the soil. The frequent rains eroded the soil, and returned crops in an ever-diminishing supply. An additional problem was one that has often been mentioned: the exhaustion of nutrients in the soil by the overuse of tobacco as the single cash crop of the Virginia planters. Avery Craven thought that tobacco had been overemphasized as a cause of decline, and that climatic conditions were probably equally guilty. This was demonstrated when the Caroline planters switched to grain crops and still could not recoup their losses.[58]

The small town of Port Royal, located immediately south of "Hazelwood", provided an example in miniature for Taylor of what was happening to the Upper South. Port Royal had been founded in 1744 by Thomas Roy, and was one of the older towns in the colony. In its early years the town had a prosperous economic life, owing to its wharf and good harbor. In those days Port Royal was a wide-open town, afraid to impose any restrictions that would discourage trade. During this time Edmund Pendleton and Roy warned against overly quick development of the town. Later, tobacco, the plantation system, and Port Royal sank in fortunes together. Except for some grain shipments, by 1830 it had become virtually a ghost town. Its population suffered chronic epidemics of yellow fever because of mosquitoes from the decaying marshes and millponds nearby. By 1830 the town had been without parson, press, church, or schoolhouse for years. Although the town was chosen to be the site of agricultural conventions after Taylor's death (in his memory), the town stood as symbolic testimony of the bad times that had come to the Upper South.[59]

Each of the three reasons that have been offered for the decline in the tobacco economy found expression in Taylor's writings. He recognized and lamented profligate carelessness that allowed animals to wander at will throughout the county, damaging themselves and the crops of others. He strongly urged that practices designed for fast profits, such as paying overseers a percentage of the crops that they exacted from the soil and the slaves under their command, would injure long-range productivity. Finally, his system of deep plowing, enclosing, and crop rotation were all attempts to reconstitute the depleted soil. The concerns of a farmer with his back to the wall, therefore, frequently emerged in his writings.

John Taylor's personal financial situation became more precarious as his region declined, adding poignancy to his worries over the economic decline of agriculture. It is true that many persons would probably have traded positions with him willingly, for he was hardly staring into the jaws of poverty; but he was worried enough that it may have given his writings a sense of purpose and tone of urgency. At any rate, they had at least the latter.

It is probable that his profits never were large after 1792. Writing to Aaron Burr, he said that "Fancy furnishes me with passions and amusements, and about one hundred dollars a year more than meets every want I have which money can gratify."[60] Taylor's wants were extremely austere, so he was probably talking about a small gross amount of cash.

The best measure of his difficulties and the fragility of his affluence is provided by an exchange of letters between Wilson Cary Nicholas and himself in the years of 1802-1809. Nicholas had asked for a large loan (around $3,000) during the late summer of 1802. Taylor replied that he had not had that much money since he left law practice. He hardly had enough to meet personal expenses, he reported. Other than his estates, Taylor went on to say, the only assets he had were in the form of loans to be paid to him.[61] Taylor went to work collecting his debts and finally put together enough to satisfy Nicholas's request by the spring of the next year. [62]

Taylor's letters to Nicholas over the next half decade were a barometer of his fluctuating fortunes. By spring 1804, Taylor reported that he had made no profit from his lands the preceding year, but a year later his affairs had improved to the point that he agreed to defer the outstanding interest payment. His only concern, he pointed out, was to provide estates for his sons, but he never had much luck in managing money for profit and might have to call on Nicholas's payment if an emergency arose. An opportunity to buy two inexpensive estates a year later caused him to ask for Nicholas's immediate payment (an amount of £954 by this time). A month later he admitted pecuninary embarassment in a plea to Nicholas for payment; he couldn't even afford to pay the fire insurance premium of $100 on "Hazelwood." Throughout the spring of 1806 Taylor attempted to collect the amount owed him by Nicholas, who finally paid it during June. By September, Taylor was flush enough to loan $100 interest free to an indebted schoolmaster. During 1807 he was able to allow Nicholas to forgo payment, but by June 1808 he was desperate for enough money to pay taxes. He hadn't sold his 1807 crop. Final settlement of the Nicholas debt dragged on several years, but Taylor never seemed to need the money so urgently as he had in 1806 and 1808. Taylor's personal problems find no overt expression in his published writings, although his private opposition to the Jefferson-Madison war measures sometimes mentions his personal situation. He changed from a qualified endorsement of the embargo, for example, to a denunciation of it for the problems it was causing farmers. It is likely that personal difficulty and the burdens of his region caused Taylor to systematize and make public his private views.[63]

The fact that Taylor thought of himself as a farmer first and a planter second was demonstrated in his public and private writings. First of all, he did not express himself as a member of the privileged few. When he talked of the five million agriculturalists in his *Definition of Parties* (1794) he was obviously referring to nearly all of the population; and later in *Arator* (1813) and the *Inquiry* (1814) he clarified his meaning by distinguishing farmers from landed gentry and including himself in the first group.[64]

In *Arator* he made it clear on the first page that he was referring throughout to two groups of agriculturalists. When he spoke of farming methods, he was referring to all states using slaves, Maryland, Virginia, and North Carolina in particular. When Taylor spoke of the political oppressions and defects of agriculture, he was speaking of farmers throughout the Union.[65]

In the *Inquiry* Taylor further refined what he meant by agriculture when he reaffirmed his belief that agriculturalists throughout the Union had common interests, and together constituted the vast majority of the population. He then specifically attacked the idea that the "landed interest" in the United States was equivalent to the English landlords. The squires were not actually farmers and actually hid behind legal tenants. He feared that the pretensions of American agriculturalists might beguile them "into the Engligh systems of legislatory ways and means for extracting wealth from labour."[66] In the United States the members of the landed interest were really cultivators and could lose only by allowing special privileges to be granted in law.

From his published word, then, it is clear that Taylor meant farmers in general when he spoke of agriculture, and that the tidewater planters were merely deceiving themselves by attempting to copy England's squirarchy. It is still possible that Taylor's private thoughts were different, and that secretly he thought of himself as a representative of tidewater aristocracy. Had Taylor copied the Adamses and kept a diary, his private opinions might be more accessible, but no diary is available. Only this advice to Jefferson regarding an appointment to office gives a glimpse into how Taylor actually distinguished himself from the old-line aristocrats of Virginia. He characterized the applicant as "very much esteemed by the old landed aristocracy of Virginia—his appointment will please them mightily . . . they are naturally republicans under our policy, and the sooner you place them in their natural station the better . . . [they are] worth converting from error."[67]

It is evident that Taylor not only considered himself separate from those he considered aristocrats, but also did not expect his actions to be automatically popular with them. It is true that this line of argument hinges on allowing Taylor to define *aristocracy*; it may be that both he and his aristocrats would fit a modern definition of landed aristocracy. Even so, it cannot alter the fact that he was no conscious apologist for the highest class as he saw it.

D. Summary and Conclusions

This chapter has examined the extent to which John Taylor may have been influenced by his intellectual and socioeconomic background.

No previous commentator on Taylor has emphasized the strong roots that Whig thought had in Caroline County and in Taylor's own family. A study of these roots provides evidence that the Enlightenment values of liberty, individualism, and rationalism were values that Taylor could very naturally have adopted.

If it can be assumed that Taylor was conforming to traditional Enlightenment values when he acted as a maverick in politics, one must question the allegation made by some commentators that Taylor's material interests made him an ideologist for tidewater gentry. First, the whole notion of a tidewater gentry is under reexamination. It may be that the material basis for class conflict simply did not exist in sufficient magnitude in Virginia before 1776 to have given Taylor much of a class bias. Second, Taylor's own status as a planter has also been clarified and qualified. He was wealthy, but this wealth was acquired by his own efforts and the assistance of friends and relatives in high position. If anything, Taylor's later attacks on the use of governmental privilege to increase personal wealth flew in the face of the methods he himself used in assembling his fortune. They were certainly not a justification of these methods. It must be admitted, however, that the Virginia aristocracy often used government to obtain personal advantages. Third, the magnitude of his wealth stopped short of making him a financial giant, and the frequent fluctuations in this wealth would have given him every reason to seek governmental assistance, if his own self-interest had been a dominant motive. Almost without exception, however, he rejected and condemned the abuse of governmental privilege.

John Taylor's Whiggish intellectual heritage, then, provided him with the force of conviction to propose a theoretical solution for all farmers' problems. Unlike most solutions before and since, it did not rely upon governmental favor. Such an aberrant attitude from a Virginia planter may well have been the cause of his frequent disagreements with fellow Jeffersonians during his career as a political partisan. Taylor carried his independent attitudes over into his theory of political parties and found that to preserve this individualism he had to change his mind about parties.

Notes to Chapter 1

1. Merle Curti, *The Growth of American Thought* (New York: Harper and Row, 1964), pp. 98–99.

2. *Inquiry,* chap. 7 passim.

3. The use of *liberalism* throughout this study should not be confused with its alternate contemporary meaning as the opposite of *conservatism.* Here it will refer to the intellectual tradition that embraces both contemporary liberalism and conservatism: a tradition that had its roots in medieval constitutionalism and that found its soul in the fight against divine-right monarchs. When this study narrows its focus to the advocates of independence during the American revolutionary period, the term *Whig* will be used, since both Loyalist theories of parliamentary supremacy and Whig theories of the British constitution were liberal. Moreover, *Whig* was a term often applied to themselves by the advocates of independence.

4. T. E. Cambell, *Colonial Caroline: A History of Caroline County, Virginia* (Richmond, Va. The Dietz Press, Inc., 1954), pp. 25–27.

5. Ibid., p. 28.

6. Louis B. Wright, *The First Gentlemen of Virginia* (Charlottesville, Va.: The University Press of Virginia, 1964), pp. 295–99, 300; Cambell, p. 28. Beverley had eccentric characteristics. He insisted, for example, on using crude handmade furniture instead of the comfortable imports he could well have afforded. He and his heirs owned 71,541 acres in Augusta County, which were sold for one shilling an acre, earning an annual profit, net taxes, of £133. Time payments were arranged for a ten-year period if the tract settled was over 200 acres; *see* Robert Brown and Katherine Brown, *Virginia 1705–1786: Democracy or Aristocracy?* (East Lansing Mich): Michigan State University Press, 1964), pp. 16–18. Beverley attacked farming based on Negro slavery, and upheld the primitive wholesomeness of the social institutions of the American Indian, including a defense of the virginity of Indian maidens.

7. Joseph Martin, *A New and Comprehensive Gazetteer of Virginia and the District of Columbia* (Charlottesville, Va.: Joseph Martin, 1836), p. 142. Caroline County did make one concession to royal opinion; it named itself after George II's Queen.

8. Cambell, pp. 83–90, 194–97. The scandal concerned Magistrate John Suttion, who had mistreated his mulatto mistress and their six children. At this time juries were the only representative institution, because elections were dominated by the propertied. Most local officials were appointed.

9. Coleman was remembered especially for his eccentric method of gaining converts. During his tenure as jailkeeper, he would convert them to the doctrines of Patrick Henry, and then "arrange" their release. See Cambell, pp. 209–211.

10. The jury was sympathetic and charged Penn a fine of one pence and twelve pounds of tobacco. See ibid., p. 228. See "The Life of John Penn," typescript of a manuscript in the handwriting of John Taylor, John Taylor Papers, Duke University Library, Durham, N.C. Penn was known to his descendants as the "dictator of North Carolina" as a consequence of his high position during the Revolution. See Capt. John Taylor (grandson of John Taylor of Caroline) to Julia L. Taylor, March 7, 1875, typescript, John Taylor Papers, Duke University Library.

11. Cambell, p. 229.

12. "The Life of John Penn," John Taylor Papers, Duke University Library, Durham, N.C.

13. Henry H. Simms, *Life of John Taylor* (Richmond, Va.: The William Byrd Press, Inc., 1932), pp. 17–18. The three parishes were: St. Mary's, the northeastern third of the county including the land later named "Hazelwood" by Taylor; St. Margaret's, the southwestern third of the county; and Drysdale, a southeast-by-northwest strip lying between the other two. See Cambell, pp. 101–2, 430. Pendleton's estate, "Edmundsbury," was located on land once belonging to James Taylor I, Pendleton's maternal grandfather, Taylor's great-grandfather, the original Taylor immigrant to America. See David John Mays, *Edmund Pendleton*, 2 vols. (Cambridge, Mass.: Harvard University Press, 1952), 1:33, 139. Although the vestry records for this period have been lost, the Pendletons and Taylors are thought to have attended an Anglican church one mile northeast of Bowling Green; see Bishop William Meade, *Old Churches, Ministers, and Families of Virginia*, (Philadelphia: J. B. Lippincott Company, 1897), 1:410.

14. Joseph Martin, *Gazeteer of Virginia*, p. 142; Cambell, pp. 94, 101–2; Marshall Wingfield, A *History of Caroline County, Virginia* (Richmond, Va.: Press of Trevvett, Christian and Company, 1924), pp. 303–15. The Disciples of Christ were also called *Campbellites* after Thomas Campbell, founder of the sect. Broadus corresponded with Andrew Campbell (Thomas's son) while in Caroline. The interpretation of the Disciples is from H. Richard Niebuhr's *The Social Sources of Denominationalism* (New York: Meridian Books, 1957), p. 179.

15. Letter from Taylor to Timothy Dwight, September 3, 1805, microfilm typescript of a letter published in the *Richmond Examiner,* June 20, 1863. Included in roll of microfilm, "Letters to Prominent Men," University of Virginia Library. Also reprinted in "A Sheaf of Old Letters," ed. David R. Barbee, *Tyler's Quarterly Historical and Genealogical Magazine,* 32 (October 1950): 82–84. Also see Taylor, *Arator,* p. 90; Cambell, p. 430.

16. Cambell, p. 432; Wingfield p. 12. On November 24, 1764, he baptized 115 Negro adults, and on March 31, 1766, over 300 more.

17. Grimes, p. 95.

18. Parrington, 1:218.

19. The complicated genealogical relationships of the Taylors, Pendletons, Pollards, Penns, and Madisons need no full elaboration here, but the major relationships are of interest. The first American John Taylor (1635–1698) had three children of importance to this study: James, John II, and Mary. James's great-grandson was President James Madison and a later descendant was President Zachary Taylor. John II was the grandfather of John Taylor of Caroline, making the latter and James Madison distant cousins. Mary Taylor married a Pendleton (as had John II) and one of her sons was Edmund Pendleton. Edmund Pendleton and John Taylor of Caroline's father married sisters, making both Pendleton and his wife blood relatives of John Taylor of Caroline. See Meade, 2:415; Simms, p. 3; Mays, 1:138–39; and Wingfield, pp. 39–40, 471. The Wingfield source must be used with caution. It is incorrect on the birthdate of Taylor, his age when orphaned, and the identities of his father and father-in-law. The most authoritative genealogical reference is Woodson T. White's communication from Joe W. Taylor, "The Taylor Family," *William and Mary College Quarterly* 12 (October 1903): 129–34.

20. James Taylor II, the father of John Taylor of Caroline, married Ann Pollard. John was born probably on 19 December 1753, and his sister Elizabeth three years later. There is considerable disagreement among the sources about Taylor's age and birthplace, and his habit of rounding off numbers when he talked did nothing to help, but most authorities agree that he was born at "Mill Farm" in Caroline County in 1753. His father died sometime during the winter of 1757. See Hunt, p. 5; Dodd, p. 214; Wingfield, p. 122; U.S. Congress, House of Representatives, *Biographical Directory of the American Congress, 1774–1927* (Washington, D.C.: U.S. Government Printing Office, 1928), p. 1,600. All of the above sources were wrong either about the date or the place, or both. The accepted date is found in Joe W. Taylor, "The Taylor Family." Edmund Pendleton, "Jr.," was also raised by Pendleton, but actually was his nephew; see Mays, 1:140–41.

21. Mays, 1:138–41. Taylor's sister married at age eighteen and moved to Kentucky. See letter from Capt. John Taylor to Julia L. Taylor, March 7, 1875, John Taylor Papers, Duke University Library, Durham, N.C.

22. Joe W. Taylor, "The Taylor Family," p. 133; Wingfield, pp. 39–40.

23. Mays, 1:355–57, 2: chaps. 4–6.

24. The Pendleton household occasionally faced financial difficulties during Taylor's boyhood, and it was a family legend that he went without shoes while attending school. Taylor inherited little from his father and spent most of that to support his participation in the American Revolution. See letter from Capt. John Taylor to Julia L. Taylor, March 7, 1875, John Taylor Papers, Duke University Library, letter from John Taylor to Edmund Pendleton, November 17, 1777, Archives of the New York Historical Society, New York City.

25. Dodd, p. 215, mentions Henry's influence upon Taylor. For the military controversy, see Mays, 2:53–54, 132, 265, chap. 11. passim. According to Mays, "Pendleton and Washington were friends of long standing" even when they disagreed on

particular issues, such as Washington's appointment as commander-in-chief; see Mays, 2:24. *See* Mays, 2:310 also for Pendleton's annual letter to Washington. Taylor's opinion of Washington is revealed in his letter to Pendleton, April 13, 1777, "Original Letters: Col. John Taylor to Edmund Pendleton," *William and Mary College Quarterly* (October 1895): 103. Other relevant discussions are Simms, pp. 18–19: Brown and Brown, pp. 286–87.

26. Letter from John Taylor to General Woodford, May 22, 1778, Manuscripts Relating to John Taylor, University of Virginia Library, Charlottesville; Mays 1:140–41; Simms, p. 4. The apparent distance between Taylor and Madison was probably partly the result of the formal style of writing popular at the time and partly the result of the real philosophic and partisan differences that split the two in 1808–1809, disturbing their relationship thereafter. Taylor attacked Madison's contributions to the *Federalist in his Inquiry* in 1814 and never passed up a chance to roast him thereafter. Chapter 2 below discusses their partisan differences and chapter 8 their philosophic clash.

27. College records show him as an alumnus in 1770, but he may have continued attending until 1771, because college records indicate that Pendleton was still paying his expenses in that year. See J.A.C. Chandler and E. G. Swen, "Notes Relating to Some of the Students Who Attended the College of William and Mary, 1753–1770," *William and Mary College Quarterly,* n.s 1 (January 1921): 40; and idem, "Notes Relative to Some of the Students Who Attended the College of William and Mary, 1770–1778," *William and Mary College Quarterly,* n.s. 1 (April 1921): 128. These college records show a balance charged to Pendleton, in September 1770, and of his still making payments for board and tuition in March of 1771. See also Simms, pp. 6–7.

28. Thomas Jefferson, "Autobiography," in *The Writings of Thomas Jefferson,* ed. Andrew A. Lipscomb and Albert Ellery Bergh, 20 vols. (Washington D.C.: The Thomas Jefferson Memorial Association, 1903), 1:3–4; Albert J. Beveridge, *The Life of John Marshall,* 4 vols. (Boston: Houghton, Mifflin Company, 1919), 1: 154–55; U.S. Congress, *Biographical Directory,* pp. 1,279, 1,323, 1,734. Taylor's grandson thought that Taylor and Marshall had attended William and Mary together, an opinion wrong by ten years. See letter from Capt. John Taylor to Julia L. Taylor, March 7, 1875, John Taylor Papers, Duke University Library.

29. Edmund Pendleton, "The History of Colo. John Taylor of Caroline County, Virginia," (1801), photostat, Miscellaneous Manuscripts, Virginia State Library, Richmond; also typescript in John Taylor Papers, Duke University Library, Durham, N.C. Since Pendleton wrote this pamphlet to defend Taylor against the charge of anarchism, it is possible that he was not bending over backward to emphasize Taylor's democratic side.

30. Ernst Cassirer, *The Philosophy of the Enlightenment* (Princeton, N.J.: Princeton University Press, 1951), p. 6; Leo Strauss, *Natural Right and History* (Chicago: The University of Chicago Press, 1953), p. 168; Peter Gay, *The Enlightenment: an Interpretation of the Rise of Modern Paganism* (N.Y.: Vintage Books, 1968, p. 77.

31. Letters from John Taylor to Wilson Cary Nicholas, May 14, 1806; June 10, 1806; August 22, 1807; February 5, 1808, in Edgehill-Randolph Papers, University of Virginia Library, Charlottesville. See also letter from Taylor to Madison, January 15, 1808, University of Virginia Library. His criticism of Madison in *New Views* can be found on pp. 26, 32, 44, 83, 90–93, 97, 162, 167–68; while his remarks on Hamilton are on pp. 64–65, 68–70, 73–75, 81, 108–9, 146, 149. His discussion of the *Federalist* in the *Inquiry* is in chap. 7, which includes Taylor's only mention of Jay's work on the *Federalist.* Jay was thoroughly saturated with monarchial prejudices in Taylor's opinion.

32. Harry Elmer Barnes, *A History of Historical Writing* (New York: Dover Publications, 1962), pp. 147, 161–62; H. Trevor Colbourn, *The Lamp of Experience* (New York: W. W.

Norton & Company, Inc., 1965), pp. 4–7, 188; Curti, pp. 128–129, 145; Raynal wrote *The Philosophic and Political Settlements and Trade of Europeans in the East and West Indies* (1771). Marshall's *Life of Washington* was a popular classic, but its Federalist bias was so notorious that Taylor probably used it as he did Hamilton: when he agreed with such men, he could be *sure* he was right. Russell is mentioned in *Inquiry*, pp. 238–39, 421; Ramsay in *Construction*, pp. 63–64, 136; and Raynal in the "Letter on the Necessity of Defending the Rights and Interests of Agriculture, Addressed to the Delegation of the United Agricultural Societies of Virginia," *American Farmer*, 3 (July 20, 1821): 433.

33. *Argument*, p. 26; *also* John Fred Bell, *A History of Economic Thought* (New York: The Ronald Press Company, 1953), pp. 90, 240–42. Malthus and Godwin are discussed in the *Inquiry*, pp. 540–45; *Tyranny*, pp. 123, 184, 208–9. The important endorsement of Arthur Young is in a letter to George W. Jeffreys, August 16, 1816, published in the *American Farmer*, 2 (June 16, 1820): 93. Saul K. Padover presented the view that Taylor was influenced by the Physiocrats in *The Genius of America* (New York: McGraw-Hill Book Company, Inc. 1960), p. 111. That view was rejected by William D. Grampp, "John Taylor," p. 260, but it was still endorsed by McConnell, p. 31.

34. *Construction*, pp. 52, 148; letter from John Taylor to Henry Tazewell, April 13, 1796, Tazewell Papers, Virginia State Library, Richmond; *Enquiry*, p. 43.

35. References to Swift are in *Inquiry*, chap. 7, passim; letter from Taylor to Thomas Ritchie, March 30, 1809, in *Pamphlet*, p. 25; *New Views*, pp. 294–99; and *Annals of the Congress of the United States*, 43 vols., *Annals of the Eighteenth Congress, First Session* (Washington D.C.: Gales and Seaton, 1856): 678. References to Cervantes are in *Inquiry*, p. 39; Taylor, *Arator*, pp. 94, 192; *Construction*, p. 205; *Tyranny*, p. 137; and *New Views*, p. 162. The references to Cervantes in "Columbus," p. 11, and "We the People" suggest Taylor's authorship of these anonymous documents, although he denied he was interested in public office at the time.

36. Bernard Bailyn, *The Ideological Origins of the American Revolution* (Cambridge, Mass.: Harvard University Press, 1967), pp. 35–54; Gordon S. Wood, *The Creation of the American Republic, 1776–1787* (New York: W. W. Norton & Company, Inc., 1969), chap. 1.

37. The writers emphasizing Taylor's connection with the Virginia landed aristocracy are Drell, pp. 285, 287–88; Dauer and Hammond, p. 402; and Mudge, p. 5. The distinction between *planter* and *farmer* is one made for this discussion. Planters were farmers, of course, but the question is whether Taylor considered himself as a member of the planter elite or a member of a profession spread throughout the United States. The Browns maintained that *planter* meant *farmer* in Virginia before 1786, p. 43. Wilbur J. Cash, *The Mind of the South* (New York: Vintage Books, pp. 4–8. Cash says that the Virginia aristocracy did not develop until after 1700. He estimated the number of genuine Southern aristocrats in 1860 as 500. Even if William E. Dodd's estimate of four to five thousand was correct, Cash argues that Virginia aristocrats alone couldn't have accounted for them. Clement Eaton's *Growth of Southern Civilization, 1790–1860* (New York: Harper and Brothers, 1961), chap. 1, passim, accepts the Virginia "country gentleman" model of aristocracy as the stylesetter for all the South, but points out its humble origins and the ease of access into it. He also singles out Taylor, Madison, Macon, and Jefferson as especially sympathetic to the simpler rural folk.

38. Cash, p. 3.

39. Drell, pp. 285–98. The Browns trace this interpretation to William Wirt's biography of Patrick Henry published during Taylor's lifetime. See Robert and Katherine Brown, p. 34.

40. U.S. Bureau of the Census, *Heads of Families at the First Census of the United States Taken in the Year 1790: Records of the State Enumerations: 1782 to 1785: Virginia* (Baltimore,

Md.. Genealogical Publishing Co., 1966), p. 9. The number of slaves in Caroline was 10,292 in 1803; the total population was 17,489. Edmund Pendleton, Jr.'s count found 1,150 families in Caroline with nearly 800 owning slaves. The slave total in Caroline in 1810 had increased by 472 since 1790, while the total population had increased by only 73. See Edmund Pendelton, Jr., *Third Census of the United States (Year 1810) for the County of Caroline, State of Virginia,* typescript, (Washington, D.C., Library of Congress, 1934).

41. Ibid.; breakdowns for the two families were: Sarah Pendleton, 46 slaves; Edmund Pendleton, Sr., 62 slaves; John Pendleton, 38 slaves; Edmund Pendleton, 25 slaves; Edmund Taylor, 59 slaves; William Taylor, 1 slave; James Taylor, 38 slaves; Reuben Taylor, 40 slaves; John Taylor of Caroline, 145 slaves. Joseph Bream's 293 slaves made him the largest slaveholder in Caroline in 1810. The breaking point of 40 slaves was chosen for convenience. The Census defined a planter as one with 30 slaves, so the number of large slaveholders would be larger by that standard.

42. Simms, p. 145. In 1798 (at field-hand prime prices) the value of Taylor's slaves would have been $21,700; in 1810, $72,500. See Ulrich B. Phillips, *American Negro Slavery* (New York: D. Appleton and Company, 1918), p. 371. Russell Kirk, *Randolph of Roanoke* (Chicago: Henry Regnery Company, 1964), pp. 131, 465. Randolph's slaves had been included in the mortgage to British creditors that Randolph had inherited. The slaves, thus, could not have been sold or freed during the large portion of Randolph's lifetime that the mortgage remained. Regardless of that, Randolph refused to buy or sell slaves as a matter of principle. He also refused to do without their services.

43. Because of the interest in the Civil War, most statistics reported in standard works on slavery refer to the 1850–60 period. Kenneth Stampp maintained that the same generalizations about slave owning can be made for the entire period of 1830–60. He reported only 10,000 families constituting the planter aristocracy in 1860. These families each used 50 or more slaves. Three thousand families owned more than one hundred slaves: See *The Peculiar Institution* (New York: Vintage Books, 1956), pp. 30–31. Statistics from a special census in the Virginia tidewater for 1782–83 reported slaveholdings on *single* plantations (sometimes the slaves owned by an absentee landlord were recorded in his overseers' names) as ranging from 108–257 in the highest ranges. See Phillips, p. 84. Considered in this light, Taylor was one of the great slaveowners of the South. Only .7% of the families owning slaves in 1860 owned 100 or more, yet he owned 145 by 1810. At the same time, he was far from the largest holder in his own immediate neighborhood.

44. Robert and Katherine Brown, p. 74 (quotation). See also pp. 72, 76.

45. Mudge, pp. 5–6. The Browns considered the planters around Port Royal in Caroline as middle sized in wealth (ibid.).

46. Mays, p. 2: 155; Simms, chap. 3, pp. 33–46. Letters from John Taylor to the Executors of Col. Buchanan of Montgomery, February 2, 1784, Miscellaneous Manuscripts, Virginia State Library, Richmond; and to Governor Henry Lee, March 10, 1792, in *Calendar of Virginia State Papers and Other Manuscripts Preserved in the Capitol at Richmond,* 11 vols. ed. William B. Palmer and Sherwin McRae (Richmond, Va.: Rush U. Deer, Superintendent of Public Printing, 1885), 5: 462.

47. Letter from Capt. John Taylor to Julia L. Taylor, March 7, 1875, John Taylor Papers, Duke University Library, Durham, N.C. Taylor's grandson said, "My Father has told me he has often seen Grand Father weighing out gold and silver to pay for his lands."

48. Simms, p. 145; *see also* Pendleton. In 1845 Taylor's estate *Hazelwood* was worth $42,435 for the land alone. See Dauer and Hammond, p. 385. *Hazelwood* became a favorite stopping place for Southern statesmen: Taylor invited Monroe to visit him before the paint was dry; see letter to Monroe, March 25, 1798, in "Correspondence," p. 270. Also see letter from John Randolph at Roanoke to John Taylor, November 13, 1810, Massachusetts Historical Society, Boston. Taylor bought *Hazelwood* from Robert Gaines

Beverley, a rakish descendant of the master of Beverley Park. See William G. Stanard, ed., "The Beverley Family," *Virginia Magazine of History and Biography* 22 (January 1914): 102.

49. Leonard Woods Labaree, *Conservatism in Early American History* (Ithaca, N.Y.: Cornell University Press, 1959), pp. 32–33. Labaree is one who believed that social cleavage occurred as a consequence of the presence of great landowners. Louis B. Wright reported the estates of some of the colonial Virginia giants as including such amounts as that owned by "King" Carter (d. 1732), who owned 300,000 acres and 1,000 slaves; William Byrd of *Westover* (d. 1704), who owned 179,000 acres; and William Fitzhugh (d. 1701), who owned 23,500. See Louis B. Wright, pp. 160, 249, 317, 346. See also Mays, 1:33; McDonald, pp. 72, 226, 275, 277; Robert and Katherine Brown, p. 36; and Eaton, *Growth,* p. 99.

50. Letter from John Taylor to Governor Benjamin Harrison, April 20, 1783, in *Calendar of Virginia State Papers* (Richmond, Virginia: James E. Goode, Printer, 1883), 3:470. After discussing the claim of his relative, Taylor stated: "As to myself (although to my capacity the claim appears to be well founded, let me repeat again, that I am not solicitous about it"). Simms, p. 15, reports a grant of 5,333⅓ acres made in 1799 to Taylor. See also Mays, 2:183–85. The Taylor-Pendleton petition was entitled, "Caroline County Legislative Petition, No. 634, June 1, 1781," in Virginia State Library, Richmond. The petition claimed satisfaction from North Carolina on the basis of "the spirit of Confed. of the Am. States which diffused a principle of general citizenship in the members of each throughout the whole. . . . " See also H. R. McIlwaine, ed., "Journal of the House of Delegates for the Session Beginning the First of March 1781," *Bulletin of Virginia State Library, 17* (January 1928), June 1 entries. Approval of the petition took ten days; see resolution of June 11 in ibid. Records of Taylor's pleading before the North Carolina legislature and its subsequent actions are reported in Walter Clark, ed., *The State Records of North Carolina* (Goldsboro: Nash Brothers, 1899), 16:44, 58; (1901) 19:31, 43; (1905) 24:447. See also the letter from Taylor to Mrs. Mary (Ayres) Bouliware, January 6, 1782, the Ayres Family Papers, 1741–1892. Virginia Historical Society, Richmond, in which Taylor refused to plead a case because of important matters pressing in North Carolina.

51. Taylor's trips to North Carolina increased his property in another way, because shortly thereafter he married Lucy Penn, John's daughter. Penn often gave them gifts, willed Taylor 15 slaves, and Lucy inherited 700 acres and 31 slaves from her brother. See "Deed Made Between John and Lucy Taylor and Their Son, Edmund," September 12, 1809, Caroline County, Duke University Library, Durham, N.C.; Simms, p. 33. Grant McConnell pointed out that Jefferson also benefited materially from his marriage, p. 17. As far as can be discovered, these few trips made to North Carolina constituted Taylor's total personal exposure to states south of Virginia.

52. Even after the North Carolina law was passed, Taylor had difficulty convincing the squatters of the error of their ways; see letter from Taylor to William Preston, June 8, 1782, Preston Papers, Virginia Historical Society, Richmond. See also Mays, 2:186; letter from Col. William Christian to Col. Sampson Mathews, December 30, 1782, in *Calendar of Virginia,* 3:406; and letter from Taylor to John Baylor, November 4, 1811, Baylor Family Papers, University of Virginia Library, Charlottesville.

53. The formative period of Taylor's thought must have preceded the debate over the Constitution and his term of office in the Senate in 1792–94, for the views he expressed by this period are virtually the same he continued to elaborate on for thirty years.

54. Merrill Jensen, *The New Nation* (New York: Vintage Books, 1965), pp. 180–81, 235, 305–7. Virginia farmers were less burdened by taxes than others because of the state's redemption of its paper money at depreciated current values; its declaring soldiers' land certificates as legal tender for debts; its abandoning of the poll tax; and its

use of the property taxes related to land values. See also U.S. Bureau of the Census, *Historical Statistics of the United States: Colonial Times to 1957* (Washington, D.C.: U.S. Government Printing Office, 1960), p. 547.

55. From 1790 to 1800, 13 of the 20 counties in Maryland and 23 of the 40 counties in Virginia lost population; see Craven, *Soil Exhaustion,* p. 119. Caroline's population stopped growing during this time and stabilized.

56. Avery O. Craven, "The Agricultural Reformers of the Ante-Bellum South," *American Historical Review,* 33 (January 1928): 302. See also idem, "John Taylor and Southern Agriculture," *Journal of Southern History* 4 (1938): 138.

57. Drell, pp. 285–98. The period of time immediately following Taylor's life found the planters in Caroline still described as living in a simple style. They lived in "ease and elegance" but there was no great "profusion of food." Despite that, what they had they served up to guests with "so little form and stiffness, that it amply makes up for all deficiencies in other respects." See letter from Briscoe Gerard Baldwin, Jr. to Frances Cornelia (Baldwin) Stuart, (n.d., mid-nineteenth century), The Stuart Family Papers, 1785–1888, Virginia Historical Society, Richmond. Baldwin had dined at *Hazelwood* while serving as a tutor in a nearby boys' academy. Carl Bridenbaugh dates the decline of the "Chesapeake Society" planters as beginning in the 1750s and in full swing by the 1760s. See *Myths & Realities: Societies of the Colonial South* (New York: Atheneum, 1974), p. 14.

58. Craven, *Soil Exhaustion,* pp. 14–16, 81. Mays thought that the tobacco plantation system was, in reality, bankrupt even before the American Revolution; see Mays, pp. 1:116–17.

59. Joseph Martin, p. 142; Cambell, pp. 174–75; Mays 1:29–30; Harvey Wish, *George Fitzhugh: Propagandist of the Old South* (Baton Rouge, La.: Louisiana State University Press, 1943), p. 13. Fitzhugh lived in Port Royal.

60. Letter from Taylor to Aaron Burr, March 25, 1803, in Matthew L. Davis, ed., *Memoirs of Aaron Burr,* (New York: Harper and Brothers, 1837), 2:236.

61. Letter from Taylor to Wilson Cary Nicholas, August 26, 1802, Massachusetts Historical Society, Boston.

62. Letter from Taylor to Wilson Cary Nicholas, March 13, 1803, Edgehill-Randolph Papers, University of Virginia Library, Charlottesville.

63. Letters from Taylor to Wilson Cary Nicholas, May 24, 1804; April 4, 1805; April 13, 1805; March 4, 1806; April 14, 1806; May 14, 1806; June 10, 1806; June 26, 1806; August 22, 1807; October 26, 1807; May 10, 1808; June 20, 1808; August 29, 1808; April 6, 1809; June 16, 1809. All of the above are in the Edgehill-Randolph Papers, University of Virginia Library, Charlottesville. See also letter from Taylor to Peter Carr, September 18, 1806, Gabriella Page Papers, Virginia Historical Society, Richmond; letter from Taylor to John Baylor, November 4, 1811, Baylor Family Papers, University of Virginia, Charlottesville. In the latter, Taylor was still complaining about his financial difficulties.

64. *Definition,* p. 4.

65. Taylor, *Arator,* p. 3.

66. *Inquiry,* pp. 618–19.

67. Taylor to Wilson Cary Nicholas, April 4, 1805, Edgehill-Randolph Papers, University of Virginia Library, Charlottesville. Taylor often communicated to Jefferson through Nicholas.

2

POLITICAL PARTIES

It is a historic irony that the independent habits of thought that came naturally to John Taylor through his exposure to Enlightenment authors, through his own family, and through the security provided by a comfortable economic station were first put to work in the hack cause of partisan pamphleteering. It is important to study Taylor's writings on parties for their bearing on his key doctrine of divided power. There can be no question but that Taylor initially looked upon parties as an evil, and always considered them a danger, but it is also true that he ultimately changed his mind and grudgingly accepted the necessity of political parties. Since his acceptance of them occurred after the development of his doctrine of divided power, it may be that his mature view was that they were a part of the same system for restraining governmental power.

This chapter will trace Taylor's descriptions of the rise of parties, the evil effects he attributed to them, and the hesitant approval he eventually gave them. It will be seen that his original opposition to parties was the direct result of his theoretical stance, and that his acceptance of parties was accompanied by a shifting of this theoretical position. In terms of his status as a theorist, this shift reveals that Taylor's sensitivity to practical politics was capable of forcing a revision in his theory. Such flexibility is not characteristic of a rigidly dogmatic thinker, yet Taylor has frequently been interpreted as such.

Notes for this chapter begin on p. 90.

A. Origin of Political Parties

Political parties were not evident in the First Congress, according to Nobel E. Cunningham, Jr. There were disagreements among individuals, but there was little consistency in their voting records and no evidence of bloc voting. By the middle of 1792 this was beginning to change and some leaders were beginning to use the term *party* and define their positions in opposition to those other leaders they regarded as opponents. By the time of the Second Congress, two rival voting groups were discernible in the House of Representatives.[1]

This was the step in party development that was occurring when Taylor replaced Richard Henry Lee as Senator in the winter of 1792. By the end of his short term of service in 1794, Taylor had become involved in the emerging party struggle. The very publication of his *Definition of Parties* in that year, for example, was a party maneuver that hoped to achieve expulsion of most of the opposition party's members from all United States legislative assembles.[2]

Taylor opened his pamphlet with a recognition of the advanced stage that party development had reached: "The existence of two parties in Congress, is apparent. The fact is disclosed almost upon every important question."[3] In his opinion it did not matter to parties whether the issue dealt with domestic or foreign policy, for "the magnetism of opposite views draws them wide as the poles assunder."[4] This division over issues within the Congress was creating problems for the entire nation because the public interest was perilously poised in the hands of two equally matched parties. "Every patriot deprecates a disunion, which is only to be obviated by a national preference of one of these parties."[5]

Taylor continued to give heavy weight to the influence of ideas in the development of political parties. The next stages of party development, he thought, were the direct result of differences in opinion over legislative issues. Above all in importance was the Hamiltonian funding system's influence over the Federalist Party. The funding of the states' debts had benefited "the 5,000" who held securities at the expense of "the 5,000,000" who had lost money through the depreciation of the original bonds and through the creation of a tax to feed a sinking fund. The Federalist Party was attempting to institutionalize its existence through the use of the same techniques that Robert Walpole had used.[6]

A further milestone in the development of parties was marked by the debate over the Jay Treaty.[7] The use of John Jay as a foreign negotiator while he was serving on the Supreme Court was opposed by Taylor, but before the treaty came up for a vote Henry Tazewell had placed Taylor in the Senate. Taylor coached Tazewell from the sidelines on the treaty, and exhorted him to turn the debate into an attempt at thorough reform after the type Taylor had advocated in his *Definition of Parties*. Taylor was frankly pessimistic that this redirection of emphasis could be achieved, because of the lack of unity among the Republican majority in the House. The very least that could be done, Tazewell was advised, was to refuse appropriations to implement the treaty. The "paper faction" of British interests would volunteer to pay the expenses out of self-interest and their treasonous connection with the Federalists would be revealed for all to see. Thus Taylor hoped to use the Jay Treaty to galvanize the Republican Party into increased unity.[8]

The parties sharpened their defenses and increased their vigor, in Taylor's opinion, during their debate over the proper role for the United States to play in world politics. In the *Defence of the Measures of the Administration of Thomas Jefferson* (1804), it was pointed out that parties had been unimportant up to the time of Washington's second election. This was "when federal principles, unpolluted by party sensations, were in the full tide of successful experiment."[9] Sympathizers with the British had already been at work, however, attempting to secure United States involvement in world affairs. The Adams administration's zeal for establishing embassies, for example, had soon drawn the country into European squabbles. The Army had been called into existence to support this involvement, and taxes created to maintain the Army. Added to these financial burdens was the Sedition Law, which had been a bald attempt by the Federalists to wipe out the Republicans.

In thrusting Americans into European politics and taxing them heavily to support these adventures, the Federalists had outsmarted themselves, Taylor noted much later with satisfaction. "The general interest was excited, though slowly, by the alien and sedition laws. . . . The laws were consigned to the grave, and the party which made them dislodged from power."[10] While the law was in its early days, however, Taylor had been less certain of its effects, and had feared that it would increase the strength of the Federalist Party. "If the mass of our citizens are now republican," he wrote, "will submission to anti-republican measures, increase that Mass?"[11]

A modern scholar agreed with Taylor that armies, taxes, and the Sedition Act were the downfall of the Federalist Party, but felt that the first two of these factors were really the most damaging.[12] Yet it is difficult to read the correspondence of Taylor and his associates for the years 1798-1800 and escape appreciating the fear they felt. They wrote as though Adams were at their elbow and Hamilton were steaming open their morning mail. Memories of this time may have caused Taylor to overemphasize the effects of the Sedition Act as one of the major influences upon party development.[13]

The stages of party development that followed the administration of Thomas Jefferson were not any more beneficial, in Taylor's opinion, than those which had gone before. Regardless of the fact that Republican Party members held the major offices at both the state and federal levels, ambition had made even them unreliable leaders.

It was at this point that Taylor first began to discuss state political parties. Midway through the Jefferson administration he had observed the beginnings of a third party, drawn from the disenchanted members of both the Federalist and Republican Parties. This party had already made itself felt in the Virginia Assembly through its defense of banking interests. A year later he counted "at least ten distinct republican Sections in the United States, enemies to each other."[14] The small parties or sections were quick to unite with the Federalists against the Republicans. These ten sections were not personal cabals, in Taylor's opinion. DeWitt Clinton, for example, was not blamed by Taylor for the parties in New York State. New York cabals were the logical products of the rewards that the governmental system of the state offered to its political officials. The office of mayor in New York City was a particularly troublesome "apple of discord." In Taylor's Virginia, he smugly suggested, men such as DeWitt Clinton would be held to their public duties and parties would be less of a problem.[15]

After the ten factions he had counted in 1807, Taylor steadily decreased the number of parties he thought active in the country. In the *Inquiry* he mentioned four political parties, two of principle and two of self-interest, but he may have meant by this four styles of activity rather than actual organizations. By the time *Tyranny Unmasked* was written in 1822, Taylor's opinion was that the Republican Party was dead and powerless, although perhaps not beyond revival.[16] During the struggle in Congress among possible successors to Monroe, which began in 1823, Taylor counted two major parties and at least four "juntos." On the Senate floor he argued that the two old parties' places had been taken by two new ones, which he compared to the "Ultras" and "Radicals" that existed in France. He aligned himself with the Radicals, and maintained that they were the true defenders of the Constitution. Even so, he thought that this group switched colors too easily: " . . . whenever the radical party are influenced by any project . . . it most judiciously picks out of its crest all the other feathers . . . mounts the white cockade and acts upon occasion after occasion with its adversary."[17] Those members of Congress who did not belong to either the Ultra or the Radical party groups vacillated in between, sometimes siding with one, sometimes with the other. Although Taylor occasionally called this residual group a "third party" or the "vacillating party" he probably did not regard them as a true political party. He did not think that this group would have any permanence, but would disappear if the possibility were removed of the House of Representatives electing the President when the electoral college failed to produce a majority.[18]

Although Taylor died at this point of development in American politics, his writings had recorded the development of political parties over a thirty-year period, from the first stirrings in Congress over foreign policy to the shifting coalitions forming about popular candidates in the 1820s. Throughout this period he saw the crucial points of development in parties as intellectual issues. Issues had been present at the birth of parties in Congress and the rise of the grassroots Republican opposition was also the result of an intellectual controversy. Although the fragmentation of the Republican Party toward the end of Jefferson's administration was more the consequence of selfishness than a difference over important issues, the defense of the Constitution became an issue again in the 1820s, and the Ultras and the Radicals took sides on that basis. Thus, Taylor considered ideas and debates to have occupied an important historic role in the growth of parties. It was only natural that his eventual acceptance of parties was qualified by the requirement that the individual not be forced to surrender his will to the will of a party majority.

B. Harmful Effects of Parties

Taylor did not change his mind much about the evil effects of parties as time went on. Even though there is evidence that he had a growing appreciation of parties in his later years, Taylor always warned of their negative effects. Sometimes the harm that parties did was intentional, and sometimes it was a by-product of their activities, but whichever it was, harmful effects had to be criticized and corrected.

Intentionally harmful effects were usually described by Taylor in terms of money. He thought that it should be clear to any but a guilty observer that the very existence of parties was an indication that someone was stealing something. Disputes between only a few individuals over money could inspire them to split the nation into parties in order to defend their personal interests, "and an appearance of this species of aristocracy, is a proof that its pablum exists."[19] Parties had taken republican institutions and created "extravagance, patronage, heavy taxation, exclusive privileges and consolidation."[20] Taylor priced the cost of these excesses at $460 million between 1792 and 1822. Parties had created this large an amount of governmental expenditure in order to make the total society dependent upon it. As with a malignant growth, the expense caused by parties could not be removed without endangering the life of the patient.

The means used by parties to encourage this governmental waste were taxes and offices. "Taxes are the subsistence of party ... [which] transfers wealth from a mass to a selection."[21] Patronage, for its part, offered a range of offices that only excited the contenders for them. There had been a doubling of patronage in the states and the federal government since the framing of the United States Constitution, he thought. But official patronage was only one side of the story, because its bad effects were not limited to the creation of offices and salaries. Officeholders in Congress were strategically placed and could use their knowledge to make speculative investments in governmentally subsidized activities such as banks. They were also privy to governmental secrets that allowed them to speculate in candidates, either by insinuating themselves into the good graces of up-and-coming politicians, or by controlling a candidate's access to the knowledge necessary to improve his position. Finally, officeholders could increase their salaries by the simple expedient of delaying the deliberations of Congress until it became virtually a standing army that never adjourned.[22]

The unintentional, harmful effects of parties were as numerous and as damaging as the direct varieties, Taylor observed. One unintentional effect was the weakening of the unity of society. There is a strain in liberal thought that has always suspected voluntary associations as competitors for the public's loyalty, and Taylor's thought was no exception. Generally this view has been based on the notion that private associations detract from the sense of community necessary for a well-integrated society. Both Hobbes and Rousseau seem to have reached such a conclusion on private associations. Taylor came to a similar conclusion when he remarked to Monroe in 1810 that the struggles for wealth and power between parties had come to dominate public thinking. As a consequence, American unity was on the wane.[23]

Instability accompanied the disunifying features of party competition. One of the first things Taylor had criticized about parties was the instability resulting from the nearly equal party groups in Congress.[24] This was a copy of the British balanced government that had only substituted parties for the classes used in England. "Power will fluctuate like wealth . . . . And every fluctuation must disorder the fanciful idea of the balance. A precise equipoise among these three interests, could not exist above a moment in an age."[25] Despotisms were stable because they were free of party spirit, but in republican systems, subject to rotation in office, parties realized their fleeting grasp on authority and tried every minute to enrich themselves. Such frenzied activity resulted in the instability that Taylor considered one of the most detrimental tendencies of parties.

At their worst, parties might cause war. Again, Taylor did not mean that parties intentionally would cause war, or even that violent conflict might result from the bitter competition between political parties. Instead, he meant that party loyalty would so cloud individual judgments that leaders might stumble into unneeded wars. In 1812, for example, he feared that Madison had so enflamed Congress with war sentiment for political purposes that war might be inevitable, regardless of what Madison really wanted. Taylor's fears on this score, of course, were well founded.[26]

Under some conditions parties could have the opposite effect of instability or war. Stagnation was also a product of party activity, according to Taylor. He first developed this opinion during his 1803-4 term in the Senate when he had been bitterly disappointed by Jefferson's unwillingness to risk unpopularity by pressing for strong constitutional changes. Taylor had complained on the floor of the Senate that both the ins and the outs had a tendency to resist such change, because the ins were benefiting then and the outs knew their turn would come. Reflecting later, he decided that all parties had followed the precedents that even their most hated predecessors had established. "Every precedent, however clearly demonstrated to be unconstitutional . . . by a party out of power, will be held sacred by the same party in."[27] No matter how much the fluctuation of parties might seem like a kaleidoscope, he warned, the pebbles causing the designs would remain the same. Parties accomplished this by convincing the gullible that the party was the government, and then by preaching Robert Filmer's doctrine of passive obedience: opposition to the government is opposition to the nation itself. Added to this deception, he pointed out, was the unwarranted confidence many placed in the good intentions of parties as organizations. All of these malpractices resulted in, first stagnation, and then unlimited government. Neither of these conditions might have been the conscious intention of parties, however. [28]

Both the intentional and the unintentional undesirable effects of parties combined to obstruct the proper functioning of American government. The growth of federalism as a system of governing, for example, had been stunted, because the Federalist Party had filled the Northwest Territory with armies and prevented settlement in order to profit from the sale of military supplies and the advantages given through British treaties. Moreover, Taylor also pointed out, parties have fostered secrecy in governmental operations in order to maintain the support that they would lose if reports on their conduct were public knowledge. The electoral processes were thwarted in several ways by parties, Taylor thought. Corruption was only the most obvious way. For example, it had not been the intention of the Constitution to allow parties to attain such an influence over the election of President that loyalties would be divided, popular election inhibited, and selection by states voting as units in the House of Representatives encouraged. Yet, parties had been able to accomplish what the Constitution had tried to prevent.[29]

Parties prevented popular control and true majority rule within legislatures, Taylor argued, because of their leaders' power over their members. Many times this resulted in a tiny minority of a legislature actually controlling the vote under the façade of majority rule. The leaders of a party could control the whole legislature by carrying a majority in their own party's caucus. In effect, this could mean that twenty-six percent of a party that composed fifty-one percent of a legislature could control the voting of that legislature. This thwarting of majority rule, of course, could not occur unless a party held a majority of the legislature, and if a party held most of the seats in a legislature, its majority decisions would almost be tantamount to those of the full membership. Taylor did not comment on the propriety of the latter situation.[30]

The ties of party loyalty operated in ways that seemed dangerous to Taylor. These loyalties spread, contaminating the judgment of governed and governors alike. Even the judicial system's independence was victimized. Not only were the judges political appointees, but party spirit had polluted the objectivity of juries. Officeholders of all stations had become so diverted by parties that their judgment was clouded to the extent that they refused to recognize national problems such as the manifest burdens of agriculture. The leaders followed erratic courses, sometimes supporting limited government and sometimes opposing it, usually depending on whether they were in or out of government. Taylor did not blame the people for becoming confused in their values and losing their ability to vote rationally, when offered such conflicting guidance.[31]

Parties finally worked the ultimate irony on themselves, Taylor predicted with some satisfaction. By rallying around great popular leaders, such as Presidents, parties often found that they had become the captives of their own creation: "Parties who corrupt their leaders . . . are punished with . . . severity. Like herds of swine, they are fed with grain or garbage, until they are fit for slaughter. . . ."[32] Even the great "democratick" leaders of history had sometimes treated their parties like hogs. Caesar had been a flatterer who had always intended to betray his followers, Cromwell was an honest fanatic who deceived both his followers and himself, and Bonaparte turned an accidentally bestowed confidence in him to despotic ends. Whatever the means used by party leaders, the effect was always the same: parties that live by fraud die by fraud.

Taylor had an eye for the richness of strategies that were used by parties to accomplish those objectives which often resulted in harmful effects. The most devious of these he attributed to the Federalists, but he was not above counseling the use of one or two of them himself during times of extreme crisis. He recorded the techniques used by Federalists in his 1794 *Enquiry into the Principles and Tendencies of Certain Public Measures.* Among them were the use of a false sense of security, indiscriminate recruitment, divide-and-conquer tactics, the corruption of governmental policies, subversive appeals, and the cooptation of popular names. False security was a relatively effortless tactic consisting simply of lulling the people into thinking parties were good for them. For example, the parties used hidden taxes so that "the community do not feel their taxes; and inferred . . . they do not pay them. A state of political apathy is most dangerous to liberty"[33] Indiscriminate recruiting was another tactic. Taylor never adopted the view that the Federalists were highfalutin snobs who went down, in John C. Miller's memorable phrase, with both their principles and their mistakes intact. To Taylor's active disgust, they grabbed supporters wherever they could by building on their natural base of die-hard Tories who had hoped to gain by intrigue what they had lost on the battlefield and by extending their appeals to more honest men.[34] By accepting recruits from the latter group, the Federalists gained members and something else. In addition, they were able to apply their third technique of dividing and conquering, because true Federalists rushed to attack a misinterpreted anti-federalism. Thus Federalists attacked their opponents, chiseled away a few true federalists from the mass that constituted the Republican Party, and then used those few true Federalists to gain more recruits. "Honest men, when deceived, are the best supporters of knavery. . . ."[35]

The Federalists used several different types of appeals in their attempts to lull the people into false security, gather recruits, and divide the opposition. Each of these appeals perverted a legitimate value that most honest men would share. The Federalists had extended their potential appeal to all men of goodwill, while being careful not to allow any of that goodwill to win out in party counsels. For example, patriotic pride in national accomplishments was corrupted either by appeals for "energetic" government, or by pointing with pride to increased prosperity over which the party had no control. Similarly, pride in President Washington's accomplishments had been used to deceive recruits to the Federalist Party. Trust and confidence in the government were worthy values, but they were especially subject to abuse: "The party call themselves the government, and then demand of the public a confidence in the magistracy. . . . faith, and not truth, is their political motto."[36] Confidence was least merited when it was most loudly proclaimed.

When the Federalists fell from power they cleverly deployed another strategy guaranteed to bring them back into favor. They kept quiet and waited for the Republicans to become degenerate by the excessively powerful governmental edifice that Hamilton's philosophy had built. The Federalists kept quiet so that "the administration may take as much rope as it will, and come to its end in the same way theirs did." [37] Federalists had planned their program well enough to be patient and wait for Republicans to join them in decadence.

The final party tactic that Taylor linked to harmful effects was the use that parties made of names. An important advantage in a political controversy, he thought, was the ability to label one's opposition. The Federalists had been able to monopolize a good name for themselves, had ridden it for all it was worth while their opposition fumbled around for a suitable alternative. But the Federalists had outsmarted themselves in this, for when they fell from power their name went with them. Thenceforth no true Federalist would have anything to do with them or with their name. "It is probable that a name, and three or four songs of popular import, would have had more weight, than. . . ."all the arguments the Republicans had used over the previous decade.[38] If the Federalists had been more careful in their choice of names, they would not have made it so difficult for true Federalists to become associated with them.

Over the thirty years during which Taylor observed, described, and participated in party development, two major characteristics of party activity attracted his attention. First of all, he was dismayed by the financial burdens that parties imposed on the rest of the country through their use of patronage, corruption, and taxes. Second, the history of parties and many of their detrimental effects hinged on the control they had been able to achieve on the use of human intelligence. Thus, the development of parties resulted from differences over issues, the Sedition Act predominant among them. In addition, parties injured the ability of individuals to use their reason in making political decisions. Worthwhile constitutional changes were discouraged, subservience to governments and parties was preached, secrecy in governmental affairs was practiced, legislatures were controlled like puppets, leaders followed erratic courses and the people were misled by these actions, and honest men were deceived by the misuse of legitimate values and deceptively named political parties into becoming the tools of parties. It was natural that, if Taylor ever became resigned to the existence of political parties, it would be on a basis that allowed him to safeguard the individual's use of reason.

C. Acceptance of Parties

John Taylor evolved from an active critic of parties to a reluctant supporter of them as unavoidable institutions. Perhaps this evolution was inevitable for one who had a program to implement but whose idea of appropriate political tactics did not include violence or coercion. Taylor eventually accepted the need to organize to accomplish his ends, but with reservations and on his own terms.

> Yet I acknowledge that I believe a sound republican party, guided by principles and uninfluenced by names, is the only substantial security in nature, for the preservation of that freedom of government we at present enjoy.[39]

Although Taylor and Edmund Burke would have agreed that when evil men have already combined, just men must also organize if the public interest is not to suffer, Taylor went further. To him, the very *ideas* of an evil combination were wrong and must be changed before any change could be expected in the actions of those who held those ideas.[40] Taylor thought that the Federalists had been the first to organize in the United States, and he always maintained that a difference in philosophy was one of the reasons that disagreements had occurred between the Federalist and the Republican Party. Parties always had to stand for something: "An administration without a maxim, would be like a ship without a rudder."[41]

Party debates were more reprehensible for their lack of fundamental meaning than for the fact that they occurred: "Parties are counsel on opposite sides, capable, by argument and reasoning, or enlightening, or by buffoonery, sophisms and perplexity, of insulting the judge." If parties could be made to stand for theoretical principles, many of their evil effects would be ameliorated.[42]

In the interest of intellectual integrity, all forms of accommodation to unsafe principles should be rejected by a Republican Party, Taylor warned. Criticism of bad policies should be practiced with vigor, and continued even if a bad policy won acceptance. This criticism should not be satisfied with an attack upon the mere effects of wrongdoing, but should penetrate to the causes of it. Prominent among these causes were differences in doctrines. Nothing would be gained by glossing over theoretical differences, and even popular publications should recognize that some intellectual issues were too important to simplify. Unless an administration's principles were correct, changing its personnel would not help: "a change of men might operate temporary public benefits, but . . . constitutional error will still ultimately prevail."[43] Again, to Taylor ideas were all-important.

Taylor may have been the first American party theorist to call for parties whose doctrines were discernibly different, but his purpose for that call differed considerably from some that have been heard since. Most appeals for party government and responsible political parties since Taylor, for example, have also called for parties that offered clear-cut intellectual choices, that is, that "made sense."[44] Usually such plans and reforms have been based on the premise that honest confrontation of party principles in debate would have a healthy and envigorating effect upon voter interest and participation. Taylor did not support ideological parties for the stimulative effect they might have on participation, because he thought it folly "to suppose that the bulk of the people are influenced by abstract political principles. . . ."[45] Instead, he advocated ideological parties for the effect that they would have on governmental policies. He was optimistic that an honest debate over the issues, and honest policies adopted as a consequence of this debate, were likely in the longrun to produce governmental actions in keeping with the public good. The people judge government by its effects, not by abstractions, and the direct application of Republican principles would bring that party into favor and keep it there. Good results flowing from correct beliefs, not the beliefs alone, were the keys to political success.

If this mistrust in popular ability to fathom political doctrines seems out of place in a man of the Enlightenment, one must remember that Taylor was a republican, not a democrat, and that many Enlightenment theorists trusted more in the reason of rulers than in that of the people. Moreover, it is a matter of degree, for it will be seen that Taylor firmly believed that popular understanding was greater in his day than it ever had been.[46]

Even though Taylor held little hope that the Federalists would ever have created many good policies, he regretted their demise. He was convinced that an honest advocacy of intellectual principles would be a safeguard against the abuse of the electoral processes through bribery or unreasoning loyalty to party heroes. Parties that differed only in degree because they followed "the policy of drawing rainbows to make converts" never earned his approval.[47] Parties could not be all things to all men, and Taylor thought that any party that deserved either his allegiance or his opposition should stand for important principles.

Late in life, Taylor's rereading of American history led him to reemphasize his opinion that originally there had been a difference in philosophy between the Republicans and the Federalists. A conflict between national and federal principles "and not an unprincipled difference, originally created the great parties in the United States," and everyone knew that either Jefferson or Hamilton would have been replaced as party leader if either had deviated from doctrinal chastity.[48] The principles had created the party leaders, not vice versa. When the Congress had been divided into two parties that were "only theoretically sectarian, and not geographically united," each might have construed the Constitution differently, but they were "honest zealots" contending for public favor on a nearly equal basis and avoiding excesses that since had discredited parties.[49] The Constitution had been in safer hands when it was being interpreted by persons who differed mainly over speculative opinions, according to Taylor, than it was during the 1820s when two geographic interests seemed headed for conflict.

Taylor's evolving appreciation for ideological parties was reinforced by the treatment he received from fellow Republicans. His appreciation of the constructive benefits of opposition grew as he found himself more and more cast in the role of a critic of fellow Republicans. Moreover, his ideas on internal party criticism allowed him to grapple with the problem of how one maintained his doctrinal purity in an organization whose chief business had to be the winning of elections.

Taylor had given some thought to the place of opposition in republican systems before 1808, when it became a matter of greater concern for him. The *Enquiry*, for example, had defended in 1794 the opposition of the Republican minority to the Federalist majority. His very definition of *party* in those early days included the necessity of opposition from other organizations, which he was reluctant at that point to call "parties". Those who oppose parties "deserve rather the appellation a 'band of patriots,' than the epithet of 'a party, they are not contending for the benefit of a party, but of the whole community."[50] Except for such early statements, Taylor did not return to the function of opposition until he was cast aside in 1808 by the monolith he had defended in its infancy as a "band of patriots."

Although he had often criticized the Republican Party before 1808, these remarks were limited to correspondence with his most trusted friends, such as Henry Tazewell. Despite these reservations he continued to regard himself as a loyal Republican, and his *Defence of the Measures of the Administration of Thomas Jefferson* was a campaign document pure and simple.

This party loyalty lasted until 1806, when Taylor began freely admitting that he wished that some of Madison's opinions were different. It was at this time that John Randolph's growing disenchantment with Jefferson's handling of the Yazoo frauds and the secret fund to purchase West Florida, resulted in an open schism. Even though Taylor had no sympathy for Randolph's personal vendetta against Jefferson, he thought some opposition was needed. "It is in the whole party and not in myself that I have more confidence than I have in Mr. Madison."[51] Let the whole party judge whether Madison's neo-Federalist opinions were consistent with the common doctrine, but first let the whole party hear the facts on both sides of the case.

From the summer of 1806 on, Taylor realized that insistence on a firm body of doctrine exacted real penalties from party loyalists. He became painfully aware that separatist campaigns were often quixotic, but felt that internal party opposition had a different function from interparty conflict: "even an unsuccessful opposition may operate as a check or an alarm."[52] He distinguished *schism* from *opposition*. Schisms occurred between men of the same political opinions, and were milder in nature, "for if they differ essentially, opposition becomes right and it is a duty."[53] Although this distinction held out the possibility of an open break with the administration over a clash of principle, Taylor was still reluctant to accept full responsibility for this. He claimed that the disparate wings of the party had been caused by the party's own internal persecution. Even though Taylor said that he feared the effects of schism ("the demon of division") even more than he feared war, he saw his choice as clear. He promised Wilson Cary Nicholas that he would use what influence he had to heal divisions in the party, but that if it ever came to a matter of principle, he would let principle be his guide. Party unity was important, but there were more important values.[54]

As the need for internal party opposition became apparent, Taylor began to give attention to the techniques for accomplishing it. First, injuries from friends stung more than those given by enemies, so internal opposition must be carefully handled. It should be practiced with restraint no matter how justified revenge might be. Otherwise, the minority who were opposing some deficiency unnecessarily hurt their cause by alienating the supporters of the administration. Second, if opposition had failed in influencing the party, the only honorable course was to continue the opposition. To do less would be an admission of error to one's conscience and all former and potential supporters as well. Third, an especially talented leader of the opposition (i.e., James Monroe) could play by different rules. He had a wider range of choices than an ordinary active member such as Taylor, and should adopt a stance that would give him the greatest opportunity to secure a respectful audience for his principles. Feigned neutrality was unlikely to be of much use to such a leader, however, for it merely alienated the administration without actively gaining the potential leader any followers. A leader such as Monroe would be better off actively opposing the administration, while remembering that the support of other anti-administration Republican factions was likely to be transient and that the support of Federalists could never be relied upon. Alternatively, he could join the administration. By joining them he would have an opportunity to change the party from within, while staying before the public eye. After Monroe

followed the latter course and was swallowed up by the Madison
administration, Taylor decided that external opposition would
have been the best course for him throughout.[55] When one
carried his opposition into an administration, he must forfeit his
status as a member of the opposition "because you must be taken
in tow by an administration party."[56] Because the responsibility
of the Republican intraparty opposition was to unveil majority
Republicanism's mistakes, Taylor warned Monroe that he could
not expect unqualified loyalty after joining the administration.[57]

Taylor's acceptance of political parties, then, was contingent
upon the party's redefining party loyalty to include internal
opposition when the party needed correction. This strategy of
opposition required a sensitive, persistent criticism, untainted by
loyalties to administration leaders on the part of the active party
member. Potential administration leaders who found themselves in the opposition had two options. They could oppose the
party from outside government, while building support, or they
could join government and attempt to bore from within.
Adopting the latter course of action, however, always separated
the opposition leader from his followers and increased the
likelihood that he would become the captive of the administration. Reform of an administration from within was a possible
tactic, but it created risks.

Even though Taylor finally accepted the existence of parties,
he never made them into and important feature of his political
theory. This may have resulted simply from the fact that he came
to accept them late in life and did not have time to develop a full
appreciation for their possibilities.

Along the way to his full acceptance of parties, however,
Taylor had proposed various reforms and strategies that would
improve the effectiveness of the party system. Among the
reforms he proposed was the abolition of the caucus system, the
exclusion of creditors from legislatures, and party realignment.
The caucus system for nominating Republican candidates was a
favorite target for Taylor, and also for the other members of the
"Old Republican" wing of the party, who had followed John
Randolph into opposition after 1806 (e.g., Nathaniel Macon,
James Mercer Garnett). Their opposition was based largely on
the fact that caucuses were secret, and therefore they stymied

the honest exchange of views that was the strongest argument for having a party system in the first place. In addition, in a one-party situation, nomination by a caucus was tantamount to election. This robbed the people of their right to select their own leaders. To Taylor it was futile to maintain that Congressmen acted in their private capacities during a caucus, because that was not the way it appeared to the public, who were impressionable. Taylor did not reject caucuses for purposes other than nominations, however.[58]

In his *Definition of Parties* Taylor had proposed a conflict-of-interest regulation that would have prevented public creditors from holding office in legislatures. By his calculation of the number of Federalist Congressmen who were public creditors, this rule would have expelled most of the members of that party from Congress. The unsporting nature of such a proposition was lost on Taylor, who found the precedent for such an exclusion in the various definitions of qualifications for office put into state constitutions. Although Taylor never repudiated this proposal, he was unsuccessful in getting anyone of importance to push for such a constitutional amendment. After awhile he stopped talking about it, but in his heart of hearts he probably never abandoned it.[59]

The only other important party reform Taylor offered was the one he tried to implement last, party realignment. Ever since the *Inquiry* (1814) Taylor had regretted the demise of the two parties of principle. The death of the Federalist Party had robbed the country of an effective interparty opposition. The remedy that Taylor proposed for this was to re-create two principled parties that would build on the base of the division between the American "Radicals" and the "Ultras," which had already emerged by the 1820s. These two new parties must be carefully named.[60] To enable true Federalists to expel the fifth column among them, an education in federal principles would be necessary: "This can only be effected . . . by arranging the advocates of each under the perceivable banners of constitutionalist and consolidation. . . ."[61] Taylor admitted that this party realignment had nearly become an obsession with him. In his last days, then, he could find no better solution for the undesirable effects of parties than to do it all over again, better.

Taylor had expressed himself on strategies appropriate for use by an honestly principled party at various times throughout his writings. Although he changed his mind on the need for parties, he never endorsed their harmful strategies, such as secrecy, patronage, misdirection of legitimate values, or complete subjugation of conscience in the name of party loyalty. These activities helped rob individuals of their ability to make rational political decisions. Instead, he preferred the cultivation of a good sense of timing and the choice of dramatic gestures that took advantage of good timing. Parties were educational institutions for Taylor, and he had great regard for the teachable moment.

Timing was a frequent concern for him, as was revealed in his advice to Monroe not to seek the Presidency in 1808; in his timing of the publication of his works so that they might have a maximum effect; and in his judgment that constitutional amendments would not receive the necessary close attention before a national election to warrant introducing them at that time. The best example of Taylor's respect for timing is the fact that the Virginia Resolutions themselves had been the product of timing. These resolutions, the doctrines of '98, were the basic catechism for the Old Republicans, Taylor, Randolph of Roanoke, Tazewell, Macon, Garnett, and their followers. Yet Taylor's plan of action in presenting these doctrines to the Virginia Legislature included several carefully synchronized steps, each one of which was contingent on the previous one's success. Taylor, therefore, was willing to allow the basic statement of Republican doctrine to be subject to the exigencies of good timing.[62]

The dramatic gesture was Taylor's logical response to a concern for good timing. The Virginia Resolutions and their consequent publicizing were one acknowledgment of this, while Taylor's attitude toward peace negotiations in 1813 was an even more striking example. He counseled Monroe, then Secretary of State, to get some kind of settlement from the British, "however slight, sense or nonsense, something or nothing,"[63] regarding the issues at stake in the war. Regardless of the benefits such a paper agreement might bring to the country, the Republican Party would benefit, because "the pleasure of getting out of the war, national pride, party loyalty, and confiding ignorance, will joyously unite in construing the pacification exactly as it pleases."[64] Although such cynical use of reason-of-state was rare in Taylor, and only commonly found in his views on foreign policy, it was an instrument that the former archcritic of parties did not hesitate to use when his party was hard pressed. Taylor's use of the technique of the right deed at the right time depended upon popular acceptance, of course, but this does not alter the fact that it could be based in deception.

Taylor's conception of parties as educational instruments made the media very important to him. On the one hand, he insisted that party debate be supportive of basic party doctrine; but on the other hand, there was a dearth of factual information that would vindicate party positions. This dilemma kept Taylor's contribution to party debate high-toned and abstract, and made him attentive to media that set off such abstractions to their best advantage.

Communication by letter had its place as a method. It is clear that Taylor's correspondence was selective. There were close personal friends with whom he was completely frank, and there were key decision-makers whose views he tried to influence with more circumspect "political" letters. These were lengthy, discursive, theoretical epistles that usually began with a statement of public opinion in Caroline County and went on to Taylor's views on current public issues. The circulation of letters was limited, and there was always the hazard in this era that they would be stolen. Therefore, Taylor proposed other media suitable for the communication of party news in addition to letters.[65]

Generally Taylor was cool to the idea of personal campaigning for votes. Such practices resulted in the very logrolling and deal-making to which he was opposed. This left representative assemblies and the printed word as methods of persuasion, two devices that were really related, since the printed debates of legislatures were one way that assemblies could be turned to educational purposes.[66]

Taylor considered newspapers as useful instruments, but warned against taking them too seriously. Directing public opinion was always an uncertain process, and the influence of presidential patronage made it difficult for publicists of opposing political views to get a hearing. Because of these limitations, sometimes the only way to be sure of a fair hearing was to start a newspaper oneself. A new publication should follow these guidelines: it should be profit-making and not kept by a party, general advertising was appropriate, it should publish news as well as party propaganda, evasion and subservience to a party should be discarded for the constant advocacy of fixed principles, and, finally, it should have an independent spirit and not hesitate to speak out on issues. If these rules were followed, newspapers could be useful.[67]

Taylor preferred to express himself through books and pamphlets more often than newspapers. These gave him more room to develop his ideas, it can be assumed, and were more fitting media for his abstract doctrines and rambling style. He refused to allow newspapers to print selections from his books (with the exception of *Arator*, which originally had been a series of essays) before the books were published in full. After all, he reasoned, a newspaper is read and forgotten.[68] Moreover, the prevalence of some paid publicists in newspapers caused some thoughtful readers to discount what they read. "The news-papers are improper channels . . . because they are a species of ephemera, and because the printers are not orthodox in general as to politics."[69] Pamphlets were better tools for persuasion, because "farcical newspaper ebullitions . . . must awaken the idea of a merry Andrew, entertaining a mob . . . whilst his accomplices are picking their pockets."[70]

One of the most dangerous aspects of newspapers was the nonresponsibility, and consequent irresponsibility, of their editors. Taylor's attitudes on the subject were influenced by the exchange of bitter letters between him and Thomas Ritchie, editor of the Richmond *Enquirer* and relative by marriage to Spencer Roane. These two founders of the "Richmond Junto" were supporters of administration Republicanism in general, and James Madison in particular. More willing than Taylor to forgive the Republican leaders for their deviation from true Republican principles, they made it hot for Taylor and John Randolph during their period of apostasy from the Madison candidacy. (A decade later Taylor and Ritchie made their peace when states' rights became a popular cause again and Ritchie came to appreciate what Taylor had been trying to say in 1808.) In the debate with Ritchie, Taylor often emphasized the unchecked influence that editors possessed. An editor's opinion on an election was his rightful property, but it was only one man's opinion: "The people have a right to change, but they ought not to be cheated into it."[71] Ritchie's opinion was "selfish," "injurious to national happiness," and "highly dangerous to republican government" because of the effective use office-holders were making of his journal. Editors and newspapers under such an influence were only propagandists for incumbents and added nothing to the discussion of public issues.[72]

Taylor lectured Ritchie on the duties of an editor, and gave particular attention to publication policies. "Open to all parties, but influenced by none" was the best motto, while an editor should take the high ground of "pure responsibility to the public good," observing "moral rectitude" in the use of his powers.[73] Ritchie had done the worst thing that an editor could do: he had defamed political opponents and then closed his newspaper columns to replies from the outraged victims. Under such a situation the freedom to publish became a license to libel, and Taylor suggested that editors be required to publish such replies. The discussions that such exchanges produced might teach the public to detect the truth, and put editors under yet another restraint.[74]

It is readily apparent from this examination of Taylor's favorable attitudes toward political parties, party reform, and party strategies that the intellectual exchange of views was his dominant concern. When parties hindered the individual's use of rational faculties, Taylor attacked parties, and when parties facilitated rational processes, Taylor supported them. A closer look at the theoretical views that underlay Taylor's change of heart on political parties is necessary for a full understanding of why he supported parties on some occasions and attacked them on others.

D. Theory of Political Parties

The theoretical conclusions that constituted the basis for John Taylor's change of views on political parties included his definition of *party*, his opinion on their inevitability, and his view of the nature of truth.

Taylor provided no hard-and-fast definition of political parties. His early thoughts on them were evolving at the same time that they were becoming institutionalized. If his use of the word *party* is fuzzy, so were the organizations. One thing is certain: political parties with mass membership were unknown in Taylor's time. It can be assumed, therefore, that his use of *party* referred to a group that was fairly limited in size.

Taylor often used *party* in combination with *faction*.[75] At times he seemed to use the two words synonomously, and it is difficult to separate their meaning. Taylor's confusion and ambiguity on this point was characteristic of James Madison, too.

Neal Riemer has said that Madison by the 1790s "still was unable to distinguish clearly between interests and parties. . . . He was, then, at this time still groping his way toward a modern theory of politics."[76] Any attempt to read rigorous meaning into the use of the terms *faction* and *party* in the writings of Taylor and Madison must be hedged with caution. Taylor's use of *faction* often signified a general sort of group whose interest in some way was set off from the public interest.[77] It was a term of scorn for him, however, and he often used it in contexts and situations that could not pause for precise definitions. His most precise statement of *fraction* was contained in an 1807 letter to Wilson Cary Nicholas, in which he said that no matter how factions might

> disorder a system of liberty, I do not think them as *deadly to it as war, armies, and debt*. . . . I have endeavored to prove that factions are artificial moral beings, proceeding from moral causes. And that none, except factions of interest, can ever be dangerous.[78]

Although this was damning factions with faint praise, it suggested that Taylor viewed factions as present in both republics and despotisms, but as "artificial" creations and not as natural groups. Moreover, he distinguished different kinds of factions, of which only "factions of interest" could be dangerous.

These views on factions sharply distinguished Taylor from James Madison on the same subject. First of all, Taylor was much less precise than Madison, whose *Federalist* essay Number Ten specified a faction as a fairly large group, either a majority or a minority of the whole citizenry, energized by a common interest that was antithetical to the public good. Thus, with Madison, all factions were potentially dangerous. He did not see in them the liberalizing effects on despotic governments that Taylor recognized, nor did he distinguish the kinds of factions as Taylor had. An even more important difference was the fact that Madison thought the "latent causes of factions are thus sown in the nature of man . . . [who has] a zeal for different opinions concerning religion, concerning government, and many other points," which included theory, practice, and loyalty to popular leaders.[79] Taylor, as demonstrated, flatly contradicted this deterministic theory of the origin of factions. He considered them universal, but *artificial*. Taylor's views on factions, thus, were loosely formulated, less fearful of diversity, and less pessimistic about the difficulty of correcting them than Madison's views on the same subject.

Taylor used *party* less ambiguously than *faction*, but here again the modern reader must bear in mind the fact that the concept of a political party was undeveloped at the time, and his definition of it sometimes varied. For example, sometimes individuals are contrasted to parties in such a manner as to imply that Taylor meant by the term *party* merely a group of individuals and was not referring to a political organization at all. Usually, however, the context clearly refers to a political group, often a group of office-holders expressing or pursuing a selfish interest. Parties were portrayed as late as 1814 by Taylor as attempting to achieve their goals with no consideration for the public interest. Similarly, at the same time he was still maintaining that the selfish interests of parties often prevented their debates from being honest enough to inform the public.[80]

Taylor was no more convinced that parties were inevitable than that factions were. He totally rejected the notion that parties flowed out of the nature of man. The very fact that party spirit had a beginning at a point in recent history, and that its spread could be observed, "violently opposes the idea, that party spirit is simply the child of nature, and evidently refers origin to artifice and management."[81] Parties as malignant as those suffered by the United States "are not natural to a republican government really dependent on natural will" and there is nothing supernatural in the "party paroxysm which now exists" either, Taylor argued.[82] If government itself had been thought by some to be a necessary evil, why should extralegal creations such as political parties be considered natural and inevitable? It was difficult enough to control government, but when parties of interest were around to encourage the bad qualities of the governors, the situation was worse.

Taylor carefully distinguished his position on the origin of party spirit from that he attributed to Jefferson, in order to demonstrate to the latter that his easygoing tolerance for differing opinions cut the ground away from any rationale for reform. Such relativistic tolerance of diversity left no standard for comparison. Party spirit, if natural as Jefferson had argued, could have been either geographic or personal in origin.

If it were geographic, its superiority in national affairs might have resulted in the lasting dominance of either the North or the South over the other. Taylor considered a permanent dominance by any section, even the South, to be the final step before tyranny. Even worse than such sectional control, however, would have been the rotation of sections in office, because the excesses of the incumbents would have led to vengeful reprisals from the outs. Geographic parties would "annihilate the chance for human happiness," Taylor argued.[83]

If parties were based in personal causes, they must arise from "interest." So what? "If the evil is in human nature, it may yet admit of alleviations. But if it springs from political encouragement, it is the work of art, and by art may be counteracted."[84] The experience of government in the American states, particularly Connecticut, proved that parties were not essential. If one adopted the position that parties were inevitable, Taylor warned presidential candidate Jefferson, he would lose any ability to criticize their bad effects. If parties were inevitable, the measures protecting the Federalist Party seemed only natural. In truth, all aspects of government were conventional.

Nor were individual men to be blamed for parties. If they acted badly, this was only the logical consequence of a corrupt political system. The motives for their behavior lay deeper in the basic relationships of the system. A simple rotation of officeholders was no substitute for fundamental reform. Rotation would "change the tyrant, but not remove the evil. . . . Saturated are preferable to hungry flies."[85] "If a good form of government too often fails, in making bad men good, a bad form of government will too often succeed in making good men bad."[86]

Preventing the birth of parties, Taylor went on, or even controlling their growth after birth, was difficult in republican systems. The vast majority of people resist being swept into active popular movements, and the enforcement of the Sedition Law made this even more unlikely. Even if the people could be welded into an effective political force, they might become another party in the process, subject to all the temptations that beset the Federalists. Party organization as such was not abandoned by Taylor, but he thought that its formative principles had to be carefully chosen, "because the individuals of a general interest cannot be cemented in the same way with those of a separate one, as there is none to supply the glue."[87] The adhesive that held parties together was the plunder they had stolen from the public treasury: to oppose such a party, a group had to find an acceptable intellectual doctrine to glue the pieces together.

The cure for party spirit was not to be found in class dominance, either. Even if farmers were given the nine million dollars that had been distributed· by funding and banking, "corruption, oppression, and party spirit" would be the unavoidable result. The point was that no single group should benefit from government at the expense of others.[88]

These three conditions: the difficulty of creating popular movements, the problem of finding appropriate organizing principles, and the impossibility of using a social group or class as a substitute for a party compounded the problem of parties for Taylor. On the one hand, he insisted that parties were artificial so that he could criticize their harmful effects, while, on the other hand, the Federalists seemed so deeply entrenched that it would take a rival party organization to root them out.

If parties were artificial creations, in Taylor's opinion, truth was not. If a party were organized so as always to support the right and oppose the wrong, it would be an acceptable safeguard against the Federalists. Since the Federalists obligingly defended the wrong side of issues, they created opportunity for a Republican opposition that could escape the harmful characteristics of parties. Thus, the dedication page of Taylor's *Definition of Parties* said that "Truth is a thing, not of dievisibility [*sic*] into conflicting parts, but of unity. Hence both sides cannot be right."[89] There was only one path to truth for Taylor (at least in the 1790s), and this implied that any compromise between the two parties was out of the question. Taylor's smugness in his ability to know which side of an issue would be right may be difficult for moderns to understand but quite in keeping with a generation that had proclaimed self-evident truths. He seems never to have questioned his ability to know the right, and this conviction led him to see political activity as easily divisible into a right-vs.-wrong dichotomy. On this basis he was willing to build a party, and his conviction that parties were artificial allowed him to approach the task optimistically once he had satisfied himself that his side was in the right. As mentioned earlier, however, in the 1790s Taylor was still reluctant to call the Republicans a "party" and preferred to think of them as a "band of patriots."[90]

Not until the Federalist Party was safely moribund did Taylor revise his notion of truth. Eventually, however, he came to lament the passing of the Federalists, which had been a party of principle and an honest advocate of constitutional monarchism. By 1814 both the Federalists and the Republicans had passed from the scene as parties of principle, leaving, in Taylor's opinion, influence seekers who played a game of ins and outs without regard to the public interest. Although none of Taylor's later writings gave so clear a definition of truth as his *Definition of Parties*, his call for two new principled parties in *New Views* suggests either that he was willing to consider the possibility that a party other than his own could be right occasionally, or that his faith in the political process, given an open and well-articulated exchange of views between parties, was such that he was willing to trust the public to appreciate the justice of his cause. The latter view is by far more in keeping with Taylor's usual doctrinaire stand, but even so, it represented a change in his previous view that party competition was unneeded because the Republicans had a monopoly of truth. Twenty years of Republican administration had convinced him that error was not the exclusive prerogative of the Federalists: it may have been only a short journey from there to the opinion that truth was not the exclusive possession of the Republicans.[91]

E. Summary and Conclusions

The problems resulting from the party struggle of the 1790s presented Taylor with an opportunity to apply his previously untested theoretical assumptions to actual political controversy. True to his Enlightenment propensities, Taylor's description and analysis of, and prescription for the problems created by political parties emphasized the role of ideas in human activity. The history of American political parties had turned largely on divisions of opinion over issues, he thought. In addition, the most harmful effects of political parties came from their tendencies to thwart the individual's reasoning processes. In order to correct the harm the Federalists had done, it was necessary to establish a philosophic position that allowed one to criticize with consistency. Since this philosophic redoubt was tenable only if Taylor could demonstrate that the Federalist Party was a man-made creation and, like all political parties, subject to human manipulation. This done, it was not difficult for Taylor to justify his personal participation in the Republican Party as a means of preserving the truth as he knew it. When he and the Republican leaders fell into disagreement over the proper application of this truth, Taylor's view of parties gave him the encouragement necessary to begin plans for the reorganization of the American party system in order to preserve the theoretical principles he cherished. Only late in his life did Taylor come to realize that truth may elude attempts to institutionalize it, and that the corrosive effects of absolute power could touch even the elect if their hold on power went unchallenged. Truth needed testing to remain healthy, Taylor seemed to be implying by his attempts to reorganize parties, and this brought him up to the brink of saying that truth was the composite of divergent points of view.

Although Taylor did not link his views of political parties to his doctrine of divided power directly, this may only reflect the fact that he accepted political parties after his definitive statement of divided power in the *Inquiry*. There are strong points of similarity between the two strands of thought. His ideas on parties and on divided power both gave heavy emphasis to the need for open governmental processes, and to the need for rational discussion and decisions to operate these processes for the public good. More fundamentally, Taylor's views on parties and divided powers depended upon the existence of a common belief system or body of doctrine. Thus, Taylor preferred political parties that were doctrinally based, and governmental systems that were firmly based in principle. For John Taylor, correct thinking was the prerequisite to correct action.

There are hypotheses that can be inferred from Taylor's ideas on parties that were not directly addressed as issues in them. These relate to the history of party development in the United States. First, the question of the origin of parties, as revealed in Taylor, gives heavy weight to the influence of arguments over policy issues that had arisen in Congress by 1793. By implication, Taylor's views do not seem to lend support to the theory that party differences had their origin in social and economic classes and sections that first opposed each other on the issue of the Constitution's adoption and then later evolved into the Federalist and Republican Parties. Similarly, Taylor's emphasis on the importance of the issue of the Hamiltonian financial program suggests that the development of parties in the United

States started at the national level over debates in Congress and later spread to the states. If it is true that the current party system is really a state, not a national, party system, it became that way after the time of Taylor.[92]

Taylor's ideological approach to party organization was an early one that developed out of the conviction that the Republican cause was just and the Federalist cause unjust, if not treasonable. Yet he came to regret the expiration of the Federalists, who had at least offered a clear alternative. This view establishes the roots of ideological parties even more deeply in American party development than the advocates of responsible party government have usually recognized. One must recognize, however, that Taylor's Enlightenment background left him freer than most moderns to expect rationalistic, disinterested discussions of public issues and agreement in the public interest. Finally, it is significant that a party meant to Taylor a fairly small core of activists and officeholders. In his day these men often turned out to be also the best educated men of the time. To such intellectual politicians, a party system energized by fairly abstract appeals was workable. Today's universal suffrage, mass electorates, and electronic media, provide an entirely different setting for ideology, and the popularization of ideology has often resulted in its vulgarization. It is worth mentioning, however, that John Taylor would have been among the last to abandon hope in the effectiveness of popular enlightenment. In fact, he pinned his hopes of limiting aristocracies on that very process.

Notes to Chapter 2

1. Noble E. Cunningham, Jr., *The Jeffersonian Republicans: the Formation of Party Organization* (Chapel Hill, N.C.: The University of North Carolina Press, 1957), 1:20.

2. Ibid., p. 22.

3. *Definition*, p. 2.

4. Ibid.

5. Ibid.

6. Ibid., p. 4.

7. Joseph Charles, *The Origins of the American Party System* (New York: Harper and Brothers, 1961), pp. 98–111.

8. Letters from John Taylor to Henry Tazewell, June 15, 1794, April 13, 1796; Tazewell Papers, Virginia State Library, Richmond.

9. *Defence*, pp. 80, 92–93.

10. *Tyranny*, pp. 324–25.

11. Letter from John Taylor to Thomas Jefferson, June 25, 1798, in "Correspondence," pp. 271–76.

12. Kurtz, p. 359.

13. Letter from Taylor to Jefferson, June 25, 1798, "Correspondence," pp. 271–76. Taylor said: "But since government is getting into the habit of peeping into private letters . . . , which may even make it criminal to pray God for better times, I shall be careful not to repeat so dangerous a liberty."

14. Letter from John Taylor to James Mercer Garnett, December 14, 1807, "Letters of John Taylor of Caroline," ed. Hans Hammond, *The Virginia Magazine of History and Biography* 52 (April 1944): 122–25.

15. Letter from John Taylor to Wilson Cary Nicholas, February 5, 1808, Edgehill-Randolph Papers, University of Virginia Library, Charlottesville.

16. *Inquiry*, p. 568. The four parties mentioned were parties of principle including monarchists and republicans, and parties of interest including stockholders and patronage appointees. *Also see Tyranny*, p. 22.

17. *Annals of the Eighteenth Congress, First Session* (Washington D.C.: Gales and Seaton, 1856), p. 559.

18. Letter from John Taylor to John H. Bernard, January 20, 1823, John Taylor Letters and Papers, Virginia State Library, Richmond; and letter from John Taylor to Lucy Penn Taylor, February 2, 1823, Virginia Historical Society, Richmond.

19. *Inquiry*, p. 567.

20. *Tyranny*, p. 89.

21. Letter from John Taylor to Thomas Jefferson, June 25, 1798, "Correspondence," pp. 271–76.

22. Letter from John Taylor to [Wilson Cary Nicholas?] November 25, 1803, Correspondence of Chancellor Creed Taylor, 1766–1836, University of Virginia Library, Charlottesville. Taylor's *Inquiry* is full of allusions to the remunerative aspects of patronage; see pp. viii, 255, 392–93, 567, 569, 575–76, and 621. Most such discussions involved political parties and other leadership groups, so the topic of patronage is also important in chapter 3 of this study. Also see *Definition*, p. 12.

23. Jean Jacques Rousseau, *The Social Contract*, trans. Willmoore Kendall (Chicago: Henry Regnery Company, 1954), pp. 79–81; and Thomas Hobbes, *Leviathan*, ed. Herbert W. Schneider (Indianapolis, Ind.: The Bobbs-Merrill Company, Inc., 1958), p. 190. Rousseau's discussion downgraded interpersonal relations for the sake of securing the advantages of a pure sense of community within the State. Each individual should be as independent of every other as possible and as dependent on the State as possible. Hobbes's discussion was in a similar vein: "For all uniting of strength by private men is, if for evil intent, unjust; if for intent unknown, dangerous to the public and unjustly concealed."

24. *Definition*, p. 2.

25. *Enquiry*, p. 49.

26. Letter from John Taylor to James Monroe, May 10, 1812, in "Correspondence," pp. 336–39.

27. *Inquiry*, p. 304.

28. *Construction*, p. 17; *Inquiry*, p. 653.

29. *Definition*, pp. 4–5; *Inquiry*, pp. 137, 609–10, 629.

30. *Inquiry,* p. 590.

31. Ibid., p. 218. Taylor's shock on the question of party spirit tainting juries was somewhat misplaced, since both his aunt and his father-in-law had been saved from severe penalties for sedition by the political biases of Caroline juries. Also see Taylor, *Arator,* p. 200.

32. *Inquiry,* pp. 516–17.

33. *Enquiry,* p. 89.

34. Ibid., p. 87.

35. Ibid., p. 88.

36. Ibid., p. 88.

37. Letter from John Taylor to James Monroe, January 2, 1812, in "Correspondence," pp. 328–29.

38. Letter from John Taylor to Timothy Pickering, February 16, 1817, Massachusetts Historical Society, Boston.

39. Letter from John Taylor to James Monroe, November 25, 1810, in "Correspondence," p. 314.

40. Burke thought party divisions inseparable from free government: "Observations on a Late Publication Intitled 'The Present State of the Nation' " (1769) reprinted in *The Works of Edmund Burke,* 12 vols., 6th ed. (Boston: Little, Brown and Company, 1880), 1:271. His definition of party included the necessity of doctrine: "Party is a body of men united for promoting by their joint endeavors the national interest upon some particular principle in which they are all agreed"; see *Thoughts on the Cause of Our Present Discontents* (1770), in idem, p. 530. His statement on the necessity of good men combining to counteract evil combinations is found in idem, p. 526. It is one of the great ironies of history that Burke, one of the first defenders of political parties, died an outcast from his party. Taylor, previously one of the great party haters, died with plans fresh for party reorganization.

41. *Enquiry,* p. 91. Almost no modern authority would accept the Federalists as the first U. S. party. See Noble E. Cunningham, Jr., *The Jeffersonian Republicans: the Formation of Party Organization, 1789–1801* (Chapel Hill, N. C., University of North Carolina Press, 1957), pp. 7, 22–23.

42. *Enquiry,* p. 85; letter from Taylor to Pickering, February 16, 1817, Massachusetts Historical Society, Boston.

43. Letters from John Taylor to Henry Tazewell, June 13, 1797 (quotation) and May 26, 1798, Tazewell Papers, Virginia State Library, Richmond. Also see letters from Taylor to James Madison, March 25, 1798, and James Monroe, January 15, 1809, in "Correspondence," pp. 291–94, 298–300.

44. Austin Ranney, *The Doctrine of Responsible Party Government* (Urbana, Ill.: University of Illinois Press, 1962), pp. 14, 20; Hugh A. Bone, *American Politics and the Party System* (New York: McGraw-Hill Book Company, 1965), pp. 655–58; Frank J. Sorauf, *Political Parties in the American System* (Boston: Little, Brown and Company, 1964), pp. 131–32.

45. Letter from John Taylor to James Monroe, January 15, 1809, in "Correspondence," p. 299.

46. Kingsley Martin, *French Liberal Thought in the Eighteenth Century* (New York: Harper and Row, Publishers, 1962), pp. 139–43.

47. Letter from John Taylor to Wilson Cary Nicholas, June 20, 1808, Edgehill-Randolph Papers, University of Virginia Library, Charlottesville. Also see letter from Taylor to James Monroe, January 2, 1812, in "Correspondence," pp. 328–29.

48. *New Views,* p. 212.

49. Ibid., p. 252.

50. *Enquiry,* p. 85.

51. Letter from John Taylor to Wilson Cary Nicholas, May 14, 1806, Edgehill-Randolph Papers, University of Virginia Library, Charlottesville.

52. Letter from John Taylor to Wilson Cary Nicholas, June 10, 1806, Edgehill-Randolph Papers, University of Virginia Library, Charlottesville. Also see Noble E. Cunningham, Jr., *The Jeffersonian Republicans in Power: Party Operations, 1801–1809* (Chapel Hill, N.C.: The University of North Carolina Press, 1963), 2:77–83; Norman K. Risjord, *The Old Republicans* (New York: Columbia University Press, 1965), Chap. 3, passim; Kirk, Appendix 2, pp. 243–91.

53. Ibid.

54. Letter from John Taylor to Wilson Cary Nicholas, October 26, 1807, Edgehill-Randolph Papers, University of Virginia Library, Charlottesville.

55. Letter from John Taylor to Thomas Ritchie, September 29, 1808, in *Pamphlet,* pp. 7–10. Letters from Taylor to James Monroe, February 22, 1808; January 15, 1809, October 26, 1810; March 21, 1811; March 24, 1811; and May 10, 1812, in "Correspondence," pp. 291–94, 298–300, 309–13, 319–21, 321–24, 336–39.

56. Letter from John Taylor to James Monroe, January 31, 1811, in "Correspondence," p. 316.

57. Letter from John Taylor to James Monroe, July 27, 1811, in "Correspondence," pp. 324–26.

58. Letter from John Taylor to Wilson Cary Nicholas, March 5, 1804, Edgehill-Randolph Papers, University of Virginia Library, Charlottesville; *New Views,* p. 280; *Annals of the Eighteenth Congress, First Session,* pp. 408–409; Risjord, p. 253.

59. Letter from John Taylor to James Monroe, October 26, 1810, in "Correspondence,"; *Definition* pp. 10–11.

60. *Inquiry,* p. 568; *New Views,* pp. 45, 51; *Annals of the Eighteen Congress, First Session,* p. 559; letter from John Taylor to Timothy Pickering, February 16, 1817, Massachusetts Historical Society, Boston.

61. Letter from John Taylor to John H. Bernard, January 20, 1823, John Taylor Letters and Papers, Virginia State Library, Richmond.

62. Letters from John Taylor to James Madison, June 20, 1793, and James Monroe, February 22, 1808, in "Correspondence," pp. 254–58, 291–94; letter from Taylor to John H. Bernard, January 20, 1823, John Taylor Letters and Papers, Virginia State Library, Richmond; letter from Taylor to Henry Tazewell, December 14, 1798, Tazewell Papers, Virginia State Library, Richmond.

63. Letter from John Taylor to James Monroe, March 18, 1813, in "Correspondence," p. 345.

64. Ibid.

65. Letter from John Taylor to Henry Tazewell, July 1, 1798, Tazewell Papers, Virginia State Library, Richmond; letter from Taylor to James Monroe, November 12, 1803, in "Correspondence," pp. 289–90.

66. Letter from John Taylor to Wilson Cary Nicholas, March 13, 1803, Edgehill-Randolph Papers, University of Virginia Library, Charlottesville; letter from Taylor to Nicholas, March 31, 1803, Massachusetts Historical Society, Boston.

67. Letter from John Taylor to James Mercer Garnett, January 28, 1818, John Taylor Papers, Duke University Library, Durham, N.C.

68. Letters from John Taylor to James Madison, June 20, 1793, and September 25, 1793 in "Correspondence," pp. 258–60.

69. Letter from John Taylor to James Madison, May 11, 1793, in "Correspondence," pp. 254–58.

70. *Enquiry,* p. 85.

71. Letter from John Taylor to Thomas Ritchie, April 14, 1809, in *Pamphlet,* p. 48.

72. Letters from John Taylor to Thomas Ritchie, September 29, 1808; March 24, 1809; April 14, 1809, in *Pamphlet,* pp. 7–10, 11–15, 44–50.

73. Letters from John Taylor to Thomas Ritchie, September 29, 1809, and March 24, 1809, in *Pamphlet.*

74. Letter from John Taylor to Thomas Ritchie, February 10, 1808, printed in *Enquirer,* March 14, 1808, Richmond.

75. *Inquiry,* pp. 72, 108, 197, 221, 512, 571.

76. Neal Riemer, *James Madison* (New York: Washington Square Press, 1968), pp. 173–74.

77. *Definition,* pp. 5, 15; *Inquiry,* pp. vii, 70, 168, 186, 432.

78. Letter from John Taylor to Wilson Cary Nicholas, November 1807, Wilson Cary Nicholas Papers, Library of Congress, Washington, D.C. See also *Inquiry,* pp. 241, 245, for apparent references to specific factions; general uses of *faction* can be found on pp. 107, 278.

79. James Madison, "No. Ten," *The Federalist* (New York: The Modern Library, 1937), p. 55.

80. Taylor never used the term *political* party in the early years of his writings, and seldom in his later life. In the pages to follow, therefore, the word *party* should not be interpreted from this narrow and more modern perspective, unless Taylor himself seems to mean this. Also see *Inquiry,* pp. 196, 392, 576, 548–49, 574, 581.

81. Letter from John Taylor to Thomas Jefferson, June 25, 1798, in "Correspondence," p. 273.

82. Ibid.

83. Ibid., p. 271.

84. Ibid.

85. Ibid., p. 273.

86. Ibid., p. 272.

87. *Inquiry,* p. 574. Letter from John Taylor to Creed Taylor, April 10, 1799, Correspondence of Chancellor Creed Taylor, University of Virginia Library, Charlottesville.

88. *Inquiry,* p. 52.

89. *Definition,* p. 2.

90. *Enquiry,* p. 35.

91. Taylor always maintained that the Federalist Party was built on a base of monarchical sentiment: "Would Mr. Jefferson or Mr. Madison have better known that Mr. King and the Adam's were monarchists, if Henry had told them so?" In this view Taylor was undoubtedly influenced by the conversation he had had with John Adams in 1794 in which the latter had advocated the inevitability of a hereditary executive and senate. See letter from Taylor to Daniel Carroll Brent, October 19, 1796, in "Correspondence," p. 267. Also see *Inquiry,* p. 568; *New Views,* pp. 48, 55, 61, 67, 86, 160–61, 213.

92. The theory that parties developed out of socioeconomic cleavages and the debate over the Constitution has many advocates. One version may be found in Wilfred E. Binkley, *American Political Parties* (New York: Alfred A. Knopf, 1959), chap. 3. Binkley said:

those militant elements of the Revolutionary or Patriot Party were the forerunners of the Anti-Federalists and eventually contributed the rank and file of the Jefferson Republicans.

The most recent and most empirical vindication of this theory may be found in Jackson Turner Main, *Political Parties Before the Constitution* (New York: W. W. Norton & Company, Inc., 1973), chap. 13. Joseph Charles, p. 92, assumed the existence of parties in the states before their development on the national scene, a view that Noble Cunningham disputed in *The Jeffersonian Republicans,* 1:7, 23. Cunningham also rejected the theory that there was any organizational transition from the Anti-Federalists to the Republicans.

3

ARISTOCRACIES

It has been demonstrated that Taylor's allegiance to a particular body of doctrine allowed him eventually to favor the use of ideological political parties. He found he could accept the existence of parties in general only after he had decided that his doctrine was more important to him than allegiance to a single party organization, that no party remained true to republican doctrine if entrusted with great power indefinitely, and that an honest debate over issues was a better way to preserve doctrine and keep it healthy than trusting to the continuation in power of a single party.

Political parties were one type of "aristocracy" and the only type Taylor ever accepted as desirable. There were several other varieties. The fact that Taylor considered most of the defects of republican government to be a result of the misdeeds of aristocracies will be discussed in this chapter. His theory of the development of aristocracies will be treated, followed by an examination of the harmful effects of each major type of aristocracy, and an analysis of why Taylor found it impossible eventually to accept all aristocracies except for parties. The central premise of this chapter is that Taylor thought that aristocractic control of governments throughout all previous ages to have resulted from the limited extent of general knowledge. The common man had come to a point where he knew enough to do without aristocracies. If this knowledge were put to work in a governmental system of divided powers, republican government and public well-being would be the results. Aristocracies would be deposed.

Notes for this chapter begin on p. 134.

A. The Concept of Aristocracy

Taylor's concept of aristocracy was both an answer to John Adams's views on aristocracy and a refinement of them. Both Adams and Taylor were aware of the fact that many of their readers would think of aristocracy in the sense that the British knew them: a nobility of feudal distinctions. Yet neither man meant only that by the term. Taylor thought of aristocracies in close association with disparities in property, while Adams considered them the result both of innate distinctions of talent, intelligence, and beauty, and of inherited distinctions of wealth and position. Taylor defined aristocracies during the course of his argument in the *Inquiry* (1814) as *"a transfer of property by law, is aristocracy, and that aristocracy is a transfer of property by law."* [1]

The concept of transferring property by law was used by Taylor to refer to any law whose direct or indirect effect was the taking or devaluation of an individual's earnings without his personal consent. Taylor adopted with this view a position close to that of John Locke, who had maintained that if the protection of property was one of the reasons men went into society, an absolute power over any part of an individual's property violated the very reason for the social compact. Locke, unlike Taylor, had gone on to hedge a bit by saying that arbitrary power over property was what he had in mind; that individual consent absolved a government from wrongdoing in the taking of property; and that in a commonwealth with elected assemblies the individual periodically had a chance to give his consent. Locke also defended monarchical governments by saying that they acted in the public interest and had institutionalized consent, or their citizens would not tolerate them. Because of his disgust with aristocracy, Taylor rejected both Locke's equivocation on the power of majority rule and his justification of monarchical forms of government. In doing this he was forced to view the people who had lived under ancient aristocracies in a less favorable light than Locke had in order to prove that the mere existence of aristocracy was a manifestation of the abuse of personal property rights. This left Taylor with the problem of explaining why the common people of ancient aristocracies had been incapable of self-government. [2]

The transfer of property that constituted the distinguishing feature of Taylor's aristocracies was accomplished through "monopolies": artificial scarcities that allowed a group to obtain higher prices or more material advantages than they otherwise could have done. Monopolists were those who owned "exclusive privileges" that allowed them to subvert the laws of demand and supply.[3]

Taylor thought that English society abounded with social orders and exclusive privileges, and that its government had been forced to recognize them or risk revolution. He did not think that the United States had reached that point yet. He cautioned, however, that every society was based on two interests: one subsisting from work and the other from legally bestowed gratuities. The most nearly perfect government had never found a way to protect itself against the second group, because government itself was part of the group that relied on law for existence.[4] Whether special interests took a civilian or military form, they were the products of human selfishness and laziness. These aristocracies were also sometimes called "minor" interests by Taylor, who thought they were constantly trying to secure either wealth or salvation without effort by sweating it from the brows of laborers or the good deeds of the well-intentioned. Corporate aristocrats sought exclusive privileges; foreign aristocracies had been taught that imperial conquest was desirable; and governmental aristocracies dreamed up impressive programs whose real purpose was to transfer property. The varieties of aristocracy had been so many, their control so tight, and the remedies for their oppressions so few, that many persons considered them inevitable.[5]

Such despondent resignation to tyranny was premature, in the opinion of Taylor, who hoped to prove that "aristocracies, both ancient and modern have been variable and artificial . . . ."[6] He thought that the truth was that rare talents were completely relative to the distribution of knowledge throughout the general population of a society. To understand Taylor one must realize that he is not talking about differentials in intelligence in his discussions of aristocracy, but of knowledge. Ignorance was the cause of political subjection, he thought, not stupidity. The people had never been wholly without knowledge: even in their most primitive state when aristocracies had robbed them of virtually half their humanity, the people had been restive. Knowledge was in a state of constant fluctuation, and by eliminating the gap between what the elite knew and what the people knew, tyranny could be erased. The present age, Taylor felt, best promised this possibility, but even former periods could have done better.[7]

Taylor was not sure that there was a hierarchy in the distribution of talent. Aristocracy was more a matter of the position one held, and how one used that position to deny access of others to knowledge. He never denied the efficacy of intelligence and knowledge in human affairs; properly employed its results were beneficial, but the magnitude of the benefit could always have been increased by wider access to information. The talented, consequently, must be held in suspicion, for they always welcomed a chance to show off, and energetic, powerful governments appealed to their vanity. At the same time they were reluctant to share their knowledge. The talented could not be ignored, Taylor thought, because they ought to govern and would govern regardless of what anyone did, but governmental systems could not depend upon such heroes always being present. Genius was bestowed very sparingly by nature. To build a government on the assumption that such statistical aberrations always would be available was to build on sand.[8]

Although John Adams had described a form of aristocracy that was completely outdated, according to Taylor's reading of history to assume that the past was finished was unwarranted. Aristocracy had not vanished, even if the kings and nobles had. "Aristocracy is forever adapting itself to the temper of the times."[9] Consequently it had undergone three transformations: "The frauds of superstition first collected the wealth, which . . . fed an aristocratical interest; then it was acquired by the force of the feudal system; and now . . . the frauds of paper and patronage" have taken over.[10] All of these forms of "nobility" had flourished through "an invasion of property."[11] To distinguish their methods, however, Taylor designated three separate ages of aristocracy. The first two ages of aristocracy, ancient and feudal, were nearly extinct, but their methods cropped up every once in awhile. Spain, for example, was governed by superstition; France and Italy by military rule; China combined force and superstition; and England had both of the first two forms of aristocracy as well as the third. In his *Enquiry* of 1794 Taylor had talked of only ancient and modern tyranny, so that his three-way classification of aristocracies of superstition, force, and fraud may have been inflenced heavily by John Adams's *Defence*. Taylor's chief purpose in discussing aristocracies, however, was not to quarrel over the number of stages of development through which they had passed, but to demonstrate that the hoary classification of governments into those of the one, the few, and the many was incorrect. In actuality all of these governments had been controlled by aristocracies that had gained power by transferring the property of others to themselves, and that stayed in power by monopolizing knowledge.[12]

The first age of aristocracy, classical antiquity, had ruling priests who had hoarded knowledge and wealth for themselves and justified their activities as the will of Jupiter. When challenged, they had hidden behind appeals for the veneration of sacred things. As a last resort they had always threatened to call down the wrath of Jupiter. This monopoly of religious knowledge denied man half of his humanity, Taylor thought. Priestly aristocracies had existed in both Greece and Rome, where they had seized the rites and offices of religion, "impressed an idea that its progeny were well born," and derived their family lineage from deities.[13] This form of aristocracy lasted through medieval times in the practices of the papal hierarchy, which was empowered to measure property on earth "by the artifice of selling heaven."[14] As time progressed, priests had become the tools of governments and were particularly useful in reinforcing public acceptance of tyrannous laws by insisting that the people respect religious codes. The very presence of religious laws had implied that the diety could be influenced by law: "The priest will learn the proselyte to govern the deity, if the proselyte will suffer the priest to govern him."[15] Yet, with all the defects of aristocracy based on superstition, Taylor conceded that it had taught moral virtues worthwhile for an age of ignorance; it had exacted only outward allegiance to its idols, while leaving the minds of its subjects free; and the constant competition between priests and kings had provided a check on governmental power.[16]

The second age of aristocracy had been the feudal system based upon conquest. Even though violence was the preferred method during this age, it had not been the adhesive that held the system together. Again, this had been property, which had to be taken from producers; two-thirds of the country's population supported the rest economically. The outward appearance of this aristocracy was "chivalry, principality, sovereignty, splendor, munificence and vassalage; its shadow, of title,"[17] but the holders of these privileges had no innate superiority: "The children of hereditary power are not tyrants from a procreative cause. They are made such by the contemplation of the power to which they are destined."[18] Nor were the governments of the feudal countries responsible: England and Italy had dissimilar governments, but similar aristocracies, owing to the monopoly of knowledge possessed by the nobility. The second age of aristocracy was enlightened by some good points: hereditary descent was less oppressive than a system that had to assert its claim with each generation; it was less expensive because the lords were supported by their manors, and the titles of the nobles were harmless and inexpensive. Open warfare, in addition, was an honest way of taking property from individuals who, at least, would know what was taken and who had it. Besides, the feudal manner of waging war did not involve many persons. Most important, a feudal government allowed the occasional expression of human interest and sympathy. No charity resulting from individual affection was allowed by the aristocracy of the third age.

The third kind of aristocracy was a carefully planned, intertwined network embodied in the Federalist plan for the United States: "Sinecure, armies, navies, offices, war, anticipation and taxes made up . . . that vast political combination . . . paper and patronage."[19] Its practitioners specialized in the obtaining of loans, banks, factories, contracts, ships, lotteries, river and road projects, "and an infinite number of inferior tricks to get money".[20] The system was a "political hydra" whose arms extended deep into the life and pockets of everyone. The secrecy and scope of this aristocracy allowed it to become much more total in its effect than aristocracies that had to stop with lip service to idols or with what could be conquered conveniently.[21]

The modern aristocrats had become the masters of the feudal aristocrats by a dual process, for which the tactics of the English Whigs served as examples. First, the institutions of feudalism had become discredited by the rising level of common knowledge. The effects of printing in spreading this knowledge and of commerce in redistributing property in Europe after the fifteenth century were instrumental in the popularization of knowledge. Second, as the forms of property changed and more and more of it found its way into the hands of aristocrats of the third age, political power followed with mathematical certainty. The wealth of this new aristocracy attracted power away from the feudal nobility. Without an independent base of power in property, feudal nobles were forced to become converts either to democracy or to the new aristocracy. Even though Taylor thought that this choice had been offered, he also thought that all of the feudal nobles and orders would soon melt into one aristocratic mass whose members would be obsessed by greed.[22]

The subversion of feudal aristocrats had been accomplished by such stealthy methods that neither the people nor the feudal aristocrats realized what had happened until the modern aristocrats had already come to control most of the property. These covert aristocrats should at least have announced their intention, Taylor maintained. Even without such an announcement, however, John Adams should have recognized that the "similitude between a stock and a feudal aristocracy is perfect," and avoided recommending a kingly executive and a princely senate in his *Defence*.[23] This quality of invisibility was to Taylor one of the most dangerous features of the new aristocracy. The only reason he had eventually accepted political parties was that their processes could be opened to public view and control. Other components of the modern aristocratic system could not be exposed to public view. Everyone had come to realize that religious and feudal aristocracies were exploiting the people, but the third form of aristocracy, "disguised in the garb of republicanism, and uttering patriotick words, joins the mob in kicking them about, by way of diverting the publick attention from itself." To think that hereditary aristocrats exhausted the possible forms was "equivalent to an opinion, that the science of geometry can only be illustrated by a square or a triangle."[24] In Taylor's opinion, the technology of tyranny had advanced ahead of the people's ability to understand it, hence popular hatred of the first two kinds of aristocracy was being used by the third to keep itself in power.

Taylor's very view of human nature may have forced him to adopt the position that there was a secret conspiracy of aristocrats behind the policy of the United States Government. On the one hand, he had an optimistic enough view of human nature to believe that civilized man had passed the point where religious and feudal aristocrats were credible leaders. On the other hand, public enlightenment had not caught up with the methods of modern aristocrats. There could be but one explanation: modern aristocrats were hiding their actions deliberately, lest they become known and condemned. Those who had seen and submitted to feudal brutality may have been wrong in Taylor's judgment, but at least they had made a choice based on full knowledge of the kind of leadership they were getting. Without awareness one had no real choice.[25]

B. Aristocracy of the Third Age in the United States

The types of aristocrats that Taylor numbered among the components of the modern form of aristocracy varied according to his interests and the prevailing issues of the time. He assumed that there would be a similarity of interest and an overlapping of membership among these various components. This mixture of aristocrats had existed from the very beginning of the modern aristocracy in the United States.

Taylor traced the new aristocracy to the 1787 Framing Convention. The delegates to that assembly had contained some sympathizers with aristocracy. A few had been honest advocates of British form, some were disappointed conspirators in a Tory plot to crown Washington king, and others were admirers of monarchical governments generally. Taylor maintained that these men had never wanted state governments, and his opinion in 1823 was that such a "consolidating project" still existed.[26]

Congress had been the crucial agency, Taylor decided, for the development of the aristocracy of the third age in the United States. Various interests had demanded satisfaction from Congress, and by its attempts to satisfy these interests had instituted a modern aristocracy. Political parties were one such interest, and the Federalists had attempted to use them to benefit themselves personally and their party as an organization. Congressmen had developed as a separate interest, and had, in turn subsidized security holders, bankers, capitalists, and pensioners. This "eleemonsynary family" had begun when certificate holders, many of them Congressmen, had been favored over paper-money holders by Hamilton's funding scheme. When the state debt was funded, one-hundred-million dollars of artificially created wealth had been immediately transferred to the holders of the state debt. The next stage of development in the growth of United States aristocracy had come when the holders of this debt had been allowed to turn their holdings into bank stock, which not only gave them more wealth for very little expenditure, but also gave them an influence over the supply of national currency. Later on, manufacturing capitalists had been protected by the Jefferson embargo and the War of 1812, so that they joined the group of privileged interests. Finally, the petitions of army pensioners had so swamped Congress's ability to legislate that pensions were granted right and left merely to get rid of the veterans demanding them.[27]

The components of Taylor's aristocracy of the third age in the United States were linked closely, then, to the activities of the national government. This modern aristocracy included groups that will be broadly classified for the purposes of this study into economic and political types. Existing along with them, but in a debilitated state, were remnants of the aristocracies of the first and second ages, which Taylor probably thought had never really gotten a chance in the New World. An appreciation of the nature, harmful effects, and techniques of each of these four subvarieties of aristocracy constitutes nearly a total picture of what John Taylor thought to be defective in United States governments.

C. Priestly Aristocrats

One might expect that Taylor would have given detailed attention to the role of priestly aristocrats, owing to the fact that Edmund Pendleton had been a last-ditch supporter of the Anglican establishment in Virginia while Taylor had been part of the movement that was seeking religious freedom. Moreover, it will be recalled that he had held membership in a parish with a skeptical tradition stood in stark contrast to the neighboring parish shepherded by the Tory Boucher. The fact is, however, that Taylor seems to have considered the fight for religious freedom nearly won. He seldom attacked the activities of particular sects, not even those of New England, whose establishment lasted much longer than Virginia's. The struggle for religious freedom had provided him with hypotheses for better understanding the methods of economic, political, and military aristocrats, but the days of priests were over.[28]

Catholics and Quakers were the only denominations criticized by Taylor. He had words of praise for the impetus toward constitutionalism that the Church had given during the Middle Ages. The Pope's activities could not be excused, however, for he had been historically "zealous to convert the heathens to christianity, and the christians to heathenism."[29] Abolitionists and Quakers, an "amiable and peaceable religious sect," had been panting for civil war for years, Taylor wrote in 1813. They had persuaded themselves that religious truth would be best served by abolitionism at any cost. "Into such fatal errors is human nature liable to fall, by its deliriums for acquiring unattainable perfection."[30] Abolitionists only wanted to use ignorant freed slaves as tools for oppressing other interests. Taylor found it interesting that abolitionists were never able to see the slavery created as a consequence of the operation of corporations, and argued that personal slavery, at least, bound the slaveowner's place in heaven to his treatment of his slaves. Thus, although there were a few religious aristocrats left and their motives were as selfish as any priests of ancient times, Taylor did not regard them as much of a threat.[31]

In keeping with the fact that he viewed religious aristocracies as virtually extinct, Taylor gave little attention to the techniques they were using. The use of religious power was mentioned by him only as an invidious standard of comparison for the practices of political aristocracies. Thus, the latter controlled information through the press as oracles had done, dispensed patronage to many sects in a fashion worse than the governments that had favored only one denomination, and offered laws touching on religion as an easier way to achieve salvation than moral rectitude. Taylor admitted that if government extended its power to matters of conscience, all other forms of tyranny would follow, but he apparently did not feel that priestly aristocrats had much of a future.[32]

D. Military Aristocrats

Taylor's view that feudal aristocrats achieved power through force might lead one to expect that Taylor would have given military aristocrats an important place in his criticism of American governmental practices. Although he did fear them, and often warned of the dangers of civil war, his fears were more specifically directed to the costs of military preparedness and the political uses of armies than to the danger of military dictatorship as such. His unfavorable attitude toward the military, when he did discuss them, could have been influenced as much by the boring period of time he had spent in the Continental Army as by any opinion that military takeover was an actual threat. As a soldier he had considered military officers "a set of Vultures," and does not seem to have modified this opinion later.[33] The only times Taylor ever supported the concept of a professional army were during the outbreak of the American Revolution and, in the last months of his life, when he voted for a multi-year military appropriation (to the disgust of John Randolph, who thought Taylor was finally getting senile). The rest of the time Taylor advocated militia instead of armies, complaining that the army would be nothing but a tax-collection agency, as it had been in the Whiskey Rebellion. He approved of Washington's frugality toward navies, but was not convinced that either Washington or Jefferson had done all they could have to support the militia. All Presidents said they favored the militia, Taylor complained, but they appropriated money for permanent armies.[34]

Taylor attacked standing armies for their cost, effects on domestic political processes, and their ineffectiveness.

The chief burden of military aristocrats was financial, not the danger of governmental control. The high taxes necessary to support armaments were crippling agriculture, in Taylor's opinion, without allowing agriculture to develop its best friend, the militia. In later years Taylor denied that the Continental Army had ever been as large as the number of persons claiming pensions for service in it. Ten thousand persons might ultimately be pensioned at an annual cost of three million dollars. At such a cost Taylor thought it would be cheaper to go back to priestly aristocrats. The final irony concerning the appeals for a larger navy was the fact that such appeals were usually voiced by persons also supporting a protective tariff. Warships would not be needed to protect merchant ships if the protective tariff was allowed to kill all useful American trade with Europe. Taylor was convinced, then, that the worst thing about military aristocrats was their cost.[35]

Taylor did not entirely belittle the danger of a military coup. He did feel that arms could be controlled only by arms, and that an army was the strongest of all factions, because it was the most disciplined and responsive to a single leader. It was more important to make the military obedient to the law than any other group. Even though no constitutional objection could be made to the raising of an army, if the purpose was the creation of a Napoleonic aristocracy, the spirit of the Constitution had been violated. There were protections against military aristocrats, however, that did not apply to other varieties. For example: military men were excluded from the legislatures; "whilst the general government may raise an army, the states may arm, office and discipline the militia";[36] and the use of military power was hard to hide, for "its manifest atrociousness would be some check upon the deed."[37]

A second important reason for subjugating military to civilian power was not "that soldiers are more cruel, avaricious or tyrannical than priests, stockjobbers or nobles, for the contrary is the fact," but that armies were separate interests subsisting off the public.[38] Their continued presence in a corrupted governmental system made them pawns in the struggle for power, and they might come under the influence of selfish candidates who would promise support of the army to get control of it. This made the army a legislative interest, and presidential patronage would be given freely as the President struggled to keep control. The struggles the presence of an army induced between its civilian masters, therefore, provided an important reason for doing without one.

A final important objection to standing armies was that they were not effective. They could not be relied upon to defend the country that had been so heavily taxed to support them. They were good only for guarding European factories from downtrodden workers, and the English had risked everything by relying on a mercenary army. The Romans before them had feared the victory of their own mercenaries almost as much as their defeat. "Besides, funding never fights for a nation in imminent danger; its wars are guided by other calculations, than those of publick safety; and the moment of peril is the moment of its flight."[39] Thus, neither the army nor its civilian defenders could be depended upon if the profit was too low.

Military aristocrats, therefore, constituted an important component of aristocracy and deserved close watching, although general human knowledge had caught up with their methods and no longer was awed by them. The expense and damage to responsible government that resulted from entanglement with a mercenary army was still a danger. "Nations who receive safety, receive at the same time a master, whether that safety is bestowed by law or by force," Taylor warned.[40]

This examination of Taylor's ideas on priestly and military aristocrats has established that he considered the aristocracies of religion a hollow threat, although the methods they had once employed had been copied by other kinds of aristocrats. Similarly, the aristocrats of force and violence had become embarrassing to the enlightened citizen of the nineteenth century. Armies were more dangerous as tangible symbols for stirring patriotism than as tools for potential dictators. Common knowledge was too refined to be taken in any longer by superstition and violence. They had lost their right to rule.

It can be charged that Taylor was too anxious to prove that aristocracies had never been justified, owing to the lack of common knowledge sufficient to control them. This orientation caused him to dismiss the threat of religious and military aristocracies in order to prove that human knowledge progressed. If Taylor had been content to settle for a static notion of human knowledge, he would have been a little more sensitive to the active threat to liberty still posed by priests and generals. New England states still had establishments, and the influence of military men on politics did not end with Hamilton's army, but lasted to Taylor's death and the ascendancy of Andrew Jackson. Yet, Taylor did not criticize these examples of aristocracies of the first and second ages, perhaps because this would have meant admitting that human knowledge had not caught up with them. If priests and generals had not yet been brought to heel, what hope could Taylor offer for stockjobbers?

E. Economic Aristocrats

Economic and political aristocrats were the actual threats to republican government in Taylor's opinion, and even though they were locked together in mutual advantage, they were jealous of each other's prerogatives, and were always stretching their imaginations to devise methods for taking property. Yet, for all their jealousy, political and economic aristocrats needed each other.

This system of aristocracy was substituting its combined intelligence for the intelligence of the people. This resulted in the destruction of the three great products of free society: virtue, produced by religion; civil liberty, produced by government; and wealth, produced by labor. Only freedom of intelligence could regain these three beneficial products, which "make up one political system, and that system, to be consistent, must adhere to one principle . . ."—a reliance on "national intelligence" rather than the intelligence of conspiracies.[41] Modern aristocrats had an advantage given them by their success: they were already in control and well practiced in outthinking and outmaneuvering the rest of the citizenry.

The knowledge controlled by elites was worthless to them unless it was put to work to bring them wealth. That was what they were really after, both as an end in itself and as a means to power. The cumulative effects of modern aristocracies were so staggering, and the details of their methods so complex, that Taylor sometimes offered aggregated estimates of their effect, measured in dollars. Their return on investment he put at twenty-six percent, twenty percent more than that of agriculture. Their cost to the country, per capita, in 1820 was four dollars in political costs and two dollars in economic costs. In 1822 the total annual cost of banking was sixty million dollars. The $416 million that had been collected in taxes, debt, and land sales since the Republic's founding had been diverted completely into aristocractic pockets. Of the sixty million dollars taken annually, twenty-eight and one-half million dollars was drawn completely from the seventeen nonmanufacturing states and relocated in the nine industrialized states. Modern aristocrats had goaded the government into living beyond its means in an attempt to institutionalize the same sort of system that was bankrupting England.[42]

The economic costs of political and economic aristocrats included, therefore, their long-range effects on the health of a country's economy. In criticizing these effects, Taylor turned to his purposes some of the arguments that had been used to deny political participation to the poorer elements of society. For example, dealers in speculative investments had no permanent stake in society. They were birds of passage who would desert an enterprise if it became unprofitable, rather than see it through to productivity. Such cowardice would ruin the very health of aristocrats and lead to effeminate manners. A further defect was that the economic freedom that still existed did so only because economic aristocrats were profiting from it indirectly. Ultimately all sectors of the economy would end up without freedom, either because the aristocrats or those whom they were oppressing would each flee to despotism for protection against the other.[43]

There were four groups of economic aristocrats that were criticized by Taylor throughout his writings. A study of their harmful effects and activities will not only lead to a fuller understanding of the problem, as Taylor defined it, but also demonstrate the importance Taylor gave to political solutions for economic problems. The four groups, roughly in the same order that Taylor discussed them, were public creditors, bankers, capitalists, and charterholders.

Public Creditors

Public creditors and national debt policies were attacked by Taylor in his early works and in the *Inquiry*. Taylor had no quarrel with borrowing as such, and he both borrowed and loaned large amounts of money, charging interest on what he loaned. Excessive borrowing by governments was another matter, however, because it had been the thin entering wedge for the entire creditor-banking-capitalist system. The funding of the state debt had given certificate holders up to twenty times what they had paid in the first place. The funding project had helped create the banking system that grew up in the same few states that housed the certificate holders, creating economic sectionalism in addition to windfall rates of return.[44]

The authority of government to borrow money was next in danger to the power to raise armies, in Taylor's opinion. A public debt was mot readily assumed by a nation during war, so those who held public obligations had an investment in past and future wars. Moreover, the longer the war lasted, the more these creditors earned, hence they would attempt to prolong wars as long as possible. A war that lasted fourteen years or so, Taylor guessed, might wipe out any possible material advantages that might have followed from it in the first place. To make matters even worse, wars instigated for the enrichment of speculators were not inspiring causes. They produced "the utmost degree of publick expense, with the least degree of publick spirit."[45]

Creditors were difficult to deal with because the normal methods of controlling aristocrats did not work, since their power was based in a status conferred by law. This political dependence, if not their guilty consciences, would lead them to corrupt the processes of government to keep the advantages they enjoyed. Dividing this power by sharing it with even more creditors would produce effects opposite to those created when landed aristocrats had vast holdings broken up by changes in the laws of inheritance. The more creditors a nation had, the more selfish were the aristocrats it had to deal with. The more it created, the more they would struggle to maintain their status as the beneficiaries of taxes paid by the productive interests in society. Theoretically if all men could be made creditors, both the seeming advantages of borrowing and the status of creditors as an exclusive interest would be destroyed. Unfortunately, the existence of a large number of creditors guaranteed that government would not be allowed to create too many other creditors.[46]

George the First and his minister, Robert Walpole, had perfected this system of buying influence. They had borrowed money for public use to buy the support the Hanover king lacked among the landed gentry. Taylor was amused that American Whigs could not learn from this English precedent that had produced such devastating results on the political influence of English Tories. Perhaps Americans had been deceived by the ability of creditors to hide behind slogans such as *faith and credit*, the *encouragement of commerce*, and the increasing need for *necessary office*. All of these were offered by the funding system's advocates as a method of avoiding criticism. Those who really believed in these principles were thus unwitting accomplices in the undermining of these very ideals. The creation and nurture of public creditors formed a policy that was rich in irony for Taylor.[47]

Bankers

Bankers were an economic group frequently criticized by Taylor. Throughout all his writings, from the earliest to the last, he attacked bankers. Banking was an interest that had unfairly claimed protection without supplying any contribution in return. It has been riveted by charters into a permanent aristocracy. He confessed once that banking was so central to economic elites that he had difficulty in distinguishing between banking and other kinds of aristocracies. The divisions within the Virginia and New York branches of the Republican Party, for example, had resulted from banking activities in both states. As a system of extortion and exploitation, banking was worse than national public debt, and could have brought the country to the same difficulties alone.[48]

There were various components of the banking system, but Taylor claimed that the most important contribution had been made by the Congressmen who had originally established the first Bank of the United States so that they might become stockholders in it. Taylor saw this as a conspiracy, and recent research certainly does not refute his judgment. Bray Hammond found that when eight million dollars' worth of bank stock for the first Bank of the United States was sold, thirty members of Congress were among the buyers. These thirty were one-third of the total membership of Congress, and constituted one-half of those who had voted to create the Bank. Hammond also reports that these charter stockholders did not even have to pay cash for more than one-fourth of their subscription, because three-fourths of the Bank's original capital was permitted by the enabling legislation to be public securities. Thus the Congressmen who, Taylor thought, had originally abused their position by funding the state debt that they owned, had compounded their guilt by using the funded debt to further enrich themselves. The governmental favors enjoyed by the bank stockholders had been passed on to a limited number of persons who had begun speculating operations that depended on the existence of banks. These adventurers had never worked, but the support given the Bank by Congress guaranteed that those depending on it would not suffer financial reverses. Such practices Taylor found plainly dishonest.[49]

Taylor was never willing to recognize any mitigating circumstances for banking. Its effects were thoroughly harmful. He discounted arguments that banks were needed, lest the country be at the mercy of foreign banks. As far as he was concerned banks were iniquitous whether foreign or domestic. Although Taylor admitted that having the Bank serve as a depository for tax revenue was convenient theoretically, he also pointed out that the location of branch banks was totally at the discretion of the Bank directors and had no relation to the Treasury's convenience.[50]

Taylor discerned six overlapping undesirable effects from banking operations. These effects were all in the influence that bankers had been able to gain—over the federal government, the supply of currency; their own banking operations, taxation, and state governments. The final difficulty was simply the magnitude of the burden imposed by banking.

The hold bankers had gained over the federal government was worse, in Taylor's opinion, than that possessed by public creditors. Creditors were always nervous about the possibility that government would repudiate its debt, and, therefore, attempted to keep government under tight control. Bankers were worse, because they often were public creditors whose greed had been stirred by the greater gains possible from banking. Thus, to an interest in controlling government they added a tendency to engage in speculative enterprises. At the same time bankers regarded themselves as a private group owing no responsibility to the public, even though they held public privileges.[51]

The second set of problems caused by the Bank resulted from its control of money. The interest that stockholders received was incomputable because it included the combined interest from public securities, bank shares, and the expansion of circulating currency beyond the actual capital resources of the bank. "It rests upon an idea called credit."[52] The danger always existed that there would not be enough specie in the banks' vaults at a time of crisis to pay outstanding claims, either because there never had been enough specie, or because it had been demanded in payment by foreigners. This completely exploded the reason for having government establish banks in the first place: when it needed help, so would they. Even if the Bank retained an adequate supply of specie, it could withhold loans and thereby influence public and private decisions. The same leverage over economic decisions could be achieved by bankers being able to demand payments in specie when their own export of specie to pay demands of foreign depositors had created a shortage of it.[53]

A third important drawback to the Bank was the secrecy with which it was able to operate, hiding its activities and records from public scrutiny. It could scatter its branches so that its money could not be counted, complicate its statements so that no one could understand them, hide its stockholders' names, and leak enough financial information to Congressmen to guarantee their support. In addition, the Bank could buy land up to an amount worth fifteen million dollars without even reporting it to the Secretary of the Treasury, who was in all other matters the Bank's taskmaster. Allowing the Bank to accumulate such enclaves of Federal land, exempt by the *McCulloch v. Maryland* decision, 4 Wheaton 316, from state taxes, could result in a new kind of feudalism. Worst of all, the bankers didn't even have the decency to spend what they gained, so that at least their consumer purchases would benefit the economy. Instead, with

Yankee parsimony, they hoarded their ill-gotten gains in secret for the day when they would be able to buy a new charter for the Bank.[54]

A fourth bad effect of banking was its tendency to control and expend taxation, as Taylor defined it. This resulted both from the fact that actual taxes had been increased to afford the extravagences that banks had introduced into government, and according to Taylor's theory, from the fact that lending and discounting operations were actually a tax. In support of the latter he argued that a circulating medium was the soul of all productive activities, and a corporation that could control it could control them. Since banks hoarded specie to back their currency, the amount available for use as currency was reduced. The profit the bank got was a tax, because labor had been robbed unnecessarily of wealth. To say that an enterprise had a choice whether or not it would pay bank fees was specious, Taylor pointed out, because any business had to have currency to live.[55]

A fifth harmful effect of banking was the way it nibbled at the powers of state governments. A state's authority to tax had been injured by the *McCulloch* decision, for example, and in this case it had happened without any indication from Congress that it had intended a diminution of state powers by the Bank charter. States were also injured by actions leading up to the *Osborn v. Bank of the United States* decision, 9 Wheaton 738, which stopped Ohio from expelling the Bank. States had to submit to the Bank or found a rival system to drain off some of its business and keep capital within the state. Unfortunately, the latter course was not open to Western states, which did not have a large number of resident public creditors and capitalists who could capitalize and manage state banking systems. Of all the Jeffersonians, few, except for Taylor and John Randolph, opposed all forms of banking, including state banking systems.[56]

A final difficulty caused by banking was the cumulative magnitude of the financial burdens it imposed when compared to the short duration of its benefits. In 1803 Taylor estimated that there were forty banks in the United States, capitalized at forty million dollars, which were gaining a fifty percent profit per share of bank stock because of their ability to generate currency through loaning. For all this expense, the benefits gained were few and temporary. Banking loans were granted only for enterprises that would turn over the money in a hurry. Lasting improvements, such as loans to farmers, tied up investments too long. Worse than this was the fact that banks paid eight percent on their stock and loaned at six. This meant that private loans to agriculture would be discouraged, because all states limited interest to six percent while a higher rate could be gotten from bank stock. To make matters worse, since banks loaned at six percent, the legal maximum, there was no possibility of secondary loans by private individuals to agriculturalists. Thus, the expense of banking operations was one of its most severe drawbacks.[57]

Capitalists

Capitalists were frequently criticized by Taylor, but his rejection of their methods was more complicated and ambiguous than his criticism of bankers. An important distinction to bear in mind throughout Taylor's discussion of capitalists is that he limited the meaning of *capitalist* to the financiers of manufacturing enterprises, excluding the managers of these factories. The latter he called "manufacturers." Capitalists may or may not have invested in manufacturing, according to the rate of return in other businesses. It was difficult for a man of Taylor's generation accurately to have described the status of American capitalism. On the one hand, Taylor certainly criticized capitalism with the model of English factory production before him (e.g., his assertion that standing armies were useful only to keep factory workers at their lathes). On the other hand, it would have been difficult to find an American enterprise that mirrored the English system until the 1850s.[58]

During Taylor's time only two systems of manufacturing were used that approached the factory system. One was the Pawtucket system, in which the factory limited itself to the manufacture of spun-cotton yarn and used the children of villagers and farmers as laborers. The families of these children completed the weaving of this yarn in their own homes, which were close by. The operator of the factory did not own it. The second system was the Waltham system, which was close to the English model but not precisely equivalent, because no permanent labor force was employed. The country girls who formed the work force at such factories returned home after a year or two when they had accumulated enough savings for a dowry. The iron, shoe, and woolen industries used methods even more primitive than those described here. Neither of these methods of production produced the abuse of workers that Taylor sometimes charged capitalists with, because no permanent labor force, dependent on wages for their total income and under constant supervision during the performance of their duties, was created. Thus, at the time Taylor lived, mercantile capitalism was defined by Louis Hacker was the only kind practiced.[59] In it former merchants, forced from commerce or leaving voluntarily by the prospect of speculative gain, would use their capital fund for various enterprises: public works promotion, real estate, insurance, banking, and manufacturing. In retrospect, it can be said that Taylor was accurate when he described capitalists as a group separate from manufacturers. The age of the entrepreneurial giants in which the financiers and the operators of factories became the same men was a later development. Moreover, these captains of industry were not drawn from the same groups that had been mercantile capitalists. It is also true, however, that Taylor was incorrect in assuming that the English factory system had already been fully implemented in the United States. Laborers were not yet a permanent labor force, nor were they subject to the conditions Taylor compared unfavorably to Negro slavery.[60]

The distinction between capitalists and manufacturers was employed by Taylor for reasons that may have been more propagandistic than anything else. He may have been trying to drive a wedge between manufacturers and the capitalists who owned the factories. At times Taylor fancied himself a true defender of manufacturers. In *Arator,* his most agrarian work, he explicitly denied that he was an enemy to manufacturing: "The fact is otherwise."[61] Taylor's attitude on this matter was reflected not only in words, but also in deeds. He had experimented unsuccessfully with some manufacturing on his own plantation, had proposed private subsidies for agricultural tool development, and was an enthusiastic booster of a plow factory owned by a relative. Taylor therefore criticized capitalist aristocrats but defended manufacturers in order to drive a wedge between them. An alliance with manufacturers did not offend him, because it was his sincere opinion that manufacturing was a form of productive enterprise.[62]

Taylor's claim that he was the friend of manufacturing was borne out in all of his writings. One of his early writings had recognized manufacturing as more useful than banking, and he thereafter pointed out that industrial technology was one type of knowledge that aristocrats suppressed. It is clear that he was referring to centralized manufacturing in these discussions, for he rejected the notion that household manufacturing would meet the demand for fabricated products. He even thought that manufacturing might become a dominant part of the economy one day, although he hoped this dominance would follow that distant day when the frontier had been settled.[63]

In line with his defense of manufacturing, Taylor criticized capitalists for limiting the amount of manufactured goods available for productive use. For example, capitalists advocated the promotion of only domestic manufacturing, even though free trade would help everyone in the long run. They had an unhealthy interest in war for the nonproductive war supplies they could sell to the combatants. The premature expansion by profit-minded capitalists into the West was another economic blunder, because no geographically large country had ever become a leading exporter. For a country to become industrialized it had to have sources of supply and markets close enough to make transportation costs reasonable, and it had to have centers of population crowded enough to force workers into a labor pool. The best way for the United States to become industrialized, in Taylor's opinion, was for it to develop its Eastern sections before spreading its population into the Western interior. Under any other pattern of development, manufacturing was not as economically sound as it should be.[64]

The labor conditions that Taylor imagined to be true of Northern factories imposed a limit on his admiration of manufacturing. He was willing for other countries to supply factory-made items for as long a period of time as possible, because of the effects of industrialization on workers. The establishing of factories required the gathering together of colonies of workers, and this forced urbanization had a series of harmful effects on them. It deprived them "of the erect attitude in society inspired by the freedom of industry"; kept them from ever becoming wealthy themselves; prevented them from learning useful trades or participating in self-government; and probably led to impoverishment and a life of crime thereafter.[65] Even if workers were somehow made the recipients of federal subsidies, such as those given capitalists through protective tariffs, they would be damaged by their loss of personality and morals.[66] Manufacturing may have been inevitable, but Taylor feared its consequences.

Another group injured when manufacturing was forced into

premature expansion was the seventeen states that had to support the cost of tariffs. The nine states that had gained from these subsidies were not even more industrialized, Taylor maintained, than certain Southern states were manufacturing was growing in strength. The nine Northern states should be careful how they used arguments supporting protective tariffs, because the Southern manufacturing states might impose tariffs against the products of the North based on the theories of protective tariffs. In his defense of manufacturing in the Southern and Middle states, Taylor must have been sensitive to the possible charge that the economic difficulties being experienced by them was the result of manufacturing. This he denied, saying not manufacturing, but the capitalistic system for financing it, was to blame for the economic problems of Maryland, Kentucky, Ohio, and Virginia. "Manufacturing is, therefore, neither the cause nor the remedy of the general distress."[67]

Taylor's views on capitalistic aristocrats, therefore, were as negative as his opinion on banks. Unlike his criticism of banks, and everything connected with them, his attack on capitalists did not extend to all participants in the manufacturing process. The managers of factories were exempt, as were the workers. Both were engaged in the creation of products of value. The last chapter of this study will discuss the fact that Taylor always endorsed honest activity that produced products or services of value.

Charterholders and Corporations

So that no aristocracy would escape verbal abuse, Taylor sometimes attacked charterholders and corporations, even though they could not be distinguished clearly from banks and manufacturing enterprises. Taylor complained that banks substituted the representation of chartered groups or corporations for individuals through the influence banks had over public officials. Taylor suggested, no doubt facetiously, that if corporations had to be represented, it would have been better to have turned over entire cities or states to them outright than to have allowed the control of the federal government, whose actions affected everyone. Taylor took issue with the unspecified opponents (possibly the court majority in the Dartmouth College case) who had argued that corporations were creations of kings, and that the British legal precedent that the king never died applied to corporations as well. Taylor pointed out that kings had abrogated corporate charters, and that, if they had not, applying a British precedent to American practice was not possible. American legislatures, unlike kings, died at every election, which required that the actions of a former legislature be subject to the review of its successor. The grant of exclusive privileges through a charter, then, was a monarchical method of making profits. Taylor recommended that it be rejected along with the other trappings of monarchy.[68]

To Taylor the word *corporation* was a legal term referring to municipalities that had "social" power. Social power was the authority to administer governmental policies, but not to restructure the governmental bodies that made these policies. This definition had been enlarged by aristocrats to include private business corporations so that it would imply that they had social power. The representation of corporations in Congress, especially through the Bank's influence, was the same thing as giving corporations the ability to restructure the federal government, because the Constitution had intended that only people be represented in Congress. In the United States, Taylor maintained, "the rights of towns, counties, or corporations, were not reserved, because they were subjects of sovereignties, whose rights were reserved."[69] Those sovereignties were the people.

In summary, economic aristocracies formed a system of private government that had corrupted talented citizens and sacrificed the public interest to individual selfishness without providing any means for popular control. Economic aristocrats had been given power over government originally through the funding system, and as they increased their hold and changed their form, their expansion was always at the public expense. No matter what their form, bankers, capitalists, and stockholders were all fundamentally dependent on governmental favors. Economic aristocrats were always forced to achieve their selfish goals through means provided by government. Thus, Taylor consistently applied his definition of aristocrats as those whose preeminence was a result of the transfer of the property of others to themselves by law.

F. Political Aristocrats

Political aristocrats and the methods for self-enrichment they controlled were essential components of the aristocracy of the third age, as Taylor defined it. Political parties were components of this aristocracy, and the objections to them that Taylor expressed have been considered in the preceding chapter. Briefly, he thought that "all parties, however loyal to principles at first, degenerate into aristocracies of interest at last ... popular parties are among the surest modes of introducing an aristocracy."[70] Taylor said this in 1814, and his opinion changed later after he had assured himself that political parties based on doctrine could be made public and responsible. His opinions of other political elites underwent no similar change.

The basic problem with political aristocrats was that officeholding separated a man from his constituency and made him part of a group of incumbents with similar interests. The interests of incumbents were often different and contrary to the public interest. For example, politicians were trained by habit to restrain emotion and act in such a manner as to achieve carefully planned ends. They lacked sympathy, consequently, for the oppressed members of society who had to pay the bills run up by aristocrats. Great political leaders also became captives of their own deceit, and suspected any critics, even friendly ones. In addition, public officials tended to have a creative bias toward projects and personnel that they had sponsored. This bias often prevented great leaders from correcting their mistakes. Still another difficulty was the fact that the profession of being a politician had little job security, hence its practitioners feared a rotation in office. There were few appeals that they considered too outrageous if the alternative was being voted out of office. Worst of all, after honest men had become disillusioned with the corruption devised by politicians to stay in office, they would abandon elections and join in the deception themselves.[71]

Types of Political Aristocrats

Although Taylor never developed a detailed classification of political aristocrats as he had for economic ones, there were certain offices that separation of powers had made inherently more powerful. Thus the President, Congressmen, and federal judges were the most important political aristocrats.

The President was so powerful that Taylor accused past ones of having corrupted electoral decisions through the very existence of their office. Lesser-known candidates fought among themselves to bask in the reflected glory of standing for election along with a popular President. Taylor found the notion of a President's "administration" a dangerous one, because it exacerbated the tendency of candidates to identify with a President. Moreover, identifying with an administration prevented individuals from being independent of mind, either as voters or as officeholders.[72]

A combination of presidential and congressional power a very few years after the founding of the country started to transfer the property of the majority to minority interests through increased taxes and other burdens. Although no presidential administration had been free of such wrongdoing, in Taylor's judgment, the administrations of Washington and Jefferson had set an example for thrift. Even at that time, however, legislators had become personally infused with a speculative spirit as a consequence of these attempts to transfer property and had been forced by interests outside Congress into further property transference. Thus, pensioners were flooding Congress's calendars during Taylor's last term as Senator, and earned his scorn for it. Although Taylor was convinced that it was wrong for legislators to mix their public duties and their private speculations, as they had done with the funding of the state debt and the founding of the Bank of the United States, change was unlikely. The longer such partialities lasted, the richer and stronger governing aristocracies became.[73]

Judges were not in the same aristocratic league as presidents and congressmen. Since Taylor maintained that judges were subject to legislative control for their misdeeds, he may have felt that it would have weakened his argument to sanctify the ermine with too much intrinsic potency. Instead, he seems to have considered the federal court's decisions as a war of ideas, to be corrected with other ideas, but of no more importance than other governmental officials gave them. He did not doubt, however, that federal judges were motivated by the same sort of sympathies that always had supported the Tory and Consolidationist cause.

The increase in judicial power that had resulted from the *McCulloch* decision was a deliberate attempt to suppress states and exalt the federal government through attacks on state laws, treasuries, and officials.[74]

Taylor's detailed descriptions of the techniques of political aristocrats were either criticisms of the conflict of interest that occurred when a public official used his office for private gain, or attacks upon the operation of policies that resulted from allowing private interests to influence legislation. Thus he criticized nearly every important program adopted by Congress after 1789: banking, taxation, debt, war, lotteries, tariffs, and internal improvements were all techniques invented by aristocrats to transfer property. One might expect that Taylor would have buttressed this thoroughgoing criticism with evidence that political deals had been made, but other than the list of creditors he presented in *Enquiry*, he did not. His logic made this unnecessary for him. He argued that similar effects flow from similar causes. Thus, if he found that a particular act of the federal government resulted in an effect similar to something that had occurred in Britain, he inferred that a similar cause was back of it. If higher taxes were backed by aristocracies in Britain, one must look behind every American tax increase for the aristocracy that would surely be there.[75]

Such standards of evidence might leave a modern social scientist with an unsatisfied hunger, but it was a way of thought quite true to Taylor's rationalistic approach. It was also a convenient approach for one who hated to leave the banks of the Rappahannock.

Motives of Political Aristocrats

Even though economic motives may have been the basic cause of the conspiracy that tied economic and political bureaucrats together, Taylor was always careful to point out that political officials controlled the means for accomplishing the conspiracy's objectives. Taylor called political motives "ambition" and economic motives "avarice," an abbreviated way of expressing his opinion that aristocrats sought both the material rewards of increased wealth and the psychological satisfaction of being able to command the activities of others. This distinction was common in the literature of the time, although few put it to the systematic use that Taylor did. Generally speaking, Taylor associated ambition with political aristocrats and avarice with economic aristocrats, but in *Tyranny Unmasked* he made it clear that there was a reciprocal relationship between the two: "If ambition is cultivated . . . with excessive power, it extorts from industry the fruits of its labor; if avarice is cultivated . . . with excessive wealth, it acquires political power to pillage industry also. Enormous political power invariably accumulates enormous wealth, and enormous wealth invariably accumulates enormous political power."[76] Economic and political aristocrats needed each other.

Techniques of Political Aristocrats

Political aristocrats pursued their objectives through several major techniques, each of which served a different purpose. These techniques included the use of law, constitutional interpretation, and patronage. Taylor's criticism of certain property-transferring laws occupied large portions of his works and included attacks on taxes, embargoes, tariffs, and internal improvements. The use of such laws was an immediate method of taking the property of others to satisfy the vice of avarice, as Taylor defined it. Constitutional interpretation was a more indirect method because it provided the means by which aristocracies could expand their power. It laid the groundwork for future laws. Similarly, patronage was useful to political elites, because it allowed them to expand their influence over governmental officials, thereby guarding against the chance that the public interest might be served in the administering of law. Constitutional interpretation and patronage, therefore, served the vice of ambition. It is obvious that the use of laws for transferring property occupied a central place in the tactics used by political aristocrats as Taylor described them. His critique of the major laws used to transfer property will be discussed next.

John Taylor limited the purposes of taxation to the raising of revenue sufficient to meet expenditures, and he insisted that even this be collected unoppressively and spent as frugally as possible. Most federal taxes did not meet these criteria. Such taxes suffered from the defects of being partial in their incidence, permanent in their duration, direct instead of indirect in their nature, and tyrannous in their effect on private property. To make matters worse, there were ways of achieving the tyrannous effects of taxation without using taxes directly. For example, taxation was often partial in its effect, because those who passed the laws did not have to pay them. Congressmen passed the laws, but except for nonprotective imposts, were not subject to the effects of them. Permanent taxes were another way that aristocrats used the power of law to enrich themselves. Taylor believed that no tax should be permanent unless it had been earmarked for purpose that was also permanent. Continuing taxes indefinitely destroyed responsibility and allowed the hoarding of power for use against peace and liberty. Among the permanent taxes, direct ones were the most detrimental to property, because they were levied on items necessary for the sustaining of life. Indirect taxes could be avoided, since they were applied to luxury items and items intended for resale, but direct taxes such as the carriage tax upheld in *Hylton* v. *United States*, 3 Dallas 171, could "rob us of the very sustenance arising from our manual labour."[77] Partial, permanent, and direct taxes were ways of transferring property, Taylor believed. He recognized that any tax transferred the amount of an individual's property that was represented by the value of the currency paid, but if an individual received something worth as much as what was paid out, it could not truly be called transfer of property. For worthwhile taxation an individual received "an equivalent in social security" that was worth as much as the property transferred by the tax.[78] When these payments went for the purpose of oppressive government and privileged aristocrats, however, taxation had become un-masked as a tyranny.

It was not necessary for taxes to be called taxes to accomplish tyrannous infringements of property. The integrated control that political and economic aristocrats were able to exert over the supply of money was a type of taxation that had to be sanctioned by laws such as those which established lending ratios. If the amount of paper currency was increased, Taylor pointed out, buyers would bid the prices of goods higher. When this occurred while the foreign markets for agricultural goods were in a depressed state, property was being transferred. In such a situation farmers had to pay higher prices and the burden of taxes was increased because they took proportionately more of the income left to farmers after paying the higher prices. Thus the effects of taxation caused by manipulations in the supply of money were actually financially more burdensome than taxation itself.[79]

Taylor had originally supported Jefferson's embargo, but by 1808 he had changed his mind. He urged Monroe, then ambassador to England, to accept a treaty that had been offered as a chance to get international trade started again. Taylor told Nicholas that the embargo was draining the Treasury while enriching smugglers, such as those on the Rappahannock River where Taylor lived. At the same time it was impoverishing agriculture and other productive economic activities. The em-bargo also was raising the prices of necessary items such as the iron that went into farm tools, thereby raising the price of tools while lowering their quality. Bad tools produced poor crops. Embargoes were merely a subterfuge for forcing Americans to support the factories owned by capitalists, Taylor concluded.[80]

Internal improvements were also a way of transferring property, even when undertaken for the most altruistic purposes. Roads and canals were offered as bribes to agriculture, so as to secure the assent of farmers to the other components of the third age of aristocracy. Yet roads and canals did not begin to reach the cause of the decline of Southern agriculture. Internal improvements were the aftermath of the speculative mood that resulted from the surplus of bank currency following the War of 1812, but Taylor charged that such projects really only enriched the contractors who built them. At the same time, internal improvements taught the federal government to live beyond its means. Of all the exclusive privileges bestowed on aristocrats, internal improvements were the most local in effect, because they were physically located in a particular place. Yet, Congress could know little about what the residents in the outer reaches of the country needed. Such an impersonal method of conferring local benefits was wrong, because it forced internal improvements on remote regions that may not have needed inproving while forcing the residents of other regions to pay for these gratuitous services.[81]

The protective tariff was a method of property transfer that Taylor insisted only helped capitalists by driving farmers out of business and increasing the dependence of the people on the federal government. All aristocrats attempted to make people dependent on governmental favors for their livelihood. Taylor's economic analysis of the tariff was more complex than a few sentences can suggest, but his reasoning emphasized throughout the tendency of tariffs to transfer property. For example, any part of a capitalist's price that exceeded what he could have received under competitive conditions was a total loss to the purchaser. Long-term benefits to the economy were not to be considered. Even though Taylor preferred tariffs to excises because they were cheaper, open to the taxpayer's choice as to whether or not he would pay them, and less violative of personal privacy to collect, he still opposed protective tariffs for their effect on property. Agricultural profits were damaged, according to Taylor, through the sealing off of foreign markets in retaliation for the closing of United States ports to foreign commodities, through increasing the costs of transportation back to the United States since ships could return only with gold in the hold instead of trade goods, through the levying of more taxes and revenue-raising devices to compensate for the money lost from imposts, and through the forcing of farmers and others in productive occupations to pay higher prices to support capitalists.[82]

Laws were the first aspect of the modern aristocratic system that Taylor attacked, but he soon came to a realization of the role that constitutional interpretation played in giving aristocrats the means to enrich themselves through law. Taylor's failure to appreciate the potency of constitutional interpretation may have been the result of the fact that in 1795 he was still hoping that the United States Supreme Court would use its powers against the carriage tax. By 1798 Taylor had become convinced that the United States Constitution had staked its existence upon the support of aristocrats and had received that support. This 1798 position was his most extreme criticism of the Constitution. Always thereafter Taylor assumed the role of friend and protector of the document, defending it against those who had lost during the 1787 Philadelphia Convention and still were attempting to impose their consolidationist views on the public.[83]

In Taylor's reckoning, constitutional interpretation was more valuable to the modern aristocrat than the control of armies. The use of force had lost its ability to frighten the common people, but constitutional interpretation had actually increased aristocratic power without increasing the possibility of popular control. The guidelines for using constitutional power had been established in Hamilton's *Federalist* Essay no. 80, according to Taylor. This essay had discussed how the declaring of congressional power supreme in an area appropriate for legislation gave Congress complete dominion on that subject. The application of Hamilton's theory, to Taylor's dismay, had vastly increased the power and importance of aristocracy in the United States.[84]

This increase of aristocratic power through constitutional interpretation had followed a well-planned progression. First, states had been persuaded that tolerance and fair play forced them to give coordinate powers to Congress in a particular policy area. Then the Supreme Court had wheeled in the doctrine of implied powers to give Congress a choice of means in the use of

not given other bribes that he had promised. Taylor quoted Jonathan Swift's "Magician's Rod" on this point, and said that the President, like Lord Bute, whom Swift criticized in this poem, often "caught his fish and saved his bait."[90] Several effects flowed from this practice. First, generally the men who accepted patronage appointments were of inferior character and likely to steal from the public if they ever got the chance. Second, when appointees were placed in office and then unsatisfied by the rewards of that office, they vastly increased their selfish attempts to enrich themselves. Third, they sometimes became ashamed of their selfishness, but their guilty consciences only led them to ever-greater stealing. Taylor saw little remedy for this. If the terms of office of appointees were shortened, their guilty consciences would only cause them to work overtime stealing. If salaries were high, the appointees were an out-and-out burden to the taxpayer, but if salaries were low, the appointees were sure to supplement their incomes from the public treasury. It would be better if all officeholders imitated Benjamin Franklin, who had never drawn salary while Governor of the State of Pennsylvania, Taylor suggested.[91]

The third characteristic of patronage that disturbed Taylor was the apparent fact that republican government was no protection against the abuses of patronage. Republics were actually worse than other governmental forms in their use of patronage: they had a larger number of persons to share in offices; access to appointing officials was easier; party spirit became a harmful reinforcement to the natural vice of avarice; the increase in the number of persons involved also multiplied the channels through which they might receive gratuities; and the rotation that occurred in office-holding simply resulted in incumbents trying to get rich quick at public expense. The very disreputability of patronage led to abuses of official position, because an honest man would take such a job only if he was desperate or too ambitious. Public criticism of an honest man who accepted a patronage job would prompt him to hide his actions, thereby taking him to the very brink of abusing his powers.[92]

The secrecy that surrounded the uses of patronage sometimes made it difficult to detect. Patronage could be dispensed by exempting a group from a generally shared burden as well as by granting them special privileges openly. Taxes were useful for this: the object of the tax could be designed so as to take the property of certain groups, the large number of collectors needed could be appointed from favored groups, and the revenue collected could be given to the favored ones in some sort of bounty. Nor did the chain of patronage stop there, for corporations could even be exempted from state taxation. This frightened Taylor greatly, because he worried that the power of incorporation might be used to achieve any sort of purpose under the implied powers doctrine. Each of these corporations then might be exempted from taxation by states. These corporations could buy real estate that would be, in effect, municipal wards of the federal government, free of the influence of state governments. An entire state might fall into the federal orbit in this manner, or at least might become dependent on federal patronage through internal improvements. Thus, Taylor feared that the combination of the techniques of law, constitutional interpretation, and patronage used by political aristocrats might result in the creation of a corporate aristocracy that would have the geographic basis of power that the other aristocrats possessed in only an incomplete form, if at all.[93]

G. Aristocratic Techniques for Maintaining Power

The techniques used by aristocrats to maintain themselves in power have been touched upon several times before; for if aristocrats increased their wealth and their influence, they had more resources to devote to their own perpetuation. Taylor observed two additional phenomena, however: the concentration of power and widespread support for the use of this power.

Power had to be concentrated into very large masses to give political and economic aristocrats the motives and the means for abusing their power. Aristocrats sought the accumulation of power for different reasons. Some had a philosophic commitment to a consolidated form of government, while others simply had tasted the abuse of power and could not break the habit. The latter group were particularly troublesome, because it did not matter whether the circumstances under which they tasted power were legitimate or not. Even if their experience with power had occurred under the safest of conditions, as legitimately elected officials held in close check by constitutional restraint, once their appetites had been whetted, a way would be found to remove constitutional limitations. Concentration of power added one other advantage to aristocratic attempts to maintain themselves: a monopoly of knowledge and technical skill. If it were not for the concentration of power, knowledge might find alternative channels of expression and develop bases of power from which to challenge aristocrats.[94]

The second requisite condition for the rule of aristocrats was based, Taylor thought, on the fact that no government could continue in office long without popular support. He insisted that public opinion was important to the success of any government. His acceptance of this principle may have been grounded in the realistic acknowledgment that monarchial forms of government had often enjoyed widespread support, or it may have been derived from John Adams's *Defence*, which had made this point. This opinion was in agreement with one of his other views, that the monopoly of knowledge possessed by aristocrats was the factor that kept them in power. This brought Taylor close to accepting the Lockian theory that even monarchies had enjoyed the consent of the social compact, but Taylor can be distinguished by his argument that the favorable public opinion that had made possible the rule of former aristocracies had been deceived by the lies of aristocrats. Regardless of which type of aristocrat was governing, Taylor thought that "neither ambition nor avarice could ever succeed in depriving nations of their liberty and property, if they did not by some artifice enlist the services of a body of men, numerically superior."[95] Even despotisms were subject to this rule.

The importance of popular opinion was acknowledged by aristocrats in the attention they gave to language, for "the hooks of fraud and tyranny, are universally baited with melodious words. . . . Fine words are used to decoy, and ugly words to affright."[96] "Security to private property" was a decoy, while "invasion of private property" was used for frightening. *Energetick government, protection and allegiance,* a *contract between king and the people,* and *order* were all terms used to attract support. Yet each of this last group of five words referred to devices used by aristocrats to advance tyranny. Taylor thus suspected aristocrats of using slogans to hide the techniques being used to subvert the very ideals expressed in the slogans. His motives for this opinion may have grown out of his rationalistic view of human nature, which led him both to doubt that the people could be completely fooled into ignoring the advance of aristocracy, and to affirm that even aristocrats had consciences that forced them to attempt to justify their activities in the name of the public interest. Taylor called these slogans a "jingle in the antithesis."[97]

One other concession offered to public opinion by aristocrats usually followed a full disclosure of an aristocracy's methods. Faced thus with popular rejection, an aristocracy would argue that the burdens they imposed were temporary. The notion of temporary burdens was absurd to Taylor, who asked, "will avarice be glutted and put to sleep by its success?", fully expecting that just the opposite would happen.[98]

Taylor's recognition of the importance of public opinion in the maintenance of aristocratic rule and of the use of language in influencing public opinion was consistent with his view that aristocracies went through a type of natural evolution. Each form of aristocracy had become outdated when its appeals lost their force. This happened when the general level of public knowledge reached the level of knowledge possessed by the aristocrats.

H. Summary and Conclusions

John Taylor was in an unusual position for a political theorist. His preferred society was within grasp, yet it kept eluding him. By the terms of his own theory American society was one of the first in history to enjoy a level of education and sufficient popular knowledge to allow republican government. He admitted that in past ages general intellectual awareness had been primitive enough to allow aristocracies to rule, but this was not the case in nineteenth-century America. This happy theory involved Taylor in a contradiction that he never seemed to realize fully, much less resolve. It was this: American society had the knowledge to be free, but it was not. According to Taylor's own doctrines, aristocratic rule should have been an absurdity.

Taylor provided only partial solutions to this problem. One answer was that his aristocracy of third age had been formed to elude the disillusionment that had caught up with feudal aristocrats. Moreover, the modern aristocrats multiplied both their forms, by splitting into various economic and political groups, and their methods, by using law, constitutional interpretation, and patronage. This shifting allowed aristocrats to keep ahead of popular understanding. Another reason that aristocrats were still in power when popular understanding should have deposed them was implied by Taylor in the importance he gave to a knowledge of the theoretical principles on which the American Republic had been founded. The use he made of these principles is more fully discussed in the chapter on divided powers, but it is significant that Taylor ultimately returned to the importance of ideas as a prerequisite for free government, given a structural framework that was largely without flaw.

This explains why Taylor ultimately accepted doctrinal political parties as a legitimate feature of republican government. Parties were the only component of aristocratic rule that could be made responsive to a body of republican doctrine. He also may have considered them a more neutral kind of organization than other aristocratic groups because their very existence did not necessarily depend on the abuse of power. No charters or public subsidies were required for parties simply to exist. Parties leashed to doctrine could also more tolerantly contain dissenting minorities within them than could a party whose sole purpose was to win and hold office, regardless of theoretical principles.

No form of economic aristocracy ever won any recognition from Taylor comparable to that which he ultimately awarded doctrinal parties. Instead, he consistently urged the extirpation of bankers, capitalists, creditors as such. He never found a way of making these groups acceptable, and he probably never looked for a way. To exist, each must live on the property stolen from others, and that disqualified them from any sort of recognition or legitimatization.

Taylor did not have as radical a solution for the problems caused by political aristocrats as he offered for the economic variety. Political aristocrats, after all, were often public officials, and for Taylor to have urged their annihilation would have involved him in a complete restructuring of the United States government. Such fundamental reform he did not think necessary, although now and then he would offer various schemes for easing the difficulties caused by political aristocrats, such as the expulsion of public creditors from Congress. He seemed convinced that the basic structure for a republic already existed. If the American people could be brought to a full understanding of the theory and the values that underlay that structure, republicanism was safe. The American system of government had already fragmented power into three branches and two levels, and into a multitude of policy-making compartments within each of these divisions. As will be seen, Taylor had no quarrel with such fragmentation. He was concerned, however, that citizens realize what principles, values, and theory were being reflected in this structure. The founding of the American Republic represented one of the few times in history that a government and its citizens had been on an equal footing in regard to knowledge from the beginning of the government. This knowledge, a summary of man's experience with free government, had been gradually evolving over the years into certain widespread beliefs about government's purpose and techniques, which Taylor called principles. It was those beliefs, set in action, which made the difference between governmental policies that supported the public interest and governmental policies that benefited a few. Unfortunately, in recent years Americans had been allowing themselves to stray from these basic values and wink at the practices of aristocracies. The harmful effects of these leadership groups, as Taylor described them, have been explored in detail in this chapter. Yet their most harmful effect, in Taylor's eyes, remains to be mentioned. The most harmful thing aristocrats could do was to discredit the wholesome republican values that alone held out the hope that aristocrats could be eradicated. Taylor was sure that John Adams's *Defence* had been an attempt to change the very way that true republicans thought, deluding them into the belief that aristocracy was natural, that knowledge was unevenly distributed, that Americans could copy British governmental practices, and that man's acts were determined by his passions and not by his free will. The danger that Adams would discredit republican principles kept Taylor up late at night for twenty years preparing a rebuttal.

Aristocracies were the bane of republican government, in Taylor's opinion. They must be controlled if individual liberties were to be protected. For this protection Taylor turned to governmental structure, only to be disappointed.

Notes to Chapter 3

1. *Inquiry*, p. 397.
2. Ibid., pp. 550–51; John Locke, *Of Civil Government*, ed. Peter Laslett, (New York: The New American Library, 1960), pp. 134–42.

3. *Tyranny*, p. 167.
4. Taylor, *Arator*, pp. 235–37; *Tyranny*, p. 131; *New Views*, p. 30.
5. *Enquiry*, p. 40; Taylor, *Arator*, pp. 94, 236–37; *Annals of the Eighteenth Congress, First Session*, p. 187; *Construction* p. 185.
6. *Inquiry*, pp. 2–3.
7. Ibid., pp. 8–10, 14, 29, 236–37.
8. Ibid., pp. 27, 236–37; *Construction* p. 249; *New Views*, p. 51. Even Adams had recognized that aristocracies were not inevitable, Taylor thought, because Adams relied on governmental structure to protect their existence; see *Inquiry*, p. 21.
9. *Inquiry*, p. 374. Also see pp. 15–16.
10. Ibid., p. 100.
11. Ibid., p. 114.
12. Ibid., p. 550; *Enquiry*, p. 40.
13. *Inquiry*, p. 20. Also see pp. 13–15, 31, 47–48.
14. Ibid., p. 387.
15. Ibid., pp. 455–56. Also see p. 459.
16. Ibid., pp. 459–60. Also see pp. 47, 454.
17. Ibid., pp. 23–24. Also see pp. 20, 120.
18. Ibid., p. 191.
19. Ibid., pp. 37, 40.
20. Taylor, *Arator*, p. 32.
21. *Inquiry*, pp. 22–23.
22. Ibid., p. 54. Also see pp. 15, 26–27, 40, 53, 55, 59, 120.
23. Ibid., p. 335.
24. Ibid., p. 74.
25. Ibid., p. 22.
26. *New Views*, pp. 20, 45, 86, 179, 289, 294. Taylor gave great weight to the opinion of Luther Martin that there had been three major parties at the 1787 Framing Convention: Hamilton's Anglophiles, Madison's Republican Nationalists, and true Federalists who opposed special privileges and supported state governments. Martin, therefore, confirmed what Taylor had always suspected: that a consolidationist conspiracy had existed since the founding of the Republic.
27. *Annals of the Eighteenth Congress, First Session*, p. 676; *Construction* pp. 317–26, 298. The term *eleemosynary family* is an obvious reference to the *Dartmouth College* decision handed down the year before *Construction* was written; *see Dartmouth College v. Woodward*, 4 Wheaton 518.
28. Franklin Hamlin Littell, *From State Church to Pluralism* (Garden City, N. Y.: Doubleday and Company, Inc., 1962), p. 7. The abolition of an establishment ended in Connecticut in 1819 and in Massachusetts in 1833. Taylor did refer pointedly to the variety of religions existing peacefully in Virginia in his angry letter to Timothy Dwight, in "A Sheaf of Old Letters," ed. David R. Barbee, *Tylers Quarterly Historical and Genealogical Magazine*, 32 (October 1950): 82–84. Taylor's explicit rejection that any form of aristocracy existed except that of armies and that of "paper and patronage" is in *Inquiry*, p. 41.
29. *Construction*, pp. 15–16.
30. Taylor, *Arator*, p. 90.
31. Ibid., pp. 90, 94–95.
32. *Inquiry*, pp. 455, 458–59, 465–66, 470, 477, 494.
33. Letter from John Taylor to Edmund Pendleton, May 4, 1777, New York Historical Society, New York City.
34. Letter from John Taylor to Captain William Woodford, May 12, 1775, Carter

Family-Sabine Hall Papers, University of Virginia Library, Charlottesville; letter from Taylor to General Woodford, May 22, 1778, Manuscripts Relating to John Taylor, University of Virginia Library, Charlottesville; letter from Taylor to Wilson Cary Nicholas, October 25, 1818, Massachusetts Historical Society, Boston; letter from Taylor to James Mercer Garnett, December 14, 1807. John Taylor Papers, Duke University, Durham; letter from Taylor to James Madison, January 15, 1808, University of Virginia Library, Charlottesville; letter from Taylor to Nicholas, April 17, 1808; Edgehill-Randolph Papers, University of Virginia Library, Charlottesville; *Definition* pp. 4–8; *Defence* pp. 68, 74–78, 82–83; letter from Taylor to Thomas Ritchie, March 27, 1809, in *Pamphlet*, p. 20. Also see letter from John Randolph to James Mercer Garnett, April 26, 1824, Letters of John Randolph of Roanoke to James Mercer Garnett, Library of Congress, Washington, D.C.

35. Taylor, *Arator*, pp. 191, 197; *Construction* pp. 274, 341; *Tyranny* p. 60; *New Views*, p. 243. The significance of the militia to Taylor is discussed further in chaps. 4 and 7 in this volume.

36. *Inquiry*, p. 375. Also see *Annals of the Seventeenth Congress, Second Session* (Washington, D.C.: Gales and Seaton, 1855), p. 7; *Defence* p. 63; letter from Taylor to Thomas Ritchie, March 27, 1809, in Pamphlet, pp. 15–21.

37. *Inquiry*, p. 242.

38. Ibid., pp. 450–51.

39. Ibid., pp. 287–8.

40. Ibid., p. 622.

41. *Construction* p. 250. Also see *Tyranny*, p. 46; Daniel J. Boorstin, *The Lost World of Thomas Jefferson* (Boston: Beacon Press, 1963), pp. 111–16, 124–33; Adrienne Koch, *The Philosophy of Thomas Jefferson* (Chicago: Quadrangle Books, 1964), pp. 34–36.

42. Taylor, *Arator*, p. 32; *Inquiry*, p. 265; *Construction*, pp. 12, 44; *Tyranny*, pp. 76–77.

43. *Enquiry*, pp. 23, 60; *Inquiry*, pp. 265, 273–74, 283.

44. *Definition*, pp. 4–11; letter from John Taylor to Wilson Cary Nicholas, March 31, 1803, Edgehill-Randolph Papers,; *Defence*, pp. 50–51; *Tyranny*, p. 52.

45. *Inquiry*, p. 251. Also see pp. 246–50.

46. Ibid., pp. 259–60.

47. Ibid., pp. 253–54, 276.

48. *Definition*, p. 16; letter from John Taylor to Wilson Cary Nicholas, June 14, 1805, Edgehill-Randolph Papers; *Inquiry*, pp. 293–94.

49. *Enquiry*, pp. 9, 17; *Inquiry*, pp. 122–23, 316–19. Also see Bray Hammond, *Banks and Politics in America* (Princeton, N.J.: Princeton University Press, 1957), p. 115. The basis of the charge of conspiracy was reinforced by the fact that Hamilton's recommendations for the creation of a bank were referred to a Senate committee that included five bankers, one of whom was Hamilton's father-in-law.

50. Letter from John Taylor to [Wilson Cary Nicholas?] November 25, 1803, Correspondence of Creed Taylor, University of Virginia Library, Charlottesville; *Construction* p. 188.

51. *Argument*, p. 23; *Inquiry*, p. 297.

52. *Enquiry*, p. 16.

53. Ibid., pp. 14, 18, 73; *Inquiry*, p. 359; *Construction* p. 180.

54. *Enquiry*, pp. 26, 65–66; Hammond, p. 233. The latter points out that the Bank directors were actually indifferent to the rechartering.

55. *Enquiry*, pp. 19, 21, 31, 74; *Construction*, p. 178.

56. *Construction*, p. 129; *Tyranny*, pp. 52–53. Jeffersonian attitudes toward state banking are discussed in Hammond, p. 221.

57. *Enquiry*, pp. 79, 81; letter from Taylor to [Wilson Cary Nicholas?], November 25,

1803, Correspondence of Creed Taylor, University of Virginia Library, Charlottesville; *Construction* p. 178; *Tyranny* pp. 60–61.

58. Hammond, p. 134.

59. Louis M. Hacker, *The Triumph of American Capitalism* (New York: McGraw-Hill Book Company, 1965), pp. 252–66.

60. Taylor, *Arator*, p. 43; *Tyranny*, pp. 55, 156, 195; Hacker Hacker pointed out that capitalists owned, but did not manage directly, early manufacturing enterprises. Thus, the country's first factory, Samuel Slater's cotton mill at Pawtucket (1791), was owned by the mercantile firm of Almy and Brown and only managed by Slater.

61. Taylor, *Arator*, p. 28.

62. Letter from John Taylor to Thomas Jefferson, May 6, 1799, in "Correspondence," p. 281; letter from John Taylor to George W. Jeffreys, March 4, 1818, printed in *American Farmer* 2 (9 February 1821): 366.

63. *Argument*, p. 23; Taylor, *Arator*, p. 20; *Construction* pp. 3–5; *Tyranny* pp. 119, 232.

64. *Tyranny* pp. 56, 119,121, 129, 192, 222, 235.

65. Ibid., p. 197.

66. Ibid., pp. 68, 120, 140; and John Taylor, "The Memorial of the Merchants, Agriculturalists, and Others, of the Town of Fredericksburgh and Adjacent Country," *American Farmer* 2 (September 22, 1820): 201–2.

67. *Construction* p. 332. Also p. 242.

68. Enquiry, pp. 13, 37; *Construction pp. 87–88*, 116.

69. *New Views*, p. 183. *Also see Construction* pp. 94–96.

70. *Inquiry*, p. 569.

71. Taylor, *Arator*, pp. 218, 235–36; *Enquiry*, pp. 36–37; *Definition* p. 11; *Defence*, p. 50; letter from John Taylor to Thomas Ritchie, April 11, 1809, *Pamphlet*, p. 43; letter from Taylor to James Monroe, October 26, 1810, in "Correspondence," pp. 306–309.

72. *Inquiry*, p. 176; letter from John Taylor to Thomas Ritchie, April 3, 1809, *Pamphlet*, pp. 30–31.

73. *Construction* pp. 2, 254, 263–64, 270, 341; *Annals of the Seventeenth Congress, Second Session*, p. 68; *Annals of the Eighteenth Congress, First Session*, p. 472.

74. *Construction* p. 189; *Tyranny* pp. 232, 279–80, 288–90; *New Views*, pp. 31, 123.

75. *Inquiry*, pp. 39, 255, 351, 386, 446; *Tyranny* pp. 52, 220.

76. *Tyranny* p. 253.

77. *Argument* p. 8. Also see pp. 7, 9, 11–12, 23.

78. *Tyranny* p. 41.

79. *Construction*, p. 328; *Tyranny*, p. 183.

80. Letters from John Taylor to Wilson Cary Nicholas, May 10, 1808 and August 29, 1808, Edgehill-Randolph Papers, University of Virginia Library, Charlottesville; Taylor, "The Necessities, Competency, and Profit of Agriculture," *Niles' Weekly Register*, Supplement to nos. 2, 3, 15, n.s. (November 7, 1818); 180. Jeffersonian attitudes toward the embargo are described by Leonard D. White, *The Jeffersonians* (New York: The Free Press, 1965), p. 424.

81. Taylor, *Arator*, p. 206; *Tyranny Unmasked*, p. 32; *Annals of the Eighteenth Congress, First Session*, p. 564.

82. Taylor, *Arator*, pp. 28, 33; *Tyranny*, pp. 118, 168–76, 242–43; *Annals of the Eighteenth Congress, First Session*, p. 564.

83. Letter from John Taylor to Thomas Jefferson, June 25, 1798, in "Correspondence," p. 272.

84. *Inquiry*, p. 211; *New Views*, pp. 146–47, 271.

85. *Construction* p. 118. Also see p. 99.

86. *Tyranny*, p. 133. Also see *Construction*, pp. 23, 27, 84, 91, 107, 117, 125.

87. *Tyranny*, p. 305.

88. *Inquiry*, p. 15.

89. *Argument*, p. 16. Also see *Inquiry*, pp. 184–85.

90. *Inquiry*, p. 185.

91. Ibid., pp. 25, 184, 228–29, 230–31, 459.

92. Letter from John Taylor to Wilson Cary Nicholas, June 23, 1804, Edgehill-Randolph Papers, University of Virginia Library, Charlottesville; *Defence*, p. 9; *Construction* p. 11.

93. *Argument*, p. 16; *Construction*, p. 89; *Tyranny*, pp. 172–73.

94. *Enquiry*, p. 87; *Inquiry*, pp. 418, 491; *Tyranny*, p. 331; *Construction* pp. 12, 249–50; *New Views*, pp. 179, 186, 202, 206.

95. *Tyranny*, p. 194.

96. *Inquiry*, pp. 558–59.

97. Ibid.

98. *Construction*, p. 212. Also see *Tyranny*, p. 221.

4

THE DIVISION OF POWER

The first three chapters have demonstrated the respect John Taylor had for the power of ideas and theories. The Enlightenment, and those who sought to implement its political phase in Caroline County, were probably of key importance in the development of Taylor's personal political philosophy. Later, when he became active in politics, it was as an ideologue who was interested more in the success of a body of doctrine than in the continuance in office of a party or group of men. As has been seen, his acceptance of political parties late in life followed his decision that they could be trusted to be the advocates of political principles. Taylor's rejection of the various forms of aristocracy was based on a respect for ideas also, for it was his opinion that knowledge was available on a wide enough basis to make aristocratic control of government superfluous. Considering the importance he had consistently given to ideas, it could be expected that their importance would have an effect on how he viewed governmental structure.

True to his belief in the importance of ideas, Taylor criticized John Adams most fundamentally because of the *Defence*'s alleged assumption that man's nature was chronically inclined toward selfishness and wrongdoing. This assumption led Adams to compare American use of separated, balanced, and checked powers to the British systems, which attempted to check the ambitions of factions by balancing them against each other. In Taylor's opinion, when Adams made this comparison he had overemphasized governmental structure at the expense of the

Notes for this chapter begin on p. 176.

role that individual choice and a republican belief system could play in a commonwealth.

The thesis explored in this chapter is that Taylor developed his doctrine of the "division of power" as a way of demonstrating that the deficiencies of American governments, whose structures he found acceptable, were the consequence of a failure to recognize the importance of ideas and values for the operation of governments. This theory was developed in opposition to Taylor's understanding of Adams's defense of governmental structure alone. This chapter suggests that, although Taylor agreed that governmental structure was important, he thought the thriving existence of a belief system that supported that structure to be indispensable for its proper functioning. In order to discuss government productively, therefore, Taylor argued that government should be judged by its acts and not by the outward appearance of its structure. If its Republican belief-system was intact, its policies were likely to be beneficial. However, when aristocrats began transferring the property of others to themselves, it was a signal that the country's belief system was under seige.

Thus, Taylor's conception of the division of power was a complex one that both reflected the experience of American governmental structures and provided a normative model for them. It will be discussed in the pages to follow that divided powers, in their structural aspect, referred to the maintenance of a system of government that divided the decision-making authority of governments: among the executive, judicial, and legislative branches of government, and within each of these branches; and between the state and federal levels of government. To these structural details Taylor added the condition that the people's will be expressed through instructed representatives and guarded by an effective militia. In its theoretical aspect, divided powers will be discussed as a central component of the republican belief system as Taylor defined it.

First to be considered is Taylor's critique of the traditional constitutional devices of separated powers, elections, and representation as insufficient bulwarks for liberty. The discussion will then turn to Taylor's doctrine of divided power, which he offered as a solution for the deficiencies of these traditional devices. The aspects of divided power dealing with federalism are discussed in detail in the next two chapters.

A. Separation of Powers

Underlying Taylor's view of separation of powers was the postulate that the people had bestowed on each officer and department of government, both state and federal, only the amount of power necessary to perform its assigned functions. If political departments did not have the independent constitutional means to protect this power and their own existence, they would be driven to combinations with other governmental branches for protection.

John Taylor's approval of separation of powers had formed a part of his thinking since the days of his law practice before he became a Jeffersonian publicist. His argument in the case of *Bracken* v. *The Visitors of William and Mary College*, December 8, 1790, clearly demonstrated this, for in it he even applied the principle of separation of powers to a private corporation, the college, whose board of trustees had attempted to limit the powers of its president. The college had been established by a charter, Taylor reasoned, and it should be interpreted as strictly as if it were a constitution establishing a government. The charter had established three separate and coordinate departments for governing the college: the trustees, the visitors and governors, and the president and faculty. The authority of each of these had been based in the charter, he argued. None could usurp another's power, for "to suppose that one creature of a political regulation, has a right to destroy another . . . is . . . opposite to the fundamental maxims of our present and former government," and Taylor was not willing to allow such disrespect for fundamental maxims, whether they were public or private.[1]

Against the argument that no such extreme independence had been explicitly included in the charter, Taylor maintained that the rules establishing this independence were fundamental, even though not enforceable through specific penalities, because infractions of theory could not be corrected by penalties applied to individuals.

Taylor's position in this case was mirrored in all his later writing on constitutions: he often inferred the existence of constitutional protections from an understanding of the alleged universal nature of government, but his use of inference left the constitutional protections for which he argued without any clear methods of enforcement.

Taylor's personal actions in public life bore consistent witness to his belief in separation of powers. For example, he discontinued his correspondence with Monore after being appointed to the Senate in 1803, because Monroe, then Ambassador to France, was a member of the executive branch. Taylor considered exchange of information between officials of two separate branches of government to be improper.[2]

Separation of powers did not always mean a rigid independence, however, for checks and balances were also necessary: all governmental agencies needed "the most efficient checks to make them all dependent."[3] The lesson of history was that an absence of a veto did not mean that a branch lacking it was government. Both in the *Bracken* case and later, Taylor argued that the theories of separation of powers and checks were larger than the express constitutional provisions authorizing their exercise.

He did not think that a department of government had to share in all the checks available to other branches, however. A disparity in power was no reason to question the independence of a branch of government that had fewer powers than another branch. Vetoes had been given only those departments of government which were part of the legislative process. The absence of a veto did not mean that a branch lacking it was dependent on the others. Thus did Taylor dispatch any arguments that the Supreme Court needed the power of judicial review of constitutionality to give it an independent status equal to that of the House, Senate, and President.[4]

Both checks and separated powers, Taylor urged, must be regarded as temporary measures that substituted for the actual ability of the people to control their government. Whether the checks were a presidential veto, bicameralism, judicial review of acts of Congress, or the resistance of a state to federal laws, each device was no more than an inadequate substitute for the people who should be controlling the government. Moreover, each device suffered from operational defects, which prevented it from being an effective substitute for popular control.[5]

The issue of possible collisions between departments was faced boldly by Taylor as a reasonable price to pay for the prevention of tyranny. The clashing among departments would be held in check by the operation of the American system of divided powers. It was more important to Taylor that the principle of "division" (discussed later in this chapter) be preserved, than that complete harmony among the departments of government be maintained: Collisions would occur occasionally, but better that than tyranny. Moreover, "should they occur, our system has provided a safe referee and impartial judge. . . ." in the people.[6] Taylor did not enjoy collisions between departments of government, however, and suspected that a prize was always at stake when these clashes occurred: "the prize can only consist of public property."[7] If each department remembered that it could be supreme only "over the persons and things specifically subjected to the limited power of each," clashes need not occur.[8] The supremacy of the people over the Constitution, and of the Constitution over all branches of the federal government was the only true standard to remember.

The appeals of various self-interested officials for supremacy were also defects that should be understood and guarded against. Each department of government easily became convinced that it was better for it to be superior than to have constitutional disagreements between departments. Each tended to judge its own orbit of influence in a self-protective manner. Any appeals by a federal department to be judged supreme in its powers when it clashed with another department's should be regarded in this light . The Supreme Court's pejorative use of the word *collisions* to discredit the necessary checking that occured in a system of separated powers was a shining example of such a bid for power.[9]

Taylor urged that those who compared the American system of checks to that of the British because of their superficial resemblance (as John Adams had done) should be judged by the eventual consequences of what they were advocating: a system of British checks in the United States would require the lower house to be šupreme. Taylor also thought that anyone who maintained that separated powers could exist without checks was also wrong: neither separated powers nor checks could exist alone. The means used by each department must be "controuled and restrained by the means of the others; because an authority capable of controuling the rest, obtained by one, destroys the grand design of either political system."[10] Checks, consisting of giving shares of one department's power to other departments, must accompany separated powers so that each department possessed the means to protect its own existence.

One must remember, however, that Taylor did not advocate that departments must possess exactly equivalent means of protecting their existence.

An operational defect characteristic of separated and checked powers that has often been criticized is the stalemate that sometimes resulted. This particularly occurs when opposing departments fall under the control of competing political parties. It is sheer speculation, of course, but it seems likely that Taylor might have approved of any governmental device that slowed down the ability of any government to pass laws that transferred property. The point is, however, that stalemate was not a reason for separated and checked powers that Taylor offered, even through he had little hestitancy about attacking the transfer of property law with all the other arguments he could muster.

In the abstract, Taylor's defense of separated and checked powers tended to support the existence of branches of government that were of equal strength and independent of each other. He did not think, however, that these branches had to possess exactly the same means for defending their independence. The discussion to follow demonstrates that Taylor did not always consistently apply this abstract theory of separated powers to the actual distribution of authority among the executive, legislative, and judicial branches of government. In fact, he played favorites.

B. Executive Power

Executive power was most extensively discussed by Taylor in his *Inquiry*, which may have been influenced heavily by the increase in presidential power that preceded the War of 1812. Taylor unfavorably compared the Presidency to older forms of oppression and thought that excessive executive power may have been the key to the increasing hold aristocracy was gaining on the country. This had been true for ancient forms of aristocracy, but "the modern struggles of reason and self government compels tyranny to drive her screws deeper into the bowels of society," thus making modern executives more dangerous.[11] Both the President and the British monarch had the same powers to appoint officers, disburse taxes, recommend laws, command armies, make treaties, and appoint legislators to lucrative offices. The concurrence of Congress in the exercise of these powers only indicated how far the growth of monarchy had extended, not that it was legitimate. If inconveniences arose over the election of Presidents, it indicated that the country had already approached too closely to monarchy and should limit the powers of its chief executive, rather than make him a genuine king by dispensing with elections.[12]

When Taylor discussed the President's powers, his descriptions did not seem unusually limited. The President and executive branch "shall be independent, not of the sovereignty, but of any other agent of the sovereign's," and he endorsed all of the powers given the President in the Constitution.[13] He recognized the moral effect that a President's use of his position of public importance could have for the Republican Party's cause, pleaded with Jefferson to use his influence in such a manner, and then urged Jefferson not to resign at the end of his second term until the Constitution had been amended to abolish aristocracies.[14]

With the succession of Madison, Taylor abandoned his advocacy of the use of presidential power, and began to condemn the effect that the high office and personality of a President might have on those attempting to identify with his party or his administration. A President should be dropped as a party leader as soon as he was elected; the concept of a presidential administration should be discontinued; and a President's powers should be limited for his own sake, because he would be torn to pieces by supporters in their attempts to make him fill the demands necessary to becoming elected.[15]

Thus, Taylor was generally fearful of executive power at the federal level. He trusted Jefferson implicitly and was willing to suppress some of his fears during the Jeffersonian administration, but as soon as Madison became Jefferson's successor, Taylor returned to his original antagonistic position on executive power.

The cabinet never received much attention from Taylor. There is no more than a mere mention in his writings of the possible role of the cabinet as a check on the President. Taylor thought, of course, that the characters of the men appointed to the cabinet were important to their roles as administrators and advisers, and that they must enjoy the confidence of the people, but he did not discuss the operations of the cabinet in any detail. This is surprising, for Taylor was quick to notice and criticize the activities of any other type of extraconstitutional policy-making body, such as the directors of the first United States Bank or caucuses for the nomination of presidential candidates. Nor can it be argued that Taylor's silence was the result of the fact that the cabinet had not yet achieved institutional status. As one modern historian has demonstrated, before Jackson's administration the cabinet had become more institutionalized than the Presidency itself. The secretaries of the various departments seemed on their way to achieving a quasi-permanent status and sometimes rivaled the President for attention. Between Jefferson and Jackson, no President appointed a completely new cabinet. It must be assumed, therefore, that Taylor was aware of the power of the cabinet, but for reasons known only to himself, did not have much to say about it.[16]

Taylor defended Jefferson's cabinet as friends of the President who were always around to criticize his actions and offer counsel, because they had been appointed for their qualifications and not their personal loyalty to Jefferson. Taylor rejected the idea that Presidents should insist on prior commitments before appointing cabinet members. Nor did Taylor think that Presidents should be held accountable for errors committed by their subordinates, although he did think that both Presidents and cabinet members should be held accountable for the costs of any actions they might take before congressional approval of their activities. He seems to have supported an exclusive discretionary right of the President to remove his appointees. In summary, Taylor acknowledged that the cabinet had an effect on presidential decisions, was not disturbed by its existence, but did not recognize in it any important check upon presidential power.[17]

Of the two legislative procedures that involved the President, Taylor criticized only the duty to inform and recommend, and that only because the constitutional phrasing, *shall*, was a mandatory blending of executive and legislative power that might prejudice the thoughtful consideration of laws. He defended Jefferson's recommendations to abolish certain taxes and the Judiciary Act of 1801, however, and thought that the President's power to recommend legislation would not represent a serious threat because of the large number of executive departments and the fact that Congress was making these departments increasingly responsible to itself.[18]

The presidential veto was viewed by Taylor as a procedure that allowed some additional control over the passage of laws not in the public interest, but he did not think that a President should interject his personal opinion of the desirability of an act in his decision of whether to sign it. Appropriations acts should be especially free of executive judgment, because the substantive judgments that they financed had already been made. Taylor praised Jefferson for not vetoing any appropriations act. By the same token, the President should not be held responsible for the desirability of every act signed while he was in office, because he simply was fulfilling a mechanical constitutional duty. Although Taylor's position was that the supremacy of the United States Constitution was only a moral one, that bound all branches of government on both the federal and state levels to its terms and established no department as the interpreter of the Constitution for all other parts of the government, he did not extend this argument's logical implications to the presidential veto. The President could not veto acts at will. Taney and Jackson argued later that the President had an obligation to interpret the Constitution independently of the opinions of the other branches of the federal government. They also maintained that the veto was available for the President to use in fulfilling whatever he deemed to be his constitutional obligation, as when Jackson vetoed the Bank recharting act. Taylor's conception of the veto was the half-step to the Taney-Jackson view, laying the groundwork for it in legal theory, but stopping short of applying it fully.[19]

The President's informal powers over Congress, obtained through the use of patronage promised by presidential candidates, were not so free of Taylor's criticism as the formal ones had been. Accepting such patronage, in Taylor's opinion, gave a legislator either a guilty feeling that he did not merit his constituents' confidences any longer, or a haughty feeling that they no longer merited his. Either way, a President had used patronage to drive a wedge between representatives and their supporters.[20]

Presidential elections were a concern of Taylor's from the time he led the fight for the Twelfth Amendment until his last year of congressional service in 1824. He feared congressional involvement in the electoral process at two points: before the actual election through the use of nominating caucuses; and after the election if it were thrown into the House of Representatives. Either situation introduced the likelihood that ambitious presidential candidates would bargain with Congressmen for their favor, thereby weakening the line of separation between the executive and legislative branches. In addition, electing by unit vote of the states' delegations in the House of Representatives allowed small state delegations, which had fewer men to bribe, to control presidential candidates. The reassembling of the electoral college would be a much better way of deciding among the front-running presidential candidates if no one received an electoral majority.[21]

The joint resolution offered by Taylor in 1823 as an addition to the Twelfth Amendment is interesting from the viewpoint of executive power for another reason which might be mentioned here. It increased the power of the President in the electoral process. The ballots of the electoral college were to be sent directly to him, and to be opened by him. No specification was made of the circumstances under which these ballots were to be opened. No longer was the Vice-President to open the ballots in the presence of the Senate and the House. In Taylor's version, it would have been the President who notified the Governors that a reassembling of the electoral college was necessary if no one received a majority. Upon voting the second time, the electoral votes again would be sent to the President. Only if this second vote failed to produce a President-elect would the election be thrown into the House of Representatives for action as prescribed by the Twelfth Amendment. Thus, Taylor had decided by the end of his life that trusting the President alone in the electoral process was preferable to a reliance upon the House of Representatives that might result in liaisons between small states and presidential candidates.[22]

The President could also violate separation of powers by exercising control over the federal judiciary, who were tortured by their weakness to implement their decisions and were always hunting for more powerful defenders. This control could be exercised in several ways, such as through the President's appointing judges in exchange for favorable court rulings. Juries might be tampered with, either through the simple creation of party spirit, which interfered with the rational deliberation required in judicial proceedings, or through the hand-picking of partisan juries through the office of the marshal. Leonard White has pointed out that presidential appointments of marshals were viewed with great suspicion by most Jeffersonians until 1800, and removals of Federalists from those posts were among those eagerly made by Jefferson when he assumed power. Taylor was convinced that the corruption of judges, juries, and marshals had been responsible for convictions under the Sedition Act.[23] His fear of presidential power was based in his conception of the characteristics of executive power in general. There were two characteristics to which he took offense.

The first was that it had an irresistible tendency to grow and accumulate prerogatives as it did. In this process executive power borrowed heavily from the secret nature of its foreign and military activities, its ability to create public support for its actions, and its inability to stop successors from falling heir to the powers accumulated by all previous incumbents. Thus, Taylor argued that executive power was incremental, so that Republican Presidents already found an institution tainted by Federalists' misdeeds when they came to power in 1801. Generally stated, Taylor's view was that executive power had been increased to suit the ambitions of individuals, but their success made the added power a permanent component of the executive office. In Taylor's opinion, therefore, the President was collecting a prerogative like the British King's, but the frequent turnover in Presidents meant that new individuals with new sets of ambitions were attempting every four or eight years to increase their power. It was only another example, in Taylor's opinion, of a governmental structure whose original purpose had been perverted.[24]

The second general characteristic of executive power was that it lacked essential attributes and could readily be adjusted to suit the requirements of any government, tyranny or republic. Executive power was not an indivisible mass, for example, "but capable of being divided . . . as society may determine to be best for its liberty and happiness."[25]

This ability of executive power to take on various forms made it difficult to keep the executive and legislative branches of a government separate.[26] The states provided good examples of how separation could be accomplished: "among several hundred state governors . . . not one . . . has appeared of kingly qualities," because of their lack of patronage powers.[27] This opinion of governors, given in 1814, represented a change of mind on Taylor's part, who had talked of elective monarchies in Pennsylvania and New York in a letter to Wilson Cary Nicholas in 1806.[28]

With surprising disregard for his previously expressed opinion that under a system of separated powers each branch of government was independent and possessed sufficient means to protect this independence, when Taylor spoke of executive and legislative powers he was capable of saying that "the legislature, as the most powerful political department, ought not to be influenced by one less powerful, because a weaker power able to make a stronger subservient . . . acquires an unconstitutional force."[29]

It can be argued plausibly that Taylor was not attacking all executive paticipation in legislative processes in this quotation, but simply those acts which threatened to dominate the legislature. After all, Taylor had explicitly defended the President's power to veto and recommend legislation. It may be that Taylor's ambiguity on this point was the result of his personal preference for the legislative branch of government, especially when compared to the executive's tendencies to accumulate power and change form. This, in spite of the fact that he also found it possible to accept, in the abstract, the proposition that the distribution of powers and means among governmental branches should be symmetrical. Taylor's preference for legislatures was also borne out by his views on judicial power.

C. Judicial Power

Taylor's concept of judicial power changed over the years. When there was a possibility that the United States Supreme Court might decide in favor of Hylton and declare the carriage tax unconstitutional in *Hylton* v. *United States*, 3 Dall. 171, Taylor was enthusiastically in favor of both declaring the tax unconstitutional and reviewing often the constitutionality of other laws so that judges would become practiced at the task. The judiciary, he argued, had been placed between government and the people to open the door of justice and to be a means of enforcing the Constitution without needing to rely upon insurrection. Such a power of review "can only become effective . . . by deciding constitutional questions, like other judicial cases. . . . The law of the Constitution is superior to the law of any legislative majority . . . a recurrence to the judiciary becomes necessary to . . . preserve the union."[30]

The refusal of the court to disallow this particular law, coupled with the subsequent political activities of some of its justices, such as Samuel Chase, who would not allow Taylor to testify at the sedition trial of James T. Callendar, may have caused Taylor to change his mind.[31]

By 1801 he had adopted the position that judicial independence did not require the permanent continuance of a judge, his office, or his salary, and by 1806 he was talking about legislative checks on federal judges. In 1807 he recommended that federal judges be made removable by joint vote of Congress and the assent of the President. Yet, he did not turn against the federal judiciary altogether, because one of the last changes he sought would have turned Congress's power to decide claims against federal officers over to the judiciary. It is obvious, however, that the changes in Taylor's views on the judiciary were even more sharp and noticeable than his ambiguous attitude toward executive power.[32]

Although circumstances later forced him to qualify his position, Taylor's final opinion on the nature of judicial power was that it was inferior to legislative and executive power. He maintained that the proper concern of judicial decisions was conflicts arising among individuals, and that the bench was without authority to act in any controversy that would have worked any major change in governmental structure or policy. Judicial power by its very nature was "imbecile" and impotent to carry out any decision, and it suffered the additional defect of not being in any way responsible to public opinion. If unchecked, judges might combine with selfish interests, and together work as effectively as any previous form of aristocracy to enrich themselves. To accomplish this the federal judiciary would need both to acquire a controlling voice in interpreting the Constitution and to bring the entire common law of England into force. With these two tools, existing controls over the judiciary, such as impeachment, would be totally ineffective.[33]

Taylor agreed with the advocates of judicial independence that the judicial system of the United States had been modeled after Britain's, and such features as life tenure, fixed salaries, and impeachment were worthwhile limitations if they were used for the purpose for which they had been designed: "The end of the British precautions, was to obtain judicial impartiality in the distribution of justice between individuals, and not . . . political departments."[34]

The English judicial system had evolved from a delegation of the king's sovereign power to various courts, and from the feudal power of barons in regard to the appellate jurisdiction of

the House of Lords. "At length the king was deprived of his
sovereign judicial power, and the House of Lords moulded into
a jurisdiction less objectionable."[35] Eventually, Taylor observed,
the House of Commons established courts to sit in judgment on
cases involving claims against the property of the nation, and the
House of Lords delegated its appellate jurisdiction to twelve law
lords. Thus, Taylor supported the independence of the
judiciary as a matter of convenience, but accepted the historical
argument that the judiciary's current power was a delegation
from the legislature, having been wrested from the executive.
The doctrine of judicial independence "does not extend beyond
the idea of their [judges] independence of any power inferior to
the sovereignty."[36] In England that sovereign power was the
Parliament; in the United States it was the people.

It had never been intended, therefore, for the judiciary to be
independent of the people. In the United States, only the
President and the Congress were subject to popular power, so
arguments in favor of judicial independence should require
total subservience to the people. If judges submitted to this test,
they could be elevated in power to the same level as the other two
branches of government. "Publick opinion is now the only
legitimate guardian of obedience to the constitution; its
sloth . . . invites . . . aberrations from it . . . which a watchful
political judiciary would detect and control. . . ."[37]

Without electoral responsibility, judges became acutely conscious of how feeble their powers were and searched assistance
from more powerful agencies to implement their decisions. This
assistance was needed regardless of whether federal judges
were able to monopolize the interpretation of the Constitution
or achieve the institutionalization of common law. With these
powers judges could afford to wait for other officials to come,
hats in hand, to bid for preferential decisions. Usually judicial
dependence upon other branches helped the President who
appointed, promoted, and patronized them with cases.[38]

Thus far, Taylor's views of the judiciary seem somewhat
inconsistent with his bold assertions of the need for separated
powers, and completely different from the position he adopted
at the time of the carriage tax. These inconsistencies in his view
of the independence of the judiciary, however, actually paved
the way for his reluctant acceptance of the federal judiciary as a
nearly coordinate branch. Even in the *Inquiry*, which contains
most of his views on the subordination of the judiciary to other

branches, Taylor sometimes criticized the judiciary's dependence on other agencies from the viewpoint of judicial independence.[39]

In *Construction Construed* Taylor still refused to consider the possibility that sovereignty could reside in the courts, and argued that it was possessed by Congress or the people, if it existed at all. At the same time he seemed to have become resigned reluctantly to considering the judiciary as an independent branch of government. The United States' policy, he said, "advances judicial power to an equivalency of independence . . . by the same constitutions, which prescribed the powers and duties of the other departments."[40] Although he believed that both state and federal judicial power applied to controversies involving individuals, individuals and governments, and states, this did not mean that the federal judiciary had any right to veto the acts of state legislatures. The veto power was never given to any group whose concurrence was not necessary to create laws. Nor did either state or federal judicial power extend to the relationships among departments of government within either level of government. If it had been intended for courts to "settle a multitude of collisions between political departments," they would have been given some tangible devices to settle these controversies.[41] If a judiciary became involved in settling the rights of political departments, the rights would fluctuage. Individual rights, which are based in the stability of governmental departments, would suffer as a consequence. Thus, even though Taylor at times may have come very close to giving the judicial branches of American governments the same independence enjoyed by the executive and legislative branches, ultimately he rejected the view that the judiciary had power that went beyond the ability to protect its own independence. "There is no difficulty in distinguishing the power of the court to disobey unconstitutional laws, from a power to govern political departments.[42]

To recapitulate, Taylor's views on the power of the judiciary to review constitutionality went through several transformations. In 1795 at the time of the carriage tax he supported such a power for the federal judiciary. In 1798 at the time of the Virginia Resolutions he seemed to believe that state and federal courts could definitively interpret their respective constitutions. By the time of his 1814 *Inquiry* he had come to doubt the power of the federal courts to do this even for the federal government: "A sovereignty over the constitution, objectionable as it would still be, would be safer in the legislature, than in the judiciary. . . ."[43] Yet, by the time Taylor wrote *Construction Construed* in 1820, he had modified his 1814 view and was willing to agree that the federal judiciary could protect its own power, but not arbitrate the disagreements between other political departments. Marshall's logic in *McCulloch* v. *Maryland*, 4 Wheat. 316, caused Taylor to revise his 1814 opinion, because he feared that Marshall was opening the door for the argument that the sheer magnitude of the federal government's power necessarily meant that it could review the acts and decisions of state governments. One must bear in mind that *Cohens* v. *Virginia*, 6 Wheat. 264, establishing the ability of the United States Supreme Court to review state court decisions, was not decided until the year after *Construction Construed* was written. Taylor apparently was willing to concede that the Supreme Court could protect itself against Congress in order to establish the argument that weaker agencies could properly preserve their independence against stronger ones. If he could get his readers to agree that might was not right, Taylor hoped that states would be safe against the power of Congress.[44]

In summary, it seems fair to say that Taylor's final view on the judicial review of constitutionality was that it could be a useful device, provided that the judiciary were held responsible to public direction and that the review of constitutionality was limited to laws passed by the same level of government to which the judiciary belonged. A final condition on which Taylor insisted was that all other branches of government have a right equal to that of the courts to decide upon the constitutionality of laws.

D. Legislative Power

Even if the judiciary had overstepped their bounds by usurping the authority of the Constitution and forming coalitions with executive power, Taylor still did not hold them primarily responsible. That was the fault of the legislature, which was inherently superior in power through its ability to create the offices judges held, its ability to impeach their incumbents, and its ability to pass the laws that they reviewed. Judges had a professional pride in entangling themselves in precedents, which sometimes accumulated and bound their hands, but Congress did not have to be concerned with consistency: "In all cases wherein the Supreme Court has been or may be charged with extending a law of Congress by construction to any unconstitutional object, Congress has a remedy in its own hands."[45] "We ought therefore to turn our attention from the judicial to the legislative power; as the latter is the real engineer by whom the pillars of our political system can be undermined."[46] Congress should be held responsible, therefore, for allowing the judiciary to misinterpret the doctrine of separation of powers in order to give themselves effective supremacy under the pretense of establishing independence.

Even though Congress was superior in authority to the federal judiciary and should be blamed if courts stepped out of line, a quasi-independent status for courts was in Congress's own interest. Congress, like Parliament, was utterly unsuited to behave as a court. Congress was internally constructed in an inappropriate manner for the deciding of particular cases. It only heard testimony on the side of the plaintiff; couldn't subject plaintiffs to costs for frivolous claims; could only award financial decisions that were subject to annual appropriation; had no rules of evidence or trials by juries; and awarded decisions without reference to any legal ruling or law. As courts, all American legislatures were "judicial monsters."[47]

Legislatures were of paramount importance to Taylor, for an invasion of their powers tainted the branch of government closest to the people. Negligence in their duties allowed other branches to accumulate superior prerogatives and become corrupt. Neither the executive nor the judiciary had such potentialities for using and losing power. If a legislature could be watched and kept independent no invasion of its realm could succeed, but legislators constantly tried to escape their duties by combining with other departments. Legislatures, even though elected, were no panacea for tyranny.[48]

Taylor did not consider Congress as an entity, but often distinguished between the Senate and the House in powers and in the extent to which he approved of their actions.

The United States Senate has often numbered among its supporters political thinkers who were jealous of the powers of states. As will be seen in the next chapter, Taylor was extremely sympathetic toward states, but he was much more reserved in his attitude toward the Senate. He accepted the fact that having the

Senate constructed as it was, was a guarantee that federalism in general and the interests of states in particular would be preserved. At the same time he regarded the Senate as "exactly analogous to the old Congress, in which each state had one vote" and was as worthless as the Continental Congress.[49] The danger in this system was that Taylor feared that the small states might dominate the Congress. The four smallest, for example, might join with the President and give away the other nine to foreign powers through treaties. He also blamed the Senate for giving states insufficient protection when the Alien and Sedition Acts were passed. The very size of the Senate made it an object of suspicion, for "the duration and small number of the Senate, affords room for more concert and dexterity, in procuring and sustaining laws favorable" to factions.[50] In order to obtain laws favorable to factions the President and the Senate could simply ignore the House of Representatives by appointing judges to the bench who could be bent to the will of the President, or by ratifying treaties that would increase presidential and senatorial power.[51]

Taylor's attitude toward the House of Representatives was more favorable than his view of the Senate. The role of the House in the election of a President if the electoral college failed has been discussed previously. This was the only criticism Taylor had of the House. Otherwise, he thought it well suited to defend the people because of its annual elections and he defended its prerogatives. For example, he was nearly alone among Republicans in wishing that the House had voted appropriations for the Jay Treaty willingly as a method of showing that it lacked the constitutional power to do otherwise and that a constitutional amendment that would have given the House foreign policy powers was necessary. In spite of his liking approval of the popular elections for the House, Taylor denied that this method of selecting Representatives implied that the people had extended an unlimited grant of power to the federal government through the House. The House was constituted as it was to make it a safe agency for originating tax bills.[52]

It can be seen from this discussion that Taylor's fears of the breakdown of separation of powers were based on the opportunity that the Senate always, and the House occasionally, presented for small states to seize control. Taylor's views on this score, then, are similar to those which moved Madison to propose representation by population in the Virginia Plan at the 1787 Framing

Convention. Both men feared the ambitions of small states. In the context of Taylor's thought this suggests that the preservation of a federated union in which all states were equal was higher in value to him than an abstract loyalty to the doctrine of separate powers.

A logically symmetrical doctrine of separated powers was not a part of Taylor's thought. He frankly thought that legislative power was superior in concept and ability. Thus, if any other governmental branch usurped legislative power it proved that a conspiracy existed: given the nature of legislative power such things could not happen by accident. His conviction that the Senate posed a constant threat of becoming an aristocracy of small states while the House was a more faithful representation of the public's will, brought him to the brink of endorsing unicameralism. At one point in the *Inquiry*, while comparing unicameral constitutional conventions to the organization of legislative bodies, he speculated that the lessons learned from conventions might provide the basis for the reorganization of legislative bodies. Conventions allowed the freest expression of election "through the organ of a single chamber."[53] John Adams's criticism of Turgot's unicameralism had been misdirected, in Taylor's opinion, because it was not the organization of the legislature but the evil moral tendencies it had generated that made Turgot's ideas unacceptable. Conventions did not excite ambitions between two houses "so the case of conventions proves the safety and utility of a single house of representatives, organized so as to suppress . . . avarice and ambition."[54] The responsiveness of legislatures to elections and their ability to be truly representative, nearly caused Taylor to discard the doctrine of separated powers. He did not do this because he was convinced that electoral procedures had their own limitations as constitutional protections.[55]

E. Elections

The presence of elections in a governmental system did not satisfy Taylor that true representation was present, for history had proved that a misplaced confidence in elections often allowed elite control. Throughout the world, for example, agriculturalists had a voice in elections, but never had any noticeable effect on policies despite their superior numbers.

Numbers alone, Taylor reminded, were never a match for a minority energized by cunning self-interest. Even though direct popular rule, or democracy, had been improved by providing for elected representatives when democracy had proved too turbulent, these elections were insufficient to control aristocracies. Taylor provided several historical examples to illustrate this point. In Rome, elections had fostered the division that arose between the people and the nobles, so that either wealth or the lack of it formed the basis for public decisions, depending on which party was in power. In England, elections had become gratuities allowed by the kings so the government could maintain its corrupt nature while claiming to be popularly elected.[56]

An electoral system could foster neither good or bad tendencies depending on how it was used. In recognizing this, Taylor insisted that election, or the right to vote, be considered a natural right. If elections were simply part of the natural order of things, the people would not become disheartened if they learned of a tyranny that used elections. Moreover, the presence of elections in a system could not be considered a special grant of power to the government from the people in that system. This would prevent aristocrats from claiming that the House of Representatives was supreme over any other branch of government, state or local, Taylor thought.[57]

Elections and other constitutional provisions were useless unless they prevented "an accumulation in the hands of an individual, an order, or a department, as will awaken man's vicious qualities," and there were several ways that this accumulation of power could make elections defective.[58] Elections themselves could become corrupted; they could convey too much power; they could provide no way of controlling an officeholder between elections; and their presence might produce a false confidence in the voter even though the government that had been elected was acting in a tyrannous manner.

Elections themselves might become corrupted either through the greed of any candidates who offer credit or other bribes for votes, or through the more serious intervention of elites created by congressional action. Such an influence Taylor attributed to Burr's Manhattan Bank, which he thought could have defeated Jefferson in 1800 if it had wanted. During Taylor's lifetime, electoral corruption seems to have been prevalent and spirited in Caroline County, but Taylor himself refused even to canvass for votes because of his conviction that the promises that resulted from such a procedure were "not only wrong, but vicious," as one pro-Taylor broadside put it.[59] Taylor may have written the broadside, however, so he did not simply sit back and wait for the public to strike like a lightning bolt.

A second reason offered by Taylor as an explanation of why elections alone were insufficient for liberty was the possibility that they would convey too much power. This in itself would stimulate the evil passions of officeholders to even greater oppressions. For example, elections used in connection with orders or nobility had never produced equally beneficial effects for all persons in the societies using them. After all, even Pompey, Caesar, Cromwell, and Bonaparte had been elected, and these elected monarchs were worse than hereditary ones. "The mode by which a tyrant succeeds to his tyranny, cannot convert oppression into justice," and elections that conveyed too much power lost the means for controlling it.[60] This was demonstrated, Taylor inferred, by the respective differences between elections for the governors of Virginia and Pennsylvania. The first promised the enjoyment of few material rewards and therefore enjoyed stable elections, while the second promised much and awakened turbulence and partisans as consequence.[61] The fact that Pennsylvania was a much more heterogeneous society was never considered by Taylor.

A third insufficiency of elections was that they allowed no way of controlling the use of power during the course of a term of office: "*A nominal election* of, and an *irresistable* [sic] *influence* over the Legislature, are things of *real* difference."[62] If a representative could draw wealth from his office, election would be destroyed, yet the people might have to retain these elected tyrants or give up self-government altogether. "Freedom is not constituted solely by having a government of our own."[63]

A final reason why elections had limited ability to safeguard constitutionalism was that an overreliance upon them would result in undesirable governmental policies. The voters might become disillusioned with elections, and shrink from the unwholesome contests. They might even submit to governmental forms they could not control at all. Nor would it take many bad experiences with elections to produce this apathy: "Be assured that a few disappointments . . . will produce an apathy, distrust, and despair among those who are guided by honest views. . . ."[64]

For the reasons enumerated above, Taylor had serious doubts

about the efficacy of elections, even when used along with separated powers, as in the United States, to preserve liberty. Elections could not guarantee that officeholders would behave as they had promised; might convey enough power to corrupt even honest candidates; were themselves disruptive contests, subject to corruption; and, worst of all, gave the appearance of republicanism to a government without ensuring any of its substance. Even if election processes could be purified, additional defects that Taylor saw in representation deserve separate consideration.

F. Representation

Representation flowed from each person's right to govern himself, Taylor thought, and from this inalienable personal right individuals constructed societies using forms to suit their particular situations. Representation was not a corporate or group-oriented process such as John Adams's proposal for the representation of social orders. From personal experience, Taylor was convinced, also, that John Adams had a secret desire to make the executive and legislative branches of both the state and federal governments hereditary.[65]

Taylor's rejection of the representation of social order did not mean, however, that he supported direct democracy. The ultimate right of the people to have government do their bidding was all he really favored. This power should operate frequently through unobstructed channels of influence on governmental officials and "whenever aristocratical influence begins, there representation ceases," although its forms may be left standing.[66]

The purity of representative forms could be injured by any kind of aristocracy. A geographical aristocracy would be the worst kind because there was no possibility that the representatives it would control could empathize with other sections of the country. No legislature had the authority to delegate permanently its representative authority to some aristocracy of their choosing, because "political power ought to be responsible, to be entrusted for short periods, to be controuled, and to be punished if abused."[67] For example, when a corporation was allowed by a permanent charter to do good or harm to a nation, legislative power had really been delegated.

Although representative, and not direct, democracy was preferred by Taylor, he did not go to the extent of Edmund Burke in allowing the representative great discretion in forming his judgments. For reasons of personal judgment, health, sympathy, and distance, representatives were often inadequate guards of the rights of their constituents. Taylor remarked once that he knew a representative who seemed to be able to form sound judgments from a combined estimate of existing circumstances and human nature, but that most persons were unable to form such conclusions "from a want of information, or from some unconscious prejudice" to which even the best-informed men were susceptible. Ill health could also injure a representatives's judgment. Taylor was the first to admit that his own interest in this world's affairs was diminished by the frequent illnesses he suffered in his old age.[68]

In choosing between representatives, a voter should attempt to learn which candidate for public office was likely to have the essential prerequisite of a representative: sympathy with his constituents' needs and interests. This sympathy could not be developed vicariously. A representative had to feel directly what his constituents felt in order to experience their desires and be able to translate them into public policy. Taxes, for example, had to be shared by the legislators who wrote them into law, as well as by the constituents who were not public officials. If not, public money would be squandered by legislators who had nothing to lose because they had nothing to pay.[69]

It was Taylor's opinion that lack of sympathy was the chief reason why the break with England had occurred: even the most enlightened British plan for governing the colonies had lacked sympathy. It had been insufficient to have some representation in Parliament. Unless all members of a legislative body had personal experience with the problems of their constituents, they should not legislate for them. In addition, any parliamentary representative who had been offered might not have been elected, would not have been a resident, and would not have been affected by the laws made for the colonies. Distance was also an important determinant of the attitudes of U. S. Representatives, because Congress met far from the homes of most of them and its sessions had become longer and longer as the years passed, so that the representatives were spending very little time in their home districts. "Congress, acting by a majority, without local fellow feeling, can never constitute a representation of the geographical interest and climates at the extremities of the United States."[70] The variety of local laws that existed in the states was "a necessary consequence of the variety in their circumstances."[71] Representatives were so limited by this background in their thoughts and biases that they would inevitably favor those interests which were closest to their own, while they would not possess the wisdom or knowledge to legislate for the particular needs of various sections of the country. It was as difficult for politicians to sympathize with that which they did not experience, as for priests to "turn bread and wine into flesh and blood"[72]

In summary, representatives often were inadequate guarantors of liberty, because their perceptions could be informed only by active involvement in the affairs of the people whom they represented. If representatives suffered personally the consequences of their actions, they would be more careful in their use of public power, but the difficulties of transportation and defective popular consultation required personal exposure to constituent interests. Most important, if a representative was personally tied to the same interests as his constituents, if his very way of thinking was the same as theirs, he could more easily be relied upon to stick to the same principles. The people had a right to expect that their representatives would be consistent in the sides they chose on public issues. If this stability was removed, the people did not have a means of judging between various candidates and might "often catch a tartar instead of a friend."[73]

The basis of representation had an important bearing on the ability of people to make their voice heard in public decisions. Even before Taylor attacked the British system of government in the *Inquiry*, he had opposed the rotten boroughs that allowed some voters more voting strength in Parliament.[74] Taylor carried his opposition to malapportionment beyond the mechanical designing of districts to also include the impact that districts had on policy. As has been mentioned, the mere form of governments never was so important to Taylor as its effects on public policy. Therefore Taylor insisted that the principle of equal representation required not just formal equality of district population, but also an equal *effect* for districts of an equal size. If public creditors had acquired an ability to control Congressional legislation that exceeded their formal, arithmetically representative strength, equal representation had been violated, and a system equivalent to rotten boroughs resulted.[75]

Taylor also used the American Revolution's doctrine of taxation to support equal representation in form and fact. He stretched the principle of equal representation to include the effects of congressional laws on matters he considered the internal concerns of individual states. Thus, if a protective tariff encouraged speculative capitalism and discouraged agriculture, the latter's interests had been injured by an unequal application of law. When Congress passed such laws it usurped the right of legislating for a particular area without allowing the residents of that area a check over the legislators involved in the decision. Thus was equivalent to the prerevolutionary British practice of virtual representation, because it substituted a theoretical concern for a constituency's interests for a workable system for allowing that constituency to express its interests directly.[76]

Taylor's disenchantment with representative procedures in their corrupted forms, however, never led him to doubt their essential worth, although he would sometimes sardonically observe that it would be better to be without elections if they had led to patronage. He was hopeful that representation and elections could be purified, but his standards for achieving this were high: annual elections and frequent rotation of incumbents; abolition of unjust tax laws; and equal representation of the people in order to give them "a real influence over the government."[77]

G. Criticism of John Adams

John Taylor developed his theory of the division of power as an alternative to the system of government he thought John Adams had defended in his *Defence of the Constitutions of the United States* (3 vols.; 1786-87). Thus, Taylor's criticism of Adams is as important to an understanding of the division of powers as is his criticism of separation of powers, elections, and representation. Taken together, Adams's defense of governmental structure and the malfunctioning of structure in practice prompted Taylor to search for a solution to the problem of free government that did not depend on structure alone.

Taylor's criticism of Adams was based on objections to his

logic, to the moral traits encouraged by the *Defence*, and to Adams's notions of property and human nature.

In Taylor's opinion, the *Defence* had encouraged undesirable moral traits when it admitted that jealousy among the three social orders (i.e., the monarch, the aristocracy, and the people) was the only way to check their powers. Taylor considered jealousy to be a dangerous and unworthy principle upon which to found a government. Governments should encourage wholesome tendencies, and the basic principles of the American system had done that, regardless of how Adams misinterpreted them. Adams should have realized that if property was not balanced equally among the three orders, the richest would automatically win out. The implementation of this principle meant that a redistribution of property throughout the world would be necessary in order to give each of the three orders their shares, so that the king, nobility, and the masses would each have a third. Such root-and-branch reform Taylor thought both impracticable and tyrannous. It would require taking property from many ordinary people. Jealousy, then, could lead to very undesirable governmental practices.[78]

Adams's most grievous error had been his dark view of human nature, which had led him to classify men into rulers and the ruled. Such an opinion so completely ignored the effects of physical or moral environment upon human nature that the only solution that Adams could offer to solve the problem of clashes between orders had been to create a third order.[79]

H. Policies, Principles, and Divided Powers

Taylor insisted very early in his career that the British practice of balancing governmental departments had been discarded by the time of the American Revolution. This had happened because of the defects mentioned above with structure and balancing, because American understanding of government was superior in Taylor's view to any that had gone before, and because American institutions had been based on the assumption that man had a volitional reasoning quality that allowed him to construct governments that would encourage morality. Man's use of his power to make moral choices helped make morality the outcome of governmental policies.

The United States had retained parts of the balancing ideas,

but improved upon them by also allowing elections that made
the people truly sovereign, by disallowing vetoes over organic
changes in the system, and by amending the Constitution
without the concurrence of any aristocratic or monarchic
orders.[80]

In sharp contrast to British practices. Taylor insisted that
American "policy" was derived from a commonly understood
body of doctrine that represented the amount of knowledge
diffused throughout the citizenry. By *policy* Taylor meant both
the structure and laws characterizing American governments.

Taylor refers so frequently to the principles upon which he
thought the American system to be grounded, that an understanding of what he meant by *principles* is essential. According to
his statement in the *Enquiry* (1794): "tho' great principles,
resulting from the constitution, as the theorems to guide our
investigations into the objects and designs of the administration"
were essential, "without a text for truth, self interest and
innovation, by their wily artifices, will slip out of our grasp."[81]
Introducing them with the words "Are not the following
propositions unquestionable?", Taylor launched into an enumeration of six principles of American government: a republican
form of government based on the people had been con-
templated by the Constitution and any administration that
eroded this dependence on the people was innovating against
the spirit of the Constitution; taxes were for general and not
individual benefit; the right of legislation resided permanently
in the people; the right was periodically delegated to representatives; "the right of election is a substance and not a form, and . . .
a legitimate representation, implies an *existing operative* principle"; and "whenever this principle ceases to exist, government is
converted into an usurpation."[82] This was the "text for truth"
that Taylor offered. He thought that these six axioms were
self-evident, but warned against complacency in affirming them:
"too ready an assent, leaves the mind unprepared to repel the
deceitful efforts, which will be made to delude it; whereas a
conviction, resulting from a deliberate investigation is hard to
shake."[83] In Taylor's early works it was sufficient for his
purposes to defend these principles as such, without reference
to divided power. By the time of the *Inquiry* his view of
government had become more complicated. In order to refute
Adams, Taylor adopted the terms *balanced* and *divided* power to
summarize the essences of the two systems.

The division of power was elevated to the level of a principle in Taylor's system, and it was also the chief descriptive characteristic of that system. It was at once one of the unquestionable propositions of the "text for truth," commanding the assent of all right-thinking citizens on normative grounds, and an empirical description of how American government operated. A capsule summary of Taylor's principles at the time of the *Inquiry* included an equality of civil rights, freedom of religion, and of inquiry, division of power, national influence or sovereignty, knowledge, uncorrupted representation, and actual responsibility.[84] Thus, the division of power became part of the axiomatic belief system that Taylor saw as undergirding the structure of American government.

Taylor deduced the components of his system of divided power from the inalienable rights enjoyed by individuals. Although he regarded the complete catalogue of these rights as too large to discuss in the 650-page *Inquiry*, the most important rights were freedom of conscience and religion, freedom of expression, the right of self-defense, and the right to enjoy the fruits of one's labor. The possession of these rights by individuals, Taylor said, "constitute[s] our most useful division of power."[85] People had governmental authority and political power based on their possession of rights. Governments enjoyed delegated powers and no rights at all.

This division between the people and government was the primary ingredient of the system of division of powers. The limited portion of power delegated to government was further divided between that given to the federal government and that conferred on the states. At the federal level, power was "again subdivided between two legislative branches, two executive branches [presumably referring to the President and the Cabinet], and two judicial branches; judges and juries; all enjoying specified powers independent of each other" (pp. 409-10). That which had been given to the states had been subdivided in different ways by different states, but roughly paralleled the six departments at the federal level. Each of the divisions between and within governments was subject to the difference between "political" and "municipal" law. Political law included those legal arrangements by which governments could be punished for transgressions against their citizens, while municipal law was that which resolved private disputes. The people were the "executive of political law, and the avenger of violations of public duties" (pp. 159-61), while governments were the avengers of private duties. The people in their individual capacities were forbidden to violate municipal law, while governments, regardless of level or department, were forbidden to change political law in any manner.

These divisions between people and governments, between and within governments, and between kinds of law established a double responsibility in which the people and the government each had obligations to the other. The responsibility of the people to the government was expressed through the "division of election," by which the people provided representatives to man the government and agreed to abide by their actions until the next election. This process prevented "the people from acting in mass against the government, under the impulse of passion" and made it difficult "to turn the people into an ocholocracy" (p. 411). The device of election gave the government assurance against the disruption caused by the physical force of random insurrections. Government, for its part, was held in check by the retention of authority and residual power by the people and the fragmented governmental structure that prevented government from acting "in mass against the people, under the impulse of avarice and ambition" through a dangerous concentration of power (p. 411).

This system of divided power was rooted in the unity of the common rights owned by each individual and was expressed by the division of responsibilities throughout all layers of government. Instead of Adams's balancing of governmental branches through the fostering of mutual jealousy, divided powers rested on the recognition by *both* the government and the people that the people retained a great mass of residual rights and that each department had its own distinct duties, its own code of "municipal law." (p. 428).

Taylor's doctrine of divided power went further than a mere exhortation that residual rights should exist, for to stop there would merely have created hollow rights, subject to the interpretation of governments. The means of actualizing these rights "consists simply in uniting the sovereign, physical and political power in one national interest" (p. 448). "National rights and national opinion, cannot really exist, without powers for defending the one, and organs for expressing the other" (p. 488). The United States policy had secured the people's will and ability to protect rights by both physical and political means: "it provided election, attempered by free discussion, as a moral mode," and "it provided a militia, as the physical mode for securing obedience to the moral means by which the will of the nation is disclosed" (pp. 488-89).

Election, therefore, served double duty in Taylor's system, for it not only secured the government against the necessity of the people's having to use mobs as the only device for popular control, but it also provided one of the means by which the people controlled the government. Taylor's faith in election was contingent upon his particular conception of the election process. He insisted that the right to instruct representatives was necessarily included in elections. The agents of even monarchic and aristocratic orders had always been required to be absolutely obedient, and they were punished when they were not. The same duty of faithfully representing the will of the creating authority was also required of the agents of the people. It did not matter that this right of instruction, or duty of obedience, was not explicitly included in any constitution. "A constitutional declaration, that duty was an adjunct of agency, would have been as absurd, as that heat was an adjunct of fire" (pp. 411-12). Saying that electing an agent did not require that he obey the constituent was equivalent to saying that a fire insurance policy "did not include an insurance against heat" (pp. 411-12). A right to instruct was included in the very definition of a representative.

Taylor never provided a satisfactory answer to the question of who would instruct the representatives. The representational unit for which elections were held could be of any size, because the right to vote was individually held and not necessarily channeled through districts. Whether representatives were elected by districts was solely a matter of convenience. The voting majority of the electing unit, regardless of its composition, was the controlling principal for all agent-representatives. The will of this actual voting majority—not that of some abstract majority of the whole public, nor that of a majority of the representatives within a legislative body—should be the sovereign controlling force: "a duty to obey the instruction of an ideal majority, would divest the representative of the character of agent, and transform him into a despot . . . under pretence of loyalty to a nonentity . . ." (p. 413).

The rights of electing and voting, therefore, could be apportioned however a society wished. In a nation as large as the

United States districts were inevitable, but once they were created, the right to instruct representatives belonged to the unit or district that elected them. Moreover, this instruction should be done by the actual voting majority in a particular election. A representative should represent the people who put him in office, not some fictional constituency such as the public-at-large or all the people in his district (p. 414).

Such a doctrine led Taylor to say parenthetically that state legislatures, which elected Senators, constituted the electing and instructing majority for them. In addition, he rejected the idea that the oath of office freed a representative from representing the actual majority of voters who placed him in office (p. 418).

Election, the *moral* mode of defining the people's rights, needed to be supplemented by a *physical* mode of accomplishing the same end, and the militia provided this. The "physical force of an armed nation, and the moral force of election and division" imposed actual responsibility and control on representatives (p. 428). The purposes of a militia were several: it protected the people against the necessity of supporting a standing army by which aristocracy would increase its foothold in the country; it protected the government against civil disturbances that would make orderly deliberation impossible; and it protected the elections, which expressed the moral will of the people in an orderly and uncorrupted fashion.

There were several additional purposes that could be served by a militia, on which Taylor was discreetly silent. A slave state had a particular interest in retaining a strong militia because of the fear of slave insurrections, particularly after the 1800 Gabriel plot to kill the Caucasian inhabitants of Richmond was discovered. This abortive massacre resulted in the organization of the one-hundred-man Virginia Public Guard.[86] In addition, the militia theoretically could have guaranteed the responsibility of public officials by the ultimate check of civil war. Taylor did not mention a capacity to wage civil war as a purpose for the militia. Civil war would be unnecessary, because, from the states' perspective, the results of it would already be achieved: federal officials would be unarmed and states would have force at their command. In a preface to his discussion of election and militia as methods of protecting the people's will, Taylor pointed out that he was "speaking of social sovereignty, and not of the natural right to resist oppression; of organizational, not of irregular remedies. The natural right appears throughout history, to be the least successful guardian of liberty, and as frequently the author as the destroyer of tyranny."[87]

In his later writings Taylor reaffirmed what he had said before about division of power, although he emphasized the historic origin of the concept and the fact that the federal division between states and the federal government had made it safe to adapt the best parts of the British system of balanced power to American use.[88] In some of his earliest writings the distinction between his concepts of division and balance was blurred, and he candidly admitted in 1809 that the unique qualities of divided power were difficult to describe. Taylor referred to the division of power very little in *Arator*, which was published in 1813, although it had been written over a period of years.

In his 1809 letters to Thomas Ritchie he related division to federal and state relations almost exclusively. During his Senate term in the Eighth Congress, Taylor used the electoral college as an example in miniature of the principle of divided power: the electors were scattered throughout the country and did not influence each other because they met in small groups and were less likely to become corrupted.[89]

In his later works Taylor turned to the consequences of the division of power doctrine in practice. He particularly objected, for example, to the confusion of it with the "sovereignty of the spheres" dicta in the *McCulloch* decision. This language implied to Taylor that governments had been invested with sovereignty, properly only the possession of the people, for the sole purpose of giving the federal government the means to enlarge its powers to a point of superiority over the states. He affirmed the obligation of political departments to defend the authority that each held from the Constitution. He suspected that the people alone could not be relied upon to supervise governmental branches, because the apparently safe governmental structure of the American system had led the public into a false sense of security. To allow the people alone to arbitrate violations of divided powers admitted that "no theory could be devised, capable of self-execution."[90]

Taylor faced up to the charge that a division of powers would cause clashes between governmental branches and among governmental levels: "The division of powers was not intended to be subordinate to a clashing of rights, but a clashing of rights was intended to be subordinate to the division of powers."[91]

Those who considered such a clashing between the federal and state governments to be too inconvenient should be careful, he warned, for the inconveniences of clashing applied as forcibly to the branches of the federal government. What if the Supreme Court disallowed federal and state clashing as inconvenient and found its own authority to inconvenience Congress or the President discarded? The dividing of power implied that each department must have the means to defend itself. Taylor thought it reasonable to assume that the 1787 Framing Convention had been aware of the difficulty of distinguishing between the prerogatives of various departments, and had therefore given them the means to defend themselves. These were means of defense only and consisted only of a veto against the aggressive use of power by a department that had stepped into another's domain. "A mutual check between powerful political departments, to be exercised by a reciprocal veto, seems to be the best theoretical principle . . . for securing liberty. . . ."[92] Its absence destroys all constitutional restraints.

Such a mutual check was available for use by all departments of the federal and state governments. Since only the people could decide whether or not a redistribution of the division of powers should be allowed, any instability or stalemate during the decision-making process was worth the inconvenience. The fact that the system forced governmental officials to respect each other meant that they might develop a sympathy for each other's problems.[93]

I. Summary and Conclusions

Although John Taylor accepted the ideal of three separate-but-equal departments in the abstract and had even applied it to the structure of private corporations, he was quite inconsistent in his application of his concept of separated powers to actual situations.

In part, this may have been influenced by the fact that Virginia's state and local governments, whose virtues Taylor defended, were imperfect examples of the use of separated powers. The unholy alliance that existed under the county court system produced a revolving circle of officials whose executive, legislative, and judicial functions were blended to a confusing extent. This suggests that Taylor equivocated on the theory of separated power because he was less concerned with it as doctrine than as a weapon to use against federal power.

On the other hand, Taylor was objective enough to realize that federalism in a large country separated the representative from his constituent, making the Congressman a fair mark for every unscrupulous President or Secretary of the Treasury who needed his vote. Thus, separation of powers and federalism were both valued by Taylor, and in a clash between the two, his view of higher public good to be served determined which he supported.

Taylor's attacks upon executive power were inconsistent, because his view of what a President should do was not greatly different from the idea held by most persons at the time. Indeed, Taylor's impatience with Jefferson arose from the fact that Jefferson refused to exploit presidential power to force through Congress constitutional limitations on aristocracy that Taylor favored. Taylor's hatred of executive power, then, was inversely related to his ability to influence executives. In his books after the *Inquiry* he was less harsh on executive power, but without being convinced that United States policy had changed for the better. In part, Taylor may have felt that if he could not influence Monroe, he might as well stop complaining about presidents and turn to problems on which he could have an effect. Or he may have felt that, if aristocracy continued in spite of Monroe, the President's role in the aristocratic system had been misjudged in the *Inquiry*. Regardless of the reason, after the *Inquiry* Taylor turned his attention to judges and legislatures more than executives.

Too much can be made of Taylor's apparent acceptance of judicial review in the carriage tax case. It is clear in context that he never meant that the judiciary would be the sole authority on constitutionality: each individual and department of government could make a separate judgment of the Constitution as it affected them. This is what Taylor claimed that the supremacy clause had intended, and his views on the matter were constant from the 1795 carriage tax episode through 1820, when *Construction Construed* was written. In the absence of any evidence to the contrary, they may be taken as his final ones on the subject. It is true, however, that at the time of the carriage tax Taylor was willing for the federal judiciary to have the final deciding voice on constitutional matters, and he did not carry that view forward. It is interesting from a modern perspective to note that Taylor's views on executive and judicial power were neither doctrinaire nor extremely limited in conception. It is clear that rejection of executive and judicial power was not a predetermined position for him. His development of it was built on honest Whig roots, but, given a different President and Chief Justice, he might well have taken a different attitude.

It is equally clear that Taylor was favorable toward legislative power. After all, his entire public service had been spent as a legislator (except for the short stint as tax-collector in Montgomery County, when he had been chased out by Indians). Taylor's bias in favor of legislatures led him to reach back in history and dust off the powers of Parliament, emphasizing its control both over the king and over the courts that had begun as agents of the king. His bias was firmly based in a belief that legislatures were the voice of the people, and he questioned the activities of legislatures that were not subject to review by the people through direct elections. Thus, the Senate, and the House of Representatives when sitting as an electoral body for United States President, were suspected by Taylor. He feared that in either of these situations the ambitions of some states would cause them to use their influence against the common interests of the whole union. Again, Taylor's love for federalism was not so great that he trusted blindly in the judgment of states. He feared the effects of state conspiracies as much as he feared aristocracies. This is a view surprising for one who was, on balance, an advocate of states' interests.

Taylor's love of legislative power did not blind him to the responsibilities of legislatures, either. He reserved his sharpest barbs regarding Supreme Court decisions not for the judges who made them or the Presidents who appointed the judges, but for the Congress, which passed the laws that the judges later rubber-stamped.

The respect for legislative power took Taylor to the brink of unicameralism. He derived examples of unicameralism from the practice of using conventions to write and ratify constitutions. If the products of such conventions had been so uniformly beneficial, he reasoned, such bodies might serve as models for the reconstruction of American legislatures. This put Taylor closer to certain Federalist theories of the union, especially Marshall's in *McCulloch*, in which state conventions had been offered as an example of the fact that the Constitution had been a product of the entire people of the union and not just of the state governments. Taylor also argued consistently that the people of the states should be conceptually distinguished from their state governments. Moreover, Taylor's rejection of Marshall's logic in *McCulloch* did not cause him to take the most extreme opposite view: that the union was the product of state governments.

Taylor's views of election and representation did not change as much as his views on separation of powers. There were two problems worth mentioning, however: instruction, and the actual meaning of representation.

Taylor gave little attention to how the instructing of representatives was to occur. The legislative process in the Virginia Assembly may have led Taylor to expect that instruction was as common or as feasible everywhere as it was in Virginia. There the county court was composed of a group of officials who usually included the county's delegation to the state legislature. Petitions would be presented by groups or individuals to the county court, which would pass upon them, sending most to the legislature for consideration, where approval by the county's delegation was virtually an assured owing to their previous agreement as members of the county court. Few other states enjoyed such internal coordination in their governmental structure, and for them instruction would have been more difficult. Taylor's only solace for them was the reminder that "the will of the majority can never be constitutionally ascertained, except through the regular organized channel for that very purpose."[94] He therefore implied, but did not specify, some sort of repetition of the electing process as the legitimate method of instructing.

Taylor's severely limited view of what government should do left him in the curious position of advocating an advanced theory of representation, based on population and purified by instruction, that would have allowed a fairly direct communication of constituent desires to representatives. Yet he expected that the message to be communicated would usually be "vote no." Starting from Taylor's premise of judging government by its effects left the possibility that only a government that was very weak could fit his definition of a *republic*. Taylor had the Enlightenment's confidence in self-evident principles of government, which allowed him to assume that the postulates of minimal government he found compelling would be shared by everyone.

To defend this Old Republican ideal of the watchman state, Taylor offered his theory of the division of powers within departments, among branches, between levels, and between the people and their governments. A popular understanding that this division was to serve the purpose of harnessing ambition, and not of inviting the various components to compete, Taylor hoped would turn American government back onto the right path. His trust in the power of ideas and theories to accomplish this prompted him to pin all his hopes on the doctrine of division. The policies of government, he insisted, were not solely the product of the structure of government, but were also derived from the principles or common beliefs that lay back of the structure. To change the policies, one had to change the beliefs.

Yet the defense of divided power put Taylor in an awkward position: if division was both a descriptive and a normative model of American democracy, what had happened to the American governmental system? After all, Taylor's own theory of aristocratic development posited the general spread of knowledge, and his principles, division of power among them, were the current embodiment of that knowledge in his time. In the context of his own system, Taylor had made aristocracies anachronisms, yet they endured.

Even though division of power was a concept that described ideas already prevalent, Taylor accepted the burden of further popularizing them, because they could not be defended against separate interests unless the public's understanding of the division of power was as thorough as this understanding of the legislative process by special interests. Knowledge could be used for good or evil, and it increased across the board. Elites had found modern methods of escaping their constitutional obligations, and the people's understanding of the proper beliefs supporting American governments was the only thing that could save them.[95]

One of the essential components of a system of divided powers was the division between levels of government, for it was at the state level that the devices of instruction, election, and a watchful militia found their primary expression; also, it was through states that the people of the United States achieved a type of communal existence.

Notes to Chapter 4

1. *The Reverend John Bracken* v. *the Visitors of William and Mary College,* reported in Daniel Call, ed., *Reports of Cases Argued and Decided in the Court of Appeals of Virginia,* vol. 3, December 8, 1790 (Richmond: Peter Cotton, 1824). This case is doubly interesting because the opposing attorney was John Marshall, and because both Taylor and Marshall took positions in argument opposite to ones they later came to hold. Marshall defended in argument the ability of an eleemosynary institution's governing board to modify the specific requirements imposed by its charter, while Taylor argued the opposite. Yet, Marshall would defend charters later in *Dartmouth College,* and Taylor would come to have the experimental attitude toward charters convenient to most enemies of the Bank of the United States.

2. Letter from John Taylor to James Monroe, November 12, 1803, in "Correspondence, pp. 289–90.

3. *Defence,* p. 35; Also see *Inquiry,* p. 417; *Construction,* p. 94; and *Tyranny,* p. 284.

4. *Tyranny,* pp. 262, 280. For an evaluation of Taylor's position in the intellectual tradition of mixed constitutions, see M.J.C. Vile, *Constitutionalism and the Separation of Powers* (Oxford: Clarendon Press, 1967), 166–72.

5. Ibid., pp. 328–29; *Enquiry,* p. 50.

6. *Construction,* p. 62.

7. Letter from John Taylor to Thomas Jefferson, June 25, 1798, in "Correspondence," p. 272. Also see *Enquiry,* p. 50.

8. *Construction,* p. 60. Also see pp. 35, 143.

9. Ibid., pp. 116, 124–25.

10. Ibid., p. 115. Also see *New Views,* p. 122.

11. *Inquiry,* p. 175. The theory that the *Inquiry* was influenced by the War of 1812 has been advanced by Norman K. Risjord, *The Old Republicans* (New York: Columbia University Press, 1965), pp. 149–50. Since Taylor himself said that the book contained nothing written after 1811, this theory may be flawed.

12. *Inquiry,* pp. 172–74, 186–87, 439.

13. Ibid., p. 202.

14. *Defence,* p. 6. Letter from Taylor to Thomas Jefferson, February 15, 1799, in "Correspondence," pp. 278–81; to John Breckinridge, December 22, 1801; ibid., pp. 284–88; to Wilson Cary Nicholas, September 5, 1801, Massachusetts Historical Society; to Nicholas April 4, 1805, and April 13, 1805, Edgehill-Randolph Papers, University of Virginia Library, Charlottesville.

15. Letter from John Taylor to James Monroe, October 26, 1810, in "Correspondence," pp. 309–13; to Thomas Ritchie, April 3, 1809, in Stanard, pp. 26–31; to Lucy P. Taylor, February 2, 1823, Virginia Historical Society, Richmond.

16. Wilfred Binkley, *President and Congress* (New York: Vintage Books, 1962), pp. 78–79.

17. *Defence,* 12–14, 25; *Enquiry,* p. 30; *Construction,* p. 305; letter from John Taylor to James Mercer Garnett, December 14, 1807, John Taylor Papers, Duke University Library, Durham, N. C.

18. *Defence,* pp. 6, 10, 13.

19. Ibid., pp. 8, 27–29, 86; *Enquiry,* p. iii, *Construction,* pp. 124–25.

20. *Inquiry,* pp. 230–31, 239–40.

21. *Annals of the Seventeenth Congress, Second Session* (Washington: Gales and Seaton, 1855), pp. 101, 195; *Annals of the Eighteenth Congress, First Session* (Washington, D.C.: Gales and Seaton, 1856), pp. 168, 408; *Inquiry,* p. 241; *New Views,* pp. 79–81.

22. *Annals of the Seventeenth Congress.*

23. *Inquiry,* pp. 21, 179, 207–19. Also see White, *The Jeffersonians* (New York: The Free Press, 1965), pp. 353–54.

24. *Inquiry,* pp. 169, 173, 187, 231–32; letter from John Taylor to James Monroe, January 31, 1811, in "Correspondence," pp. 315–19.

25. *Inquiry,* pp. 201–2.

26. Ibid., p. 20.

27. Ibid., p. 88.

28. Letter from John Taylor to Wilson Cary Nicholas, May 14, 1806, Edgehill-Randolph Papers.

29. *Inquiry,* p. 227. Also see pp. 102, 186.

30. *Argument,* p. 4. Also see *Hylton* v. *the United States,* 3 Dallas 171.

31. Albert J. Beveridge, *The Life of John Marshall* (Boston: Houghton, Mifflin Company, 1919), 3:190–91.

32. Letter from John Taylor to John Breckinridge, December 22, 1801; *Defence,* pp. 35–36; letter to Wilson Cary Nicholas, October 26, 1807; Edgehill-Randolph Papers; *Annals of the Seventeenth Congress, First Session,* p. 67; *Annals of the Eighteenth Congress, First Session,* p. 472.

33. *Inquiry,* pp. 183, 205, 207, 221, 225.

34. *Construction,* p. 260. Also see *New Views,* p. 123.

35. Ibid.

36. *Inquiry,* p. 202.

37. Ibid., p. 211.

38. Ibid., pp. 202, 207, 210, 214–15, 217, 219–20; *New Views,* p. 12.

39. *Inquiry,* p. 218.

40. *Construction,* p. 58.

41. *Tyranny,* p. 266. Also see p. 280 and *Construction Construed,* p. 85.

42. *Tyranny,* p. 265. Also see pp. 283–84.

43. *Inquiry,* p. 211. Also see, pp. 203–4; *Debates in the House of Delegates of Virginia, Upon Certain Resolutions Before the House* (Richmond, Va.: Thomas Nicholson, 1818), December 20, 1798.

44. *Construction,* pp. 108, 124, 135–36, 140; *Tyranny,* p. 282; *New Views,* p. 253; *McCulloch* v. *Maryland,* 4 Wheaton 316; *Cohens* v. *Virginia,* 6 Wheaton 264.

45. *Inquiry,* p. 290.

46. Ibid., p. 288.

47. *Construction,* pp. 263, 271–74; *Tyranny Unmasked,* p. 98.

48. *Inquiry,* pp. 233, 304, 322, 494, 527.

49. *Construction,* p. 105.

50. *Inquiry,* p. 598. Also see *Definition,* p. 13, and *Debates in the House of Delegates,* December 13, 1798.

51. *Inquiry,* p. 626.

52. Letter from John Taylor to Henry Tazewell, April 13, 1796, Tazewell Papers, Virginia State Library; *Annals of the Eighth Congress, First Session,* pp. 93, 100, 115, 124, 183, 186, *Construction,* p. 106; *Annals of the Seventeenth Congress, Second Session,* p. 195.

53. *Inquiry,* p. 152.

54. Ibid.

55. Ibid., p. 176.

56. Ibid., pp. 412–13.

57. *Inquiry,* pp. 413–14; *Construction,* p. 71.

58. *Inquiry,* p. 176.

59. Letter from John Taylor to Henry Tazewell, April 13, 1796; *Inquiry*, p. 351; "We the People," Caroline County Broadside, 1803, University of Virginia Library.

60. *Inquiry*, p. 330.

61. Ibid., pp. 135–36, 169–70; letter from John Taylor to Henry Tazewell, May 26, 1798; Tazewell Papers, Virginia State Library, letter to Thomas Ritchie, March 27, 1809, in Stanard, p. 16; *Annals of the Eighteenth Congress, First Session*, p. 387.

62. *Definition of Parties*, p. 14. Emphasis original.

63. *Tyranny*, p. 114. Also see p. 104; *Inquiry*, pp. 318, 326–27.

64. Letter from John Taylor to Wilson Cary Nicholas, April 14, 1806, Edgehill-Randolph Papers. Also see letter from Taylor to Nicholas, March 31, 1803, Edgehill-Randolph Papers; letter to Thomas Ritchie, September 29, 1808, in Stanard, pp. 7–10; *Inquiry*, pp. 151, 245; *Construction*, pp. 29, 281.

65. Ibid., p. 412; letter from John Taylor to Daniel Carroll Brent, October 9, 1796, in "Correspondence," p. 267.

66. *Annals of the Eighteenth Congress, First Session*, p. 687.

67. *Construction*, p. 186.

68. Letter from John Taylor to James Monroe, November 24, 1811, in Hans Hammond, ed., "Letters of John Taylor of Caroline," *The Virginia Magazine of History and Biography* 52 (April 1944): 126.

69. *An Argument on the Constitutionality of the Carriage Tax*, p. 11; *Construction*, p. 270; *Tyranny*, p. 318.

70. *Annals of the Eighteenth Congress, First Session*, p. 564.

71. *New Views*, p. 252. Also see *Construction*, pp. 58, 296, 303.

72. *New Views*, p. 240. Also see p. 195.

73. *Construction*, p. 68.

74. Letter of John Taylor to Daniel Carroll Brent, October 9, 1796; *Defence*, p. 27; *Inquiry*, pp. 19, 638–39.

75. *Definition*, pp. 6, 8, 16.

76. *Annals of the Eighteenth Congress, First Session*, p. 388.

77. *Inquiry*, p. 582.

78. Ibid., pp. 75–76.

79. Letter from John Taylor to Daniel Carroll Brent, October 9, 1796; *Inquiry*, pp. 3, 83, 101–3, 113, 126, 133, 141, 256, 403.

80. Letter from John Taylor to Daniel Carroll Brent, October 9, 1796.

81. *Enquiry*, p. 5.

82. Ibid. p. 6.

83. Ibid. See discussion of republican influences on Taylor in the final chapter.

84. *Inquiry*, p. 406.

85. Ibid., pp. 85, 171, 448, 471.

86. Clement Eaton, *The Freedom-of-Thought Struggle in the Old South* (New York: Harper and Row, Publishers, 1964), pp. 89–90.

87. *Inquiry*, p. 416.

88. *Construction*, pp. 61–62.

89. *Enquiry*, p. 49; Taylor, *Arator*, p. 42; letters from John Taylor to Thomas Ritchie, March 27, 1809; March 30, 1809; April 3, 1809, in Stanard, pp. 16, 19, 26, 29. The March 30 letter also connects division of power to property. Also see *Annals of the Eighth Congress, First Session*, p. 115.

90. *Construction*, p. 277. Also see pp. 84, 117; *Tyranny*, p. 256.

91. *Construction*, p. 163.

92. *Tyranny,* p. 282. Also see pp. 141, 322–23; *Tyranny,* pp. 255–59; *New Views,* p. 218.

93. *New Views,* pp. 190–91; 241–42.

94. Alpheus T. Mason and Richard H. Leach, *In Quest of Freedom* (Englewood Cliffs, N.J.: Prentice-Hall, Inc., 1959), p. 254.

95. *Inquiry,* p. 399.

5

FEDERALISM

JOHN TAYLOR'S doctrine of divided power requires a detailed examination of federalism, since the division between the state and federal levels of government was one of the primary components of that doctrine. His application of that theory to political controversies touching upon disunion will be considered in the next chapter.

Although in the *Inquiry* (1814) Taylor's doctrine of divided power included separations within and between branches of the same level of government—between the state and federal levels of government, and between the people and all governments— the latter two components were associated first with the term *division of power*. In his 1809 debate with Thomas Ritchie, Taylor had often used the term in a sense equivalent to his use of *federalism*. Even though his conceptualization of divided power had become more elaborate by the time of the *Inquiry*, it seems fair to say that to Taylor *divided power* usually meant the unimpaired operations of federalism. The details of this association form the substance of this chapter.

Taylor's understanding of federal systems had unique features because of the special emphasis he gave to the role of popular understanding in perpetuating a federal system. On the other hand, even though he believed that division of power had produced federalism in America, he acknowledged that a similar understanding of man's right to self-government, tem-

Notes for this chapter begin on p. 212.

pered by a realization that safeguards were necessary against man's selfishness, might produce a different kind of republic in a smaller country. He always seemed to be at a loss for examples of other kinds of republics, however.[1]

Taylor's theories on federalism ranged over its causes, advantages, the nature of the Union, and the division of authority between the states and federal government. Taylor maintained a consistent point of view in discussing most of these aspects of federalism.

A. Causes of Federalism

Taylor derived the origin of federalism from both conventional and natural causes, devoting his greater attention to the latter.

In arguing for the conventional, man-made causes that resulted in the formation of the American federal system, Taylor disagreed with Montesquieu, Rousseau, and Hume, who had argued that republican government had to be limited to, or was most naturally found in, small countries. Taylor and the many Founders who agreed with him on this point argued that many eighteenth-century writers had been ignorant of federal organizational techniques and had too hastily concluded that only governments relying on physical force could govern large territories. By definition such governments could not be republican. Taylor thought that these misimpressions had been popularized by the "enemies of a republican form of government."[2]

Taylor agreed with the defenders of small republics that such commonwealths maximized communication between the governors and the governed. He also maintained, however, that the ingenious American invention of linking many independent republics into a federal system had obviated the older rule about distance requiring force. The adoption of federalism, Taylor seemed to be saying, was an act of will not dependent upon any economically or historically determined forces. Yet American federalism had built upon sound economic and historical foundations.

Taylor offered a number of arguments for the artificial causes of federalism. First, he maintained that the arguments the colonies had used against Great Britain were relevant to the relationship of the states and the federal government. Second, he argued that the dissimilarities in customs, climates, and occupations throughout the states made the federal government incompetent to legislate intelligently and uniformly for all. Third, he suspected that vanity would never allow Congressmen honestly to admit that they had an inadequate understanding of local conditions: they would simply legislate pigheadedly to prove that they could do it. Such stubbornness, Taylor warned, might lead to effects comparable to those when the French Assembly freed the slaves of Santo Domingo without knowledge of local conditions. Fourth, and closely related to the last point, he was convinced that the representatives from one state simply could never know enough to govern other parts of the country. This final argument, of course, comes very close to saying that the administrative conveniences of federalism were merely an honest recognition of deeper, more fundamental loyalties, which would find expression regardless of whether a system was federal or not. In Taylor's opinion the preference of the residents of a state or a particular region for the interests that concerned them most directly had been imprinted by God in the different economies with which He had supplied the states and in the propensity for self-interest that He had given all men.[3]

Cultural differences were among the natural causes of federalism discerned by Taylor, and his awareness of these differences crops up several times during his career. His personal correspondence during the American Revolution indicated his first awareness of cultural differences among the states, but events were moving too quickly for him to have time to draw these impressions into any consistent statements. On the one hand, he complained that Northern campaigns were simple façades to cover a quick attack on Virginia by the British, and that enlistments were few in states north of Maryland. Those who enlisted in Northern states, moreover, were ruder than Virginians. On the other hand, Taylor was impressed with Pennsylvania's war efforts. Moreover, his sympathy for Virginia's plight did not deter him from leaving the state militia for a congressional commission when it was offered. It is true that the 1781 "Remonstrance," written by Taylor for communication to the Continental Congress, had expressed Virginia's increasing disenchantment with the bonds of "federal union" because she had been left to face the British alone. But the timely intervention of Northern troops made the sending of the remonstrance unnecessary and Taylor never referred to it afterward.[4] His awareness of cultural differences is best revealed in those letters which discuss with great affection the condition of his Virginia volunteers: his home state was first in his affections although more because it was home than because it possessed any innate superiority.[5]

This state patriotism was not a narrow attachment to home and hearth, for later he did not hesitate to advise friends, because of the added prestige of Richmond, to locate business enterprises in Richmond instead of nearly Fredericksburg. He also rejected the notion that a small village was in any way analogous to a total society and economy, because a division of labor and a need for some industrialization were manifest. Thus Taylor seems to have rejected extreme decentralization in politics and economics.[6]

What Taylor recognized in himself he expected of others, so he warned against the dangers inherent in local attachments or patriotism at the same time he defended their inevitability. Local attachments or state pride could cause a banding together within a geographic section, and a consequent discrimination against other areas. The issue of state rivalries was faced directly by Taylor during his management of the Twelfth Amendment's progress through the Senate. His position on the issue was one very similar to Madison's in the 1787 Virginia Plan: Taylor attempted to muster large-state support for the amendment by pointing out the dangers of giving small states, which contained a minority of the total population, too large a voice in the choice of the chief executive. Parliamentary elections controlled by such small minorities had led and could lead again to monarchial privileges if many elections were thrown into the House.[7]

Even though he recognized state rivalries as natural and inevitable, he tried to minimize them. In the debate on the Twelfth Amendment, for example, he insisted that "the controversy is not between larger and smaller States, but between the people of every State and the House of Representatives," and that allowing the latter unlimited power to foment divisions such as occurred in the House choice of President in 1796 and 1800 was detrimental to all states.[8] In the *Inquiry* Taylor emphasized the unifying theoretical principles and interests that bound the states together and did not discuss rivalries among states. He returned to the subject of rivalries in *Construction Construed* and *New Views*. In the former he maintained that uniformity of law was difficult to obtain because of the different interests, habits, and opinions in the states. To force any state to surrender its identity might result in civil war, would certainly result in chains, and could only result in a toleration at best of the institution of private property. In *New Views* he attacked the Missouri Compromise for having stirred violent state and local sympathies, which were best left alone, and which at any rate were the only qualified judges of their own interests. Throughout his life Taylor maintained a realistic attitude toward state loyalties that recognized and defended their inevitability while simultaneously attempting to put them to work for either nationalistic purposes such as the Twelfth Amendment or particularistic purposes such as the Missouri question.[9]

Differences in loyalties from state to state were based on geographic and economic conditions that had produced common beacons of self-interest separating the residents of each state from those of all other states. The tendencies created by these interests had been reinforced by the creation of legal boundaries forming political communities in which the residents had taken pride: "It is not in human nature to possess equal affection for a distant country, as for that of its nativity and abode."[10] More reinforcement for state loyalties was provided by the fact that state governments differed in characteristics and policies, thereby helping to perpetuate state differences.

In his later works Taylor reaffirmed that the states embraced a "great variety of local circumstances" and pointed out that the geographic sections into which the United States had been divided by nature had resulted in a beneficial assignment of functions to these sections.[11] If each would pursue its comparative advantage, the greatest good for all would result. He reminded other states that the natural relationships that existed between states could work in reverse: for example, the Western states would suffer with the Southern if they attempted to take advantage of their geographic position or to develop an economy for which they were not suited. Free trade among diversified sections of the country, not economic balkanization, would put state differences to beneficial use. He distinguished his free trade views from those of capitalists, however, who supported free trade only for domestic commerce. Capitalists were a small minority of the population in a minority of the states, hence their economic interests could never become a natural state interest. He thought that the maintenance of a pluralistic economy did not require the toleration of economic privileges such as protective tariffs, which undercut the independence of states.[12]

At the same time, state loyalties and the natural effects of geography upon men's interests influenced even the attitudes of capitalists. In *New Views* Taylor flatly stated that human nature could be permanently affected by geography and these underlying predispositions would evidence themselves, regardless of the position or title one held.[13]

Even the consolidationist actions of the federal government reaffirmed the prevalence of geographic influences. Funding, banking, the Sedition Law, and presidential campaigns; the settling of Western lands with the people taken from a few states (especially from Virginia); and the Missouri issue had all favored some states at the expense of others. Likewise, each of these policies had vindicated the importance of geography. Even in a consolidated republic such attitudes would exist and make any unity spurious (p. 262).

Even though Taylor derived the natural origins of federalism from state loyalties based on economic interests, pride in different territories, and the differential effects of governmental systems, he thought the adoption of a federal system to have been an act of will that placed local interests in separate states. Taylor preferred to think of the development of different state interests as accidents that had been turned to good purposes by deliberate effort: "our division into states, induced us to consider the hostile principles of power . . . in a geographical light, yet our decision was rather the result of an improvement in political knowledge, matured by reflection in experience, than casual." (p. 239) Only the expression of state interests through formal governmental structures and processes ever earned Taylor's approval. The origin of federalism, then, was a harmonious blending of natural and volitional factors.

B. Advantages of Federalism

John Taylor's very limited view of the proper uses to which governments might be put did not often lead him into lengthy descriptions of the advantages of a particular form or structure, but his admiration for federalism was so great that he permitted himself some words of praise in its behalf. Federalism was the logical culmination of a division of powers; it avoided the coercive governmental enforcement practices that would have been required had it not existed; it allowed states to act as safety valves; and it taught and expanded the principles of republicanism while providing laboratories for experimentation with governmental programs.

Federalism amplified the division of powers and controlled the harsh governmental policies used by aristocrats by reducing the stakes available for speculation. The larger the amount of power that would be available for control, the greater the efforts would be to seize it. Taylor credited the Framers with the foresight of having seen that great power would be an irresistible temptation. This led them to reserve powers to the states, which they thought more trustworthy in the use of power than the Federal Government. Federal officials did not have "a greater mass of intelligence" than their state counterparts, but did have greater temptation to abuse their power, while state officials were "beneficient angels" who had the power "to do much good, and but little evil" (p. 199).

Another advantage that the federal system offered was that it created two more protective layers for divided powers: no officer, department, or level of government could alter the political law that had been established and that sustained the division, without stirring up the wrath of other departments. Had it not been for federalism, the harsh governmental practices necessary to control large foreign countries would have been necessary in the United States. Peace and unity were the advantages to be gained from federalism, and the opposite conditions would have followed an application of the British, French, or German forms of government to the United States (pp. 179, 199, 201, 254, 292).

European countries might have had social classes that were antagonistic to each other, but these classes lacked a geographic base. The members of one class could mingle with the members of other classes and, as a result, the class differences could be muted by individual friendships. Although the states were cultural, and therefore social, entities, Taylor pointed out that they had a definite geographic basis. There were fewer contacts among the residents of states than among the members of classes, and therefore fewer friendships. Consequently, the geographic dispersion that had helped create state loyalties helped also to preserve them. Without federalism, only a recourse to arms would settle controversies arising out of congressional ignorance and lack of sympathy for the problems of local areas. He warned that resorting to arms to settle state disagreements was not only unsettling, inconvenient, and brutal, but historically it had proved ineffective (pp. 186, 237-39, 242-43, 260, 290).

The presence of state governments unified in an amicable bond of fraternity allowed a series of safety valves for the hostilities and tensions that built up in any society. Taylor did not regard the states as jealous armed camps, but their different interests and loyalties based on these interests could spark disagreement. The Framers had recognized this, he thought, and made the interests of the states the basis of the Union, instead of turning their backs on the jealousies and pretending they were nonexistent. He willingly accepted the inevitable consequence of a system founded on an equilibrium of mutual hostility and thought that the collisions that would occur were a virtue: "the absence of collision from a concentrated supremacy, is exactly the vice which engendered all its oppressions" (pp. 250-51). The existence of states gave the people regular channels for influencing the public affairs and governmental structure of the union, while the state governments allowed the population within each state an outlet for their frustrations. Pretending that the people were some sort of organic entity that had a life separate from the individuals who composed it was, in Taylor's opinion, a mistake. It ignored the difficulty that ordinary people faced in attempting to organize for political action, and the fact that it was easier to organize on a state basis than a federal one (p. 187). The rights of the people could find appropriate protection only through state governments: "which will act with most knowledge, discretion, legality, and effect, in maintaining the rights of the people, mobs or state governments? In a country so extensive as the United States, we must have one or the other . . ." (p. 188).

In hoping that the states would serve as "safety valves" for internal frustrations, Taylor was trying to contain political and economic tensions within a state and avoid transmitting them to Congress for solution. That simply spread the burden of coping with local problems over the entire country: "Local interests . . . will go to war with each other in Congress, the causes of their hostility, intended to be removed by the union, will be revived . . . and both will generate new battles" (p. 262). Even worse than the disruptions created when the states failed as safety valves would be a capability in the federal government to solve state problems, because that also increased its abilities to control all of their actions. The best policy was to let the state governments act as safety valves and let off the gas of exclusive interests, for "while these safety-valves are kept in operation, and the gas is thus discharged, the country will go on well enough."[14]

There is ample evidence that John Taylor considered the existence of states as an opportunity to experiment with the further development of republicanism, and his derivation of the three stages of aristocracy from the level of knowledge existing during historical epochs undoubtedly led him to look forward to such experimentation. For example, he recognized cultural differences among the states but did not propose that manners unfamiliar to him be eliminated. On the contrary, he even attempted to send his sons North and abroad to schools so that a respect for different life-styles would be part of their education. In a political sense, he supported the creation of new states in order to increase experimentation with republicanism. Such new states must be annexed by republican measures as he understood them, however, and he opposed the taking of Canada by force during the War of 1812 and the imposing of conditions on Missouri before allowing it in the Union. Taylor often used state governments as illustrations. The *Inquiry* is full of approving references to the techniques various states used to select judges, the length of office of governors, the use of rotation in office, and the presence of plural executives. The state of Virginia, naturally, was often offered as an example of various beneficial governmental practices, as was Connecticut; but Taylor used states as bad examples, too. For example, his objection to the power of New York's governor was noted in the previous chapter on political parties; and the state of Rhode Island, which Taylor thought a hotbed of bankers and capitalists, occasionally earned his scorn. He endorsed such *avant-garde* experiments as the state's lending paper currency at interest in Pennsylvania and unicameralism in Vermont.[15]

There can be little doubt that Taylor thought the differences among states could serve as useful instruction to others, but he never gave any attention to how states might share this knowledge or to the dangers and difficulties of others in implementing their experiences. His most concise statement on learning from state experiments was made in 1818, when he proposed that the Virginia agricultural society use the state as a proving ground for new developments—for "water, wood, iron, coal, and a wide communication with the state, decide it to be the proper place for experiment"—and that the society subsidize the experiment.[16]

The attitude of Taylor on experimentation, however, was limited from the outset. He did not want government at any level to be very active, so that the experiments he thought most worthwhile were those which contributed to the science of keeping government modest in size and ambition. Nonetheless, Taylor's opinion of the appropriate bounds of state governmental actions stretched to include clearing river beds, establishing schools, safeguarding the property rights of illiterate Indians, subsidizing ferries, and establishing town development corporations. These actions represented the outer limits of governmental action in his opinion, however, and if state governments began transferring property by law he was as quick to criticize them as he was to criticize the federal government.[17]

One conceivable advantage of federalism was ignored by Taylor, for he never discussed the positive opportunities that states might offer for the development of a sense of community and civic responsibility among their citizens. Either Rousseau's general-will or civic-religion concept might have served as a point of departure for an examination by Taylor of what the good life was like within the communities of the states whose existence he defended. For example, one might speculate that it would have been only natural for him to have extended his division of powers doctrine to the relationship between states and municipalities, but he did not use the state and federal division as an analogy. Rather, he took the traditional position and asserted that municipalities were creatures of their states and totally dependent upon them. Nor was he overly concerned with ethnic minority groups within states. He seemed to have had a certain regard for the American natives still surviving in Virginia, was sympathetic toward the German-speaking residents of the Shenandoah Valley, and was active in working for extension of the suffrage to include Piedmont and frontier Virginia. He had no sympathy for anything approaching proportional representation within a state's voting system, however, and personally saw to it in the election of 1800 that the Virginia Federalists' votes for presidential electors were wiped out by an at-large voting system that kept the Federalist enclaves in their place.[18]

C. The Concept of Nation

Taylor amplified his conviction that human nature was affected by geography and that each state contained men with different interests by his use of the concept *nation*. There seems to be no precedent or parallel for his use of this term, and he never supplied a definitive explanation of which groups could or could not constitute nations. At various times during his life he used *nation* to refer to the entire population of the United States, the population of foreign countries such as England or France, a college, racial groups, occupational groups, and spawning herrings.[19]

Regardless of these inconsistencies, in Taylor's middle and later works the term *nation* always was used to distinguish people from their governments and was usually used in a context that left no doubt that states and nations were equivalent terms. The following discussion will document the importance of the concept of nation to his doctrine of divided powers.

Taylor left no ambiguity on the question of whether or not nations could ever be confused with governments. Regardless of any other meaning he ever gave the term *nation*, he never used it to mean governments.

> The doctrine "that nations ought to stick by their govern-ments" right or wrong, is apocryphal where the sovereignty of the people exists. Are governments the best judges of national interests? No. . . . How are the degrees of liberty and tyranny graduated? From free discussion and national will, down to passive obedience.[20]

Here the word *nation* is not given any particular geographic, class, or economic connotation. It simply refers to people as distinguished from their governments and that is the definition on which Taylor ultimately decided.[21]

The concept of nation filled a gap left in Taylor's system by his insistence that self-government by political entities flowed from man's individual right to govern himself. This idea would have left Taylor's concept of popular sovereignty as a very individual right and thrown the full burden on the individual to make his weight felt in public affairs. In addition, such an individualized expression of popular sovereignty might have cleared the way for an intellectual defense of a consolidated republic instead of the federal one Taylor favored. Any kind of tyranny could be justified in the name of popular sovereignty if it could be defended by the argument that it had resulted from the people's consent to a social compact. To avoid this, Taylor offered the alternative solution that any compact that had been made was made among the people who formed themselves into a political society or "nation." The political society thus created was paramount and the government its agent, but through the exercise of the individual right of self-government, even the political society could be dissolved by its contracting parties. Until its dissolution the political society as such would be the master of the government.[22] No government could have a part in any social compact at any time: "the ancient notion of a social compact between nations and their governments or monarchs, alone sufficed to corrupt them."[23] Either party to a contract between nations and governments could interpret the terms of the agreement. In the case of a social compact this could lead to tyranny.

Taylor expounded the attributes and the functions of nations at various times, carefully distinguishing between them and the governments that were their servants. He reified the nation as "both a natural and a moral being"[24] having both physical and political powers which must enjoy uninterrupted possession of each to remain free. The national will and national reason were supposed to be communicated through electoral procedures and protected by the militia. The only way to do this in the United States was through regularly organized elections. Mere theoretical responsibility of a government was insufficient.

Taylor also insisted that nations, like individuals, possessed an undelegated set of rights that they must be allowed to enjoy separately from government. From this vantage point a nation was "an intellectual and political being. Thinking is as necessary to a body politic, to enable it to shun evil and obtain good, as to any other reasonable being" (p. 482). This judgment was best exercised by the nation itself if its happiness were to be the ultimate goal. Sedition laws, established religions, and standing armies had often been used to keep nations in servitude, denying them the enjoyment of their rights by substituting the judgment of an aristocracy for that of the nation, and by monopolizing the flow of knowledge that would have given nations the facts necessary to cast off their oppressors (pp. 446-47, 484, 488-89, 512).

A nation had to possess a strong code of political law (i.e., constitutional structural and procedural limitations) to protect its rights, but it must understand "its interest, at whatever degree of virtue or corruption it may be stationed, in fact or in theory" (pp. 438-39). This understanding could be helped by "permanent standards for measuring power and property" (p. 386). Nations had often lost their freedom by accepting fluctuating standards that impaired their ability to understand what was happening to them.

Although nations and governments must be separate, there should not be an antagonistic relationship between the two. Unity should be the goal, but when it was not obtained it was not automatically the government's fault. Good or bad principles were infused into governments by constitutional frameworks, which controlled them more surely than by education, a government "corrupted by an infusion of bad principles, can more justly complain of the nation for making it wicked, than the nation can complain of the government for making it miserable" (p. 167). Nations guarded this political framework, and it was their duty to see that it operated correctly. The right to adopt new governments and fundamentally change old ones was "held by nations, and not by governments or individuals . . . the social rights of nations, cannot be destroyed by political laws . . . (p. 498).

Two characteristics of nations resulted from their independence and self-sufficiency. Each nation was a total community composed of people of all ages "and as one generation passes away, another succeeds, having the same wants, and the same capabilities."[25] Each of these total societies was constituted of individuals in relation to each other and existing at the same time. Even so, mutual harmony based on a specialization of economic activities should be pursued: it was stupid for each to follow a policy of economic isolation.[26]

There were guidelines that nations could follow in deciding whether their independence had become illusionary through the tyrannous policies of their governments. For example, when a nation began to depend upon the transfer of money to capitalists through the use of government to achieve economic progress, or when governments could freely claim that they conferred protection and wealth unassisted upon nations, a nation was not free. The criteria for judging national freedom were outgrowths of the beliefs of the people in frugal government: "All reflecting individuals, except those bribed by self interest" would support frugality and attack the transfer of property without consent. A government that believed the opposite stood judged by its own acts as a tyrant.[27] When this happened a nation had lost its liberty. In order to prevent such a loss, a nation's attention to public affairs must be great, but this required that "national questions ought to be candidly and fairly stated to obtain a genuine national opinion."[28] If there had been any hoarding of information for the advantage of a particular group, the threat to national freedom was great. It was also important that the facts presented to the nation not be phrased in an overly complex manner.

Taylor never dealt directly with the physical or social characteristics of all the possible kinds of nations. He did say that societies or nations could "give legislation whatever form they prefer" and use either representative or directly democratic forms. If they chose the latter the government would not constitute a separate interest.[29]

D. The States as Nations

As time went on, Taylor increasingly tended to identify nations with states, to the exclusion of any other groups. Only a few times before the *Inquiry*, and only once in it, had he combined states and nations. In the *Inquiry* he had said:

A nation has been considered as a moral or political being, capable of opinion, will and sovereignty. States, are nations.[30]

After the *Inquiry* he consistently referred to states in this manner, although he never excluded the possibility that nations could take other forms. For example, he did not discontinue his use of *nation* to describe the whole population of foreign countries. Each American state nation was a unified entity and contained "no inimical ingredients, willing to sacrifice it to another state, because of its unity as a moral being."[31] Nations had natural rights more manifestly evident than those possessed by individuals, because nations could exist independently of each other while men were tied together by mutual relationships that sometimes blurred the limits of individual rights. Although Taylor's use of *nation* as a term equivalent to state was often repeated in his later works, he felt that nothing proved the existence of state nations any better than the fact that they had created governments at a point in time. The fact that all of the state nations were "communities . . . each constituted of a distinct people" had been proved by the fact that each had chosen a slightly different form of government when governments were created at the time of the Revolution.[32]

As colonies the states had been "imperfect" nations, but "by the revolution, each became a perfect individual nation, possessed of all the natural rights of nations."[33] The Constitution recognized states as nations. The commerce clause described the nationhood of states as being equal to that of foreign nations and Indian tribes. In addition, the very word *federal* often used to refer to the American Union was a recognition that "state sovereignties really existed. It implied a league between sovereign nations."[34]

In seizing upon the term *nation* for application to states, Taylor soundly rejected the reverse thesis that there ever had been such a thing as an American nation composed of the whole population of the country. It will be remembered that in his early writings he had occasionally talked of an American nation, but after the *Inquiry* he refused to concede that such an entity had ever existed. He opposed the notion that Congress could be considered as a national legislature, although he had called it that in early years himself.[35] An American nation had not been created in 1789, the states had never associated themselves since into one, Congress could not exercise general or national powers of legislation, and the fact that the House of Representatives was elected by the people in a direct manner was no indication that it represented or derived any powers from a single American nation. "The notion that the twenty-six States are but one nation, is similar to an assertion that the . . . principalities of Germany . . . constitute but one nation." Everyone knew they were separate.[36]

Although no one can doubt that Taylor's sympathies were with the state nations he described, he was quick to recognize that extreme fragmentation could lead to difficulties. The federal government had been created to ensure that no "geographic majority" or sectional interest should gain the ability to dispense "injustice, oppression or ruin" to other geographic interests. Since the independence and self-sufficiency of nations made it difficult for one nation to oppress another directly, this exploitation usually occurred through federal legislation. On balance, however, he thought the advantages of such a system far outweighed the disadvantages.[37]

E. Sovereignty and State Rights

Taylor's concept of nation was not fully developed until it was joined with the need to use the term *sovereignty* in countering arguments mustered by Marshall and other Federalists in defense of the growth of federal power. Throughout the *Inquiry*, Taylor had refused to use *sovereignty* in any sense except that of *popular sovereignty*, meaning self-government. He offered no extended definitions or discussions of sovereignty until *Construction Construed* (1820), but seems to have changed very litle in his opinion on this subject over the years.

Taylor's full discussions of sovereignty never firmly asserted its existence. This hesitation resulted from the fact that the term implied superiority and subordination to him and, therefore, had limited applicability to a land where equality was one of the ruling principles. In reference to sovereignty, Taylor said: "I do not know how it has happened, that this word has crept into our political dialect, unless it be that mankind prefer mystery to knowledge; and that governments love obscurity better than specification."[38] Taylor referred to no particular authors in his discussions of sovereignty except for a quotation from Coke in reference to English sovereignty being unlimited except by the impossible. "By referring to the English books and practices, from which it is borrowed, for its interpretation, it turns out to be synonimous with despotism" (p. 33).

Sovereignty also implied an indivisibility that may have been applicable to Roman emperors and popes who had contended for the same unit of sovereignty, but not for the United States (p. 26).

In actuality, the idea of sovereignty had been stolen from the attributes of God, who alone deserved to be thought of as sovereign. "Imitation and ignorance even seduced the English puritans and the long parliament to adopt the despotism they resisted . . . and caused them to fail in accomplishing a reformation for which they had suffered the evils of a long war" (p. 26). Kings, popes, bishops, presbyteries, and the Long Parliament had demonstrated what man would do with the powers of Providence (p. 26).

The use that had been made of sovereignty in international law had no applicability to domestic affairs, because in its international context the term had been intended for civilizing the relations between countires, not for "increasing domestic oppression, by dissolving restrictions imposed for the security of civil liberty" (p. 279). Taylor referred to sovereignty as "imaginary," and felt that the discussion of it had been deliberately diverted from its references to God and international law by the friends of despotism, who framed political discussion so as to question which *form* of government possessed sovereignty rather than asking whether any possessed it. Terms such as *sovereignty* and *corporation* had been put to work in such discussions because they had politically neutral common meanings that could be expanded for despotic purposes (pp. 279-80).

If the term *sovereignty* had to be applied to the United States, Taylor insisted that it be applied with the same connotations of superiority, subordination, and indivisibility that defined its use in other countries. For example, sovereignty was possessed either by the people or by Congress, because under the rule of indivisibility it could not be possessed by both. If those who agreed with Marshall wanted to dust off the term *sovereignty* and apply it to the United States, Taylor insisted that they use the term as it was understood in Europe. Thus defined, it was impossible for the Marshallians to claim that supremacy and sovereignty existed both in the people and in the laws of Congress: what was supreme was sovereign and what was sovereign had to be indivisible (p. 27).

Taylor's own reluctant acceptance of sovereignty at times seemed not to be consistent with the rules that he insisted sovereignty had to follow (i.e., be supreme and indivisible). The state constitutions had bestowed sovereignty upon a majority of the state's population, and the United States Constitution had made the people in the states and the state governments supreme. Since, however, "neither the state nor federal governments received any powers except as trustees," actually sovereignty boiled down to the majority of the population in each state. Taylor sought to "prove that the right of self-government, or sovereignty, if the right should be so called, resides in the people . . .", but he thought it in order to refute the theory that the federal government was sovereign (p. 38). He disregarded the distinction "between the rights of sovereignty and of self-government . . . and in accordance with common language, use [d] the term 'sovereignty' as an attribute of the right of self-government, and only applicable to the people" (pp. 32-33).

In order to use the concept of sovereignty against the Federalists, Taylor was forced to give it a different definition. The Federalists tended to interpret sovereignty as the ultimate authority in a political system that must go unchallenged either by word or deed. Taylor, on the other hand, interpreted it as the people's constituent power to form a government.[39]

Nothing would prove the existence of a sovereign community more definitively, Taylor said, than the creation of a government by that community. "Sovereignty is the highest degree of political power, and the establishment of a form of government, the highest proof which can be given of its existence."[40] The state majorities had not only created the federal government through exercise of their separate sovereign capacities, but also reserved powers to demonstrate that their creation had not been given sovereignty.

The states received no sovereignty from the federal Union, because their sovereignty came from the Declaration of Independence and was not relinquished by forming the Union. Taylor offered many proofs of state sovereignty. State sovereignty could be derived from the common definition of the word *state*; from the notion that the Union was a league of sovereign states; from the superior authority that state legislatures and conventions had over the 1787 Constitutional Convention as a transmitter of sovereignty; from the fact that the Paris Treaty recognized the states individually by name; from the hold over their territory that states retained through Article 1, Section 8, Paragraph 17; from the alleged fact that the Swiss and Dutch confederacies were precedents for the retention of individual state sovereignty in a federal union; and from the retention of arms by state militia forces.[41]

All of these arguments in defense of state sovereignty are more or less plausible and unexceptionable for a man of Taylor's time and opinions. When the discussion passed beyond a mere defense of state sovereignty to the substantive meaning of that concept, however, his ideas must be examined with particular care. Taylor was very precise about what he meant by a *state*, even if he did vacillate on whether sovereignty was too dangerous a term for practical use. In one early discussion, he had defined a state as including the people, territory, capital, stock, and revenue of a geographic section. Almost without exception in his later discussion, however, he limited the definition of *state* to *its people alone*, who collectively exercised as a nation their individual rights in establishing a government. He understood the Tenth Amendment, reserving power to the states *or* the people, as an attempt to link the two, thereby establishing a definite meaning for the word *state*, which had not been defined carefully in the preceding sections of the Constitution. As a geographic term *state* might refer to land, but Taylor wanted its political reference reserved to mean the people of a territory "united by mutual consent into a civil society."[42] It is evident, therefore, that when Taylor referred to state sovereignty he did not mean the powers of state governments, but the power of self-government possessed collectively by the people of each state. He often drew a sharp distinction between the people of a state and their government, and insisted that the two should not be confused.

State governments were less likely than the federal government to violate the practice of and belief in the division of powers, but they were by no means innocent of such transgressions. If state governments were made dependent upon federal sources of revenue, their wholesome dependence upon the people of each state would be gone. Or, if the notion that the people had surrendered their sovereignty to state governments took root, the people could become slaves to their state governments. In addition, the state legislatures' influence over United States Senators made the latter especially suspect, because they were removed from the direct control of the people. When this happened, responsibility suffered even if the states were the electing bodies.[43]

Taylor took special exception to Madison's view of states because Madison had distinguished them from the people of the country as a whole. In fact, Taylor urged, there was no dichotomy: "The fact is, that the people and the states are one and the same. . . . When we speak of Pennsylvanians or Virginians, it would be absurd, if these people had not constituted themselves into states. The state of Pennsylvania means the people of Pennsylvania."[44]

Each of the great charters of American republicanism verified this opinion, Taylor argued. Neither the Declaration of Independence, the Articles of Confederation, nor the Constitution allowed amendment by a simple majority of all the people of the Union, but each one would have done so if people were different from states.

Taylor's concept of states as sovereign peoples, as nations, casts new light on the term *states' rights*. First of all, this was not a term that had any great significance to Taylor. He sometimes used it, but it never attained the frequency of use or the special meaning that he assigned to *nation* or sovereignty. If a great nation was made up of smaller nations, "it must absorb the same right of self-government in its component parts."[45] "All State rights are rights of the people," Taylor insisted, and they were held by the state-nations separately.[46] There was no undifferentiated mass of states' rights in Taylor's conception.

Although Taylor never abandoned the notion that states were equivalent to the people of those states and distinguished from their governments at all levels, he sometimes seemed to waver in his conviction. It has been noted that Taylor's early writings were sometimes inconsistent with his later ones. So it was with his concept of states, for he said in his *Enquiry* (1794) that the "state legislatures are the people themselves in a state of refinement, possessing superior information. . . . They are annual conventions subject to no undue influence . . . and actuated by the motive of public good."[47] His most extreme rejection of the separation between the state governments and the people came during his defense of the Virginia Resolutions, when he offered the possibility that the United States Constitution could be amended without recourse to special conventions, since the states had been the original contracting parties and their legislatures had the authority to speak for them. Taylor did not deny during the debates that the people had been parties to the contract, but he had originally supported language that said that the states "alone" were the contracting parties.[48]

In his works following the raising of the Missouri question, Taylor showed an increasing preference for merging the concepts of the people of a state and their respective state governments. In *Construction Construed* he specifically renounced the "idea sometimes advanced, that the state governments ever were or continue to be, sovereign or unlimited," but three years later in *New Views* he defended the choice of United States Senators by state legislatures as truly the choice of the states-as-people.[49] He obliterated the distinction between state legislatures and conventions that he had insisted on one year before: "both State legislatures and state conventions, are representation of State sovereignties, equally competent to express their will."[50]

In summary, although Taylor's affection for the separation between state nations and their governments seemed to have weakened, he never referred to state governments as sovereign, nor to state rights as a single, common, undifferentiated mass. The people of each state had formed the federal compact independently, and they retained most of their rights independently, because only the owners of rights (i.e., nations) were fit to guard them.[51]

F. The Nature of the Union

Taylor thought that some of the terminology used in establishing the Union should be reexamined in order to recover its pure meaning. For example, the term *United States* was an endorsement of his view of the Union, because it referred to more than one state, rejecting the existence of any single united *state*. The term also intimated correctly that there first had to be states for them to be united. An added dimension to this term was the fact that *United States* implied a coordinate relationship among its partners. The Framers of the Constitution had intended this coordinate relationship and they had never intended to equip the federal government "in all the panoply of means, implication and inference" of a giant, dwarfing the state governments by comparison.[52]

Another important term was *union*, although Taylor never adopted a perfectly consistent definition of it himself. At first he claimed that the term was never used to describe a combination of individuals, and, therefore, would not have been used if the Constitution had instituted a consolidation. The choice of the word itself demonstrated the clear intention of the Framers to continue the limited sort of government begun under the Articles. Later Taylor was forced to admit that *union* could have various "inexplicit" meanings, including "a perfect consolidation."[53] Since *union* was an ambiguous term, however, it could not be used to justify consolidation any more than it could be used to defend federalism. To determine the meaning of *union* in its American context, therefore, one must abandon conventional usage and return to its use at the political birth of the country, when separate and independent state sovereignties were acknowledged most clearly.

Although the Constitution had laudably fostered union among the participants in the federal compact through Article 1, Sections 8 and 10, and the Tenth Amendment by uniting states against foreign aggression, preventing geographic conflicts among states, and drawing a plain line of demarcation between the states and the federal government, the separate states still existed as independent sovereignties.[54]

The word *federal* was also a crucial term; it had been borrowed from international usage and referred to a joining together of independent sovereignties for some specific and limited purpose. "The federal is not a national government; it is a league between nations."[55] "It implies a league between sovereign nations, has been so used by all classes of people from the commencement of our political existence down to this day."[56] It would have been inappropriate for any of the equal partners to such a union, or for the artificial partner created by the American Union, to interpret its power so as to nullify the prerogatives of the superior equal partners.

In the light of this understanding of *United States, union,* and *federal,* the three purposes of the Union could be understood and, once understood, preserved by popular support. The Union was, first of all, intended to form and maintain a compact, as evidenced by the guarantee of a republican form of government to free and independent states whose powers were reserved in the Tenth Amendment. Second, the Constitution was intended to organize a government, limited by the terms of the compact. Finally the Union did intend to allow the federal government to establish laws relating to individuals (a view that Taylor originally seems to have rejected when Edmund Pendleton urged it upon him in 1788), but only within a framework delegated by the states.[57]

Taylor's understanding of the nature of the Union allowed him to reject quickly many of the arguments for consolidation current in his time, which interpreted constitutional clauses relating to the "people of the United States," "posterity," federal powers over land, and supremacy of federal laws and treaties.

He claimed, for example, that the Union had been a compact between the states as nations and not the act of a combined American people voting for convenience in states that served as geographic districts. The Constitution itself had recognized this when it talked of securing liberty for a "posterity." Taylor thought pieces of territory could not have posterity, refusing to recognize that a combined American people could have posterity even though voting in districts. Even though states were people in a basic sense, they retained control of their territory. The federal government, consequently, did not have the necessary powers for a truly national control over the country's land. It could not, for example, alter a county, incorporate a town, divide a state, or acquire land without state consent.[58] The Marshallian doctrine of supremacy was explained away by Taylor in the following fashion: even though it was true that the Constitution was supreme, it was supreme over the acts of *both* the states *and* the federal government, and neither had the authority to judge the extent of power of the other under the Constitution. Taylor claimed that this interpretation had been the clear intention of the Framers, because they had rejected Edmund Randolph's "national" plan in favor of one that placed the "supremacy" of the Constitution in its place.[59]

Taylor did not spend much time on the less frequently used arguments for consolidation that drew on clauses relating to federal power over the District of Columbia, the guaranty of a republican form of government, or the argument that calling the Framing Convention had dissolved the states as political bodies. The unlimited power over the District of Columbia, for example, was a specific exception and a clear example that this grant of power was for limited and special purposes only. The republican form guaranty imposed a duty on the federal government but did not convey any powers other than those explicated in the Constitution. In fact, the Constitution said that the "United States," and not their creation, the federal government, guaranteed a republican form. How this guarantee would be implemented Taylor did not say, although he may have looked upon the guaranty as simply the duty to protect states from invasion. As for the argument that the 1787 Framing Convention dissolved the states, the action of that body in returning its product for state review was the most effective refutation of this notion.[60]

G. Distribution of Authority

Taylor never specifically listed the respective powers of the federal and state governments, probably because he thought that the powers of the first were limited to the express provisions of the Constitution and the powers of the second were unique to each state and too numerous to list. Also, Taylor's opposition to the transfer of property by law led him to a severely limited conception of what *any* government should do. Even though the federal government was limited by express provisions and the spirit of the Constitution, still, only the people of states were sovereign. Neither state nor federal governments should pass legislation favorable to particular groups.[61]

Although he provided no complete discussion of the allocation of powers between the state and federal governments, fragments provide some indication of what Taylor thought. The "necessary and proper" clause was important. "Necessities are, strictly, things unavoidable," but as governments became larger, whims became necessities and all sorts of internal concerns, such as local legislation, roads, food production, and manufacturing, became necessities, "because there is nothing [to] which war, commerce and taxation may not be closely or remotely connected."[62] Actually, *necessary* should have been interpreted only so as to implement the powers listed in Article One, Section Eight of the Constitution: *necessary* was the Framers' way of saying that Congress was limited to the expressly delegated powers. Since it was unthinkable that the Constitution would favor one level of government over another, the "necessary and proper" clause introduced a rule of reason by which to judge the constitutionality of federal activities, even when they were directly derived from expressly delegated powers. Thus federal power was limited by the spirit of the Constitution, which supported the purpose of strong and independent states; the expressly delegated powers itemized in the Constitution; and by judgments whether the exercise of a delegated power, even though for purposes sympathetic to independent states, was necessary.[63]

The clauses that dealt with the "common defense and general welfare" were also interpreted in a restrictive manner by Taylor, who insisted that the phrases did not convey unlimited powers and that the terms *common* and *general* were clear indications that actions taken under this authority could not primarily benefit individuals.[64]

On the powers of land acquisition and ownership, Taylor's views were less clear. There was no doubt in his mind that the states had possessed complete powers over land before the Constitution's adoption. Yet in 1803 he argued that a combination of the treaty and war powers gave the federal government the right to acquire lands not already within the boundaries of the United States. Later he maintained, as has been seen, that the states controlled the territory of the United States, and their separate territories could not be carved up into new states, or be transferred to federal ownership, without their consent.

The meaning of the commerce clause was derived by Taylor from its specific context: foreign nations, Indian tribes, and commerce among the states had been united in one article, because federal commerce power touched all of them equally. If it could not regulate the internal affairs of foreign nations or Indian tribes, it could not interfere in the domestic concerns of individual states. Even in this limited sense the commerce power could not justify activities designed to favor one occupation or region by levying burdens on others. Congress's power of taxation (and Taylor expected most uses of the commerce power to be a type of taxation) was limited: there could be no direct taxes without apportionment, no export taxes at all, and no preferential treatment given the ports of any single state.[65]

His interpretation of the goals of the commerce power resembled pre-Revolutionary doctrines that Parliament could regulate trade but not tax for revenue: he admitted that foreign nations must be discouraged from obtaining unjust advantages over the United States. The federal government must be able to mount an appropriate response. It must also be able to prevent geographically advantaged states from exploiting their locutions at the expense of other states. The power to regulate commerce among the several states, therefore, was an exclusive power of the federal government, and not concurrently shared by any state. Taylor's first reaction to the *Gibbons* v. *Ogden* decision was that it supported him by adopting the view that roads and canals were internal, and thus reserved completely for the regulatory action of the states. Taylor was mute on the nationalistic concurrence of Justice William Johnson (Jefferson's first court appointee) in the *Gibbons* case.[66]

The taxation power and the power to suppress insurrections

were coordinately possessed by the state and federal governments, but all other powers in the Constitution were distributed on an exclusive basis to one or the other. This meant that neither the federal nor state governments could nullify the taxing powers of each other. Taxation was the life's breath of government that sustained its existence. In a federal system it must provide an independent souce of revenue by separating tax bases, thereby providing a means for resisting the encroachments of federal or state power. Taylor eagerly identified with the state of Maryland's contention in *McCulloch*, even though that side's argument had been ruled unconstitutional. He did not suggest how the decision should be reversed.[67]

Continuing his discussion of concurrent tax sources, Taylor boldly attacked the "power to destroy" argument by pointing out that a tax for revenue (e.g., Maryland's tax on the Bank of the United States) was not an attempt to destroy the federal government. If any tax became oppressive there were regular parliamentary and electoral procedures for correcting it. Besides, what *was* a power in the federal government to categorically abolish a state tax, if not a power to destroy? The argument that the federal government could not rest easily with the knowledge that states could destroy it was entirely spurious: states could also destroy it by not electing Senators. Like it or not, the federal government had to trust the states, and if it could do so with the election of Senators it could also do it with concurrent tax sources.[68]

As with all delegated powers, a federal tax had to be scrutinized for its actual incidence and real purpose before Taylor was willing to judge its constitutionality. Most critics of the protective tariff, for example, were at a loss for constitutional arguments to use against it, because the federal government could unquestionably levy imposts. Taylor never allowed an important issue to rest on the shaky grounds of popularity, subject to the disposition of a majority. To Taylor, if a practice was wrong, it must be pronounced *constitutionally* wrong, in order to demonstrate that the principle was without institutional footing in American values. He attacked the tariff as a direct capitation tax, an export tax, and a bounty for certain ports, all of which were forbidden by the Constitution in clear language.[69]

Thus, Taylor's view of the distribution of authority between the federal and state levels of government used the Constitution's common-sense meaning at the time of ratification merely as a point of departure for such additional limitations as whether an action was "necessary," whether it interfered with the states' control over territory, whether it regulated their internal activities by claiming they were commerce, and whether it violated Taylor's particular version of concurrent taxation.

H. Clashes and Concurrent Powers

In giving precedence to the supremacy of the Constitution and denying the ability of any branch of either the states or federal government to construe the relationships established by the union, Taylor was led to a discussion of the inevitability of clashes between members of the federal system. This clashing could and did occur throughout the American system of divided powers, he maintained, but only disputes arising between the federal and state governments were publicized by con-solidationists. To say that the American system of government provided no way to guard against accumulations of power in the hands of a few, required that the system must return to the people for organic change every time a dispute arose between departments of government. Taylor was never one to object to organic change, but even he found too frequent a resort to it inconvenient. Nor was he willing to admit that enlightened framers of the Constitution would have established such an unwieldy procedure.

A clash between state and federal powers arose when both simultaneously taxed, regulated, or otherwise touched the same object with legislation. In Taylor's opinion, neither level of government was forbidden from passing or administering constitutional laws. The existence of a rivalry would not emasculate the federal government, Taylor argued, because it could still exercise all legal federal powers, including partial jurisdiction over individuals. After all, state officials had sworn the same oath to protect the Constitution as federal ones, and, therefore, could not obey unconstitutional laws, whether they were state or federal. The creators of the Constitution "refused to invest the federal legislative, judicial, or executive departments, with a negative over state laws or judgments, and relied upon the mutual control of political departments . . . for its preservation."[70] Neither level could review the actions of the other, but both were subservient to their interpretation of the Constitution.

If an occasional clash resulting from the simultaneous exercise of state and federal powers was the price of a federal system, Taylor thought it a small one to pay. He was confident that any unbiased view of American history would agree that American unity would not have been weakened if federal banking and lottery laws had been unenforceable in two states. Both the state and Federal levels had kept the Constitution "in a vast majority of instances," and had acted moderately. In fact, "mutual moderation is . . . the general effect of our system, and occasional excess an inconsiderable exception."[71] This mutual moderation was the result of the system of divided powers and various beliefs that were part of that system, such as the moral equality of states and the deference or "sympathy" shown to each level of government by the other. The same moderation that marked the system of divided powers during harmonious times would be an important reserve in times of disagreement. If Congress passed a law that was unconstitutional in a state's judgment, that state must refuse to obey the law. The ensuing clash of opinion could be settled only by reason and discussion.[72]

Despite Taylor's assurances that clashings of power would occur infrequently, any casual examination of how he divided authority among the federal and state governments reveals such a limited conception of federal power that frequent clashing would have resulted.

Taylor's construction of the Constitution turned it into an inverse hierarchy of powers, all of which reinforced state powers and downgraded federal power. The Union was merely an extension of the revolutionary Confederacy, and federal power had been limited because it was delegated. This limitation had been explicated by the reservation of powers to the states in the Tenth Amendment. The limitations on state powers found in the Constitution were merely evidences of the powerful nature of the states: they were so strong that they had to be limited. In Taylor's opinion, then, the powers of states were vindicated both by the sections of the Constitution that recognized these powers and by the sections that limited them.

The results of constitutional limitations on state power were three classes of powers: one exclusively federal, one exclusively state, and one exercised by both. In the case of a dispute over whether one or other levels could exercise a particular power, "we have only to discover whether a state or federal act conforms to its classification, and not whether the exercise of one power is inconvenient to another."[73] The federal government's limitations actually helped preserve its powers, because its exclusive powers were expressly stated and difficult to challenge, while the general powers of the states were fair game for the advocates of a consolidation.

Concurrent powers might be looked on as "spheres" Taylor said, adopting Marshall's analogy, and, like a solar system, needed balance, discipline, and restraint. The notion of a "sovereignty of the spheres," however, was mischievous. Both the federal and state governments were limited in the sense that only the people were sovereign. Since the people of each state formed an entire political entity or "nation," sovereignty often wore a provincial costume. In actuality, however, there was a comparable sympathy for the federal government. Thus, if either level passed a law that eroded the sympathy shown by the people for the other level, the law in question had broken down the wall of division between federal and state powers. Taylor considered it thoroughly possible that such a law might be within the literal power of the level that enacted it, but if the effect of the law was to break down federalism, it was as unconstitutional as if it had been specifically forbidden.[74]

It can be seen from this discussion that Taylor interpreted the Constitution as flexibly as his most inventive Federalist enemies did, with the difference being that the presumption was always in favor of a state power as far as Taylor was concerned. "If words are to be tortured or borrowed, let it be done to sustain, not to subvert the essential principles of our political system; if we continue to love that, which other nations admire."[75] Where Marshall or Hamilton used a common-sense definition of terms such as *necessary* to enlarge federal powers, Taylor used the inverse construction: if a federal power would not have withstood a common-sense agreement by the Framers that it was explicitly permitted, it was proscribed. Thus, the question to be asked regarding the bank was not whether regulation of currency could be conveniently achieved through a special-purpose corporation but whether the bold statement that the federal government could create corporations would have been permitted by the Framers. Under this method of construction, if a federal law was wrong in *spirit* it was unconstitutional, even if it used constitutional means. This was not strict construction, but the Federalists's flexible construction turned back on them.[76]

I. Summary and Conclusions

John Taylor's theory of federalism was built upon his conviction that federalism was the natural result of economic interests, local attachments, state pride, and other influences that had created cultural differences among states. He did not however, offer a deterministic theory of the origin of federalism, but continued the Enlightenment's approach to political problems, which had characterized his intellectual background, had allowed his acceptance of ideological parties, had formed the basis for his theory of the development of aristocracies, and had permitted his belief in the persuasive power of republican principles to mobilize fragmented governmental structure into a system of divided powers. Instead of considering federalism the predetermined result of such natural causes as geographic size or economic differences, Taylor insisted that the system's adoption was an act of will that put the natural differences among states to work in the service of federal union. Natural causes had some influence, but they were not the whole story. Taylor stood in the ebb tide of the Enlightenment, and he still maintained that man could accept or reject those forces as he wished.

In keeping with the fact that Taylor considered the adoption of federalism to have been an act of will, he stressed a variety of advantages which had resulted from it. He pointed out to the unconvinced that federalism helped control and moderate the exercise of power by dividing the size of the spoils among the partners to the Union. He also said that federalism allowed regular channels for governing remote parts of the Union, which under any other system would have required the use of force. Moreover, the operation of state governments served to filter internal discontents so that they did not become countrywide in their effects. Finally, Taylor looked benevolently on the experimentation with republican forms of government, life-styles, and human rights that federalism would allow. He drew the line, however, at most experiments in the positive use of governmental power to cure environmental and economic ills.

The legacy of Locke and the other social compact theorists presented Taylor a difficult problem, which he responded to with his concept of nation. It is possible that the ratification of the Constitution appeared to those nurtured on social compact theories as a tangible example of one. The salient aspect of this compact had been the creation of the federal government, and it may be that Taylor resented the featured place this government received. If so, Taylor's concept of nation served well to put the social compact a historic step back from 1789, thereby placing state nations in the position of having been the original American contracting parties. The people of a region, sharing similar life circumstances, had formed little societies or "nations." These nations were also called "states," but were not to be confused with the state governments that nations had established later for their convenience and protection.

Considered in this light, Taylor was not able to read much meaning into the term *sovereignty*. He rejected the idea that any government had ultimate power, and since he did not believe there was any such thing as an American nation, by implication he also destroyed the possibility of any sovereignty of the United States according to international law terminology.

John Taylor carried his presumption of state superiority into discussions of the distribution of power among the partners to the Union. Whenever he could interpret the Constitution to amplify the power of states, he did, hence his interpretations of such terms as *United States, posterity, commerce among the several states,* and *common defense and general welfare.* When the words of the Constitution failed him as a source of support for state power, he rose to the challenge and insisted that the spirit of sympathy and mutual understanding among the partners to the Union was the higher purpose of the Constitution, which even the expressly authorized powers must reflect.

There is much that is incomplete in Taylor's theory of federalism. He was more willing to leave loose ends than a rigidly systematic theorist should be. Three of the most important difficulties in his ideas on federalism were his doctrine of nations as social compacts, his near-acceptance of the logic of Adams's system of balanced powers, and the ambiguity of his notion of clashing governments.

Nations were Taylor's answer to the social compact, but he merely ignored the problem of obligation that had concerned most other theorists of the social compact. The relation of the individual to the nation and the mechanisms that might be used to ensure the aggregation of individual wills into a national interest were almost totally ignored by Taylor, and he completely ignored speculation on the conditions and procedures that might justify the reassertion of an individual's right to self-government and the dissolution of political society. If an individual withdrew, would it return all men to anarchy? The answer seems to be that Taylor never really believed that there had been any sort of historical compact: he often qualified a discussion of the concept with adjectives giving the impression that he thought the notion outdated or imaginary. Nations were at least partly the products of social and economic conditions, which formed the only building blocks popular sovereignty had to work with. Drop-outs from the social compact could not occur if the compact was fictional. Had Taylor truly examined the problem of obligation and consent in his doctrine of nations, he might have been forced to reexamine the county court system of state and local government in Virginia, the virtues of which he often extolled, and the practices of which violated nearly every aspect of his system of divided powers. Yet, his view of the compact that formed the Union was one that left a greater place for consent and choice.

As the growth of American federal power increased through congressional and judicial actions, Taylor more and more came to accept the inevitability of clashes between the states and the federal government. His 1814 *Inquiry* had been full of criticism of John Adams, who had allegedly posited a system based on the assumption that men were rotten to the core and that their vice and aggressiveness could be controlled only by balancing off the jealousies of one group against another. Instead of this, Taylor offered divided powers, an attempt to demonstrate that virtue and cooperation could form the energizing force for a governmental system. Taylor never lost his faith in cooperation and virtue, but he came to have a greater respect for competition between the two levels of government after 1820.

In part this change in attitude may have resulted from the fact that between the *Inquiry* (1814) and *Construction Construed* (1820) the decisions in *Martin* v. *Hunter's Lessee, McCulloch* v. *Maryland, Dartmouth College* v. *Woodward,* and *Sturges* v. *Crowninshield,* along with the 1816 Protective Tariff Act and the Missouri Compromise, had all been handed down.[77] Taylor may well have wondered whether these assertions of federal power did not call the efficacy of cooperation into question. By 1820 he had accepted clashing between states and the federal government as an inevitable consequence of divided powers and had even read it back into the intentions of the Framers. Although he still denied that he had accepted checks and balances (because he had placed sovereignty in the people and not in any governmental agency, thereby dampening the jealousies of competing departments), the impression lingers that he expected clashes to occur fairly often. His strictly limited conception of the powers of the federal government would have precipitated clashes without end.

The final difficulty with Taylor's theory is the indeterminate rule that governed the process of clashing between levels. He hoped that clashing would not occur, but if it did, it did. At that stalemated level Taylor left the matter. Barring a change of heart by one or the other of the clashing governments, or a constitutional amendment, no resolution was possible. In the absence of any supreme authority to interpret the Constitution, each department followed its own interpretation. Taylor proposed no general rule for handling these disagreements, and considered instead that the Union and the federal idea were both big enough to contain such diversity.

The ambiguity and reluctance to press for some sort of resolution to state-federal controversies were demonstrated by Taylor's theories and actions during actual situations when states and the federal government were in disagreement. For a better understanding of how Taylor applied his tolerance of clashing to actual situations, and for an appreciation of the purposes he saw for the Union, an examination of his reactions to dangers to the Union is necessary.

Notes to Chapter 5

1. *Inquiry,*, pp. 413–15.

2. Ibid., p. 646. Also see *Argument,* p. 7; Neal Riemer, *James Madison* (New York: Washington Square Press, 1968), pp. 36–38.

3. *Inquiry,* p. 252; *Construction,* pp. 57–58, 300–302; *Tyranny,* p. 340; *New Views,* pp. 240–41, 288.

4. "Remonstrance to Congress Regarding the Indifference to the South's Plight," reprinted in *Tyler's Quarterly Historical and Genealogical Magazine* 12: 39–41.

5. Letter from John Taylor to Edmund Pendleton, May 4, 1777, in Hammond, pp. 1–2; letter from Taylor to Pendleton, November 17, 1777, ibid., pp. 2–4; to Cap. William Woodford, May 12, 1775, Carter Family-Sabine Hall Papers, University of Virginia, Charlottesville.

6. Letter from John Taylor to James Mercer Garnett, June 28, 1806, William Garnett Chisholm Papers, Virginia Historical Society, Richmond; *Tyranny,* pp. 231–32.

7. *Annals of the Eighth Congress, First Session* pp. 99–101, 114–16, 180, 183–84; *Construction*, pp. 18–19; *New Views*, p. 266.

8. Ibid., p. 183.

9. *Construction*, pp. 18–19; *Tyranny*, p. 266.

10. *Argument*, p. 7.

11. *Construction*, p. 18.

12. *Tyranny*, pp. 36–38. Also see discussion of capitalism in chap. 3 above.

13. *New Views*, p. 262.

14. *Annals of the Eighteenth Congress, First Session*, p. 387. Also see *Construction*, p. 103; *New Views*, pp. 187, 246, 250, 262.

15. *Definition*, pp. 10–11; letters from Taylor to Wilson Cary Nicholas, June 14, 1805; May 14, 1806; October 26, 1807; Edgehill-Randolph Papers, University of Virginia Library; letter from Taylor to Jefferson, June 25, 1798; *Annals of the Eighth Congress, First Session*, p. 188; Taylor, *Arator*, p. 44; *Inquiry*, pp. 84, 158, 169, 189, 209, 213, 600; *Construction*, pp. 22, 40, 62, 95, 274.

16. John Taylor, "The Necessities, Competency, and Profit of Agriculture," *Niles Weekly Register*, Supplement to nos. 2, 3, 15, n.s. (November 7, 1818), p. 179.

17. *Definition of Parties*, pp. 4, 13–4; letter from John Taylor to James Monroe, May 10, 1812, in "Correspondence," pp. 336–39.

18. *Journal of House of Delegates*, 1797 (Richmond: Augustine Davis, Printer, 1798), December 16, 1797.

19. *An Argument on the Constitutionality of the Carriage Tax*, pp. 20, 23; letter from Taylor to Henry Tazewell, June 13, 1797, Tazewell Papers, Virginia State Library, Richmond; *Enquiry*, pp. 13, 21, 24, 54, 90.

20. Letter from John Taylor to Thomas Ritchie, April 7, 1809.

21. Examples of this use of *nation* may be found in the following: letter from Taylor to Thomas Jefferson, June 25, 1798, in "Correspondence," 271–76; *Enquiry*, pp. 3, 27; letters to Thomas Ritchie, March 24, 1809 and March 27, 1809, in Stanard, pp. 14–15, 20; letter to Monroe, March 18, 1812; *Inquiry*, pp. 39, 50, 162, 166–67, 171, 178, 205, 207, 210, 214, 215–16, 222, 230–31, 245; *Construction*, p. 186; *Tyranny*, pp. 15, 27, 54, 165.

22. *Inquiry*, pp. 171, 177, 412, 415–16 417.

23. Ibid., p. 424.

24. Ibid., p. 449. Also see pp. 171, 419.

25. *Tyranny Unmasked*, p. 250. Eighteenth-century thinkers, especially Jefferson, commonly believed that earth belonged to the living and that the latter had the right to use the earth as they saw fit. Taylor's concept of *nation* may have been an attempt to translate this respect for the current generation into a more institutionalized form. Taylor believed that each generation was likely to have the same attitudes, however, while Jefferson once thought that a revolution once in a generation would not be a bad thing. Jefferson did not expect, then, that generations would share attitudes. See Adrienne Koch, *The Philosophy of Thomas Jefferson* (Chicago: Quadrangle Books, 1964), pp. 140–41.

26. *Tyranny Unmasked*, pp. 71, 125; Taylor, *Arator*, p. 24.

27. *Tyranny Unmasked*, p. 295. Also see p. 237.

28. *Construction*, p. 119. Also see *Tyranny*, pp. 249, 293.

29. *Inquiry*, p. 413.

30. Ibid., pp. 504–5.

31. Ibid., pp. 571–72. Also see *Argument*, p. 16; letter from John Taylor to Henry Tazewell, March 24, 1794, Tazewell Papers, Virginia State Library.

32. *New Views*, p. 9. Also see *Annals of the Eighteenth Congress, First Session*, p. 684; "A

Letter on the Necessity of Defending the Rights and Interests of Agriculture," *American Farmer*, 3 (July 20, 1821): 133; *Construction*, p. 242; *Tyranny*, pp. 65–66; *New Views*, pp. 13–15, 98, 162, 194–95.

33. *Construction*, p. 171.

34. *New Views*, p. 6.

35. *Construction*, pp. 189, 235–36; *New Views*, p. 13.

36. *Annals of the Eighteenth Congress, First Session*, p. 684. Also see *New Views*, pp. 93, 175, 191, 224.

37. *Construction*, p. 235; *New Views*, p. 286.

38. *Construction*, p. 25.

39. *Argument*, pp. 16–7; *Enquiry*, p. 43; *Annals of the Eighteenth Congress, First Session*, p. 563.

40. *New Views*, p. 9. Also see p. 36.

41. Ibid., pp. 37, 171–177, 182, 189, 208, 213, 226, 232, 244; *Construction*, p. 142.

42. *Construction*, p. 42. Also see pp. 47–48, 304; *Argument*, p. 29; notes from Taylor to James Madison, [1799?], Madison Papers, Library of Congress.

43. Letter from John Taylor to James Monroe, January 2, 1812, in "Correspondence," p. 328; *Inquiry* pp. 395, 489–90, 503–6, 511, 571–72; *Construction*, p. 60; *New Views*, pp. 259, 329.

44. *New Views*, p. 231. Also see p. 89.

45. *Construction*, p. 47.

46. *New Views*, p. 96. Also see p. 200.

47. *Enquiry*, p. 55. Also see letter from John Taylor to Thomas Ritchie, March 27, 1809; *Argument*, pp. 28–29.

48. *Debates in the House of Delegates of Virginia, Upon Certain Resolutions Before the House* (Richmond, Va.: Thomas Nicholson, 1818), December 20, 1798; December 21, 1798.

49. *Construction*, p. 143.

50. *New Views*, p. 174.

51. *Construction*, pp. 45–46, 57, 144.

52. Ibid., p. 42. Also see pp. 94, 107.

53. Ibid., p. 43.

54. Ibid.; *New Views*, pp. 1–2, 37, 263.

55. *Construction*, p. 234.

56. *New Views*, p. 6.

57. Ibid., p. 136.

58. Ibid., p. 98.

59. Ibid., pp. 17–18, 20–23, 189, 290.

60. Ibid., pp. 185; 207; 226; 234.

61. *Construction*, p. 74.

62. Ibid., pp. 168–70.

63. Ibid., pp. 165–66.

64. *Construction*, p. 164; *Enquiry*, p. 6.

65. *Annals of the Eighth Congress, First Session*, pp. 50, 53; *Tyranny*, p. 189.

66. *Annals of the Eighteenth Congress, First Session*, pp. 563–64; *Gibbons v. Ogden*, 9 Wheaton 1; Randolph G. Adams, *Political Ideas of the American Revolution* (New York: Barnes and Noble, Inc., 1958), pp. 91–100.

67. *Construction*, pp. 153–54, 163, 165, 219; *Tyranny*, p. 189.

68. *Construction*, pp. 150–52.

69. Ibid., pp. 91, 93, 96, 150–51, 163–65, 221–22.

70. *New Views*, p. 151.

71. Ibid., p. 250.

72. *Construction*, pp. 158, 171; *Tyranny Unmasked*, pp. 168–69, 321; *New Views*, pp. 150, 244.

73. *New Views*, p. 275. Also see *Construction*, p. 55; *New Views*, p. 155.

74. *Construction*, p. 99; *New Views*, p. 265.

75. *Construction*, p. 140.

76. Ibid., p. 168; *New Views*, p. 267.

77. *Martin* v. *Hunter's Lessee*, 1 Wheaton 304; *Dartmouth College* v. *Woodward*, 4 Wheaton 518; and *Sturges* v. *Crowninshield*, 4 Wheaton 122.

6

DANGERS TO THE UNION

TAYLOR'S theory of federalism made it easy for him to accept situations in which state and federal powers conflicted and neither side was willing to back down. Full appreciation of his easygoing acceptance of these "clashing" situations can only follow an appreciation of what he considered even more dangerous threats to the Union.

Among these dangers were the utter impracticability of consolidation, the possibility of civil war built upon a base of sectionalism, and state-federal clashes over the interpretation of the Constitution. The first two of these were grave dangers, but the third Taylor viewed as an opportunity as well as a danger.

A. The Danger of Consolidation

The dangers to the Union that Taylor thought were being fostered by the policies of the federal government have been mentioned in previous chapters. They included the disunifying effects of political parties interested in patronage, and the selfish activities of various other elite groups that were seeking economic goals. He had a grudging respect for the unerring accuracy with which these groups had struck at the very parts of the Constitution that had been written to secure the common interests of the states. For example: banks had usurped the

Notes for this chapter begin on p. 233.

taxing power, road appropriations had been based on the war power, gratuities had made the power to appropriate money a virtual lottery among competing groups, and monopolies had resulted from the power to regulate trade and the authority to admit new states. The four essential principles of American liberty had been violated by these practices: no longer were state constitutions the act of the people; three-fourths of the states were no longer the judge of whether the Constitution should be amended; the definite division of powers between the states and the federal government had been abolished by the latter's ability to construe "state rights" to its own advantage; and finally, the independent right of a state to its own revenue source had been. nullified by the decision upholding the Bank of the United States.[1]

The ultimate dangers of the consolidated form of government to which these measures were bringing the United States were both individual and political. Individually there would be an increased tendency to take property from those who had created it and distribute it to those who had not. Politically the results would be the opposite of those which consolidationists intended. If the federal government gained the power to distribute rewards and immunities to promote economic activities it would become the sole redresser of grievances. Congressional proceedings would no longer be moderated by the filtering influence that the representation of state interests in state governments provided. In a consolidation local interests of the most parochial variety would stride the halls of Congress demanding satisfaction. No aggregation and compromise between interests would be provided. Under a consolidation the only standard of success for Congressmen would be their ability to secure favors.[2]

Consolidation in the United States would always be an impossible solution because of the natural causes of federalism. If a consolidating conspiracy had won in the 1787 Framing Convention, Taylor argued, it would have found only that it could not have obliterated the local interests established in the various regions of the country by nature. The great variety and dispersion of economic interests throughout the states would make it impossible for consolidationists to favor one interest without favoring one section. The favoring of one section would breed envy among the others. The country would tend to become three great regions, divided along sectional lines. Local dissatisfactions would accumulate to the point where they would be uncontrollable by laws and judgments and require the attention of a mercenary army.[3]

Those who debated these arguments against consolidation by pointing out that Congress was not preoccupied with the local affairs of the District of Columbia, refuted themselves, in Taylor's opinion. If a Congressman who lived one-half of every year in the District of Columbia neglected that city, how could he be expected to legislate intelligently for remote sections of the country in which he had no personal interest? Moreover, Taylor warned the residents of small states, although the large states had been magnanimous so far with their smaller counterparts, in a lottery of selfishness the large states could not remain on the sidelines. Their ambitions would be excited, and the small states would surely be swallowed.[4]

It was obvious to Taylor that a consolidated republic could not exist in a country as large and varied as the United States, although the constant erosion of private property might prevent a truly republican federal system from being successful as well. Even in a consolidation the natural tendency of men was to favor what was dearest to them. In a consolidation, Congress would be the country's city hall and the battleground for all its interests. Consolidation could never exist long under such circumstances; in the long run it would dissolve into anarchy and, following that, tyranny.

Even though the efforts of consolidationists and aristocrats were doomed to eventual failure, they posed a quiet threat to the present Union in another way. As the federal government ventured into more and more publicized activities, the attention of the people would be directed to it and they would forget the value of states. The assault on state rights, moreover, always hit one state at a time and was noticed by hardly any others. The activities of state governments were mundane, if important, and did not attract attention. States protected rights, solved crimes, promoted good manners, and administered municipal regulations, while ambitious men drove the federal government into more exciting activities. Taylor offered the example of road projects, which some were urging the federal government to begin: if states could not be trusted to build their own roads, it was questionable whether they could be trusted with anything. If state governments were to be viable units, they must have activities comparable in importance to those of the federal government. The only solution for this problem that Taylor could find was to cut back the federal government's size until it was more comparable to that of the states.[5]

B. The Danger of Civil War

No discussion of John Taylor's thoughts on the dangers to the Union can ignore the question of his attitude toward civil war. No other states' rights theorist came so close as he to defending both the possibility of some form of nullification and the ultimate right to resort to force. John Randolph and Alexander Stephens considered nullification an absurdity, but secession merely the mid-nineteenth-century version of the right to revolution so cherished by the patriots of Lexington. Calhoun, on the other hand, attempted to formulate nullifying procedures for guaranteeing the existence of sectional minorities, which would make civil war unnecessary. Taylor flirted with both doctrines, but adopted only the rhetoric of each.[6]

John Taylor's conviction that the American Republic was an experiment in republicanism that had never before or since been duplicated had important implications for his discussion of civil war. Much of his discussion of the superiority of the American nation emphasized its uniqueness and argued that former governmental systems were inapplicable to the United States. He did not doubt that the old countries of Europe watched the United States with envy and attempted to put provocateurs among the people of the United States in order to overthrow the country. These foreign countries could never have devised such beneficial institutions. The American nation had been appointed by God to spread the true doctrine of free, inexpensive, mild government; it was the Switzerland of the world.[7]

The founding of the American nation, however, had followed a bloody civil war, which he never hesitated to use for moral precedent. This revolution had been legitimatized by the Declaration of Independence, which Taylor considered a constitutional document of binding authority. In his view, the Declaration had established independent and legally equal states, joined together by some common interests, fellow-feeling, and little else. Taylor thought that the Revolution had been a civil war caused by economic exploitation, harsh taxation without consent, and the envy of England. He did not ignore the detrimental economic effects of the Revolution, and he did not attempt to glorify it as a crusade even while fighting in it, but its symbolic value remained a keystone of Taylor's appeals to men of whose opinions he was uncertain.[8]

The Revolution remained the great unifying symbol for the American people at least through the first two decades of the nineteenth century. As such it lent credibility to any cause that could use it as an appeal. The right of revolution, moreover, was deeply rooted in the conventional wisdom of this period. It had been recognized in the *Federalist Papers*. So honored was it as late as the 1830s that Martin Van Buren succeeded in having President Jackson amend his nationalistic 1832 proclamation on the South Carolina nullification ordinance by supporting the right of revolution in a newspaper essay published the following year. American revolutionary appeals were especially well suited for Taylor, who may have fallen prey to the habit of reflecting on his youth during his December years and whose authority on public issues was undoubtedly enhanced by frequent reminders that he had been a revolutionary patriot. Even Thomas Ritchie deferred to Taylor on this basis during their bitter 1809 exchange. Finally, it also may be that Taylor's continuing reference to the American revolution was a poignant hint. Such civil wars, he may have been warning, were the natural consequence of discriminatory economic policies.[9]

But whether this was a threat on Taylor's part or simply a word to the wise, it is evident that he endorsed neither civil war nor disunion. He thought the right of revolution unworkable, unreliable, and often mischievous. "Tumulity [turbulence], it was known, only served to invite a repetition of injury" he counseled his fellow Virginians even during the hot debates over the Alien and Sedition Acts in the Virginia General Assembly[10] He denied in later writings that states had the constitutional power to maintain any sizable armed force or the military and diplomatic authority to deploy it. He recognized that the Articles of Confederation had been a compact between state governments, and were therefore less stable than the Constitution, which was a compact between the states-as-people. Even though he warmly supported an occasional healthy clash of powers between the federal and state governments, he feared any situation that would force people to choose between their loyalty to the federal government and their loyalty to their respective state governments. "I earnestly hope that the ever-to-be-avoided contest will never occur."[11]

Only in the stormy years of the Adams administration did Taylor ever flirt with the idea of secession, and then it was suggested as a theoretic possibility, mentioned in passing without endorsement. He also once suggested in an early pamphlet that, if a Federalist majority ignored the Constitution and interfered with a state majority's prerogatives, an individual had the obligation to interpret the Constitution for himself and refuse obedience to the government. It was at this same time that Taylor refused the offer of Rufus King and Oliver Ellsworth to lead a Southern attempt to dissolve the Union, so he himself was not ready to refuse obedience to the federal government. Refusing by force of arms was an even more extreme position and did not play a part in his thinking that time or any other.[12]

Hypothetical prophecies of civil war and violent strife were often used by Taylor as arguments against governmental features he opposed, but in these discussions he was expressing his opinion of what might happen, not what he wanted to happen at all. The possible causes of civil war were many, in his view, and they included many of the defects of the federal government mentioned in previous chapters: financial burdens, state differences in interests and manners, and defects in federal governmental structure. Less tangible factors, such as the loss of public spirit in Congress, the increasing jealousy between North and South, and the refusal to defend the literal meaning of the Constitution were all forces for civil war.[13]

The nearest that Taylor ever got to a doctrine of civil war was his concept of a state right of self-preservation. Comparing this alleged right with civil war might be incorrect, because Taylor explicitly rejected the type of sectional wars that most twentieth-century Americans would associate with civil war. Taylor's endorsement of civil war seemed to be limited to a justification of a state-by-state defense of the territory of each if invaded by federal troops. It was strictly an attempt to defend state territory against an invading army.

During the debates over the Virginia Resolutions in December 1798, Taylor explicitly denied that the Republicans were taking the first steps toward the civil war. War could not happen, *unless* Congress should attempt to control public opinion by force. The entering of a state by federal troops could be justified only if a state had invoked the Constitutional clause guaranteeing protection for a republican form of government. In his later works Taylor continued to deny that the federal government had any legal authority to coerce states by force, because similar sanctions had been proposed in the 1787 Philadelphia Convention and had failed to carry. At the same time he often mentioned a state's "natural right of self-defense."[14] It is probable that Taylor's concept of a state right to self-defense was derived from the standard right-to-revolution argument as it was understood at the time. Even James Madison in his later, most nationalistic years admitted that such a right must be upheld.[15]

Taylor's advocacy of a militia as a protector of the rights of the people who had organized themselves into nations has already been discussed. Nations and a strong militia were closely linked in Taylor's system of divided powers. Taken alone, the importance Taylor gave to the militia could be considered an example of his willingness to accept the possibility of civil war. It cannot be questioned that the existence of militia forces provided the means for civil war that standing armies would not have. Considered in the context of his time, however, Taylor's acceptance of the militia was quite ordinary. Virtually all of his contemporaries gave at least lip service to the advantages of the militia. Their common admiration was based more on a fear of standing armies than on any expectation that the militia would be used in civil wars. As was seen in an earlier chapter, Taylor's hatred of the cost of armies probably took precedence over any fear of their power. Although he did not discount their power entirely, he generally considered paper and patronage aristocrats more dangerous than military ones.[16]

Some commentators have seen the threat of civil war in Taylor's discussion of the state right of self-defense found at the end of the chapter on the Missouri question in *Construction Construed*. A recent interpretation of this passage has suggested that Taylor was referring only to the right of each state to deal independently with domestic strife, such as slave revolts.[17] This localistic focus of the right of self-defense may have been Taylor's main emphasis, but it does not adequately explain his statement in the same passage that, by the right of self-defense "nations are justified in attacking other nations, which may league with their foes to do them an injury. . . . they are justified, if they see danger at a distance, to anticipate it by preparations.[18] Pressed to the extreme, preemptive warfare may have been among the arsenal of defenses a state could bring to bear in order to ensure its own domestic tranquillity. The militia provided the tangible means for a state to defend itself. Indeed, Taylor's doctrine of state self-preservation seems to have taken the place in his three later works that had been previously occupied by the militia; little specific mention of the state right is made before 1820, and the militia is seldom mentioned after the *Inquiry* and *Arator*.

The right of self-defense was a mutual one, given both to states and to the federal government. Such a balance of terror may seem inconsistent with Taylor's previous warnings on the dangers of competitively balanced departments, but the ambiguity was removed when Taylor went on to say that this division of physical power was a symbol of trust given by each level of government to the other. Unlike balanced powers, parallel systems of arms were not intended for use.[19]

By dividing the military power of the country in this matter, the Constitution gave explicit consent to its use for maintaining state existence and implicitly denied that the Supreme Court could take by inference what the rest of the federal government would have to fight for. This dual military power was safe, because it had never been the intention of the Framers that it should be used: "The states have retained a right to defend themselves, if invaded by a federal army, because the constitution was not to be construed by force."[20]

In summary, John Taylor's views on civil war were phrased in the language of an aging revolutionary who worried that the policies of the federal government were bringing the country to the brink of a violent disaster that was completely avoidable. Among with other members of his generation, Taylor talked of a right to state self-preservation, but limited its application to occasions when states were being invaded or when invasion was imminent. Resort to civil war was not, therefore, a tactic recommended by Taylor in any but the most extreme circumstances, circumstances that most of his contemporaries would have agreed justified the use of force.

C. The Danger of Sectionalism

There is much evidence that Taylor personally was no sectionalist. There is no evidence that he had much familiarity with any part of the South below northern North Carolina, and his impressions of that region were collected as a moon-struck bachelor in the 1780s. He recognized his deficient knowledge of the South by refusing to give specific advice on agricultural systems except in the Virginia-Maryland tidewater regions. Although he permitted himself some uncomplimentary remarks about the Northern mercenary armies during the Revolution, and took a few swipes at Calvinism in a scorching reply to an arrogant letter written to him by Timothy Dwight in 1805, he seemed personally free otherwise of any bias against Northerners. Evidence of this is provided by a letter written a few months before his death to a fire-eating granddaughter who had written him that she hated Yankees: "But you should hate nobody. May it not be better for me to make a speech on their side, if they are endeavoring to cure the Ladies of their love of finery . . . ? It often happens that we change our opinions, and heartily repent of them."[21] What if she met a rich young Yankee bachelor, and someone slipped him her letter! Taylor did more than refrain from hating Northerners himself: he defended their life-style and apparently did not even care if his granddaughter married one.

Even though his own resentment against policies supported by some Northerners did not harden into sectional bias, Taylor became more and more alarmed over the growth of sectionalism after 1814. The Constitution had been written, Taylor thought, with an eye to the possibility of sectionalism and had included the limitations on interstate compacts as a means of thwarting such a development. Yet the combination that had agreed to the settlement of the Missouri question was nothing more than an informal interstate compact, forbidden by the Constitution. The Missouri Compromise institutionalized the balancing of power that the *Inquiry* had criticized. Its result would have been to divide the country into two parties worse than those which had warred against each other in England because of the "hideous feature of being geographical."[22] There was nothing wrong with a section's enjoying honestly acquired pecuniary advantages, but the manufacturing states were luxuriating as a consequence of the transfer of property. Not only were their benefits ill-gotten, but they had tainted honest professions by bribing the wool and hemp farmers with tariff protection. The West, Taylor warned, would be foolish if it did not recognize that the sectional hatred of the South being fomented by Northerners was for the latters' own advantage.[23]

New Views, Taylor's last book, spoke strongly against the evils of sectionalism. Using the analogy of Swift's *Tale of a Tub*, Taylor likened the North to Peter, who wished to decorate his father's coat with spangles such as the protective tariff and internal improvements; the Southern sectionalists to "mad Jack," whose "disorganizing fury" wanted to rip his father's coat into pieces; and men in the middle to Martin, who tried to save the coat by simplifying it without damaging the fabric. Taylor obviously considered himself in the last category.[24]

In attempting to discourage the sectionalism that he feared was bringing civil war, Taylor was hindered by the chronic problem that the only remedy he ever offered for the defects of the American system was the purified operation of that system. Thus, the only cure he could offer for sectionalism was federalism: "it is now demonstrated that geographical combinations founded in a similarity of interests, are the evils in the future to be apprehended."[25] Yet federalism had not proved sufficient to discourage the development of sectionalism in the first place.

D. The Danger of Clashes in Interpretation

Even though Taylor supported the right of individual states to forcibly resist a federal invasion of their territory, this was not his preferred defense for the federal system. After all, he had offered federalism as the cure for civil wars caused by sectionalism; the normal operation of the system could hardly have relied upon the condition it was designed to prevent. The ultimate weapon, which he sometimes called the "moral" right of self-defense, or "mutual vetoes," was discussed in passages that were hammered into a different shape to suit the purposes of Calhoun, the great nullifier.

Taylor's proto-nullification doctrines were founded in his claim that the states had the constitutional authority to defend their territory, and in his firm belief that the supremacy clause had only moral sanction. "It is a moral and not a personal supremacy which is established."[26] All parties to the Union and its creatures, even federal judges, were entitled to interpret the

Constitution, but none of their decisions was binding on the others without a return to the original parties for a resolution of conflicting opinions:

> Opposition must therefore be constitutional. They [states] may even oppose armies to armies. Why then may they not array laws against laws, and judgments against judgments? This is the very remedy contemplated by system compounded of co-ordinate and divided powers, against wars with guns and bayonets.[27]

Both the federal government and the state governments, therefore, could interpret the Constitution, but neither could interpret it with binding force for the other. The ability of states to interpret the Constitution did not have to be specified in the document, because it was a product of reserved powers. The states had been careful to avoid such itemizations of power lest the inference be drawn that only the powers mentioned were reserved. Nonetheless, Taylor urged, states had the power to interpret the Constitution.[28]

Taylor stretched his imagination to argue for the legality of this moral right of self-defense, claiming that Alexander Hamilton's *Federalist* essay "Number Twenty-eight" must have been referring to such a power when it mentioned the capacity of state legislatures to discover federal usurpations: why discover usurpations if states were impotent to correct them? After all, the states had been the contracting powers behind the Constitution, and the power to create could be the power to destroy if that consent were withdrawn. Whether this withdrawing could be done by a single state, or only by all of them in the amending process, Taylor never made clear.[29]

To defend the federal government's enforced supremacy of the Constitution under the premise that any excesses created by the practice would be corrected by the "American people" was hogwash to Taylor. The American people could not mobilize to make their opinions known in any way except through an unruly mob, and a state legislature's enactments were preferable to that.[30]

Instead of emphasizing each state's individual ability to withdraw its consent to the federal union, its right to forcibly resist, or even its ability to pass laws in conflict with federal laws it considered unconstitutional, Taylor stressed the amending process to the Constitution as a regular corrective procedure when federal and state power clashed. From his earliest works on, Taylor considered a responsive amending process the truest guard against civil war, and he advocated its use to solve state-Federal disagreements.[31]

This use of the amending process, however, was given some unique characteristics. Taylor's conception of states as individual nations required that he also make room in his theory of federalism for the possibility of dissent by individual states. The reserved powers of the states were not aggregated: each state exercised those which had relevance to its own traditions and needs, which may or may not have been the powers important to other states. Conflicts between the reserved powers of all states and the federal government, therefore, would not often happen. Seldom would more than one state have a conflict over a single issue with the federal government, and the very state differences that made federalism desirable would make a flocking of other state's to the dissenter's defense unlikely. In practice, this meant to Taylor that a state could continue a practice that clashed with the federal government's interpretation of the Constitution as expressed in a law or a court decision until two-thirds of the membership in Congress decided that the state's activities should be controlled by a constitutional amendment. The state's activities did not nullify the federal government's, nor did one state's expression of opinion necessarily mean that any other states would agree with it. It simply meant that, when disputes arose over constitutional interpretations, both the states and the federal government would have the authority to judge the meaning of the Constitution separately and their judgments could be overridden only by a formal constitutional amendment.[32]

Taylor's experience with the Virginia Resolutions suggests that he also thought clashing could occur through a mere declaration of disagreement with federal practices. It is, of course, true that Taylor was not primarily responsible for the wording of the resolutions that he ushered through the Virginia House of Delegates in the winter of 1798-99, but his *Enquiry* (1794) had anticipated this process when he proposed using state legislatures for "explanations of the constitution, according with its spirit—its construction when adopted—its unstrained construction now—and with republican principles."[33] Moreover, a letter written by Taylor during the summer of 1798 might well have been the stimulus that led Jefferson to think of using state resolutions in the first place. "The right of the state governments to expound the constitution, might possibly be made the basis of a movement towards its amendment," Taylor had said in the letter, and he suggested that if that did not work, then the states could proceed to amend the Constitutions by using the state conventions that had been the contracting agents to the Constitution, "and possessing the infringing rights, may proceed by orderly steps to attain the object." Although Taylor's opinions turned against his own advice for some reason during 1798, he was reconvinced of the advisability of state resolutions by Wilson Cary Nicholas in the fall of 1798.[34]

A similar use of state legislative resolutions had been made the previous year, and Taylor had participated in this. The issue involved was the indictment of Congressman Samuel Jordan Cabell under the Sedition Law for communications with his constituents that Federalists found objectionable. A resolution critical of this indictment as a violation of separation of powers was proposed, but debate broke out over whether a state legislature was authorized to make constitutional judgments about the federal government. Taylor voted to censure the court's action against Cabell, but voted against sending the resolution to the United States Senate, demonstrating his conviction that a state legislature was wholly competent to make an independent judgment on the constitutionality of a federal action against a federal official.[35]

The Virginia Resolutions were a similar experiment, founded in the belief that Congress had overstepped its constitutional bounds in passing the Alien and Sedition Acts, because they could be used to smother any sort of dissent. As Taylor explained to Jefferson:

> it was my project, by law to declare the unconstitutional laws of Congress void, and as that would have placed the state and general government at issue, to have submitted the point to the people in convention, as the only referee.[36]

When pressed during debate on the Virginia Resolutions on why they did not take the form of a proposed amendment or of a call for a constitutional convention, Taylor stated that his faith in public opinion was so great "that he doubted not but that the two reprobated laws, would be sacrificed to quiet the apprehensions of a single state, without the necessity of a convention."[37] He refused to accept the criticism that the Virginia Resolutions might end in civil war, insisting that such a drastic measure was not intended and would not follow. The worst that could have happened was that Congress would have ignored the petition of Virginia and not repealed the Sedition Act. In that eventuality, three-fourths of the states might be forced to call a convention. It seems likely, from Taylor's firm statement, that he intended to both force the issue of the Sedition Act and then decide its constitutionality in a general convention. Yet he was personally responsible for stripping the Virginia Resolutions of any language that could be interpreted as substituting the law of Virginia for federal law. Taylor himself moved to strike the phrase *and not law, but utterly null, void and of no force or effect*[38] from Madison's draft of the Virginia Resolutions. It is clear from an explanation of his intentions that he later offered to Madison that he did not believe that the Virginia Resolutions were an attempt to nullify federal law:

> that the state governments neither created nor can abrogate the federal compact, and that the people of the states did create, and may abrogate it [no one doubted] . . . nothing could have been more unimportant . . . than to announce that the people of the states were parties to the constitution. Every body acknowledged it.[39]

If the Virginia Resolutions were examples of Taylor's doctrine of moral self-defense for states, the mechanism that would keep federalism alive and the passions of sectionalism subdued, several generalizations can be made about the doctrine. It neither involved the use of civil war nor did it even necessarily have to lead to an amendment. It is obvious, however, that Taylor hoped that usually it would lead to Congress's changing its mind, and, failing that, a convention and amendment. He probably meant to use the processes provided in the Constitution for calling a convention, but a 1798 letter to Jefferson said that three-fourths of the states could call a convention if Congress ignored the Virginia Resolutions. Since under the Constitution only two-thirds of the states needed to petition Congress to have a constitutional convention called, Taylor may have been referring here to the original constituent majority of the Union. He may, of course, merely have confused the procedures. If he was proposing an extra-constitutional route for amending the Constitution, his doctrine was quite radical. It implied that the states retained their abilities to function as separate agents after the Constitution had been ratified, and outside the processes established by it. If Taylor intended such a novel theory of amendment, he never elaborated it after this 1798 letter.[40]

The event in American history that most closely paralleled the Virginia and Kentucky resolves was the Hartford Convention. Taylor did not approve of it and looked upon it as an attempt to destroy the Union. Even he, however, could not ignore the similarity between it and the events of 1798-99, and he admitted the similarity by maintaining that the opposition to the Sedition Act had been worth the Hartford Convention.[41]

E. Summary and Conclusions

John Taylor was able to accept the clashing of opinion between states and the federal government because he thought that such disagreements were preferable to the other dangers that threatened the Union.

The danger of consolidation found Taylor developing a theory that allowed him to claim that he was only trying to save the aristocrats from themselves. In his opinion the interests and cultural differences that had made the creation of nations so natural would cause trouble after a consolidation was formed. Such local interests would not go away but would demand satisfaction at the highest levels of government. Every petty interest would become a national problem. Consolidation, therefore, was a self-deception on the part of those who hoped to institute the British system of balanced orders in the United States: in a country as large as the United States, civil war and probably despotism would be the inevitable consequences of trying to administer everything from Washington. Believing that the alternative to a stout resistance of unconstitutional laws by states was a short-lived consolidation, Taylor considered the inconveniences arising from confrontations between the state and Federal government a reasonable price to pay for the preservation of freedom.

Civil war was feared by Taylor, yet he insisted on a concurrent power over arms by the federal and state governments. This was necessary so that each government could moderate its ambitions in light of the means of resistance possessed by the other. Although Taylor's frequent references to the American Revolution or to the possibility of civil war may tend to give him the appearance of approving of violence, he did not. The nearest he ever came to approving of civil war was in his state right of self-preservation doctrine, but even there the violence would have been confined to the defensive use of state forces to repel territorial invasions by federal troops.

Sectionalism was a great danger, in Taylor's opinion. He often warned against it and did not qualify his criticism by any attempt to put sectionalism to work in his theory. Instead, he rejected all sectionalism, whether of the Northern or Southern variety. Why he objected to it is a difficult question. After all, the three major sections of the country seemed to share the characteristic that he had considered essential for the creation of nations: homogeneity of economic, geographic, and cultural conditions. Probably his refusal to accept sectionalism arose from complex motives that included a simple love for the state system and his place in it as a Virginian, a desire to keep governmental power as small and close to the people as possible, and a conviction that the sections were being formed were the result of aristocratic transfer of property.

What Taylor called the moral right of self-defense or the ability of both the state and federal governments to interpret the Constitution to suit themselves, was the only republican alternative Taylor could think of when faced with a choice among consolidation, civil war, sectionalism, or some form of tyranny. He recognized that a concurrent power to interpret the Constitution would result in inconveniences, but he accepted it nevertheless.

This concurrent power of interpretation must be acknowledged in retrospect as the half-step toward later nullification doctrines, because it opened for question the actions of the federal government and suggested that there was some other course of action open for a state than submitting to federal actions it considered unconstitutional. On the other hand, it is apparent that Taylor's ideas of this moral right may owe much to the general climate of opinion of his generation, which accepted the right to revolution as a matter of course. When both Taylor and James Madison agreed that the republican theory of natural rights demanded an alternative to tyranny outside the confines of governmental structure, one may assume that there were men in the wide gap between these two who also shared this belief. Moreover, in practice, Taylor's conception of the concurrent ability to interpret the Constitution relied heavily on either constitutional procedures, such as the amending provisions, or harmless procedures, such as mere declarations of disagreement. In either case Taylor was willing for the judgment of a single state to be reviewed by the judgments of two-thirds of Congress and three-fourths of the states. He trusted in the basic reasonableness and fellow-feelings of men to suspend noxious federal measures voluntarily, if they could just be shown the error of their ways.[42]

The concurrent ability to interpret the Constitution, then, would often result in a difference of opinion to be settled by popular actions within the confines of the Constitution itself. As Taylor said to Madison, he never assumed that the Virginia Resolutions promoted the idea that state governments could abrogate the Constitution or the federal compact. In a letter written before the debate over the Virginia Resolutions, Taylor spelled out his plan for implementing them, which included: passing an act to secure freedom of debate in the legislature "by aid of the habeas corpus"; extending that same act's coverage to all Virginia citizens; approving the Kentucky Resolutions; compiling an anthology of the Virginia, Kentucky, and habeas corpus acts; and distributing ten-to-twenty thousand of these anthologies to stimulate popular discussion of the issues involved in the Alien and Sedition Acts.[43]

It is apparent, thus, that the Virginia Resolutions were not intended as a means of nullifying the Alien and Sedition Acts. Taylor himself had seen that language to that effect was removed from Madison's draft. Nor did the Virginia Resolutions have to lead to an amendment of the Constitution.

Taylor did not say whether he thought that state laws that contravened federal actions, or mere appeals to reason such as the Virginia Resolutions would be the most frequently used method for checking the centralization of government at the federal level. It is apparent, however, that whichever one of these devices was used, concern for the preservation of the Union and the supremacy of the Constitution as he interpreted it, were Taylor's higher purposes. Ultimately he was willing to surrender a state's solitary judgment to the review of its fellow states and the Congress. The Union was worth more to Taylor than a single state's opinion. The procedure for reviewing a state's opinion was very cumbersome, but it was based on the literal words of the Constitution and therefore provides a glimpse at what a Union without Marshall might have been like.

Taylor's system thus far is coherent. His ideas on political parties are meaningless without knowledge of his impressions of aristocracies and his attribution of rational malevolence to them. The misdeeds of aristocrats, moreover, led him to discuss the constitutional devices necessary to control them, and to finally decide that only federalism was sufficient to preserve republicanism. Not only did federalism scatter governmental power, but it made this power easier to watch by keeping in being institutional devices for correcting abuses.

Ultimate moral and philosophic questions emerged at each level of this system, and it will become clear in the next chapter that Taylor discussed governmental practices only to create the kind of atmosphere in which man's use of reason could be used to explore the productive use of nature to sustain a shared existence with friends and companions.

The struggle to preserve constitutionalism was not, therefore, a hollow one, but a struggle for the freedom from restraint that was necessary to pursue more important goals.

Notes to Chapter 6

1. *Construction*, p. 215; *Tyranny*, p. 285.

2. *New Views*, p. 247.

3. *Ibid.*

4. *Construction*, pp. 224; *New Views*, pp. 207, 247, 262; *Tyranny*, pp. 333–34.

5. Letter from John Taylor to Thomas Jefferson, June 25, 1798, in "Correspondence," p. 271; *Construction*, pp. 107, 284; *Tyranny*, p. 165; *New Views*, p. 203.

6. Alan P. Grimes, *American Political Thought* (New York: Henry Holt and Company, 1955), p. 285; Russell Kirk, *John Randolph of Roanoke* (Chicago: Henry Regenery and Company, 1964), pp. 76, 94.

7. *Argument*, pp. 26–27; *Enquiry*, p. 49; *Defence*, p. 136; letter from Taylor to James Monroe, March 12, 1812; Taylor, *Arator*, pp. iii–iv; *Construction*, p. 2; *Tyranny*, pp. 251, 345.

8. Letter from John Taylor to Captain William Woodford, May 12, 1775, Carter Family-Sabine Hall Papers, University of Virginia Library, Charlottesville; *Argument*, p. 7; *Enquiry*, p. 22; *Tyranny*, pp. 33, 185–86; *Construction*, pp. 13, 19, 52, 54, 56, 62, 70; *New Views*, pp. 2, 36; *Annals of the Eighteenth Congress, First Session*, pp. 600, 682.

9. Merrill D. Peterson, *The Jefferson Image in the American Mind* (New York: Oxford University Press, 1962), p. 60. See Hamilton's "No. Twenty-Eight" and Madison's "No. Forty-Six" in *The Federalist*.

10. *Debates in the House of Delegates upon Certain Resolutions Before the House* (Richmond, Va.: Thomas Nicholson, 1818), December 20, 1798.

11. *Construction*, p. 156. Also see p. 43; *Argument*, p. 4; *New Views*, p. 156.

12. The threats to secede came in letters from Taylor to Henry Tazewell, June 13, 1797 and July 1, 1798, Tazewell Papers, Virginia State Library, Richmond. The first mentioned disunion as a preferable alternative to monarchy.

13. Letters from John Taylor to James Monroe, March 25, 1798 and April 29, 1823, in "Correspondence," pp. 268–70, 348–53; *Argument*, pp. 4, 23–29; *Definition of Parties*, pp. 3, 5; *Construction*, pp. 68, 233; *Tyranny*, pp. 282, 299; *Annals of the Eighth Congress, First Session*, pp. 99, 115–16; *Annals of the Eighteenth Congress, First Session*, pp. 251, 564.

14. Letter from John Taylor to Henry Tazewell, June 13, 1797, Tazewell Papers, Virginia State Library; *Argument*, p. 4; *Debates in the House of Delegates*, December 20, 1798; *New Views*, p. 291.

15. Neal Riemer, *James Madison* (New York: Washington Square Press, 1968), pp. 179–80.

16. Samuel P. Huntington, *The Soldier and the State* (Cambridge, Mass.: Harvard University Press, 1959), pp. 166–69.

17. Keith M. Bailor, "John Taylor of Caroline: Continuity, Change, and Discontinuity in Virginia's Sentiments toward Slavery, 1790–1820," *The Virginia Magazine of History and Biography*, 75 (July 1967): 290–304.

18. *Construction*, p. 314. The "danger at a distance" argument is quite close to *Federalist* "No. Twenty-Eight" and "No. Forty-Six."

19. *New Views*, pp. 71, 233.

20. *Ibid.*, p. 233.

21. Letter from John Taylor to Lucy P. Taylor, February 22, 1824; Virginia Historical Society, Richmond. The letter to Dwight followed the latter's scornful reply to an earlier letter from Taylor, which had suggested that Northern and Southern students should study in each other's homelands in order to foster national unity. Letter from Taylor to Timothy Dwight, September 3, 1805, "A Sheaf of Old Letters," in David Rankin Barbee, ed., *Tylers Quarterly Historical and Genealogical Magazine*, 32 (October 1950): 82–84. Letters from Taylor to Henry Tazewell, April 13, 1796 and June 13, 1797, Tazewell Papers; letter to James Madison, June 20, 1793, in "Correspondence," pp. 254–59; *Cautionary Hints*, p. 8; letter to Thomas Jefferson, June 25, 1798; letters to Wilson Cary Nicholas, March 5, 1804 and May 28, 1804, Edgehill-Randolph Papers; *Defence*, pp. 44–47; letter to Monroe, February 22, 1808, in "Correspondence," pp. 291–94; letters to George W. Jeffreys, March 4, 1818, and October 28, 1818, in *American Farmer* 2 (February 9, 1821): 366, and (February 23, 1818): 380.

22. *Construction*, p. 292. Also see pp. 236, 295–96; *Inquiry*, p. 294.

23. *Construction*, pp. 18, 231, 236, 291–96; *Annals of the Eighteenth Congress, First Session*, pp. 677, 686; *New Views*, pp. 188, 287.

24. *New Views*, p. 315.

25. Ibid., p, 85.

26. *Construction*, p. 123; *New Views*, p. 163.

27. *New Views*, p. 71.

28. Ibid., p. 255.

29. Ibid.

30. *Tyranny*, p. 263; *New Views*, pp. 70, 187, 274.

31. *Enquiry*, p. 65; *New Views*, pp. 137, 249.

32. Ibid., pp. 255–56.

33. *Enquiry*, p. 65.

34. Letter from John Taylor to Thomas Jefferson, June 25, 1798. Also see Sarah Nicholas Randolph, "The Kentucky Resolutions in a New Light," *The Nation* 44 (1887): 382–84.

35. *Journal of the House of Delegates,* 1797 (Richmond, Va.: Augustine Davis, 1798), December 28, 1797.

36. Letter from John Taylor to Thomas Jefferson, December 18–21, 1798, in "Correspondence," p. 278; *Debates in the House of Delagates*, December 13, 1798.

37. Ibid., December 20, 1798.

38. Ibid., December 21, 1798.

39. Notes from John Taylor to James Madison, [1799?].

40. Letter from John Taylor to Thomas Jefferson, February 15, 1799, in "Correspondence," p. 280.

41. *Construction*, p. 296; *New Views*, pp. 216–17.

42. Riemer, pp. 178–79.

43. Letter from John Taylor to Henry Tazewell, December 14, 1798, Tazewell Papers.

7
AGRARIANISM AND SOCIETY

The theory of divided powers, built as it was upon faith in reason and the creative power of man to shape his environment, was the supporting structure of Taylor's whole system of thought. Taylor devoted most of his writings to the evils of aristocracy, which the division of powers was intended to prevent through correct governmental structure, electoral processes, and belief in Republican principles of government. A characteristic feature throughout the aspects of his writings considered in preceding chapters was his unwillingness to put the faith he had in man's creative ability to work in constructing a detailed prescription for governmental reform.

The reason Taylor refused to pin his faith on the manipulation of governmental structure was that he considered government to be a means to the general goal of a harmonious society of productive individuals, and not a substitute for that goal. Since the general goal of an agrarian society was within reach, elaborate tinkering with governmental structure was unnecessary.

The story of the eighteenth century's love affair with the cult of nature has been too well told by Carl Becker and Ernst Cassirer to require detailed repetition here.[1] Briefly, the Enlightenment broke the connection between theology and science by substituting natural concepts for theological categories. Thus, a future state of harmony between men was the substitute

Notes for this chapter begin on p. 259.

for salvation, virtue for grace, a remote Prime Mover or Author of Creation for God, and nature and her laws for the authority of church and Scripture. These concepts were popularized by the interpretations of the social implications of Newtonian physics that received such wide distribution during the eighteenth century. Through Newton's popularizers, nature was seen as a matter of apples and prisms. The laws governing such ordinary objects were within the grasp of even ordinary men. Nature provided a medium in which man's mind could interact with the process of God. Where Newton and Descartes had begun with the description of natural processes through their careful erudite mathematical formulae, the crowd soon followed with a descriptive science of nature that had no time for mathematical proofs.

This descriptive phase of the Enlightenment seems to be that most characteristic of Taylor and his contemporaries. Their vision of a harmonious society that would achieve a natural equilibrium if man would simply stand out of the way gave them comfortable, if modest, substitute for utopia. Moreover, their very way of life lent urgency to their interest in nature: for John Adams, Jefferson, Randolph of Roanoke, and Washington, agriculture was both hobby and vocation. (For Madison and Monroe it had the importance of a vocation but was more often treated as a hobby). This fascination with the laws of nature may explain Taylor's reluctance to offer grand plans for the reform of government: the perfection of government was not the point. The study of nature and the application of this learning to man's well-being was, and if agrarianism were allowed to flourish, everyone benefited.

A. The Economy of Nature

The Enlightenment view of nature, as discussed by Daniel Boorstin, is well represented in Taylor's agrarian writings. The view of nature accepted by Taylor and the other members of Jeffersonian Circle stemmed from the conviction that all life was bound together in an unbroken chain, in which each link had a function related to the whole, no link had ever been duplicated, and no link had ever passed from existence. As Boorstin points out, Jefferson confidently expected that the mammoth fossils exhibited in Peale's museum would be verified by living specimens when the interior vastness of the American continent had been fully explored.[2]

Although Taylor did not doubt that man could force nature's hand (for example, tyrants could "raise cities in deserts"), he thought that the most productive course was to allow nature to be the guide.[3] When one followed nature, he came to realize that agriculture began the productive efforts that later made technological innovation and urbanization possible. If nature was the guide, agricultural methods must be as varied as nature's circumstances. Taylor never thought that the specific details of even his most successful agricultural experiments would have much application beyond the boundaries of Virginia and Maryland. His application of this attitude toward nature sometimes actually prevented advances in agricultural science. In describing the types of vegetable cover suited for different soils, for example, he pointed out that each type of soil must have a cover suited for it: "the entire vegetable creation must contribute towards sustaining this hypothesis, or it must fall."[4] He also traced stomach ailments to the immediate cause of improper diet, and he rejected the notion that minerals could be worthwhile soil additives because they were located below the earth's surface instead of on top, where the Creator put what He wanted used as manure. Although Taylor rejected the belief common in his time that swamps should not be drained because they provided the atmospheric elements needed for plants to breathe, he justified drainage with the argument that the Author of Creation would not have left man the choice of breathing swamp air or eating bad food.[5]

Although Taylor tried to apply the laws of nature, when he could not apply them he put his faith in the inventiveness of man to provide for himself. Thus, even though nature had given crops and stock such as tobacco and sheep, both of these were hardly worth raising. Moreover, nature's real bounty could be wasted if man did not attentively manage it. Diligent efforts could provide a surplus that rewarded the cultivator. Included in these diligent efforts were tools, houses, labor, and fertility. Three of these required human effort exclusively, and human effort could improve the fourth, fertility, through the use of enclosing.[6] Dramatizing the fact that Taylor was less wedded to the economy of nature than some Jeffersonians was the fact that

Taylor did not believe that the mammoth was still living. His chain of being had some closed links.[7]

The key to Taylor's system of agriculture, therefore, was his belief in the sufficiency of nature to provide when she was aided with a little ingenuity. For the farmer the most important element in nature was the atmosphere, not the soil. The soil was only as rich as the atmospheric nutrients it contained, but it was not the only source of these nutrients. Both the air itself and the vegetables that drew nutrients from air were sources of nutrients for crops. The vegetables would return nutrients to the soil as they decomposed. All such dressings for the soil Taylor called "manure": "Manure is vegetable matter, and of course vegetables are manure."[8] To use these vegetable sources of nutrients, Taylor advocated "inclosing" or plowing under successive covers of various plant types in order to build up, over a course of years, a residue of rich nutrients. "The system of inclosing, [is] to manure the earth by its own coat of vegetables."[9] The United States had wasted nearly three-fourths of the manure that the earth had provided for them, largely through the use of the three-shift system, which rotated Indian corn, wheat, and pasturing on the same plot. The first two crops extracted much from the soil without adding anything, while the pasturing of animals merely beat the ground flat, diminishing the surface area exposed to atmospheric nutrients. Deep plowing under vegetable cover and the four-shift system were each a partial salvation for the injured land.[10]

Other agricultural panaceas favored by Taylor may have caught his eye because of their close relationship to natural processes. The most important of these reforms was the practice of "live" fencing: the substitution of cedar hedges for wooden or "dead" fences. For live fences Taylor saved his most ecstatic prose, and it does not overstate the case to say that live fences were as important to him as all other agricultural and political reforms. "Throughout the world, countries enclosed by stone or live fences, and those enclosed by dead wood, exhibit the contrast between cadaverous decripitude and blooming youth."[11] Wealth, national strength, and liberty resulted from the use of live fences, because they did not need constant repair. Labor would be saved that could be diverted to enclosing, the destruction of crops by straying animals would be stopped, and the loss of these wandering animals would be eliminated. If apple trees were added to the cedar, live fence rows could also provide a beverage better for the drinker than liquor. The labor saved was considerable, because Taylor estimated that ten percent of the average planter's time was spent on fence repair: thus, the use of live fences would free thirty-five days a year which could be spent on the intricacies of inclosing. As a bonus, the wood formerly used in dead fences could be plowed under and become another type of manure.[12]

Overseers and sheep had little place in a system of well-managed agriculture. Each violated the laws of nature. Taylor's renunciation of each was important. Overseers were not rejected for their treatment of slaves, but because they were commonly paid on a commission basis. This led to hit-and-run professional attitudes, causing them to do what they could to produce fast bumper crops without regard to the exhaustion of the soil. After ruining a farm, they moved on. Sheep ruined farms not merely because of their grazing habits, but because an economy based on them led to industrialization and ruined agriculture, as England's legislation protecting the wool industry demonstrated. The South would be better off if it could do without all sheep except the number necessary to satisfy a taste for mutton. "It may be owing to this animal that the independence of one country is almost overthrown, and of the other tottering."[13] and it would have been better to trade with England for wool than to turn American cornfields into sheep pastures.

Seen from the perspective of following nature, Taylor's hatred of overseers and sheep made sense. The first ruined nature's bounty with get-rich-quick exploitation, and the other resulted in governmental interference in natural agricultural processes. Yet, by limiting entrepreneurial incentives and limiting the South to cotton as the chief cash crop, Taylor was helping preserve the homogenous economy on which Southern "Mad Jack" sectionalism was based.

In brief, Taylor summarized his system of agriculture as the channeling of natural laws into courses beneficial to humans through the application of three virtues: *liberality* in giving back to nature what she had provided, *foresight*, and *unduplicated effort*.[14] Examples of the application of these virtues included, respectively: unstinting use of manure; use of the four-shift system; and use of live fences rather than the constant repairing of wooden ones.

B. Agriculture and the Good Life

Although natural forces were persuasive guidelines for Taylor as a farmer, the ultimate significance of agricultural life for him did not lie in a slavish copying of nature out of some sense of mystical obligation, but rather in the value that property had for those who owned it.

He thought that love of property was a wholesome passion that could be channeled to form the basis of the good society. This was true for several reasons. Even though he acknowledged that the social compact and the popular sovereignty on which it was based were valuable (if fanciful) concepts for visualizing the respective obligations of government and the people, the people had not given up everything in the name of popular sovereignty. The social compact had stopped short of property rights. The taking of private property such as land, money, and the purchasing value of money for private purposes was never justified, although the use of taxation for social purposes could be. The owners of property would be more active participants in republican processes because they had something at stake, and their watching of government would keep it honest. Property owners would favor the classic processes of civility, such as the rule of law, sanctity of contract, and stable government. At the same time they would recognize appeals to these virtues that were really masks for tyranny, special privileges, and governmental experimentation.[15]

The protection of property was of importance to individuals because the creation of its value was an individual matter: "Gain can never arise out of nothing. . . . It must therefore be the product of labour, and labour only; and that which produces the gain, must of course bear the loss."[16] Wealth could be properly looked upon as surplus labor. Taylor gave assent to Locke's theory that labor created value, that this labor was an individual matter, and that individuals who had contracted into society for greater benefit would not have given either that society or its government the power to usurp what it had been formed to protect "As nature compelled man to acquire in order to exist, his acquisitions from his own labour are his property, according to the law of his maker; since man must have existed before society."[17]

Taylor did not believe that labor applied to land was necessarily the only way the honest property was created, and he proclaimed his love for the other productive interests of society, among which he numbered manufacturing, commerce, and crafts. Of all the kinds of property, however, land was the most reliable producer of wealth, and its successful cultivation was the best encouragement for all other productive enterprises. Most of the property that was produced was made possible by agriculture. The return of investment that land yielded, however, was not the most important reason for being a farmer.[18]

The enjoyment of property allowed an individual to gather satisfaction from his life in a manner that simultaneously improved him physically, psychologically, and intellectually, while it produced goods of value to society. Moreover, the profession of farming did not unduly penalize the individual of humble origin, the orphan who acquired six plantations assured. Cultivation required healthy labor, which improved the body.

It also provided psychological gratification, because it required the fitting of ideas to substances, of substances to ideas, "and a constant rotation of hope and fruition. The novelty, frequency and exactness of accommodation between our ideas and operation, constitutes the most exquisite source of mental pleasure."[19] Men were stimulated to industry through this process, and their knowledge was increased by their use of new methods to increase their property. Even though these technological innovations might be devised by the more intelligent, they could be put to work readily by the ignorant, preventing the growth of agricultural elites. Unlike other realms of human endeavor, new agricultural knowledge could not be hoarded, possibly because the results of this knowledge were very visible as successful harvests.

The attempt to make a fortune through agriculture improved one morally, also. Both agriculture and the Divinity had as purposes the feeding of the hungry, the clothing of the naked, and the giving of drink to the thirsty. Thus, agriculture constantly reinforced the moral virtues, which were the "passports to future happiness":

> the divine intelligence which selected an agricultural state as a paradise for its first favourites, has again prescribed the agricultural virtues as the means for the admission of their posterity into heaven.[20]

It should be noted that this passage, which has been offered as an outrageous example of Taylor's love for farmers, favored the *virtues* promoted by agriculture, and not farmers to the exclusion of any other group. These virtues were, as mentioned before, liberality, foresight, and unduplicated effort.

Moreover, Taylor argued that agricultural property could not be abused as other kinds of property often had been. With agriculture one could never take time out to plot the downfall of someone else: agricultural property had to be used or be lost.

Property that did not have these characteristics did not deserve the name of property or the protection of government. The abolition of primogeniture and entail laws in the states had prevented the growth of a landed monopoly, and similar legislative actions should be taken against any other form of spurious property that threatened to become a monopoly, for example, funding of the state debts or the various monetary activities of bankers. "All societies have exercised the right of abolishing privileged, stipendiary or factitious property, whenever they become detrimental."[21] The only encouragement that should be offered to private property holders by government was security in their possessions when these possessions fulfilled the beneficial purposes of property.

Even though Taylor had supported the abolition of feudal land laws and had advocated the limitation monopolistic corporate property such as the Bank of the United States, he always based his arguments in a defense of true kinds of property against the encroachment of these false kinds. He specifically rejected all sorts of leveling doctrines and claimed that aristocrats would have been happy with the strong governments that property redistribution would require. William Godwin's doctrines, offended Taylor in particular, because Godwin had argued that a division of property, not power, was necessary. Taylor thought Godwin should have recognized that a division of power was the only way to safeguard individuals in their justly acquired property. Actually, both levelers and paper aristocrats were cut from the same pattern: each wished to transfer property by law, and each needed the existence of the other to frighten people into supporting them. Leveling philosophers should have distinguished useful and pernicious kinds of property, instead of proposing methods for sharing all of it. Instead, they had so tainted the concept of property that many young men had come to hold it in contempt and had not developed the attitudes necessary to support contracts. Since most civil rights were measured by money, such a young man "tramples upon most. . . . he cannot live by rules he hates and breaks. He who dissipates his property, dissipates also his virtue and honor."[22] Leveling and financial speculation should both be rejected, because they advocated an artificial distribution of property. True general well-being was achieved only through the free competition of productive enterprises that harnessed the base passion of selfishness and turned it toward productive activity.

Unless monopoly was threatening, Taylor urged that the enjoyment of property not be censured. Needs called productive industry into existence, and they had to be gratified occasionally or industry flagged. This was one important criticism of the tariff: by limiting the luxuries that were imported, personal incentives to produce were whittled down.[23]

Although the enjoying of property might seem a variety of hedonism and an encouragement of a vice, Taylor feared the evil tendencies of being without property much more than he did those of having a little extra. Subsistence living soaked up all a man's spare time so that he was "less industrious in the preservation of liberty." Poor housing, especially, instilled "a pernicious wandering habit . . . because nothing worth retaining is surrendered, and no evil, not already endured is anticipated."[24] A pauper could barely make a living and never learned the skills necessary for holding public office; therefore he missed out on a vital part of citizenship. A man who was dependent upon wages, moreover, could be forced below the subsistence level by illness or other misfortune. He was led in desperation to a life of crime. In general, a life without property independent of the control of others deprived a man "of the erect attitude in society inspired by the freedom of industry."[25]

Even if poverty was inconsistent with freedom, Taylor did not suggest any easy way to overcome it. A return to agrarian life based on the improvement of the land's fertility, which in turn must be based upon a proper understanding of nature, was his only program. He was opposed to charity as a solution for poverty, because it hurt both the giver and the receiver. The giver was entitled to no praise for giving away money to gratify his own vanity, while the receiver was often dissipated by handouts and had less incentive. The whole process of charity was unproductive, for it merely exchanged money without creating wealth. Taylor followed his own advice in this and would sometimes loan money to help out a friend in need, but he seldom offered charity and he did not want to be identified when he did.[26]

C. Agrarianism and Society

Just as nature was the key to agriculture, agriculture was in turn the key to a properly constructed society. Throughout his life, Taylor insisted that the interest of agriculture was the interest of the entire country and that it could not be at enmity with the public good. In the first place, there were so many farmers that their interests very nearly constituted the public interest; and, second, farmers were the customers of the few other interests and dependent on their existence and good will. This predominance of agriculture was likely to remain for centuries for two natural reasons: the amount of land available and its consequent cheapness; and the fact that man naturally wanted a home, independence, and leisure more than wealth for its own sake.[27]

The economic and social importance of agriculture required of it duties that extended to the support of government, to the encouragement of commerce, to the sustenance of the learned professions, to the introduction of the fine arts, and to the support of the more useful mechanical employments.[28] Putting this attitude to work, Taylor worried that his opinions might be unreasonably biased in favor of agriculture, and sometimes called his readers' attention to that possibility, exhorting them to watch him closely. Although he had confidence in the superiority of agriculture, he was not so blinded by passion that he ignored the fact that other professions had more power, even if agriculture was more widespread. Agriculture "must be rich to be powerful, and she must be powerful to discharge faithfully the sacred obligation she owns to society, by constituting the majority."[29] The problem was that agriculture was not rich but poor, and getting poorer.

In short, some of the conditions impoverishing planters were mistakes that they had themselves committed through the use of overseers, the three-shift system, tobacco, sheep, and wooden fences. Other problems had been caused by federal adoption of banking, funding, tariffs, and other special privileges.[30]

A third group of difficulties was caused by the frontier.

Taylor's love of nature did not lead him to romantic visions of frontier life in the midst of fertile, untracked wildernesses. Agriculture was based upon the fertility of the soil, and towns were based upon agriculture. The frontier was exerting a pull upon the farm population, which led lazy men to refuse to use scientific, but painfully slow methods of building up the soil's quality. Instead, they merely migrated to the frontier in order to start the same wasteful process again. The extra expenses that the federal government had placed upon agriculture had made proper farming methods such as adequate storage shelters too expensive, and this also forced many to go West. Finally, the natural trait that made man a land owner by choice and a wage laborer only by necessity had caused a wasteful quest for western lands exemplified by the exploitative settlement of western New York State. This sort of "Genesee" fever was causing thousands to emigrate from the seaboard to the interior, but Taylor feared that after resources became depleted it would be too expensive to be a farmer and men would turn to manufacturing. If they did that before agriculture had allowed cities to develop, the manufacturing would fail for lack of markets. In such a situation Taylor pointed out that the Virginia farmer was faced with three choices: a voluntary banishment from nation and friends; "a banishment from heaven," the result of changing from an honest profession to a speculative one; or exertion of a virtuous mind and body in the rebuilding of Virginia soil.[31]

Although the practice of agriculture depended heavily upon the guidance that nature could provide, Taylor never believed that agriculture could be freed entirely from governmental assistance, nor did he limit this assistance to the state and local levels. His *Inquiry* and *Arator* were intended as the twin pillars of a system of thought that would provide the intellectual justification for a society that was predominantly, but not exclusively, agrarian. Taylor first turned from agriculture to the political solution at the time of the Sedition Act: "can we, when our house is on fire, be solicitous to save the kittens?"[32] The political solution to agriculture's problems because more important to him as time went on. Such political intervention took two forms: the abolition of special-interest groups, and forms of direct governmental assistance.

The abolition of special privileges was required because the thined soil of the American continent and its lowered fertility argued against burdening agriculture as England had done. In

England it had caused increased immigration, decreases in land fertility, sales of landed estates, and the dwindling of landed gentry. Repeal of the relevant laws would prevent armies, tariffs, and paper frauds from burdening farmers. Just as important would be the periodic review of all laws, to consider whether or not they deserved continuance. The long-run consequences of governmental patronage would most likely be either the complete enslavement of agriculture, or an increased ability in Congress to subvert the federal system by exercising powers properly owned only by the states. If either happened, farmers would become listless producers interested only in a scuffle for appropriations.

More positive governmental assistance included a range of projects. At one time, Taylor wanted the federal government to create a "tool office," to serve as an "inverse" patent office to prevent the monopolization of technological discoveries in agriculture science; to collect foreign models of tools; and to publish reports on the research and development of new inventions. Admitting that such an "un-patent" office might not be practicable, Taylor also advocated state loans to inventors for the encouragement of tool development. Positive state laws were also advocated by Taylor, which would have required fences, the penning of livestock, and the punishment of owners for allowing their livestock to forage on farms belonging to others. He had no objection to a state law requiring that property owners keep drainage channels free of obstruction to aid the reclamation of swampland; Pennsylvania had such a law and, in his opinion, it worked well.[33]

Even the sensitive area of slave ownership should not be free of state governmental regulation if the regulation supported the long-range interests of slaveowning. A bad code of local laws allowed unsettling contacts between slaves and freedmen, which interfered with work and increased the prices of agricultural products. Slaveholders should be forced to remove runaway or thieving slaves from the scene of their trespasses, lest others be encouraged by their example. Should the state "require a farther limitation of the prerogatives of ownership, public and private good will unite in their recommendation of such a measure."[34]

Another action that should be taken by government was reversing the court decision that had disallowed a federally endowed agricultural society because of the necessity for keeping faith with patent holders. Taylor did not specify whether or not this society should be given subsidies for encouraging agriculture, but he did think such groups essential if agriculture was to avoid being thrown defenseless against the combined might of self-interested aristocracies.[35]

A farmer's communion with nature did not ensure political wisdom as well. Farmers were "political fools": they scarcely knew how to talk to their representatives because of their provincial manners. The remedy lay in reciprocal efforts: agriculture should inform itself on political problems (by reading, for example, the *Inquiry* and *Arator*), and representatives should learn of agriculture's problems by personally experiencing this sort of work. Agricultural societies, whether recognized by the government or not, should attempt to become political action groups, electing only those persons who were uncorrupted by vice and knowledgeable about agricultural matters.[36]

Until farmers gained the knowledge necessary to participate effectively in politics, their best hope was a strengthened militia. Not only would this force be available to protect farmers' rights in any crises, but the militia's very existence would compensate for the lack of cleverness on the part of farmers. In the councils of power farmers would be treated with respect for the damage they could do, if not for their intellectual contribution to the discussions. Experience with use of this power would also serve farmers well when they achieved the knowledge and political mobilization necessary to make their political influence commensurate with their numbers. Having suffered in the wilderness as a stepchild interest, farmers would understand the problems of minorites and possess the means to defend them.[37]

D. Slavery and Agrarianism

Taylor's theory of agrarianism has proved consistent thus far with his Enlightenment background, and largely consistent with his criticism of aristocracy, and with the governmental and intellectual safeguards he considered necessary to combat aristocracy. The attention Taylor gave to slavery was another matter, however, and his consistency weakens at this point. Most associates of Jefferson were troubled by the problem of slavery, and Taylor was no exception. Their sympathies were tugged and pulled in several directions: Jefferson himself seemed to have weakened his earlier egalitarianism on the issue after the Compromise of 1820. Many Virginians gave intellectual assent to the idea of gradual emancipation although recent critics have charged that Virginia's liberalism on this score has been over-rated. Regardless of the emancipationist convictions of his fellow Virginians, Taylor accepted the institution of slavery un-apologetically for the short run, and held out the possibility of emancipation only at a time in the remote future.[38]

Taylor defined slavery in abstract terms from his earliest writings, always leaving open the possibility that the institution's effects, if not its actual form, might be suffered by groups other than Negroes. In this way he redefined the institution in order to implicate Northern abolitionists. "Slavery is only a domination of an artificial, over the natural interest of a nation."[39] He distinguished "direct" slavery, which included both the form and the effect, from "indirect" slavery, which was achieved by using patronage and public debt to transfer property. He became one of the first to compare the plight of factory workers to the Negro slaves, whom he considered better off. The latter increased freely, their condition was softened by the solicitous concern of their owners, their food and clothing were free, and they were carefree and cheerful. From the very beginning of his public writings, therefore, Taylor defensively attempted to turn anti-slavery arguments back upon their authors. If this was less than a full application of his own advocacy of substantive equality, and less than an imaginative theoretical response to a looming social problem, it did not completely deny Negro slavery's undesirable effects, it merely maintained that these effects were not limited to Negro slavery.[40]

Taylor several times explicitly discovered any personal liking for Negro slavery on either moral or economic grounds. "Be it not be supposed that I approved of slavery because I do not aggravate its evils, or perfer a policy which must terminate in a war of extermination."[41]

These disavowals occurred in the midst of discussions of scientific farming and, considering the audience, probably represent Taylor's completely candid opinion offered at some risk of popularity. But he also said that slavery was "a misfortune to agriculture, incapable of removal, and only within the reach of palliation." He claimed that all economists had agreed that slavery was the least profitable method of agriculture.[42]

Although Taylor seems to have thought Caucasians superior in intellect to Negroes, he did not consider this as an excuse for the White population's "converting to its own use the labour of Africa."[43] Instead, he implied that the inferiority in intelligence was associated with the institution of slavery: "Would the intelligence of the Negroes in Africa be diminished by freedom of labour?"[44] What was needed to face the problem of Negro slavery was realism, and an ability to be satisfied with half measures:

> The fact is that Negro slavery is an evil which the United States must look in the face. To whine over it, is cowardly; to aggravate it, criminal; and to forbare to alleviate it, because it cannot be wholly cured, foolish.[45]

There were several things that could be done in order to improve the unsatisfactory and inefficient institution of slavery. In the long run, both Europe and America could look toward the establishment of a colony of free Negroes in a fertile part of Africa that would soon achieve self-sufficiency. "Slavery might then be gradually re-exported, and philanthropy gratified by a slow reanimation of the virtue, religion and liberty of the Negroes. . . ."[46] Although Taylor gave very little attention to this colonization plan in his writings, scattered passages throughout his later works give some indication that he thought slavery had a limited lease on life and would be abolished by the states themselves, in time.

During the long interim while slavery would still be a fact, Taylor may have hoped to phase it out through the improved management of agricultural resources, improving farming so that more could be produced with fewer slaves. Taylor's use of manures allowed him to increase his acres under cultivation from one per laborer to four, and he was confident that eight per worker was possible. Even though he refused to be dogmatic about the number of slaves needed per farm, and did not hesitate to put old men, old women, and children to work in the fields at light work, he also believed that the use of live fences would reduce the need for all field workers.[47]

Taylor advocated better treatment for slaves, but for reasons that dash cold water on any hopes that his unfulfilled promise of equality might find outlet in humanitarian sentiments. One treated slaves well for the same reason that one treated livestock well: "liberality to slaves and working animals, is the fountain of their profit."[48] By supplementing necessities with comforts, the affections of slaves would be secured: happy slaves would be productive slaves. Mistreating slaves lost profits through the diminishing of health, strength, alacrity, and the increase of disease, short lives, dejection, barrenness, and injuries. Taylor prescribed modest capital investments for the maintenance of slaves. Food was useful as a means for disciplining slaves, and the withholding of food and the selling of malcontent slaves were the only disciplinary methods he recommended.[49]

Taylor thought that the proper management of slaves was impossible under the constant harrassment of agitators, abolitionists, and religious zealots. The constant threat of invasion or insurrection created a security problem that diverted attention and resources from productive uses. The creation of a third force in tidewater society made up of free Negroes and mulattoes was especially dangerous. Freedmen constantly caused problems among slaves, lived upon stolen goods, and were driven by their lack of political and social rights to a life of idleness. Both freedmen and plantation owners would be better off if Congress would buy some land and offer it to the freedmen.

During Taylor's time Caroline freedmen often raised hogs by allowing them to roam at will, a type of foraging that was one problem that led Taylor to advocate live fences. In spite of his antipathy to freedmen, the only direct action he seems to have taken against them was to sign a petition to the state legislature asking that Port Royal be allowed to hire a hogcatcher.[50]

His sentiments may have run deeper. Keith Bailor has pointed out how vulnerable the planter was in tidewater Virginia, often outnumbered by his slaves and remote from other white men. Although, upon the sketchy evidence available, Taylor's relations with his slaves seem to have been harmonious, his emphases upon the militia and a code of local law to regulate the punishment that masters could inflict on slaves may have indicated his fears of slave uprisings. The example of what happened in Haiti was used by him fairly often, yet he did not mention the Denmark Vesey plot of 1822 in Charleston, whose conspirators were said to have been in touch with the freedmen in Santo Domingo, nor did Taylor ever mention the 1800 Gabriel attempt to kill the white inhabitants of Richmond.

Moreover, his emphasis on the militia does not seem closely correlated with these events.[51]

If he attacked slavery as unproductive, Taylor also had words of praise for it when his contemporaries hesitated to consider it as anything other than an embarrassing necessity. His defense of slavery anticipated both the constitutional and practical defenses used often later.

The constitutional arguments were based in the fact that the Constitution recognized slavery through the three-fifths representation ratio. If slavery had such constitutional protection, it could not be abrogated by any other provision in the document. As with all his constitutional interpretations, Taylor extended this argument to include the indirect effects of other constitutional provisions. If officials said they were not interfering with slavery as an internal institution, but then took action that indirectly hurt it, they had acted unconstitutionally. Congress could not use its taxing powers, its war powers, or its power to admit states into the Union as instruments for abolishing slavery. The guaranty of a republican form of government flowed from the United States as states, and not from the federal government. It was no basis for emancipation.[52]

If Congress left slavery alone and abstained from matters such as the Missouri Compromise, slavery would not disturb the peace of the Union. Taylor considered the banding together of states in Congress to pass the Missouri Compromise as a violation of the constitutional provision against interstate compacts. For such a purpose the Hartford Convention had been preferable: at least it had frankly stated that its intention was to form an interest separate from the rest of the country. The fact was that no balance between slave and free states could be maintained, because slavery was not permanently fixed to any region.[53]

Taylor's other defenses of slavery supported its desirability as a natural institution, its moral benefits, its innocence of intended wrongdoing, the dangers of any alternatives, or maintained that it could be regulated intelligently only by local laws. Point by point his defense explicitly refuted Jefferson's chapter 18 on slavery in *Notes on Virginia*.

Slavery was natural, in Taylor's eyes, because of the differences in racial appearance. Frank Tannenbaum has suggested that social acceptance of racial integration depends upon the prevailing concepts of human beauty. He points out that Latin countries such as Brazil freed their slaves later than the United States, but accepted them into society sooner, partly as a consequence of more cosmopolitan aesthetic standards created as a consequence of having had a large group of freedmen. Taylor lacked such cosmopolitan tastes, and maintained that beauty and "deformity" were as naturally coexistent in the animal world as virtue and vice in the moral world: "One cannot be destroyed without the other" in both worlds. He thought mulattoes "monstrous" in appearance.[54]

The only religious defense of slavery Taylor offered was that God would not require the unreasonable paradoxes of emancipation and racial war, yet the second followed the first inevitably. Enrolling the Deity upon the slaves' side could only result from "inattention to his own attributes."[55] Taylor never used Scripture to justify slavery, as was done later.

Races were meant to be separate, or nature would not have made them so different in appearance. Negro freedmen could never have a separate political existence in the United States, because their color would give them away if they tried to push their interests secretly and few Caucasians would support them openly. If party slogans had caused excitement in the past, "no doubt can exist of the consequences of placing two nations of distinct colours and features on the same theatre, to contend, not about sounds and signs, but for wealth and power."[56] The example of Santo Domingo was often used as proof that two races could not live on an equal basis in a state of peace, but Taylor realized that, once a large number of slaves had become free, the values of a republican system would make it impossible to withhold either property or equal political rights from them. If equal rights were withheld, they would be ripe for subversion and demagoguery, but with equal rights they would keep trying to subject Caucasians to their rule.[57]

Slavery taught certain beneficial moral virtues to the masters. Even though Taylor had attacked the evil moral principles he imagined that the factory or wage system encouraged, he did not recognize or discuss at length any harmful effects on private morals brought about by slavery. The contrary was true:

> slaves are too far below, and too much in the power of the master, to inspire furious passions; that such are nearly as rare

and disgraceful towards slaves as towards horses; that slaves are more frequently the objects of benevolence than of rage; that children from their nature are inclined to soothe, and hardly ever suffered to tyrannize over them . . . fewer good public or private characters have been raised in countries enslaved by some faction or particular interest, than in those where personal slavery existed.[58]

Human slavery was better than indirect economic slavery, which did not allow an individual master to build up a personal relationship with his sentient possessions.[59] The Greeks and Romans, after all, had used an advanced system of slavery, and produced more patriots than even the slave states had. Even the latter had already produced men such as Jefferson, who demonstrated in his own person a refutation of his arguments against slavery in *Notes on Virginia*.

Both partners to the master-slave relationship were innocent, and should be absolved of any blame by Northern agitators. The ancestors of slave-owners, after all, had not been the ones who had stolen Negroes from Africa: "If some remnants of such monsters exist, they are not to be found in the Southern quarters of the union."[60] Constant agitation and pointing the finger of guilt at slaveholders might even cause them to take stronger measures to ensure their hold over their slaves.

Taylor leveled both general and specific criticisms at abolitionist agitators. Among his general comments were the charges that abolitionist fanaticism had occurred only because the North could no longer profit from the slave trade. If abolitionists needed a crusade, why couldn't they direct their attentions to slavery in Brazil, Cuba, or Africa, which would help trade and not be an attack upon fellow Christians. Slaveowners in those foreign countries were so by choice and not by chance, as was the case in the South.[61]

Agitation was shortsighted, because a policy of emancipation that hurt three-fourths of the Union would hurt the remainder. If all slaves were freed, Northern cities would soon face the immigration of "thieves, murderers and villains," even though slavery had taught Negroes to behave better. Such a mass of ignorant freedmen would easily become as subject to the will of Northern demagogues as they had ever been to Southern slave-masters.[62]

Abolitionist propaganda might have an unforeseen effect stretching beyond the probable wrongdoing of freedmen and the resentment of their former masters. If the Northern factory worker got wind of this rhetoric, the abolitionist might find himself confronted with a Northern emancipation movement. "It is prudent, when a resolution is taken to set fire to some body's house, to go far from home, lest the flames may reach our own, as the wind is apt to change." [63]

It was also absurd for abolitionists to attack the master's hold on the slave with dogma about freedom of conscience. Where is freedom of conscience under a plan of forced conversion to abolitionist morality? The French had tried to legislate morality in Santo Domingo and found it impossible to make people happy. The natural right to express one's own conscience would be violated if abolitionists had their way. Such legislation did not have the knowledge of local conditions necessary to make laws abolishing slavery work. Those who knew slaves well, knew that "converting black slaves into good patriots . . . was visionary." [64]

This view of Taylor's dramatizes the inconsistency of much Jeffersonian thought on slavery. With surprising ease he was able to defend the right to own slaves on the grounds of a natural right, without troubling himself over whether Negroes had consciences and natural rights, too. His was the individualism that marched to a personal drum, and the basic similarities in the form of their arguments kept men such as Taylor and Thoreau from ever hearing each other, because each was convinced that he embodied individualistic freedom while using similar natural right appeals.

Individualism required self-government, self-government required "nations," and nations possessed the right of self-defense. Both preemptive warfare and internal security measures were justified in the name of national self-defense, Taylor warned northern critics.

> The right of self-defense applies to that situation, of the necessity for which the parties exposed to the danger are the natural judges. . . . I leave to the reader the application of these observations. [65]

What happened to slaves was the South's exclusive business. The application of natural rights and individualism required nothing less.

E. Summary and Conclusions

John Taylor's theory of agrarianism provided a compatible extension of the protections he had devised for republicanism as a governmental system. The agrarian life was what he was saving man's liberty for and the agrarian life-style, in turn, complemented the division of powers by maintaining a wide diffusion of wealth and supporting a militia to guard liberty.

Bound to a vision of nature as a harmonious network of interrelated laws, Taylor literally built his ideal agrarian society on a foundation of manure, because the prerequisite for Agrarian happiness was a clockworklike series of crop rotations and fencing practices that would establish each plantation as a separate ecology, providing by its natural operation for all the wants of its inhabitants. The contemplation of and experimentation with these natural processes gave man the immediate satisfactions necessary to provide him with a sense of personal worth through accomplishment. The processes detrimental to agriculture were those which somehow upset the balance. To Taylor agricultural experimentation was not a matter of what man did to conquer nature, but of discovering nature's laws and trying to augment their tendencies in incremental ways.

The *laissez-faire* stance that Taylor assumed toward government was mirrored in this system of agriculture. In both cases the key to well-being was the discovery of appropriate natural laws and the adjusting of one's behavior accordingly. The natural laws of government were the text of truthful principles considered in preceding chapters; those of agriculture, the practices that implemented the theory of atmospheric organic nutrition. It is apparent, therefore, that Taylor's reluctance to propose a grand design for the reform of government was not at all inconsistent with his view of man as the creative gardener who could accept or reject the laws of nature as he willed, but who had to accept the inevitable rewards or punishments that followed his decision. Taylor used the same calculus to judge government and economics, and, in either case, he judged the whole system by the beneficence of its results and not by its superficial aspects. The standard of value to be used was an absolute one decreed by the political and physical natural laws that governed the universe.

Taylor was no determinist in his belief in natural laws. Not only did man have the ability to accept or reject the natural axioms, but the key to their operation lay in his choice. Possibly *law* is too strong a term to describe these axioms: Taylor's principles and agricultural truths were really *tendencies*, which would operate as constants if man adopted them. Thus, the structure of a system of divided powers was impotent unless the operators of the system believed in its principles. Similarly, Virginia could allow agricultural decline to continue or she could do something about it.

Man's partnership with nature created both his knowledge and the value of his property. Neither could be increased by law, and to try was to set government against nature. By thus holding nature off at arm's length, Taylor was able to avoid the severe problems of theodicy that haunted many Enlightenment think-ers. If nature were given too strong a role in the operation of the world, they found, it was difficult to escape the inference that whatever was, was right. Some conservative thinkers such as Adams, Bolingbroke, Hume, and Swift were willing to accept this inference, but many were not. In Taylor's view, nature's potential was unrealized, and he fell back on the experience of history to determine which of man's actions had proved workable in the past. He was definitely not willing to accept evil in the world as a given.[66]

By accepting the authority of nature as susceptible to de-velopment, Taylor preserved man's ability to choose right from wrong. By positing the labor theory of value and an agrarian economy he provided man a naturalistic source for knowledge, pleasure, and humanitarian values. But Taylor's solution to the problem of theodicy involved him in the most serious contradic-tion of his system: the moral place of the slave.

Taylor's occasional utterances on slavery suggest he really had no settled opinion on the institution. He was capable of recommending the colonization of freedmen and the virtues of slavery within the same book, but for the most part he simply ignored the issue. For, whatever peace that may have given his conscience, his silence destroyed the theoretical system he advocated on two grounds: equality and property.

Taylor's theory of aristocratic development, it will be recalled, depended on the increasing enlightenment of the general population. By saying that the people governed by ancient tyrants simply had not known better, Taylor avoided saying, as Locke had not, that the people sometimes consent to unrepubli-can rulers. By saying that man's knowledge had increased to a point of such substantial equality that aristocracy was all but unthinkable, Taylor successfully discredited the moral right of aristocrats to rule in the modern age. But apparently the progressive forces of enlightenment or the doctrine of substantial equality did not extend to Negro slaves. If Taylor considered slaves fully human, he never explained why they did not share in the natural right of self-government that all other men possessed as a consequence of their being.

Had Taylor not put forth a doctrine of substantial equality among individuals' abilities, he might have escaped contradiction on the issue of slavery. But he had said that superior abilities were based on knowledge and that no "certain state of knowledge, is a natural or unavoidable quality of man. As an intellectual or moral quality, it may be created, destroyed and modified by human power."[67] Without this doctrine Taylor lost his main argument to use against John Adams's theory of aristocracy. It is ironical that both John and John Quincy Adams were able to maintain a belief in moral equality but *in*equality in abilities that allowed them decisively to reject slavery.

The second contradiction faced by Taylor on the issue of slavery was the result of his labor theory of value. According to this doctrine, the labor of slaves created value. In fact, this value added to the property of their masters, but there was no theory offered by Taylor that explained why this should happen. Slaves, presumably, enjoyed their work and were stimulated by it as the master was. Yet, they worked for no more than a subsistence, while the owner accumulated as much as possible. Taylor did not entertain the possibility that he and his fellow planters were aristocrats, but they obviously were engaged in transferring wholly the value created by the slave to themselves through the use of laws that held him in bondage. This transfer of value should have been particularly noticeable in the case of slave propagation: there, clearly, slaves were creating value for the master without any effort on his part other than the purchase of a Negro couple under a system of law that made their issue his property.

Taylor nearly ignored the possibility that farmers could be aristocrats. He recognized that the feudal system had landed aristocrats and called them "aristocrats," but he thought that farmers in the United States were cultivators and much too numerous to be an aristocracy. Landed aristocrats were really absentee landlords, in Taylor's view. If a man worked his own farm, he was no aristocrat, not even if he spent much of his time in Congress attacking bankers.[68]

Taylor's inadequate handling of the issue of slavery may have been partially reinforced by his conceptualization of the forces of production. As was seen earlier, Taylor's concept of capitalists did not recognize entrepreneurship as a separate factor of production. He looked upon money and equipment as capital, but he looked on the managers of an enterprise as labor in the same sense as the cottage system had considered as labor a farmer and his wife who made shoes for a distributor in their own home. The thought that a plantation bore a greater resemblance to a factory than to cottage industry, in its diversification of skills, and probably surpassed the primitive industries of the early 1800s in this regard, seemed never to occur to Taylor. He conceived of the slave master as other than labor and, consequently, seemed to have put slaves in the same economic category as equipment and beasts of burden. In his frame of reference slaves were not "labor"; they did not work, but were used precisely as beasts of burdens were. Although Taylor discussed the use of slaves in chapters entitled *Labour*, it is clear that he was comparing them to beast labor that was his to command without question or consent. Visualized as capital, it did not seem inconsistent to Taylor that slaves worked and created value, but never owned. Neither did his horse, "Doctor."

The reliance on natural laws that so characterized the Enlightenment had a direct effect on the Age of Romanticism that followed. By minimizing man's ability to shape the forces of nature, some thinkers explained the presence of evil in the world. Had Taylor retreated into determinism he would have had a ready-made defense of slavery. Other defenders of slavery did just that, for example, German-educated Thomas Dew, who defended slavery as natural. Taylor was never willing to surrender man's responsibility, but he never explained it either.[69]

Notes to Chapter 7

1. Carl L. Becker, *The Heavenly City of the Eighteenth-Century Philosophers* (New Haven, Conn.: Yale University Press, 1932), pp. 33–70; Ernst Cassirer, *The Philosophy of the Enlightenment* (Princeton, N.J.: Princeton University Press, 1951), pp. 37–92.

2. Daniel J. Boorstin, *The Lost World of Thomas Jefferson* (Boston: Beacon Press, 1963), pp. 37–53.

3. Taylor, *Arator*, p. 207; letter from John Taylor to George W. Jeffreys, August 16, 1816, *American Farmer* 2 (June 16, 1820): 93.

4. Taylor, *Arator*, p. 68.

5. *Ibid.*, pp. 59, 70, 102, 130, 161–62, 181–82, 203; letter from John Taylor to Wilson Cary Nicholas, August 29, 1808, Edgehill-Randolph Papers, University of Virginia Library, Charlottesville; letter from Taylor to George W. Jeffreys, January 8, 1819, *American Farmer* 2 (March 9, 1821): 397.

6. John Taylor, "The Necessities, Competency, and Profit of Agriculture," *Niles Weekly Register*, Supplement to nos. 2, 3, 15, n.s. (November 7, 1818), p. 179; letter from Taylor to George W. Jeffreys, October 6, 1817, *American Farmer* 2 (January 26, 1826): 348–49; letter from Taylor to James Mercer Garnett, January 28, 1818, John Taylor Papers, Duke University Library, Durham, N. C.

7. Even though Taylor denied that the mammoth still lived, he rationalized the beast's extinction by saying that it had been destructive; *Tyranny*, p. 113. For other missing links in the chain of being see Taylor's comments in "Artificial Grasses," *American Farmer* 1 (November 12, 1819):259–62; "The Necessities, Competency, and Profit of Agriculture"; letter to George W. Jeffreys, March 7, 1818, *American Farmer* 2 (April 20, 1820): 30; letter to Timothy Pickering, February 16, 1817, Massachusetts Historical Society.

8. "The Necessities, Competency, and Profit of Agriculture," p. 178.

9. Taylor, *Arator*, p. 84.

10. Letter from John Taylor to Timothy Pickering, February 16, 1817, letter to George W. Jeffreys, August 1, 1817, *American Farmer* 2 (October 13, 1820): 230; "Artificial Grasses."

11. Taylor, *Arator*, p. 233.

12. Ibid., pp. 69, 145, 186, 228; letter from Taylor to George W. Jeffreys, March 2, 1817, *American Farmer* 2 (September 29, 1820): 212.

13. Taylor, *Arator*, p. 140. Also see p. 57; *Construction*, p. 88.

14. Taylor, *Arator*, pp. 184–86.

15. *Inquiry*, pp. 329, 561, 636; *Construction*, p. 78; *Definition*, p. 9.

16. *Enquiry*, p. 10.

17. *Inquiry*, p. 636.

18. Ibid., p. 333; *Tyranny*, pp. 194–99, 208.

19. Taylor, *Arator*, p. 188.

20. Ibid., p. 189. Also see p. 190; "The Necessities, Competency, and Profit of Agriculture"; *Inquiry*, p. 364; *Tyranny*, pp. 178, 208, 364.

21. *Inquiry*, p. 562. Also see pp. 85–86, 128, 258–59, 262, 553–54; *Argument*, pp. 21–23; *Enquiry*, pp. 62–63.

22. *Inquiry*, p. 329. Also see pp. 85, 563–64, 635.

23. Ibid., p. 282; *Construction*, p. 29; *Tyranny*, p. 62; John Taylor, "The Memorial of the Merchants, Agriculturalists and Others, of the Town of Fredericksburgh and Adjacent County," *American Farmer* 2 (September 22, 1820): 201–2.

24. "The Necessities, Competency, and Profit of Agriculture."

25. *Tyranny*, p. 197. Also see pp. 139, 196. *Enquiry*, p. 31.

26. Letter from John Taylor to Peter Carr, September 18, 1806, Gabriella Page Papers, Virginia Historical Society, Richmond; *Construction*, p. 316.

27. *Definition*, p. 9; John Taylor, "A Letter on the Necessity of Defending the Rights and Interests of Agriculture," *American Farmer* 3 (July 20, 1821): 431. Economic developments during Taylor's lifetime did little to challenge his agrarian assumptions: from 1790 to 1820 the urban population increased from roughly 5 to 7 percent. In 1820 approximately 70 percent of employed workers were engaged in agricultural occupa-

tions. This held constant up almost to the time of the Civil War. U. S. Bureau of Census, *Historical Statistics of the United States: Colonial Times to 1957* (Washington: U. S. Government Printing Office, 1960), p. 72.

28. "The Necessities, Competency, and Profit of Agriculture," p. 180. Also see Taylor, *Arator,* p. 20; *Tyranny,* p. 119.

29. Taylor, *Arator,* p. vi.

30. Ibid., pp. 26–27, 145, 224.

31. Ibid., p. 5; letter from Taylor to Timothy Pickering, February 16, 1817; letter to George W. Jeffreys, August 12, 1818, *American Farmer* 2 (February 16, 1818): 374; letter from Taylor to ____, August 3, 1801, Massachusetts Historical Society; "The Necessities, Competency, and Profit of Agriculture," p. 178; *Tyranny,* pp. 120–21.

32. Letter from John Taylor to Thomas Jefferson, December 18–21, 1798, in "Correspondence," p. 277; letter to Jefferson, February 15, 1799, ibid., pp. 278–81.

33. Taylor, *Arator,* pp. iv–vi, 17–18, 31, 206, 209–11; letter from Taylor to Thomas Jefferson, June 25, 1798, in "Correspondence," pp. 271–76; letter from Taylor to Thomas Ritchie, March 30, 1809, in Stanard, p. 22; *Tyranny,* p. 155, 224; *New Views,* p. 268.

34. "The Necessities, Competency, and Profit of Agriculture," p. 179; Taylor, *Arator,* pp. 60, 172, 206.

35. Ibid., p. 219.

36. Ibid. p. 38; "A Letter on the Necessity of Defending the Rights and Interests of Agriculture," p. 431. Despite his disapproval of the exploitative practices of the frontier, Taylor was not squeamish about legally defending a settler who had seized his claim by force from another; see *Hamilton* v. *Maze,* June 1791, in Daniel Call, ed., *Reports of Cases Argued and Decided in the Court of Appeals of Virginia* (Richmond, Va.: Robert I. Smith), vol. 4. Taylor disapproved of Marshall's holding in *Fletcher* v. *Peck,* 6 Cranch 87. If Taylor wrote *Cautionary Hints,* he also thought large-scale land settlement to be the beginning of an American squirearchy. See pp. 8–11.

37. Taylor, *Arator,* pp. vi. vii, 35–36, 42, 195, 198, 236–39; letter from John Taylor to James Mercer Garnett, January 28, 1818; letters from Taylor to James Monroe, March 25, 1798; February 27, 1806; July 27, 1811, in "Correspondence," pp. 268–70, 290–91, 324–26.

38. Clement Eaton, *The Freedom-of-Thought Struggle in the Old South* (New York: Harper and Row, Publishers, 1964), pp. 19–20; Herbert Aptheker, *Nat Turner's Slave Rebellion* (New York: Grove Press, 1966), p. 1.

39. *Enquiry,* p. 58.

40. Letter from John Taylor to Henry Tazewell, April 13, 1796, Tazewell Papers; letter from Taylor to Timothy Dwight, September 3, 1805, in David Rankin Barbee, ed., "A Sheaf of Old Letters," *Tylers Quarterly Historical and Genealogical Magazine* 32 (October 1950): 82–84; "Letter on the Necessity of Defending the Rights and Interests of Agriculture," p. 431.

41. Taylor, *Arator,* p. 54.

42. Ibid., p. 48. Also see letter from Taylor to Timothy Dwight, September 3, 1805.

43. *Construction,* p. 250.

44. Ibid.

45. Taylor, *Arator,* p. 93.

46. Ibid., p. 49. Also see *Construction,* pp. 233, 294, 296, 314.

47. "Artificial Grasses," p. 261; letters from John Taylor to George W. Jeffreys, August 1, 1817; August 12, 1818; April 16, 1819; *American Farmer* 2 (October 13, 1820): 230; (February 16, 1818): 374; (March 23, 1821): 415.

48. Taylor, *Arator,* p. 185.

49. Ibid., pp. 96–97, 184.

50. Caroline County Legislative Petition, December 9, 1816, Virginia State Library, Richmond; *Argument,* p. 20; *Construction,* pp. 284, 310.

51. Eaton, p. 90.

52. *Construction,* pp. 167–68, 291, 294.

53. Ibid., pp. 296–8.

54. Taylor, *Arator,* pp. 54, 91. Also see Frank Tannenbaum, *Slave and Citizen* (New York: Vintage Books, 1946), pp. 121–23.

55. Taylor, *Arator,* pp. 53–54.

56. Ibid., p. 90. Also see p. 53.

57. Ibid., p. 91.

58. Ibid., p. 53.

59. Ibid., p. 94.

60. Ibid., p. 93; *Construction,* p. 301.

61. *Construction,* p. 293.

62. Taylor, *Arator,* p. 92.

63. *Construction,* p. 293.

64. New Views, p. 277.

65. Construction, p. 314. Also see Taylor, *Arator,* pp. 48, 90, 218–19.

66. Becker, pp. 69–70.

67. *Inquiry,* p. 9.

68. *Inquiry,* pp. 335, 349, 553.

69. Carl L. Becker, *The Declaration of Independence* (New York: Vintage Books, 1942), p. 247.

8
CONCLUSION

A. Summary and Conclusions

THE study of the intellectual influences on John Taylor revealed that the forces which usually mold a personality— family, education, professional training, friends, in-laws, and community environment—all combined to form a comprehensive Whig backdrop for Taylor's own ideas. Tories were being run out of Caroline County before the Revolution began, and the most conservative men around were revolutionary patriots. Some of the most radical people around were his relatives. Moreover, there was a literary tradition in the country that reinforced a Whig orientation. Although Taylor was exposed somewhat to the views of Tories, it may be that his attitudes had been molded long before that into such a rigid Whig mold that he did not pause later to question his assumptions. Also reinforcing this rigidity was the fact that many of the Republic's founders were cosmopolitan in idea and experience: Adams, Jefferson, Jay, Franklin, Hamilton, Monroe, and Marshall had all experienced travel and life abroad. Others, such as James Madison or John Randolph, went to Northern schools. Taylor, by contrast, formed his ideas in the backwash of the Enlightenment and may have maintained them out of a provincial stubbornness; he may have feared there would be nothing with which to replace them if any were surrendered.

One is forced here, again, to consider the similarity of John Taylor's ideas and those of the English republican tradition. In almost every important way they were similar. The English Republicans attacked the Walpole Administration as a conspir-

Notes for this chapter begin on p. 316.

acy that had been corrupted by patronage and bribes to follow the King's wishes without deviation. The King's friends were seen as worse than misguided; they were thoroughly debased. Their sense of morality had been dulled by temptation. The Republicans were fond of criticizing the government from two sources of authority. Most basic was the knowledge of morality and human rights that God had implanted in each human heart. Their faith was in an intuitive form of natural law, which Staughton Lynd has seen as derived more from Rousseau than Locke, whose sensationalist psychology left standards of value to be determined by convention and government. The second source of authority was the study of history, especially a romanticized Saxon golden age, when men had been less corrupted and when their sense of morality operated more freely.[1]

Taylor had nothing to say about the Saxon golden age, but did assume that persons of his generation would be able to tell right from wrong by the exercise of their reason. His view of the operation of intuitive rational morality seems very close to that described by Lynd as derived from Rousseau through Burgh and Price. Morever, Taylor continued to look back to a golden age of his own choosing: the American Revolutionary era when persons had exercised moral choice free from the contamination of personal advantage and had therefore been able to agree on the meaning and benefits of republicanism. In a sense, John Taylor is the last of the Coffeehouse Radicals who had made life miserable for Robert Walpole. Taylor simply cast John Adams, Alexander Hamilton, James Madison, and John Marshall, in turn, for the role of Walpole.

Taylor thought he saw another grand conspiracy in the making, one equivalent to that which had kept Robert Walpole in power. As with the first, Taylor thought the conspiracy of his day was eroding liberty through the corruption of morality. He was saddened that the men who had in their youth been very critical of the use of patronage, speculation, and corruption were insensitive to the same tendencies in America. Not only had the Federalists, such as Adams, forgotten the ideals of the American Revolution, but the Jeffersonian Republicans of the 1820s, such as Madison, had forgotten the same ideals they had defended against Adams in the late 1790s. When Taylor used the term *the Principles of '98* or *Republican Principles*, then, he may have been referring to the century of development from the

Walpole Administration in England to the Monroe Administration in the United States, and to the continuing Republican opposition that had fought for the right throughout this period and had usually lost.

Taylor's socioeconomic background was varied enough to allow him to take a wider view than that of his own economic class alone. He was a self-made man whose fortune in land and slaves was truly large, but not so large that he needed to look upon himself as one of the leaders of a privileged class. Moreover, both the general agricultural decline of the Upper South and the precarious nature of his personal wealth reinforced Taylor's feelings that he was a member of an oppressed class. The agricultural and political solutions that he saw as inextricably linked were always phrased so as to appeal to farmers generally, or, in his more expansive moods, to all producers in general. John Taylor's ideas may have served the interests of an economic class, but they were phrased so as to appeal to most of the population of the United States.

Intellectually and professionally, then, John Taylor's thought emphasized individualism and independence within the limits of the ideal of harmony in nature and society. Politics and economics were linked—more than they should have been—and it was necessary to change political practices to regain the promise of America.

John Taylor's status as a theorist probably stands on the weakest ground when it comes to his views on political parties. It was in reference to these that the most observable change occurred in his thought. Although he had begun as an unyielding advocate of his interpretation of truth and refused to believe that truth could take any other form, the demise of parties during the Era of Good Feelings and the continued health of the energetic federal government caused him to revise his views. He seems to have come to realize that truth was best protected by having an opposition party, which could replace incumbents who had become corrupted. So long as these parties were ideological or doctrinal in nature, Taylor was willing to allow them. To any who might consider his approach to parties a reasonable choice for a committed intellectual to make in the twentieth century, it should be pointed out that Taylor's party was a tight group of activist scholars and not a group with a following comparable to that of a modern party. In accepting Taylor's views on parties, one should probably be prepared also to accept the same view of the mind that he did. He fully expected that the only discipline binding ideological parties would be each individual's allegiance to a common body of doctrinal principles. Party government could occur only as long as the members of the party agreed. Taylor thus carried over to his view of parties the presumption that, if trust and common belief in idealogical principles existed within a party, internal party dissent could be allowed without punishment. Although he did not have well-developed state parties with which to work and, hence did not think of allowing internal party dissent to be channeled through some form of federal party structure, as he had for the government, he did borrow from his concept of divided powers to find a rule that allowed dissent within the structure of a party. It was simply that dissent should be allowed and countered only with arguments, not with patronage or other material sanctions and rewards. It is not surprising that Taylor, who believed that the laws of nature governed the agricultural and economic worlds, eventually came to accept free trade in ideas within and between political parties.

John Taylor's diagnosis of the problems of the United States led him to attribute virtually all public, and a significant number of private problems to the selfish activities of aristocrats. In describing these power groups he combined several conclusions about politics into a limited program of reform which he expected would be achieved better through the general en-lightenment of mankind than through governmental structure.

If his evaluation of the harmful effects of aristocracies was correct, Taylor could have chosen three major conceptual alternatives. One, that aristocrats were superior individuals, was the one that John Adams accepted. No one feared the effects that these superior individuals could have more than Adams, but Taylor apparently felt that it would concede too much to admit that the aristocrats he hated were permanently superior in ability. The second alternative, economic determinism, was also rejected by Taylor. He could have considered the political influence that came from economic power as unavoidable. He rejected such materialism, and affirmed a duality between man's moral or intellectual capacity and his physical being. The very reason that the *Inquiry* had been written was to reject John Adams's expectation that man's greed and ambition were constants that governmental structure had to prevent. Taylor chose a third alternative, the increasing enlightenment of mankind, which led ultimately to equality. This allowed him to explain adequately how aristocrats had been able to establish themselves in power, which a doctrine of complete and immediate equality would not have permitted, while permitting him to point to a day in the near future when popular enlightenment would become so thoroughly diffused that aristocracies would be absurd. For the present, Taylor set equality on as strong a footing as possible by claiming that substantial widespread equality in abilities was already the case; that republican government was possible with the amount of equality that existed; that modern aristocrats had many bad moral qualities, which belied their surface superiority; and that if modern aristocrats had not learned to hide their methods behind funding, banking, charters, and similar devices, they would have been deposed already.

Taylor applied this doctrine of aristocracies to the history of the United States, which in his opinion had been characterized by a steady evolution of aristocrats. Using political means such as laws, constitutional interpretation, and patronage, aristocrats avariciously sought economic goals and ambitiously pursued political ones. Yet, the sense of morality they shared with all men kept reminding them of the natural harmony that had been broken by transferring property to themselves. This required them to publish justifications of their actions. Such rationalizations deceived no one, however, and their own bad consciences kept dragging them back to their misdeeds and to continual attempts to justify them as beneficial to the public interest.

Taylor, therefore, provided an early theory of the "iron law of oligarchy" without accepting the oligarchs as inevitable. He noted the existence of aristocrats, but he did not celebrate their accomplishments. Moreover, he derived both the power and the eventual downfall of aristocrats from the same source: the diffusion of knowledge. A monopoly of this knowledge was what had kept aristocracies in power over the ages, but its popular increase through education, the printed word, and free trade would eventually rival and overtake that possessed by aristocrats and would discredit their ideological justification for ruling.

Taylor devoted himself to the task of helping to expose modern aristocrats. His lack of interest in any grand scheme of governmental structural reform only reflected the fact that he thought the abolition of aristocracy would be sufficient to restore the natural social, political, and economic balance that their selfish projects had upset. This balance would be restored automatically when general knowledge of the methods of modern aristocracy was achieved and the aristocrats were limited in power.

Taylor's view of human nature led him to emphasize the power of persons to exercise moral choice. People knew the difference between right and wrong if their ideas were not confused by falsehoods and deceptions from outside sources. In a sense, the conspiracy that Taylor thought he had uncovered among aristocrats was also a product of moral choice. Aristocrats had the power to choose virtuous, simple, Republican government, but did not. Instead, they had chosen a governmental conspiracy to enrich themselves, and then began to deceive the small producers who created the wealth. The aristocratic conspiracy was no accident. There was little room in Taylor's moral universe for any accidents, perhaps because they would have broken nature's balance. Whether or not an aristocratic conspiracy actually existed was almost irrelevant to someone of Taylor's orientation. His optimistic view of the progress of the human mind measured against the hard times that agriculture was experiencing required a conspiracy, if only as an intellectual fiction. The lack of an aristocratic conspiracy would have raised serious questions about the very view of human nature that Taylor accepted. He needed a serpent to explain where all those apple cores had come from.

Taylor's approach to the problem of aristocracies, in broad outline, was similar to that adopted by an important group of modern students of social stratification and "power structure." The charge has been made by Nelson Polsby that many of the power-structure studies formulated their research problem and devised measures in such a fashion that the findings were self-fulfilling prophecies.[2] Taylor and the power-structure theorists shared at least the initial assumption that leadership groups existed. Taylor, of course, was unapologetically prescriptive in his approach, in that regard resembling C. Wright Mills, but it is possible that even more empirical students such as Floyd Hunter may have conducted studies using hypotheses that were self-fulfilling prophecies. To the extent that the expectation of rationality in man has generally projected the existence of a power structure, it may be possible that the diagnosis of problems by American reformers, and the actions taken as a consequence of the diagnosis, have often attacked apparent leaders whose power was symbolic at best. Such may have been the case with the Populist and agrarian reformers considered later in this chapter.

The public burdens that John Taylor traced to the activities of political and economic aristocrats led him to a reexamination of the constitutional procedures of American republicanism. Although he conceded that those who had formulated policies and American constitutional forms had learned from English antecedents, he thought that that the New World's statesmen had vastly improved on what their Old World predecessors had done. Taylor credited the increased diffusion of knowledge, more responsible legislatures, and invention of federalism with these improvements.

Among the many ideas he had herded together in his doctrine of divided powers, the most important were his convictions that governments should be judged by their policies, that traditional structural forms had serious defects, and that the proper functioning of a republican system depended on its ideological basis.

Taylor's insistence that governments be judged by their effects and not by their structure distinguished him from older theorists, who had traditionally been interested in structure. The classification of governments into the one, the few, and the many was an analytical practice at least as old as the Platonists. Liberal theorists such as Hobbes, Sidney, Locke, Harrington, and Rousseau had all prescribed structural details, although the extent to which structure dominated in their theories differed. Compared with his predecessors, Taylor probably came closest ideologically to Harrington, because of their appreciation of the effects of property relationships on republicanism, and to Machiavelli. Machiavelli appears to have been the first "policy scientist," willing both to accept governmental structure largely as he found it and to devote his considerable talents to helping the governors achieve goals as they visualized them. Machiavelli and Taylor are similar in that each broke with the tradition of emphasizing structure. By logically extending some of Taylor's less guarded statements regarding structure, one might infer that he would have accepted a monarchy or an oligarchy so long as their effects were acceptable to him. The inference would make the analogy between Taylor and Machiavelli closer, but, in fact, Taylor completely banished that possibility by defining all nonrepublican governments as a form of aristocracy and by defining aristocracy in such a way that its effects could only be harmful. Taylor's doctrine of divided powers gave him the conceptual ability to step back from the actual operating practices of American governmental institutions, to closely survey the principles that had been intended in American governmental structure, and then to offer suggestions as to where the connection between the principles and practices of government had broken down. In this his method somewhat resembles that of Montesquieu, except that Taylor deduced his principles of government from self-evident rationalistic truths and Montesquieu from cultural preferences embodied as the spirit of the laws of any particular state.

Turning to the structural details that had been invented to keep the governors honest, Taylor was unsatisfied. In respect to separation of powers, he had an admiration for the independence of departments of government and their individual ability to protect that independence. However, he refused to take a doctrinaire approach to separation and checks and balances. A precise equivalency in power, which teased the mind with the neatness of its symmetry, was rejected by Taylor, who looked upon checks as flowing out of the regular procedures used by each department. To him a check was not a device that allowed a department to dabble in the affairs of other agencies, but the unchallenged authority of each department to exercise those powers which generically and historically belonged to them. Thus, he was willing for the President to propose and veto legislation, for executives had earned that privilege, but they should not use those powers to gain an influence over legislators. The participation of the judiciary, on the other hand, was not required in the legislative process, and they had no powers in that area. Courts could decide particular cases, but the rulings should apply the law to particular situations and certainly should not formulate new, judge-made laws. On the other hand, there were few powers Taylor was not willing to trust to popularly elected legislatures, although he did have reservations about the Senate. For example, it did not use popular elections, and Senators served for long terms. They should be guided, therefore, by the will of their constituents, the state governments that had chosen them. Since these state governments were popularly elected, they could not have intended any aristocratic purposes. Thus, when Senators acted in aristocratic fashion they were in violation of their instructions. It is clear that Taylor's view of separated powers was influenced by his preference for elections: the closer a branch of government came to being popularly elected, the more Taylor trusted it.

Yet, he had qualms about elections as such. Elections must be judged by their effects and if they resulted in concentrated power, they were malfunctioning. Such distortions could occur easily if election campaigns became corrupt, if they transferred too much power, if there was no way of controlling candidates while in office, and if the people became disillusioned and joined in the corruption. Representation was the goal of elections and when it did not occur, the people were being cheated of a precious right. Thus representation achieved in Taylor's eyes the status of an individual natural right. The representation of a social class or an economic order was rejected by him whether it took the form of virtual representation, rotten boroughs, or an informal influence over Congressmen by the Bank of the United States. Representation, too, was judged by its fruits: if it operated in an unequal manner so that one privileged interest was favored, it was not effective.

Throughout his criticism of the traditional devices of constitutionalism, Taylor feared that the appearance of republicanism would be mistaken for its reality. It was ironical to him that the very devices that had been forged in the struggle to abolish priestly and feudal aristocrats were being used to shield the activities of their modern equivalents. The popularity of elected leaders, such as Cromwell, Walpole, or Napoleon, had never proved any safeguard against such aristocrats. It was not enough that government look beneficial; it must also act that way. Both the electorate and the officials must affirm by their deeds the principles they already knew in their hearts.

Thus Taylor offered the division of powers as an attempt to articulate the ideological ground of being for the American governmental system. Such an effort was doomed to failure by definition if it improvised greatly on the existing structure. Taylor did not improvise: "This essay does not aspire to the honour of proposing a new political system."[3] Instead, he generalized the values expressed in various organizational arrangements, pointing out that the primary division was between the people and government, *any* government. Subsidiary divisions existed within departments and between levels of government. The protection of the rights of the people was the purpose of government, which meant refraining from intervention in natural market forces and property relation-ships. Affirmation of the superior prerogative of the people helped institute wholesome motives inside and outside of government, but the instruction of representatives so that their actions could be controlled while in office was also essential. Moreover, a strong militia to guard the rights of the people from military coercion was needed.

Taylor was keenly aware of the symbolic importance of governmental forms and worried that bad policies flowing from good forms could discredit the latter without removing the former. Government rested on a latent system of belief that would only be eroded by actions inconsistent with it. Taylor never doubted that all Americans would acknowledge the self-evident truths he found compelling. A consideration of the list of axioms he presented requires the judgment that he was probably right in assuming that these values were widespread. Many undoubtedly still are, although the Enlightenment's confidence that men can agree on the definition of these values is gone, along with the expectation that there is a harmony between individual self-interest and the public interest. The very ability of language to convey the same meaning to persons accepting the same rhetoric is subject to severe doubt. Yet, Taylor's view that all government was based on widespread assumptions concerning its purpose, that imbalances in the extent to which these assumptions are reflected in governmental policies can create tensions, and that the forms of republicanism can shroud the substance of tyranny may be applicable to any time.

Federalism was a vital part of Taylor's theory of divided powers, for the division between the federal and state govern-ments provided both a safeguard against concentrated power and the means for expressing the will of the people through the constitutional communities, which he called nations.

Taylor put his system of federalism on the strongest possible standing by maintaining that it had been both natural and a product of choice. He maintained that states were cultural entities with a background of shared values. At the same time, his recognition of the differences between federal and state governments did not deter him from expecting that they could be harmonized by human effort into a governmental system entrusted with specific powers to act in matters that affected the interests of all the states. Even though historical factors had created the states, Taylor credited the American improved understanding of government with having had the genius to combine them into a workable system of government.

He thought the adoption of federalism offered several advantages that otherwise would not have been available: first, in reduction of the amount of power any American government possessed, thus dampening governmental tendencies to break faith with their people; second, in the existence of state governments that were united in sympathy and interest with local conditions. A final advantage lay in the fact that states could learn from each other's experiences with various governmental structures, processes, and services. Taylor often used such factual examples in his discussions, not limiting his choice of good examples to Virginia, or even to the South.

The key to Taylor's system of federalism was his doctrine of nation. By linking the natural causes of federalism with the social contract theories common to his time, Taylor was able to argue that each of the American states was a separate nation that had formed its state government and then joined with others to form the federal government. A nation, then, was the people of a state in their combined roles as the product of a particular cultural and historical development and the constituent group that extended its consent to governments deserving of it. State rights, in Taylor's opinion, referred to the individual rights of self-government channeled through state nations. No governments had rights.

This concept of nation was Taylor's substitute for the society hypothesized by social contract theorists. For Taylor it was not a question of society, but societies. No government could have a part in the formation of these groups. In offering this version of the social contract, Taylor did not seem actually to believe in the historicity of social contracts but implied instead that, since the states were already communities at the time of the American Revolution and each citizen within them had the right to self-government, each nation was superior to both its own state government and the federal government that was formed later. He hesitated to call this authority to govern *sovereignty*; instead he considered it simply the ability to form governments. He had little use for the term *sovereignty*, which by his definition required an indivisible ultimate authority in governments. He preferred to divide delegated authority and denied that any group other than the people of each state-nation could have ultimate authority.

Nations made divided powers possible, because nations were the supporters of the militia and the electing bodies that manned the state and federal governments. At the same time the division between the nation and its governments was a pledge to governments that their constituents would use regular electoral procedures, not mobs, to control governmental actions.

The American Union was a compact between states as nations—the people acting in their combined cultural and constituent capacities. The terms of the Union did not require nations to give up their right to self-government, although they had willingly surrendered some specific powers to form the sphere of authority possessed by the federal government. Taylor examined the clauses in the Constitution that Federalists had used to expand the powers of the federal government and applied a test of intent to the exercise of even expressly delegated federal powers. He found that the Constitution allowed federal tariffs, but he believed that if a tariff discriminated against a particular group of state nations, it violated the spirit of mutual sympathy that should exist between the states and the federal government. Therefore he sometimes declared expressly delegated powers unconstitutional.

If any level of government, or any department within each level, achieved the power to review the activities of another level or department, the delicate arrangement of divided powers would be threatened. Thus Taylor insisted that the supremacy of the Constitution had moral, but not legally enforceable, authority over the federal and state governments. Each level had the duty to make the Constitution's intent supreme; to surrender this obligation to another agency would be a betrayal of trust. The actions of state governments were, therefore, exempt from the review of the federal government and vice versa.

Given Taylor's belief in the independence of state and federal governments under the Constitution, and the fact that his opinion of the proper activities of any government was very limited, it was inevitable that disagreements would arise between the federal and state governments. His belief in the compelling force of reason to resolve disagreements among individuals allowed him to expect fewer confrontations between state and federal governments than would some of those who did not share this faith, but even he cheerfully admitted that clashes would occur. Each level of government must have security against possible usurpation of power by the other. The concept of mutual veto took four forms in Taylor's thought, although he never clearly distinguished the conditions governing the use of each. In a confrontation each level could do as it pleased without regard to the opinion or activities of the other; an aggrieved government could issue appeals to other members of the Union to add their moral support to its cause; the issue could be resolved definitively through the regular amending process; and, in a violent crisis during which a state was invaded by federal troops, it could forcibly resist. Note that Taylor did not offer compromise as a solution, as Calhoun later did. Taylor's rationalistic view of truth did not leave much room for compromise. He had faith in the ability of a just cause to win wide acceptance on its merits alone, particularly if those merits were publicized through such devices as the Virginia Resolutions. No satisfactory resolution of disagreement would be achieved, however, by surrendering half of a just cause.

The alternatives to mutual vetoes were all much more dangerous to the peace of the Union. They were, in fact, some of Taylor's ideas on the natural causes of federalism turned inside out. Thus, consolidation was dangerous, not just because it concentrated power in one government, but because state interests would still be present and the central government could only resort to force to secure compliance. Another danger was the fact that no safety valves would be present to filter out local interests. Each parochial interest would carry its cause to Congress and the peace of the Union would be disturbed by petty issues. The danger of sectionalism was also inhibited by the presence of states, because they were communities unified by a commitment to republican principles. Sectionalism had no such commitment and was motivated completely by self-interest. Strong states were a cure for sectionalism.

Taylor's frank acceptance of clashing between levels of government is at odds with modern notions of "marble cake" federalism, its layers stuck together with a frosting of cooperation. One commentator called it a "fantastic picture of a fragmented governmental system. . . ."[4] Taylor was embarrassingly eager to accept the logical consequences of concurrent powers, and his views are at odds with most constitutional theories that have assumed, since *McCulloch*, an ultimate authority in federal laws, treaties, or court decisions. In the area of clashing powers, however, the theoretical assumptions expressed in landmark Supreme Court cases and in the actual operation of the American governmental system may be creatures of different worlds. In practice, the federal government has often found concurrency an inevitable, convenient, or even desirable manner of operation. Thus, even though the *NLRB* v. *Jones and Laughlin* decision left almost no important economic activity free from the influence of federal commerce power, in practice there has often been a concurrent exercise of commerce power, as with state, federal, and local taxation of interstate commerce.[5] Convenience has also resulted in a division of labor unjustified on the ground of abstract constitutional theory alone, as with the preponderance of state regulations in the areas of highways and insurance. In addition, the federal government itself has found the concurrent exercise of federal, state, or local powers an acceptable course of action in such areas as freedom of access to public accommodations and housing, water pollution control, and firearms regulation.

Taylor's notion of concurrency may have been irrelevant to the subsequent course of American constitutional theory, but this is very different from saying that it was unworkable in principle. When Taylor defended the clashes that occurred when a state passed a law to check or duplicate a federal law it considered unconstitutional, he was merely proposing a patchwork variety of regulations that often accepted in practice today. An important difference arises from the fact that modern practice often adopts a variety of paths to the social policy goal, while Taylor often rejected any energetic use of governmental power. He did not, for example, advocate a state banking system to displace the Federal one; he disliked *all* banks and subsidies as a transference of property by law.

As a method of resolving state and federal disagreements, Taylor's resort to the amending process seems very cumbersome. In recent years the amending process at the state level alone has taken as much time as four years for the Twenty-Second Amendment and as little as nine months for the Twenty-Third Amendment.[6] The Supreme Court's authority to police the boundaries of the federal system can result in a much more expeditious settling of federal and state disagreements. The potential the Supreme Court possesses in this regard, however, should not be mistaken for its normal operating procedures. The progress of landmark court decisions through various levels of appeals usually takes years and the creation of a body of precedent that sets the scene for such a major departure takes even longer. Consequently, the mere cumbersomeness of the procedure suggested by Taylor does not distinguish it from the existing system as much as might initially be thought.

The arguments for federalism offered by Taylor are still valid, although experience has probably proved that the ability of federalism to filter interests is accomplished at the cost of its ability to provide experiments in republicanism. The federal system has proved in practice to be different in one other major aspect from the way Taylor conceptualized it. He seemed to think of the system as containing a limited amount of power: if the federal government grew in energy, it must be at the expense of the states. Actually, both the federal and the state and local levels have grown in power, and the exercise of power by one level has often increased the range of choice, authority, and means of the other level.

Taylor's theory of divided powers was related to his agricultural writings in several ways. First, an agrarian society in a country with an abundance of land would automatically give republicanism a widely diffused property base. Agrarianism ensured that the general interest of society would be nearly the same as the expressed interests of all American farmers. Second, working with the laws of nature in an agrarian setting stimulated the intellectual activity that had proved to be the foe of all kinds of aristocracy in ages past. Third, a farmer's life required the daily practice of those principles necessary for the success of a republican government. Liberality, foresight, and unduplicated effort were the virtues Taylor expected both statesmen and farmers to practice, and when the statesmen were farmers the transference was natural. Fifth, the life of a tidewater farmer who implemented Taylor's program of deep plowing, four shifts, and live fences might become so profitable that he would have time for public service, and his service would be improved by the fact that a prosperous farmer in a society of farmers would be interested only in the public interest. Sixth, the agrarian society would form a compatible setting for the maintenance of a militia and the instruction of representatives united in self-interest with their constituents by the fact that they all shared the same local problems. The final way that division of powers was served in Taylor's agrarian writings arose from Taylor's using basically the same approach in both politics and farming. In both realms he advocated the creative, uninhibited use of man's reason to discover nature's laws. When they were discovered, he usually encouraged man to adjust his behavior in a manner compatible with them. Just as nature's laws governed agriculture, the principles of republicanism were considered controlling in the political world. Either set of laws could be ignored, but only at the cost of prosperity and happiness. Republican principles came in both particular and general varieties— particular in that each state nation had different circumstances and, therefore, a different understanding of human rights, and general in that they included a commitment to the principles of division that maintained each state's particular existence and rights.

Taylor's ideal, a society of agrarian yeomen, smashed logically on the rock of Negro slavery. Taylor never applied the labor theory of value, the equality of individual abilities, and the right to self-government to the slave. It seems never to have occurred to him that the planter was transferring the property of slave labor to himself and thus stood judged by Taylor's own system as an aristocrat. Plausible reasons can be offered for Taylor's negligence on this point, chief among them the fact that he considered his personal field work as labor's contribution to the factors of production and that of the slaves as capital. There can, however, be no excuses that save the logical coherence of his system. Although Taylor's system was among the most egalitarian in Western political thought, it proved inadequate to deal with the problem of slavery on any but the most extreme long-range terms.

B. The Problems of Intellectuals and Morality

There are two themes that cut across various aspects of Taylor's thought and deserve mention. They are the problems of the intellectual in politics and the effect of government on morality.

One of Taylor's chief aims was to put the farmer-intellectual in politics. However, he worried about what government and intellectuals did to each other. By his personal example and with his expressed admiration, Taylor favored scholar-activists, but he did not consider all intellectuals suited for public service.

Both lawyers and speculative philosophers were rejected, the first for the tendency to trust in the precedents of the past, the other for the tendency to be too utopian and abstract. Moreover, governmental service had a detrimental effect on some intellectuals, who lost the ability to evaluate objectively their own work as a consequence of the decisions they made in public office.[7]

The ideological party was, of course, one of Taylor's solutions to the dilemma of how an intellectual could contribute to government without becoming overcommitted. He advised the intellectual to protect his ability to make a contribution as a thinker by keeping his distance. One had an obligation to fight for candidates who offered the best chance of implementing the ideological program favored by the intellectual, but after the election, incumbents must be scrutinized with care. As he said to Monroe:

> I hereby give you notice, that you are not to infer . . . that I will join a party yell in favor of your administration; No, no, the moment you are elected, though by my casting vote, carried a hundred miles in a snowstorm, my confidence in you would be most confoundedly deminished, and I would instantly join again the republican minority.[8]

Taylor assumed that the very process of achieving knowledge enabled its holders to make correct political judgments. Such a joining of the *is* and *ought* has always been characteristic of natural law thinking in general and of the rationalism of the Enlightenment in particular. The impact of positivism on twentieth-century political science has caused some to question whether it is ever the duty of science to pass from description, measurement, analysis, and prediction to prescription. Such questions did not disturb Taylor, who simply assumed that human rationality was an expression of the law of nature. Without some such attempt to bridge the *is* and the *ought*," the political choices of intellectuals must be assigned a value equivalent to that of all other intelligent citizens. Taylor's example as a scholar-statesman is one that is difficult for activist intellectuals to ignore, but it can be accepted only at a philosophic cost.

If John Taylor disliked an aspect of government, he attacked it in depth, offering as many arguments as he could muster. Unlike many liberal thinkers, Taylor did not leave his fight against centralized power at a mere attack upon tyranny and proposals for reform. He went on to speculate about what strong government did to its subjects. Throughout his writings he expressed the conviction that government and other institutions with public roles influenced individual conduct and private morals through the examples they offered. The moral impact of institutions was a major theme of John Taylor. His consideration of this impact put him a notch above those who have merely attacked excess power without detailing, either what made it harmful or what to do with a free life once it was secured.

Taylor's idea of *moral* bore the distinct imprint of the eighteenth century. On the opening page of the *Inquiry* he stated that man was composed of both matter and mind. Of the two, mind was by far the more powerful, for it could reflect on the qualities of matter, whereas matter could not reflect on anything. "Therefore," he wrote, "as we cannot analyze mind, it is generally allowed to be a supernatural quality."[9] Human activities arising from the mind's power of abstraction, and man's ability to choose among alternatives were *moral* activities. Taylor reserved the words *natural* and *physical* for extensions of matter, and linked the religious nuances of the term *moral* with man's ability to exercise free choice.

This led him to attack as immoral three kinds of laws: those which encouraged competitive, selfish, private morals; those which limited the power of thought, because Taylor's rationalism expected that men could think their way to ethical truth; and that which attempted to substitute the authority of government for that of an individual's own conception of God[10] Given the modest size of government in Taylor's time, and its lack of social policy activities based on value and moral commitments, the fears Taylor voiced regarding the moral impact of government are even more relevant today than they were then. The stakes are much larger today in the struggle for public subsidies than he could have imagined, and the struggle is more observable among organized groups that feel little need even to phrase their demands in the rhetoric of the public interest. Taylor's second fear, infringement of the individual's ability to think his way to truth, is a problem only for those who believe that it is possible for truth to be achieved and applied through a rational process of individual discovery. That may be no small group. It might include, for example, not merely believers in natural law, but also absolute idealists, scientific naturalists, and pragmatists. Each of these philosophic positions holds hopes that humanity can be served by a process of enlightenment that might be interrupted by government. Taylor judged such an interruption of the process of moral discovery to be the very essence of immorality. Taylor's views on religious freedom are somewhat unusual for one of his orientation. Generally speaking the American Enlightenment was characterized by deists, who defended the social control that religious training brought, but who had little concern for organized religion as such. Taylor defended religious freedom, however, from a rhetorical viewpoint, which would appeal to denominations and sects. Whatever his personal beliefs, he looked upon himself as trying to save God from the twin impieties of laws that attempted to force beliefs down the throats of heretics and of laws that favored religion in general. The first assumed that God was a bad salesman who needed help, and the second that, if all the religions existing in the United States were equally valid, none could be. Secular practices that promoted respect for everybody's God really satisfied no one's.

Taylor never questioned the premise that government should have some kind of moral effect, but he was anxious that this effect be beneficial and not forced. He was not an advocate, therefore, of a completely minimal and ethically neutral polity, but he came close to this. He attacked governmental practices that legislated moral choices for its citizens in the name of someone's concept of fairness or decency. Any government that makes such moral choices proved itself to be an atheistic rival of God's sovereignty and that of the individual believer. Such coercion violated freedom of religion for all who were adherents of a denomination that prescribed moral conduct. Public humanitarianism denied both the freedom and expression of religious faith. In constitutional jargon, Taylor probably would have found the modern use of the Commerce Clause to be at war with the First Amendment. This is a degree of abstraction to which few would follow Taylor, but his insight that large government cannot act without teaching its citizens by example is a valid one that merits greater appreciation and is likely to find it in the post-Watergate-Chappaquiddick-Lockheed era.

Although he wanted government to do very little, his acceptance of the notion that government was a teacher of ethics makes his thought a natural bridge to a view of government that looks upon itself as having a moral obligation to solve social problems or even as an instrument of moral and social change. To the extent that more and more areas of public policy are resolved and placed "above" politics—as foreign policy, municipal government, Social Security policy, and civil service appointments have tended to be in recent years—official standards of conduct and conflict-of-interest considerations both increase in saliency. Eventually these standards and considerations may return to the importance in public affairs they held in Taylor's time, when government was doing very little.

C. Taylor and His Critics

At the beginning of this study the various interpretations of John Taylor offered by previous commentators were discussed. All of these had a common defect: reluctance to treat Taylor's theory as a comprehensive system of thought that covered a wide range of topics in an integrated fashion. But Taylor's doctrine of divided powers does just that, and it establishes his title as that of political theorist rather than mere ideologist. In fact, the more the ideological content of Taylor's thought is examined, the more it is apparent that his doctrines of aristocracy and of the-states-as-people required philosophic commitment to eventual substantive equality and to popular self-government—both very large investments. It may be that only the misunderstanding of Taylor's theory by his contemporaries gave him any status at all as an ideologist. Yet, it was the ideologist that most of Taylor's commentators discussed.

Whatever misunderstandings Beard introduced, for example, may have been corrected by his subsequent critics, but in the light of more recent research into the intellectual legacy of Caroline County it is a fair question whether overcorrection of the Beard thesis may not have taken place. Beard may have been right, but for the wrong reasons. Taylor may be considered the defender of republicanism, or even of democracy, but more for his epistemological assumptions about the growth of human knowledge outpacing the ability of aristocrats to create myths legitimatizing their right to rule than for his critique of the harmful practices of aristocrats.

The deficiency of the Mudge analysis lies chiefly in the fact that it made too limited a use of Taylor's works, making no effort to test his theories for consistency over time and providing few comparisons. Baritz restated some of Taylor's ideas well, but gave insufficient weight to his theory of aristocracy and his belief in the basic equality of men. Taylor's views on political parties were left largely unexplored by both of these critics.

Bailor has boldly argued for an interpretation of Taylor's ambiguous warning in chapter 15 of *Construction Construed* that would redeem Taylor from the taint of being a secessionist. Bailor's analysis must be accepted with qualifications, however, both because his interpretation of Taylor's meaning is still open to question and because the philosophical implications of Taylor's acceptance of slavery on the doctrine of equality were still unexamined. Bailor never explained, for example, the meaning of Taylor's sanction of preemptive warfare among nations in chapter 15. Although Taylor's agricultural experiments diminished the number of slaves needed to till each acre, Bailor may be inaccurate in assuming that Taylor meant to phase out slavery by this means. Taylor might simply have acquired more land.

The interpreters of Taylor as a state rights theorist have fallen short because of their lack of attention to what he meant by *state rights, nation, state,* and by their insufficient demonstration of how his doctrine of divided powers related to his theories on the causes, advantages, and dangers to federalism. Moreover, Taylor has often suffered from a careless linking of his thought to secessionist and nullificationist thinkers, as a later section of this chapter will demonstrate.

The interpreters of Taylor as an economist, Craven and Grampp, each found Taylor deficient in a particular aspect. Craven thought Taylor's deficiency was the overemphasis he placed on the nutritive role of the air and soil, which excluded his appreciation of the importance of plant diseases. Grampp criticized Taylor for misunderstanding the purpose of Hamilton's funding plan: Taylor thought that Hamilton's funding was to establish a permanent debt and a sinking fund to finance further speculative ventures of governmental officials. In part, Taylor's deficiences may have resulted from the fact that Taylor could be expected single-handedly to push the frontiers of knowledge only so far: Craven and Grampp seem to accept this view. It is a persuasive explanation, but the reason Taylor could go no further than he did is more basic. He overemphasized soil because of the importance he gave to the providence of nature, and he misunderstood governmental debt because of the universal applicability he gave to his theory of aristocracies. To appreciate Taylor as a technician, one must understand his total philosophic outlook.

All previous commentators on Taylor have relied heavily on a history-of-ideas approach that considered Taylor important more for what he could add to an understanding of the schools of Jeffersonianism, agrarianism, and states' rights than for what he said in itself. He has often been characterized either as a representative of what Jefferson *really* would have said if he had not been forced by public duties to compromise, or as the most articulate spokesman for early states rights theories and the predecessor of Calhoun. It would be futile to argue that Taylor had no effect on Jefferson and Calhoun, but it is also true that they had a not-often-recognized impact on him. Regardless of Taylor's influence, however, no commentator can be excused from examining Taylor's ideas for their own value. Reexamination has been necessary, therefore, because few of his commentators treated Taylor as a political theorist with intrinsically important ideas, and none as a theorist with a range of ideas covering most important political problems whose solutions are still elusive. Because Taylor was a theorist and not merely an ideologist, it is necessary to determine what ontological, metaphysical, and epistemological baggage must accompany any ideas borrowed from him. One cannot easily adopt Taylor's ideas on separation of powers, ideological political parties, state rights, or any of his other fundamental doctrines without being forced to adopt at the same time his entire rationalistic method of thought. Surprisingly, the chief inconsistency of his system for Taylor is not one that need concern moderns. If he had attempted to justify slavery in any important manner, it might have made his system completely inapplicable. Calhoun went much further than Taylor in this regard. Since Taylor largely ignored the problem of slavery, he never attempted to limit his ideas of natural rights and popular sovereignty to Caucasians. Just because he did not apply the labor theory of value or natural rights to slaves is no reason to repeat his inconsistency.

D. Comparison with Contemporaries

John Taylor's status as a political theorist of considerable consistency and breadth of vision has been studied in previous chapters by an almost exclusive focus on Taylor's own writings. Those who have interpreted Taylor as simply representative of various social movements such as agrarian reformism, states' rights, or Jeffersonianism have done him injustice. This conclusion is made explicit by comparing Taylor's system with the ideas of other Jeffersonians and John Adams. The question of Taylor's influence on Calhoun, since it occurred in the late 1840's if at all, will be considered in the next section.

The similarity of Jefferson's and Taylor's ideas is often taken for granted, or the differences explained, when recognized, as owing to Jefferson's need to compromise principle during a busy political career. It must be admitted that Jefferson's three decades of public life required adjustments and compromises, but Taylor spent over a dozen years in state and national office. The fact is that they both made compromises, and Taylor's participation in the passage of the Twelfth Amendment and his defense of the purchase of Louisiana, tariffs, and embargo indicate that he was flexible, like Jefferson, and in the same direction. At the same time, Taylor always attempted to retain his ability to dissent. After 1804 he increasingly began to do that, as far as Jefferson and Madison were concerned. That there were similarities between Jefferson and Taylor cannot be denied, but the assumption that the ideas of Jefferson led directly and uniquely to Taylor is less tenable.

Jefferson and Taylor apparently were never close friends who frequently exchanged views. Moreover, each man seems to have assumed greater agreement between them than existed. Each seemed to accept the general agreement of the other as vindication of his own views. Consequently, late in life Taylor was overheard wishing that Jefferson would come off his mountain and restate the principles of 1798.[11] Since these principles had been interpreted at least partly by Taylor's defense of the 1798 Virginia Resolutions, Taylor's wish came close to hoping that Jefferson would vindicate Taylor. Jefferson seems to have been an obliging individual who liked to get along with people—with Taylor, with Madison, and with John Adams, and, to their mutual horror, all at the same time. This strained the abilities of even Jefferson, who was forced to protect himself against being drawn into every petty quarrel among his friends and followers. Consequently, Jefferson's warmest words of praise for Taylor were written to Thomas Ritchie: "Colonel Taylor and myself have rarely, if ever, differed in any political principle of importance. Every act of his life, and every word he ever wrote, satisfies me of this."[12] Thomas Ritchie may have been taken aback when he heard that Jefferson approved of "every word" Taylor ever wrote. By implication this meant that Jefferson approved of the ripping attack that Taylor made on Ritchie in 1809 when Ritchie was assuming the role of self-appointed defender of the Jefferson-Madison administration. Moreover, these words of praise for Taylor were written as advance praise for *Construction Construed*, which Jefferson had not yet even read. Even more significant was this sentence from the letter to Ritchie; "So, also as to the two Presidents, late and now in office, I know them both to be of principles as truly republican as any men living."[13] Since one of these men was Madison, whom Taylor numbered among his most important intellectual enemies, and the other was Monroe, who was the object of Ritchie's 1809 criticism, Jefferson's praise may have been difficult for Ritchie to understand. Despite his praise for the work, Jefferson declined to write a letter of introduction to *Construction Construed,* because previous authors had misrepresented him on occasion.

Jefferson praised all of Taylor's later works (including *Construction Construed* after he had read it) and did not hesitate to recommend them to his correspondents. He once suggested that a copy of *Construction Construed* be furnished all state legislators as a manual standing instructions. On another occasion he said that he never endorsed anything that was not in *Construction Construed*, but he declined to defend it in the newspapers. It is probable that Jefferson accepted Taylor's writings so readily after retirement, especially after the Missouri Compromise, because he was himself moving toward a more sectional position. It was then that he became interested in founding the University of Virginia as a refuge against the corrupting effects of Northern schools.[14]

Jefferson admitted to Ritchie that Taylor's *Inquiry* had caused him to change his mind on a few points. He especially delighted in Taylor's criticism of John Adams's system of orders (contained in the *Inquiry*, which Jefferson did not read until 1816), even though Adams had indicated in an 1813 letter to Jefferson that he agreed with Taylor's indictment of banking. Taylor had sent Adams advance copies of the *Inquiry* in 1813, but he did not send a copy to Jefferson until 1816. There is no evidence to indicate that Taylor ever solicited Jefferson's opinion on any of his other books, although his early pamphlets may have been reviewed by Jefferson.[15]

At the same time that Jefferson was praising *Construction Construed* to Thomas Ritchie, he admitted to Spencer Roane, Ritchie's brother-in-law, that not all of the book's ideas were acceptable to him. He did say, however, that *Construction Construed* did contain the "true political faith, to which every catholic republican should stedfastly hold."[16] Regardless of this warm recommendation, when Taylor himself finally asked Jefferson about endorsing political works, the latter still declined to go on record. It seems fair to say, considering the range of political figures who earned Jefferson's approval and the mixed feelings he displayed in respect to Taylor's views, that the general tone and orientation of Taylor's works were what Jefferson admired. He still had reservations about their specific contents.[17]

The specific points of agreement and disagreement between Jefferson and Taylor related to their views on secession, human nature, aristocratic practices, governmental structure, and farming.

The exchange of letters between the two men in 1798 over secession was caused by a misunderstanding. Jefferson thought Taylor had endorsed secession because he had seen a smudged copy of a letter written to a third person in which Taylor seemed to say this. Jefferson wrote a conciliatory letter to Taylor urging patience. Time would bring the republicans to power, Jefferson said, because parties and disagreement were endemic in human nature. If the Union were broken, on the other hand, even North Carolina and Virginia would find things about which to disagree. Taylor, for his part unaware of Jefferson's misreading of his previous letter, assumed that Jefferson wanted to argue about the origin of political parties, but in the course of responding agreed that a "southern aristocracy oppressing the northern States, would be as detestable, as a northern, domineering over the southern states."[18] They agreed, then, that the Union was worth preserving.

On human nature, they were less in agreement. As Adrienne Koch and Daniel Boorstin have each pointed out, Jefferson was a sort of materialist who looked upon thinking as a form of action.[19] Taylor, on the other hand, was more of a dualist, who believed not only that human choice was possible, but that government should protect it. His chief criticism of John

Adams's *Defence*, it will be recalled, was that it instituted a policy of determinism that assumed that people would always act aggressively in any governmental setting. Jefferson was very reluctant to believe that government could be changed by the sheer force of argument. He really did not believe in the short-run ability of ideas to get results. In Jefferson's opinion, a man's ideas did not change quickly, because more was involved than a simple effort of will. To Jefferson an opinion was a kind of behavior pattern or habit, and new opinions had to be practiced. Jefferson thus was tolerant by necessity: he felt that there was little he could do about contrary opinions but wait them out. Taylor had more faith in the evangelical power of ideas and less patience with those who disagreed with him, including Jefferson. He wrote Jefferson and pointed out that the latter's opinion in the same 1798 that party spirit was based on the natural variety of opinions among people was dangerous. Even if party spirit were based in human nature, Taylor warned, it might be possible to change human nature. Moreover, the manifest truth of republican principles would ensure that even pessimists on the subject of man's nature could support republican government.[20]

Aristocratic practices, especially banking, found Jefferson and Taylor in only general agreement. Jefferson claimed that he and Taylor had always agreed on banks, but they had not. Taylor condemned all banks, while Jefferson, at least temporarily, defended state banks. On the subject of funding, Jefferson and Taylor both started out opposing the accumulation of a sinking fund, Taylor because he thought it was expensive, and Jefferson because he did not believe in one generation's tying the hands of posterity with debt. Jefferson ultimately changed his mind and supported using the sinking fund for internal improvements, pending a constitutional amendment. Jefferson came to a reluctant acceptance of manufacturing and supported protective tariffs on certain commodities. His acceptance of internal improvements particularly revealed his difference from Taylor: Jefferson urged a correspondent to real Taylor's *New Views* as an orthodox interpretation of the Constitution while urging the same correspondent to return to Congress and vote for a constitutional amendment that would allow internal improvements. At the same time, the author of *New Views* was in the Senate earnestly trying to implement his book by speaking against internal improvements! Jefferson and Taylor were in general agreement on the practices of aristocracies, but Jefferson eventually came to accept the view that America must be economically independent of the Old World. If this meant manufacturing, and he admitted it did, he was ready to accept it, capitalists and all. Along with acceptance of manufacturing went, for Jefferson, acceptance of the tariff. Taylor, on the other hand, had never rejected the need for manufacturing, but did reject the role of capitalist financiers and protective tariffs. Consequently, both Jefferson and Taylor came to accept a more modern view of the economy than one based on simple agrarianism. Jefferson based his view on a sort of "fortress America" concept while Taylor continued to believe in the benefits of comparative advantages and free international trade.[21]

Jefferson and Taylor were in close agreement on governmental structure and procedures throughout their lives. For example, both opposed long terms of office for the President and considered upper houses as tending toward aristocracy. In 1824, however, Jefferson endorsed popular election of the President by the people as embodied in a draft constitutional amendment before Congress. The chief opposition to that amendment in Congress was offered by Taylor, who was pushing at the same time for his own revision of the Twelfth Amendment, which would have increased the power of the electoral college. Jefferson also differed with Taylor in suspecting the judiciary of being a "subtle corps of sappers and miners" who were attempting to overthrow the Constitution.[22] He exonerated the President and Congress of guilt in this matter. It will be remembered that Taylor laid the blame for aristocratic advances on the shoulders of Congress, not federal courts. The response that states should make to these attempts to destroy the Constitution was described by both Jefferson and Taylor in such metaphoric terms that it is difficult to determine exactly what they meant. Taylor had talked of mutual vetoes and the right of self-defense and Jefferson talked of every individual's raising his arm in defense against federal usurpers and of meeting invaders "foot to foot." At the same time each believed that convictions regarding true republican principles were the most important defenses. Jefferson thought *Construction Construed* would provide the states with such an understanding of federalism that the battle against federal usurpation would be half won if the book were widely distributed.[23] Jefferson's conception of the Union

was almost identical to Taylor's, as revealed in this letter to
Spencer Roane:

> It is a fatal heresy to suppose that either our State govern-
> ments are superior to the federal, or the federal to the states.
> The people . . . have divided the powers of government into
> two distinct departments . . . in differences of opinion be-
> tween these . . . the appeal is to neither, but to their employers
> peaceably assembled by their representatives in convention.[24]

Jefferson and Taylor seemed less close on the subject of Virginia
local government, because Jefferson criticized the county court,
while Taylor supported it. Neither Jefferson nor Taylor was
worried over the fact that the county courts combined in their
operations all the powers and functions of local government
with no concession to separated powers; Jefferson, at least, did
worry about the fact that its officials were not elected. "I
acknowledge the value of this institution" he said. "It is their
self-appointment I wish to correct."[25] On the subject of governmental structure and procedure, then, Jefferson and Taylor
were in disagreement on minor points (election of the President
or the culpability of judges) but in close agreement on the crucial
issue of the nature of the Union. The blind spot Taylor had for
the division of powers at the local level was shared by Jefferson,
although the latter did want some sort of rotation in office.

   In agricultural matters Jefferson and Taylor were both
experimentalists. Jefferson accepted Taylor's theory of atmospheric nutrition and agreed that the best way of improving crops
was by getting out of the way of nature's laws. Nature's own time,
not human treatment, was what the land needed, in Jefferson's
opinion. Thus Jefferson used a six-shift system of crop rotation,
while Taylor used a four. This led Jefferson to advocate the use
of larger tracts of land. He seems to have been influenced more
by Physiocratic theories than Taylor, who diverged from them
by considering the rent paid on land equivalent to the interest
paid on loans, and by his Lockean belief that wealth was created
by labor. Jefferson quoted Physiocrats approvingly; Taylor did
not. Moreover, Jefferson's view of a nation of freehold farmers
led him to propose cheap land for frontier settlement, while
Taylor believed the precipitate development of the frontier to
have been an important cause of Virginia's agricultural decline.[26]

There were profound disagreements between Jefferson and Taylor on the subject of slavery. As was discussed in the last chapter, Taylor's defense of slavery was built, point-by-point, on a refutation of Jefferson's views. While recognizing its defects, Taylor maintained that slavery also had certain positive aspects. Jefferson recognized only the former. Yet Jefferson, even more than Taylor, proposed a system of agriculture that relied upon the cultivation of huge tracts of land, probably requiring the efforts of slaves. Jefferson did at least manumit five slaves in his will; Taylor freed none.[27]

A comparison of Jefferson and Taylor reveals less similarity than would have been expected from previous interpretations of Jeffersonian thought. There is evidence to suggest that the influence, to the extent that it existed, flowed from Taylor to Jefferson more often than from Jefferson to Taylor. Jefferson admitted, for example, that the *Inquiry* made him change his mind on a few points that he had previously not seen clearly. The strongest similarity between the two was their common acceptance of the states and the federal government as coordinate partners to the Union. The differences between the two were several, but, most fundamentally, Jefferson can be characterized as a naturalistic thinker who was bound even more than Taylor to the laws of nature as he conceived them.

Whether the issue was the origin of parties, size of farms, or equality of slaves, Jefferson was true to his naturalistic assumptions, which gave his thought the peculiar quality of being both deterministic and tentative. Jefferson seems always to have been in a state of anticipation waiting for nature to make up "her" mind. Since it was "her" decision that ultimately counted, Jefferson did not always find it necessary to have a settled opinion himself on particular issues. Whether the issue was crop rotation or public opinion, Jefferson was willing to wait on nature's laws.[28] Taylor maintained a more creative role for man than Jefferson. After all, Taylor was never at a loss for opinions and was always willing to try to convince others through the sheer force of argument. Thus, on the issues of human nature, origin of parties, or agriculture, Taylor argued for a more creative role for individuals. When it came to the matter of slavery, Jefferson was truer to his egalitarian assumptions, while Taylor held back from recognizing either the master's creative ability to change the institution or the slave's creative role in value.

This comparison of Taylor and Jefferson was required because of the often-alleged similarity of their views. A comparison of Taylor and Madison is required because of Taylor's opinion that Madison was a formidable intellectual and political adversary whose influence in the Republican Party was dangerous. The fact that Madison, even more than Jefferson, can be considered the founder of the Republican Party was never considered by Taylor.[29]

Yet, before Taylor's break with Madison in 1806, the two often worked together. Taylor submitted drafts of the *Enquiry* to Madison, who revised it to Taylor's satisfaction. Madison valued Taylor's support in the United States Senate and the Virginia House of Delegates and wrote several times to Edmund Pendleton encouraging Taylor's participation in national politics. Pendleton's opinion was highly valued by Madison, and the former's death in 1801 may have marked the beginning of the disagreements between Taylor and Madison. They of course worked together on the Virginia Resolutions: Madison wrote them, Taylor defended and reinterpreted them, and then both worked together in the 1799-1800 session of the House of Delegates, which saw the submission of Madison's 1800 report on the Virginia Resolutions.[30]

Taylor had begun to suspect Madison's orthodoxy in 1797 when the latter voted in favor of a congratulatory proclamation to President Washington, but his real opposition grew out of his reading of the *Federalist* in 1806. At first his criticism was general, suspecting Madison of admiring the British system of government and of showing lack of vigor in pressing for constitutional reform. By the time of *New Views*, however, Taylor had gained access to Yates's notes of the Framing Convention, which convinced him that Madison's ideas had always been heretical. He objected most stenuously to *Federalist* essays "Number Thirty-nine" and "Number Forty-five," in which Madison had discussed the nature of the Union and the role of the judiciary.[31]

Taylor thought that Madison and Hamilton had adjusted their arguments in the *Federalist* to appeal to two parties that had not won out in the Framing Convention: republican consolidationists and monarchists. Madison had represented the first group, Hamilton the second. Both had written the *Federalist* essays with schemes for strong government warm in their minds and first in their sympathies. Madison had signed the Constitution only out of a desire to do something to strengthen the

Confederacy and would have preferred, in Taylor's opinion, a much stronger government. Taylor found Madison's "mixed" theory of the Union—that the Union was partly federal and partly national—an ambiguous doctrine from which both true federalists and consolidationists could take heart. This theory, combined with his statement in the same essay that the *American people* had ratified the Constitution, called into question his devotion to a federal system. Taylor thought the term *American people* had been used to discredit the fact that the only people that legally existed in the United States were those organized as state-"nations." Madison's theory of the Union falsely gave him the appearance of being moderate, since only a ratification by "nations" could have been granted under the Articles of Confederation. When Madison said in the Federalist that the House of Representatives would draw its power from the people of America, he revealed his bias. The House had no power, regardless of its basis in elections, that had not been given it by the Constitution. Taylor also disputed Madison's use of the word *corporation* to refer to states. *Corporation* implied that states were no more powerful than municipalities.[32]

Taylor and Madison had clashed on the state-and-people issue as early as 1800, when Madison asked Taylor to explain why the word *state* had been used in the Virginia Resolutions without reference to the people of those states. Taylor answered that states meant people and that everyone knew that; elaboration was unnecessary. From a twentieth-century perspective, the differences in Taylor and Madison's understanding of the nature of a state do not seem significant. Each recognized that a distinction should be made between a state's government and its people, but Madison seems by *state* to have meant state government, while Taylor used it to mean only the people. At the same time it cannot be denied that Madison's view of the Union envisioned a much more energetic central government than Taylor was willing to allow. Neal Riemer, a sympathetic interpreter of Madison, has admitted that Madison's statements during the 1830s that the Virginia Plan had never intended a stronger Union than was actually created may have been untrue. However, there is no reason to believe that Madison intended a consolidated form of government devoid of states.[33]

The second prong of Taylor's attack on Madison revealed a strong difference between them. In *New Views* Taylor noticed that Madison agreed with Edmund Randolph's defense of a strong judiciary, a bias that Taylor felt was manifest in the call of *Federalist* "Number Thirty-nine" for an impartial, federally created tribunal to settle jurisdictional clashes between the federal and state governments. Taylor feared that Madison meant for the Supreme Court to have this role. Taylor was right.[34]

Madison scarcely bothered to defend himself against Taylor's attacks in *New Views*. On the nature of the Union, he said in response only that the word *national* in the Virginia Plan was never meant to endorse a completely consolidated government, that it simply intended to establish a government that could operate on individuals for specific and limited purposes.[35] As was mentioned earlier, Taylor and Madison were in basic agreement on the fact that states' government should be considered separately from the people of each state.

On the subject of judicial review, Madison, in effect, admitted that Taylor had interpreted him correctly. Madison defended the Supreme Court's review of state laws by stating that even Edmund Pendleton had once agreed that there should be the possibility of appeal from a state's highest court to the United States Supreme Court. Moreover, he produced a copy of Taylor's *Argument on the Constitutionality of the Carriage Tax* and claimed that Taylor had at one time considered the Supreme Court in such a light himself.[36] To Jefferson he said:

> Believing, moreover, that this was the prevailing view of the subject when the Constitution was adopted . . . I have never yielded my original opinion, indicated in the "Federalist," No. 39, to the ingenious reasonings of Col. Taylor against this construction of the Constitution. . . . the abuse of a trust [by the Supreme Court] does not disprove its existence.[37]

Ultimately, therefore, Madison admitted that there was a gap between his and Taylor's view of the role of the judiciary, and by this admission also distinguished himself from Jefferson, who felt even more strongly about judges than did Taylor. Although Madison did not directly answer Taylor's charge that he was ambiguous on the nature of the Union, it seems clear that there was a strong difference between the two on this matter. In his last months Taylor stated that Madison really could not have believed that the Supreme Court should have the power of reviewing state laws, but is is clear from Madison's correspondence at the time that he meant just that.[38]

Madison's *Federalist* essay "Number Ten" was never discussed by Taylor, although it is clear that here, too, there was a strong difference between the two thinkers. Madison believed that faction was natural to the nature of man, as did Jefferson. Taylor's view was contrary to this. Madison worried about the disruptive effects of faction, but he thought that disagreements were inevitable and beneficial when not carried to excess. Riemer points out that Madison looked to the very number of interests in society, especially religious sects, to prevent the formation of majority tyrannies. In their acceptance of social diversity, Jefferson and Madison may have represented a later stage of the Enlightenment than Taylor, who seems to have thought that harmony was rather easily obtained by the ready application of republican principles. From his view in 1794 that "Truth is a thing, not of dievisibility into conflicting parts, but of unity," until his attack on sectionalism in the last chapter of his last book, Taylor held faith in man's rational capacity to avoid disagreements.[39]

Taylor's influence on other Republicans is somewhat problematical. Among his most frequent correspondents were Wilson Cary Nicholas and John Randolph of Roanoke. Yet, Nicholas was always sympathetic to the national wing of the Republican Party and supported issues and persons Taylor did not. Nicholas also was a supporter of banking. Randolph and Taylor often exchanged letters and agreed on many issues, but Taylor explicitly rejected the contention that he had any influence over Randolph's opinions and regretted the latter's inclination to indulge in ad hominem attacks. In later years Randolph came under the influence of the writings of Edmund Burke and orthodox Christianity, so that the tone of his writings changed even more. Unlike Taylor he eventually came to oppose change as such, to suspect written constitutions, and to oppose any inroads on the property of Virginia plantation owners. Taylor, on the other hand, never opposed change, although he was cautious about the motives of some who wanted it, thought a frequent resort to constitutional amendment was necessary to settle state-federal clashes, and supported the abolition of primogeniture and entail. Randolph's opinions on slavery were varied, but for a time at least he enjoyed considering himself the theoretical enemy of the institution. Moreover, his slaves were freed in his will. Randolph thought nullification a constitutional absurdity and Taylor supported mutual vetoes, but to the extent that Taylor's vetoes relied on the amending process, his views were completely constitutional and not nullification as understood in the 1830s. Randolph's opinions of Taylor's works were always pungent. It was he who suggested that the second edition of the *Inquiry* be translated into English, and he advised Taylor that the publication of *New Views* was inadvisable: it was too bitter an attack for even Randolph![40]

Taylor's influence on other followers of Jefferson is even more difficult to trace. Those politicians from Virginia and North Carolina—known at various times as "Old Republicans," "Quids," and "Radicals"—often voted the way it can be assumed that Taylor would have voted. Given the fact, however, that such literary giants as Randolph and Adams had difficulty reading and understanding Taylor's works, the extent to which the members of this group were really acting under the specific influence of some of Taylor's more baroque theories may be open to question. Nathaniel Macon is sometimes compared to Taylor, yet no correspondence of theirs seems to have survived, and Macon sometimes differed with Taylor on important issues, such as the election of Madison in 1808. Macon and Taylor's views on slavery may have represented more closely the planter outlook than those of Jefferson. Macon was a political power in his own state as leader of the "Warren Junto," and had little cause to appeal to Taylor's authority for ideas to buttress his power. Taylor enjoyed a great revival in the Virginia tidewater after the publication of *Construction Construed* and made his peace with his archrivals of the Madison campaign of 1808, Thomas Ritchie and Spencer Roane. These two, who controlled Republican politics for years in the Richmond area, came to a new appreciation for state rights after the decisions in *McCulloch, Martin* v. *Hunter's Lessee*, and *Cohens* v. *Virginia*.[41] Yet, again, the extent to which they really accepted Taylor's specific doctrines, or the extent to which they simply used him as a fellow ideologist who, unlike themselves, had an unbroken record of loyalty to states' rights, is open to question. The only safe generalization that can be made at this time regarding Taylor's influence on his contemporaries is that Jeffersonianism in Virginia was a cloak of many colors whose wearers sometimes shifted their views to suit time and circumstance. Taylor's thought was a largely consistent body of doctrine, parts of which they always accepted, but containing other parts they would accept only when the occasion demanded. Unfortunately for Taylor, those who accepted his influence always seemed to do so while they were out of power.

Ironically, John Taylor may have influenced his prime intellectual antagonist, John Adams, more than he did those who claimed to be followers of Jefferson. His attack on Adams in the *Inquiry* drew thirty-two letters in reply from Adams, who devoted the first twenty-one of the letters to criticizing the first eight pages of Taylor's *Inquiry*! If Taylor had spent twenty years taking him apart, Adams explained, it was only fair that Taylor listen patiently while he put himself back together. Taylor's influence, however, was largely a negative one, which caused Adams to restate with verve and clarity his doctrine of aristocracy, giving it perhaps a more democratic cast than before, but otherwise disregarding Taylor's theoretical ideas on aristocracy. Taylor's criticisms of aristocratic practices, on the other hand, Adams accepted wholeheartedly. Like Taylor, Adams opposed banking practices. Adams also found *Arator* an admirable book, although he disapproved of Taylor's having mixed politics into it. Adams was gratified to see that some of his protests had taken root by the time *New Views* was written, for in this book Taylor treated Adams's theories with respect greater than he showed for Madison. Taylor and Adams developed respect for each other as a consequence of their exchange of letters late in life, and Taylor praised Adams's role in the American Revolution. Yet Taylor never abandoned the view that Adams had originally been a monarchist. This did not prevent him from considering John Quincy Adams, whom he also suspected of once having been a monarchist, for President, because Taylor thought that the early days of the Republic had seen many monarchists who later changed and proved their worth. Perhaps it is just as well that Taylor did not live to hear John Quincy's inaugural address; its extreme nationalism would have sent him into a searching reevaluation of the role of Adamses in history.[42]

A few of Adams's criticisms of Taylor merit notice. These dealt with Taylor's terminology; his assumptions about the naturalness of governmental institutions, slavery, and aristocracy; and the connection he drew between knowledge and republicanism. First, Adams found Taylor's use of abstractions such as *moral liberty* mystifying and refused to use them. It is still a valid criticism of Taylor that he simply assumed that everyone would know what he meant by such terms as *moral, republican, nation,* and *state*. Second, Adams found Taylor's refusal to discuss governmental forms nothing more than a refusal to recognize that such forms had existed and that the structural features of aristocracy, democracy, and monarchy were reflected, in a perfected form, in the Constitution. Third, Adams's criticism of Taylor's status as a slaveholder was oblique, but unmistakable. Adams suggested that the inevitability of aristocracy would be proved if Taylor chose thirty of his "domestics" at random and constituted them into a republic for test purposes. An aristocracy would soon result. At another point he voiced the hope that Taylor would attempt to spread knowledge as much among his "domestics" as he said that it had been spread throughout the world. With such remarks Adams could not have escaped making his point that slaves were capable of aristocratic ability, self-government, and learning. Fourth, Adams did not quarrel with Taylor's assumption that aristocracy could be based on a transfer of property, but he insisted that Taylor ignored other sources of aristocracy, such as land, sex appeal, and heredity. He pointed out something that Taylor never discussed: Taylor was an aristocrat by land, slaves, and the fact that he had married a rich wife. Was it not true that most landed aristocrats were Tories? Finally, Adams rejected Taylor's conclusions on the spread of knowledge and the consequent decline of aristocracy. Knowledge was always a possession of the few, and that was a good thing. If all men were Newtons, they would starve. He warned Taylor that it was a mistake to assume that virtue inevitably followed knowledge. Even though it was inevitable that knowledge be a possession of the few, the few should be carefully watched so that they did not abuse their trust. Trusting in the press to spread knowledge, Adams continued, ignored the fact that possessing information made one an aristocrat by intelligence and having enough seed capital to start a newspaper made one an aristocrat by wealth. When Taylor assumed that knowledge could be equally divided, Adams implied, he simply made it easier for aristocrats to control government.[43]

There were points of similarity between Adams and Taylor other than those noted above. Both assumed that aristocracy was a recurring institution, although Taylor hoped that it could be controlled. Both men, however, also thought that superior ability and knowledge were what had ruled the world in the past, and that governmental forms were only reflections of this fact. Moreover, each man gave a political connotation to his definition of aristocracy: for Adams an aristocrat was one who could influence one vote besides his own; for Taylor he was one who had taken the property of others through law. In both cases the emphasis was on the *intellectual* ability of aristocrats: Taylor's aristocrats monopolized knowledge, while Adams's influenced others to vote with them or for them.[44]

E. Influence on Successors

The legacy of John Taylor has been a mixed one that developed from various emphases in his thought. There is evidence, and it has long been assumed, that Taylor's effect was limited to the development of states' rights and Southern sectionalism. This study reopens the question of separatism. On the basis of what he said, rather than what he was alleged to have said, there seems no good reason to conclude that his relevance was limited to Southern separatism, or to emphasize it.

It was to be expected that Taylor and Spencer Roane would have had similar ideas after *Cohens* v. *Virginia* awakened Roane to the danger of federal power. Roane, like Taylor, believed that states were entities separate from their governments and that the Union was a compact among the states as people. Roane, as chief justice of the highest Virginia court, took a dim view of review of his decisions by the Supreme Court, and agreed with Taylor that such review was unconstitutional. Roane seems to have tiptoed closer to a doctrine of secession than Taylor, but in so doing he was not applying Taylor's mature ideas, for he died before *New Views* was published.[45]

Justice Peter Daniel's view of federalism has been compared with some justice to Taylor's. John P. Frank gave Taylor credit for having influenced Daniel on the subject of banks. If Daniel was influenced by Taylor, he provided a bridge to the Jacksonians, for Daniels became an ardent supporter of Jackson and Van Buren. As such, Daniel supported Jackson's views, including a rejection of nullification. On the court, however, Daniel spoke for a concurrent state commerce power. Daniel did not refuse to review the decisions of state courts, thereby departing from Roane and Taylor, but he did interpret the diversity-of-citizenship clause in such a way that he managed to avoid deciding on the substantive issues in reviewing many state actions.[46] Since Daniels insisted on *complete* diversity, including all of the stockholders of a corporation, there were few cases that he would consent to review.

The writer with views most similar to Taylor seems to have been Abel Upshur, whose 1840 criticism of Justice Story's *Commentaries* presented a theory of the Union that rejected any sovereignty but popular sovereignty and that regarded the states as people instead of governments. Upshur's earlier defense of limited suffrage in the Virginia Constitutional Convention of 1829-30, which relied on the idea of economic interest instead of natural rights, seems unrelated to Taylor, however.[47]

There were several strains in Taylor's thought that are distinctly different from those developed in the South prior to the Civil War. There was, for example, Taylor's belief in natural rights and governmental principles. As was seen earlier, his belief in the universally binding force of certain abstract republican values was much more pronounced that that of Jefferson or Madison. Yet, Calhoun deduced government from essentially hedonistic principles and Fitzhugh denied equality altogether, not even leaning on the biological argument of race as a crutch. Taylor's ambiguity on the question of sovereignty posed another difficulty for any Southern sectionalists trying to implement his theory. If Taylor's system was built on state rights, it was a conception of states as people, and he really could not find a place for sovereignty in the picture. As a theory of state rights, therefore, Taylor's ideas were inadequate in a practical sense. It was difficult to build a workable cohesive state opposition to Federal actions on a base that held that the rights of one state could be completely different from that of another—that they were, in fact, separate nations. Taylor's respect for the Union and refusal by word or deed, even when given the chance as in 1794, to advocate disunion with honor, demonstrated his antipathy to separatism. The most fundamental difference between Taylor and the Southern separatists, however, is that they were sectionalists who spoke for theories that wiped out the communities of consent Taylor had called nations. No one deplored sectionalism more than Taylor, who had described the dismal prospects for freedom when three great sections stood poised to leap at each other's throats. He thought a balance among sections was as bad as a balance among orders: a neat equilibrium tempted rivals to try to get the upper hand by a sudden move. Morality suffered under such temptations because jealousy and suspicion won out. Liberty would suffer, too, because three great sections would leave the nations, which had socioeconomic identities and needs, without any effective government to serve them.[48]

The most important of the Southern thinkers after Taylor was Calhoun. Taylor and Calhoun were acquainted and Calhoun visited Hazelwood at least once in his attempt to enlist Old Republicans in his campaign for President in 1824. This visit met with mixed success, because Taylor tentatively decided to support both Calhoun and Adams, not indicating any preference between them for top position on the ticket. He did not approve of Calhoun's liking for the Navy and suspected that Calhoun would give the federal government supremacy in any clashes with states. On the other hand, Calhoun did respect the federal-state division of power, had never been a monarchist, and was correct on the Missouri question, since he was a slaveowner. These were all points in his favor. It should be noted that when Calhoun won Taylor's approval he was still a nationalist who had supported the second Bank of the United States, the Bonus Bill, and the tariff of 1816. Taylor never knew Calhoun as a sectionalist, whose conversion to that cause has been associated with the 1828 reprinting of the Virginia and Kentucky Resolutions and the 1832 discovery of Jefferson's original draft of the Kentucky Resolutions.[49]

There were certainly points of similarity in Taylor's theory and that set forth in Calhoun's *Disquisition* (1853).[50] For example, both treated the officials of government with suspicion because rulers had often developed interests separate from and contrary to those of their constituents. Controlling such men required constitutions, in Calhoun's opinion. Taylor, in a similar vein, thought that the problems of government could be solved by creative men endowed with the correct republican values. Both men criticized, without rejecting, certain traditional constitutional procedures. Elections were criticized as sufficient to put men in office, but insufficient to control them once they got there. Written constitutions were criticized by both men as inadequate, because liberty had to be safeguarded by more powerful procedures than the written word alone. Similarly, both men found separation of powers inadequate, because even in a system using it, the personnel of government would still be an interest separate from the people. The greatest similarity between the two thinkers, however, was that each was willing to allow federal and state powers to contradict each other without any definitive immediate resolution.[51]

Beyond this, however—that both men were content with uncertainty of procedure when conflicts arose among the federal partners—Taylor's theory of mutual vetoes and Calhoun's of the concurrent majority form a study in contrasts. Taylor described his theory in terms of procedures established in the Constitution for adopting amendments. Although he never provided a scenario for how a federal-state conflict would occur, the following is a probable sequence of events: one level of government, state or federal, might act in a manner inconsistent with the other level's interpretation of its power. The dissenting level of government would then simply act to its satisfaction under its interpretation. If the aggressor were the federal government, any state might simply disobey the objectionable ruling or law. If the offended party were a state, it could memorialize other states, explaining its position and seeking their support. These states could act as they chose. In the case of the Maryland tax on the Bank of the United States, for example, no other state might have imposed a tax on the Bank, and it might have refused to pay the Maryland tax. The issue would have been stalemated, but only insofar as the State of Maryland was concerned. If a more definitie decision was required, the issue could be taken to Congress and resolved through the amending process established by the Constitution.

Calhoun had something more far-reaching in mind, for if *one* of his interests should disagree, unanimity was required before the disputed activity could continue. Taylor's mutual vetoes might slow down federal or state governmental activities, but would not stop them altogether. Calhoun's concurrent majority was a blackballing technique that would bring the federal government to a halt as far as the disputed issue was concerned, until the "conservative principle" of compromise was achieved.[52]

This difference between the two went deeper than the question of how intergovernmental conflict should be handled. The two possessed distinctly different approaches to politics.

Taylor built his theory on the foundation of the individual's right to self-government, expressed through nations that were constitutional communities unified by socioeconomic similarities. These nations had found it convenient to establish regional and central government. None of these structures were economically determined. Even though nations had socioeconomic identities, they were able to rise above the problems of other states and the federal government. Actions that would threaten other parties to the Union would be avoided and decisions made in the public interest would be pursued. For Taylor it was not so much a question of compromise, which implied a bargaining situation among antagonists, as an expectation that common belief in the axioms of republicanism would create a mutual empathy, which would preserve the harmony of the Union by avoiding intergovernmental clashes in the first place. Taylor's confident belief in the power of republican principles to keep government on the straight path was fundamental to his theory.

Calhoun started from entirely different premises: he thought man social by nature and government of divine origin. In both situations, there was less choice exercised by Calhoun's man than by Taylor's. Although Taylor's nations were a conceptual half-step away from the social-contract theory that gave men a medium in which to survive if government had to be disciplined, they were still only a half-step and no more than Locke himself had taken. Calhoun turned his back on the social contract, for he realized what Taylor apparently did not: to base government on equal rights raised serious questions back on the plantation. Once Calhoun had put society and government on the same footing and found a hedonistic basis for the separate interests that existed in society, there was no good reason for him to equate those interests with states. Interests might be states but, they could be geographic or socal groupings of any size. For all his disavowal of natural rights and the social contract, such an anarchistic premise actually took Calhoun back to the state of nature in his logic, for it left him without an argument to use against oppressed minorities in the South. It would surely have caused difficulties for Taylor because it justified the existence of sectional interests organized to pursue their own self-interest and not under the restraint of any government. Not only did Calhoun justify the existence of interests whose competition would create the aggressive moral climate that Taylor disliked, but the whole Calhounian system was erected on a view of man that required this sort of behavior. Calhoun's faith in governmental structure to balance off the cronic evil tendencies in human nature had more in common with John Adams's mixed government than it did with Taylor's divided power. It was such a trust in structure and reluctance to acknowledge the role that a consensus on rationalistic republican values could play that had caused Taylor to write the *Inquiry*. Therefore, when the *Inquiry*'s rejection of the balancing principle is added to *New View*'s horror of sectionalism, it may be concluded that a system like Calhoun's was what Taylor feared, not what he wanted.[53]

If the conclusions that the Southern way of thought before the Civil War advocated sociological determinism, sectionalism, sovereignty of governments, and inequality, and that it attacked natural rights and the social compact are true, it is clear that Taylor's effect on the "reactionary enlightenment" was limited to such generalities as a common regard for state power. The ties that weakly connect Taylor to Southern sectionalism and slavery should not prevent a consideration of his influence on other schools of thought.

The great area of policy agreement between Taylor and the Jacksonians suggests possible influences in that direction. This is particularly true in view of the fact that several of Taylor's friends, such as John Randolph, Nathaniel Macon, and Littleton W. Tazewell, and acquaintances, such as Thomas Ritchie and Peter Daniel, all became supporters of Jackson and Van Buren. Although Arthur Schlesinger, Jr., appreciated the similarity between the views of Taylor and those of the followers of Jackson, he was not impressed with the amount of direct influence Taylor had. It may be that Schlesinger was saving Jackson for more worthy influences. Yet, there were many similarities between the two bodies of thought. Considering that the Jackson period produced no single thinker who spoke with authority for the diverse range of Jacksonian thought, it might well have been that Jacksonianism traveled on borrowed and left-over ideas, Taylor's among them.[54]

There was, first of all, a similarity of tone between Taylor and the Jacksonians: when the latter talked about "monster banks," "Paper Dynasty," "avarice and ambition," and "scrip nobility," they sounded much like Taylor. [55] When Taylor had used such terms, his use of them was practically unique. The point here is not that the Jacksonian terminology was taken from Taylor, although it may have been, but that there was a common moral indignation behind the writings. Taylor and the Jacksonians knew who their enemies were and set out to smash them without second thought. Moreover, the Banks of the United States gave them specific foci for their discontent. When Taylor attacked banks, he had often been alone in his misery. The Jacksonians accepted similar ideas as conventional wisdom. In accepting the same conclusions, if not the actual writings that contained them, they followed Taylor in attacking modern aristocracy. Both the Jacksonians and Taylor built their theories on the fear and resentment experienced by groups disadvantaged by prevailing social conditions. Their analysis of the causes of their difficulties led them to suspect a particular institution in whose operations they detected conspiratorial tendencies. In attacking these conspiracies, Taylor and the Jacksonians advocated a very similar political program: limits on corporate charters, suspicion of paper money, dislike of public enterprises, and reduction of the tariff. There was a reformist bent to Jacksonianism that went beyond Taylor by preferring regulation of corporate activities even if this required increasing the power of the federal government. Even though Jackson and his followers reaffirmed their beliefs in state powers, unity and the Union were also valued, for as both Taney and Jackson pointed out, there was no stopping point for disunion. The sectionalism of today might become the anarchy of tomorrow, without any change in the doctrines that had justified sectionalism. Both Taylor and the Jacksonians emphasized popular sovereignty above, perhaps, any other political value, including the Union and states' rights. Here also the Jacksonians and Taylor shared common ground. The Jacksonians went further than Taylor in widening the franchise, but even in this respect Taylor was advanced for his time. Among the Jacksonians Taylor can best be compared to Roger B. Taney and William Leggett.[56]

Much of Jackson's theory was derived from Taney, either directly as a ghostwriter or indirectly as an adviser. Taney, like Taylor, looked on struggle over the Bank of the United States as the recurrence of problem that other countries had faced: whether the wealth of a free people would become concentrated in the hands of a few. Both men looked on the question as a struggle between single economic class and the rest of the people, not as one between classes or interest groups. At the same time each believed in private property and the right of its holders to expect protection from the government. With both men it was a question of protecting rightfully acquired property from conspiracies that always seemed to be trying to take it. The idea of the public good possessed by both men was closely connected to the concept of legitimate private property, and when either supported the regulation of property, it was for the sake of making it more secure for those who had actually earned it.

Taylor preferred state and local regulations, such as drainage laws, slave codes, and grazing limitations, but he was willing to support federal regulations if a sufficient good—such as expelling public creditors from office—could be accomplished. Similarly, Taney supported state regulations but was willing for federal regulations to be imposed rather than having the holders of special privileges go unregulated. Thus his decision in *Bank of Augusta* v. *Earle* refused to extend the protection of the privileges and immunities clause to corporations. He refused to accept Marshall's formulation that the federal commerce power and the state police powers were separate things, and instead argued for a concurrent state-federal commerce power and a police power that was completely possessed by states. He silently concurred in *Cooley* v. *Board of Wardens,* which, while it did not establish a state commerce power on the full basis he would have liked, still had the subsequent effect of allowing states great latitude in regulating commerce. Taney undoubtedly approved of this, but his subsequent decisions revealed no change in his opinion that the clashes that resulted between the states and the federal government would be best settled by elected legislators. Neither Taney nor Taylor was awe-stricken by the concept of the inviolability of contract—for example, Taney's decisions in the *Charles River Bridge* and *West River Bridge* cases, and Taylor in reference to the Yazoo land frauds—but neither was either one contemptuous of contracts. Both tended to choose state sovereignty over property rights when the two clashed and the institution of slavery was not being questioned. It is true that the Taney ruling in *Dred Scott* was a use of federal power, but in declaring the Missouri Compromise unconstitutional, he merely came to the same conclusion Taylor had in 1820, although Taney's rationale was a defense of property and Taylor's a defense of state sovereignty. Faced with the opportunity of using the power of the Supreme Court in this manner, Taylor himself might have returned to his opinion on the carriage tax. It was, after all, the use of the federal judiciary to review state laws and court decisions to which Taylor objected most strenuously.[57]

There was, therefore, much in the general tone of Taney's approach to governmental problems that was similar to Taylor's opinions. Both men were Southerners and slave owners who nonetheless valued the Union. Both men were wedded to the defense of private property, but were equally dedicated to the criticism of what they considered to be artificial and illegitimate forms of property. Each had an ability to see beyond superficial appeals to commonly valued institutions, such as property and contracts, and the courage to discriminate between acceptable and unacceptable forms of these institutions. Each was willing to take the risk that he might be misunderstood by those who did not have the patience for neat distinctions.

The influence of Taylor upon William Leggett, the spokesman for New York Locofocoism, is a matter of record. Leggett himself praised Taylor's writings and regretted that they had not found wider audiences. Leggett was "an unconditional, almost obsessive advocate of laissez faire."[58] His editorials in the New York *Evening Post* and *Cleveland Plain Dealer* revealed an overriding faith in the order of nature, based on an assumption of equal rights. As an advocate of minimal government, Leggett outstripped Taylor by opposing governmental post offices, the licensing of businesses, and even the use of government to break up the monopolistic combinations both Leggett and Taylor hated. In Leggett's opinion the laws of supply and demand would destroy monopolies if government would get out of the way. Any sort of exclusive privilege bestowed by government interfered with Leggett's interpretation of these laws and was opposed by him. He even proposed that corporate charters be handled by a single enabling act that would extend to all corporations the privileges given piecemeal to some. It was to be expected that Leggett would oppose the type of monopoly and exclusive privilege represented by the second Bank of the United States, and his visions of a tight-fisted conspiracy controlling banking operations recall some of Taylor's criticisms of the same thing. Even Leggett's terminology was similar to Taylor's, for he called monopolists *aristocrats* or *scrip nobility*. When Jackson retired from office Leggett congratulated him, not for what he had done, but for what he had prevented. The chief evil avoided under Jackson's guidance, Leggett said, was further innovation by the aristocrats, who had controlled government up to that time. In sounding that note, Leggett seems on the brink of a frequent theme of Taylor's: a vision of an agrarian, small-producer society as the only really worthwhile type. Leggett came to this conclusion by two routes. First, he criticized developing economic institutions so thoroughly that he left little to admire, although he professed to be the friend of banks and corporations in their purified form. Second, he so trusted in economic laws to correct economic ills unassisted that he was indifferent to such emerging institutions as labor unions, which possibly could have helped to purify corporations. These two themes made it appear that Leggett really considered only an agrarian society as a reasonable choice. In so doing he had come full circle and had adopted Taylor's conclusions as well as his assumptions. Having started out to apply Taylor in an urban setting, Leggett found that a rigid application of the laws of free trade kept leading him back to agrarianism.[59]

After the decline of Jacksonianism and Southern nationalism, it becomes very difficult to argue for Taylor's direct effect on the thinking of individuals. It was, after all, the initial assumption of this study that Taylor has been a neglected thinker to some extent. Moreover, the orgy of idealism and organicism that followed the Civil War, and the influence of German idealism, which had begun before the Civil War with the transcendentalists but continued afterward with Bancroft, Burgess, Lieber, and Ely, among many others, produced systems of thought uncongenial to Taylor's.[60]

It is therefore necessary to recast the approach to be used in studying Taylor's influence on the latter half of the nineteenth century. His ideas fed into a stream of Jeffersonian and Jacksonian ideals that have periodically served the cause of agrarian and Populist reform, but it is difficult to point to any particular thinkers who were heavily influenced by him. One might think that Henry George, for example, who was quick to acknowledge his debt to Jefferson, might have added Taylor's name to the list of economists cited in *The Science of Political Economy* (1897), but such was not the case. Yet, there were certain aspects of George's thought that might have built on Taylor. Both recognized that value could be produced from activities other than agriculture, and accepted the labor theory of value. Both men started from assumptions of equal rights, associated human progress with the growth of reason, and preferred the use of local government for local problems, and a federal government that was as small as possible. Taylor and George feared monopolies, and even though George's solution of nationalizing natural monopolies such as railroads was one that Taylor probably would not have presented, it is also true that Taylor preferred having banking operations as a governmental operation rather than in the hands of some quasi-private corporation. The effects of such corporations of democratic processes, interested as they would be in their self-interest, were too dangerous to risk. Neither man trusted to republican governmental forms alone to guarantee the existence of a happy, productive society: the distribution of wealth was just as important. The similarities between Taylor and George, therefore, are very general ones. George's single tax, the confiscation of all economic rent as unearned income since God and not man had made land, was probably not one that Taylor could have favored. Yet, by going just one step further in Taylor's own egalitarian assumptions and adding that *only* that property which has been created by labor can be owned, George's conclusions could appear reasonable to one holding Taylor's assumptions. Moreover, it should be remembered that only the title to the land itself was ever to be nationalized under the George plan; such improvements and personal property as landowners had added would continue to be theirs to enjoy.[61]

To carry an investigation of Taylor's influence further than George requires virtually abandoning any direct influence from Taylor's works and relying on similarity of ideas alone. Such was the case with Thorstein Veblen, who may never have heard of Taylor, but who had certain comparable ideas. Veblen's system, like Taylor's, was deduced from axioms, although Veblen dressed them in scientific garb by calling them instincts. His instincts of workmanship and idle curiosity created throughout all his writings a presumption in favor of those who were the producers respectively of wealth or ideas. Like Taylor, however, Veblen recognized that all individuals were tempted at times to take the easy way out and take the wealth created by the purer expression of instincts in others. Taylor and Veblen both believed that certain institutions were created to accomplish this robbery, although they were not mature enough during Taylor's time to allow him to describe more than their beginnings. When he criticized cabals of bank directors or stockholders, he could not have anticipated the complex institutions that would develop from those roots by the turn of the nineteenth century. Taylor and Veblen both attacked the powerholders of their day for the same reasons: they were unsuited for their positions; their activities created burdens for the masses actually producing the wealth; these same activities encouraged imitation by the masses, who would consequently be slow to depose their rulers; and the process of creating economic goods enlightened and liberated the mind, fulfilling personality. Taylor and Veblen would have disagreed on the actual qualities possessed by those in control. Taylor thought that they were skillful because of their monopoly of knowledge, but that they had bad morals. Veblen thought them incompetent in their knowledge of technology, but skilled in the arts of salesmanship and control. He refused to talk about morality. Taylor and Veblen also used language in a similar fashion, either by drawing humorous analogies that degraded enemies while teaching a moral lesson, or by giving ordinary words special meanings so as to lure readers into agreeing with them, whether or not they really did. Thus Taylor compared the banking system to prostitution and Veblen compared businessmen to toads; Taylor's *nations, states,* and *aristocracies* have meanings special to his system, and Veblen gave *consumption, emulation,* and *leisure* meanings all his own. Even though Veblen was skilled in the analysis of an urban society in whose productive capacity he found much to admire, fundamentally what he expected the "machine discipline" of that society to produce was a reemergence of the primitive values that were innate in man, and that had been smothered by institutions. It was a moral, if not a technological, return to an agrarian society.[62]

Taylor has shared the contradictions as well as the programs and analyses of various agrarian reformers. His equivocation on the question of racial tolerance is one that has been shared by various agrarians such as Ignatius Donnelly, Theodore Bilbo, Mary Lease, and Tom Watson, each of whom combined the Jeffersonian and Jacksonian ideals of a harmony of economic interests and status, class, and racial prejudices, with religious prejudices and status resentments. As Richard Hofstadter said, "There was something about the Populist imagination that loved the secret plot and the conspiratorial meeting."[63] This was as true for Taylor's analysis of the Federal Convention with its republican and monarchist consolidationist conspiracies as it was for Populism's distrust of Wall Street. The agrarian reformer has often attributed to foes a height of cunning that closer investigation has found improbable if not imaginary. It may be that achieving reform requires such optimism regarding human reason that logic and habit require that the same assumption of rationality be applied to one's enemies. Certain forms of racial and religious hatred, of course, have had real economic bases, such as the fear of inexpensive Negro, Chinese, or southern

European labor by indigenous working classes. V. O. Key, Jr., even conceded the Populist assumption of elitism when he maintained in *Southern Politics* that delta Bourbons had consistenly followed a rule of divide and conquer between poor whites and Negroes. But regardless of the sociological reasons, it is a significant and ominous fact that the American agrarian tradition has continued Taylor's mistakes as well as his visions.[64]

F. Future Research

This study has been limited to the writings of John Taylor and any other thinkers necessary to understand Taylor. By building on the findings of this study, one should be able to investigate certain issues further. These issues fall into the following groups: further research on Taylor himself; comparisons of Taylor and other thinkers; and substantive hypotheses for research not necessarily related to Taylor.

Although an attempt has been made in this study to present as comprehensive a view of Taylor's ideas as possible, there are several gray areas left that deserve illumination. There were, first of all, his ideas on international relations. A supporter of the American Revolution, Taylor was a vociferous critic of the War of 1812. Although his views on that war have been included when they related to his criticism of what was wrong with American society, it has been difficult to avoid the impression that there was some inconsistency in Taylor's views of international relations, which deserves separate attention. This is true because Taylor seemed to have no axioms for foreign policy as he did for the domestic arena. A separate but related issue is the source of the natural rights philosophy used by Taylor. What theory of natural rights provided him axioms for domestic policy but only expedience for foreign policy? Third, the whole question of intellectual influences on Taylor is one deserving more intensive investigation. His library was split by the terms of his will among the members of his family, and an examination of their wills might be able to trace much of it. Similarly, the holdings of libraries to which he had access might be helpful, including the library of William and Mary College while he was a student there and the library of Edmund Pendleton. Fourth, it is clear that certain literary writers had a special appeal for Taylor, and the philosophic implications of that appeal may be important. Of those writers, Cervantes and Swift head the list. Fifth is the matter of the lost years in Taylor's life. It simply does not seem reasonable to assume that he should suddenly blossom as a full-fledged political theorist in 1793 and within a year's time produce his *Definition of Parties* and *Enquiry*. William Dodd said that Taylor had written against the adoption of the Constitution as an Anti-Federalist, but none of this is known today.[65] A perusal of Anti-Federalist literature, especially letters to newspapers in the Fredericksburg area, might turn up one or more lost essays. Probably there are also letters of Taylor included in unindexed family collections that will be coming to light. For example, there is an eight-year gap in the Taylor-Monroe correspondence for 1815-1823, which seems strange, considering the closeness of their relationship up to 1815 and after 1823.

Comparisons of Taylor's views with those of others could build on several of the suggestions just mentioned, particularly that dealing with Jeffersonian views on foreign relations. If Taylor did publish as an Anti-Federalist, moreover, a comparison of his insights with others of that persuasion would be very valuable, especially since he outlived most of the Anti-Federalists. Similarly, a much less impressionistic comparison of Taylor with any or all of the Jacksonians, agrarians, or states' rights schools of thought would be valuable. A survey is particularly needed in the last case, owing to the lack of any definitive work that is also comprehensive. Finally, Taylor's ideas on principles appear to be an early statement of the role of myths in modern society, and they evidence less concern for the mechanistic trappings of checks and balances than one might expect from an advocate of state rights. It is possible that other thinkers have been similarly maligned. It is recognized now, for example, that Calhoun thought that the concurrent majority was only one of several ways by which societies had attempted to control their rulers.[66]

Taylor's writings provide several historical hypotheses. Some of these have been pointed out previously, but the most important among them are probably Taylor's implications for the study of parties and elites. Taylor's ideas on parties suggest that the assumptions that parties resulted from economic origins, began in the states, or began over the division in opinion over the Constitution may be in error. He seems to agree with those who find the origin of parties within national legislatures. Taylor's ideas on aristocracy suggest that the criticism of elitist activities in the United States has roots that are deep, but that the presence of the elites may, to some extent, have been created by policies adopted by the critics when they came to power. Taylor's doctrine that governments had moral effects on their citizens is an interesting and, if true, vitally important insight. Empirically, the effects of governmental actions on the values and ideas of individuals could be measured with attitudinal surveys. For example, has Watergate set a bad example for individual ethics? Normatively, the concept of government as the teacher of morals reveals that the morally neutral liberal state may be a fiction, regardless of the actions or intentions of its rulers. Moral implications may be drawn inevitably from both actions and refusals to act. This raises policy questions for the planning of governmental social service programs, for no longer will it be possible to simply free people from various limitations on their political and economic choices. If Taylor was correct to any significant extent, it will henceforth be necessary to plan governmental services with an eye to what people are being freed for.

G. Concluding Note

John Taylor's doctrine of divided powers gathered together the disparate strands of his thought into close association, if not a seamless web. Thus, the social and intellectual backgrounds that had given him the financial and ideological freedom to assert his individualism were conditioning influences that freed Taylor from everything but the influence of the agrarian society he loved. He equated its virtues of the highest in Heaven, its ecology with the highest purposes of nature, and its culture with the good life of productive activity.

Taylor thought that the leaders produced by such societies had to be scientists and scholars to manage their land, but they could not farm in peace owing to the intrusions of government. They must participate in government, but the effects of narrow partisanship on intellectuals were always unpleasant. Instead, they should become committed only to parties with a body of principled doctrine, and even then guard against subservience to the officeholders of that party.

In their lives as farmers, Taylor hoped that members of this agrarian class could ameliorate slavery by improving the land so that it needed fewer slaves. Although both master and slave derived material and moral benefits from slavery, it was an inefficient institution and unnecessary in the long run to sustain the planter-scholar life.

In their lives as statesmen, Taylor urged the agrarian leaders to realize that governments influenced private morals by the examples they offered. The establishing of a single religion or the patronage of many was equally harmful to the individual citizen.

At the outset of this study the goal of exploring the theoretical consistency of Taylor's background influences, and his doctrines on parties, aristocracies, governmental structure, and agrarianism was set. The consistency with which they were integrated was taken as the measure of a political theorist. Although the high degree of consistency that Taylor maintained in discussing his views seems easily to qualify him as a theorist, his doctrines were not fully synchronized because of his ambiguity on the issue of slavery.

It is a double irony that Taylor's system should founder on this issue. First, his doctrine of actual human equality was his most original idea and is fundamental to an understanding of his stages of aristocracy. Failure to develop the concept of equality, then, injured his system at its most important point. Second, not only did he avoid a full discussion of equality, but he actually proposed a social system that looked as aristocratic as the Hamiltonian commercial system he had attacked. His planter-scholars were scaled-down aristocrats, to be sure, but he did ultimately resort to elitist appeals to save the society he loved. Equality went by the board and his system with it. Had he adequately been able to explain the situation of the Negro, he might have saved his version of pluralism from charges that it was merely a defense of the planter aristocracy. He did not, however, and his views on slavery have become inextricably combined with federalism.

A fair assessment of the experience of the American Negro since Taylor, however, must expand the indictment of federalism to include public and private policies and agencies at all levels of government and in all sections of the country. Few institutions have adequately dealt with the legacy of slavery. Since Taylor's system no longer bears any unique relationship to racism it may be possible to look on his conception of federalism from a different perspective.

Federalism was, to Taylor, part of a larger system of divided power that separated governments from their sovereign people so that the governments might be controlled more easily. The people were organized into regional communities that he called *nations*. These nations were not to be confused with state governments, but were the ultimate constituencies for both the state and national levels of government. The nations preserved a common understanding of republican principles, which included a deep belief in the importance of the system of divided powers, the right to instruct representatives, the right to defend from attack by the use of a militia, and the right of a nation to conduct its own affairs with its own understanding of its powers under the U.S. Constitution unless a constitutional amendment forbade it. The most important part of this system of divided power was belief in and application of the moral truths that supported republicanism. Taylor held the view characteristic of the early rationalistic phase of the Enlightenment which assumed that persons could readily agree on a common standard of right and wrong if their reasoning powers could be freed of self-interest and passion.

Taylor's satisfaction with an ambiguous division of power in the federal system may strike modern tastes as either naive or dangerous. Modern commentators have learned from decisions of the United States Supreme Court to expect that federal-state conflicts must be reconciled by general rules of law. Yet, the day-to-day operation of cooperative federalism probably implements as much of Taylor's loose system of overlapping authority as of landmark court decisions that leave no intergovernmental conflict irreconcilable.

Lest the reader think that the days of federalism and decentralized pluralism are over, he is urged to consider the assumptions of public choice policy analysts, black power and community control ideologists, metropolitan federationists, libertarian theorists, sunbelt populists, and the advocates of revenue sharing. At this writing, interest in governmental pluralism comes from all points of the ideological spectrum and seems to be increasing. However, the creation of any viable formalized pluralism, whether it occurs at the regional, state, metropolitan, city, or neighborhood level, may need to recapture the civility, tolerance for diversity, and search for the public interest that John Taylor insisted on. The fact that the day may have passed when such common agreement on moral values can be achieved or even imagined may be beside the question. John Taylor's most important contribution was the reminder that the citizens of a federal republic may need to believe in and practice the same moral values. Lacking that, coercion, centralization, corruption, or disunion may be the only possible alternatives in the long run.

Notes to Chapter 8

1. Bernard Bailyn, *The Ideological Origins of the American Revolution* (Cambridge, Mass: Harvard University Press, 1967), pp. 35–54 and *The Origins of American Politics* (New York: Vintage Books, 1968), pp. 38–52; Gordon S. Wood, *The Creation of the American Republic, 1776–1787* (New York: W. W. Norton & Company, Inc., 1969), chap. 1; H. Trevor Colbourn, *The Lamp of Experience* (New York: W. W. Norton & Company, Inc., 1965), pp. 27–32; Staughton Lynd, *Intellectual Origins of American Radicalism* (New York: Vintage Books, 1968), pp. 18–37; Pauline Maier, *From Resistance to Revolution* (New York: Vintage Books, 1972), pp. 27–46; R. R. Palmer, *The Age of the Democratic Revolution: The Challenge* (Princeton, N.J.: Princeton University Press, 1959), pp. 213–17.

2. Nelson Polsby, *Community Power and Political Theory* (New Haven, Conn.: Yale University Press, 1963).

3. *Inquiry*, p. 387.

4. M.J.C. Vile, *Constitutionalism and the Separation of Powers* (Oxford: Clarendon Press, 1967), p. 172.

5. *National Labor Relations Board* v. *Jones and Laughlin Steel Corporation*, 301 U.S. 1.

6. U.S. House of Representatives, 90th Congress, 1st Session, *The Constitution of the United States of America* (Washington: U.S. Government Printing Office, 1967), pp. 18–23.

7. *Defence* pp. 15, 23–24, 32–33, 54; letter from Taylor to Henry Tazewell, April 13, 1796, Tazewell Papers, Virginia State Library, Richmond; letters from Taylor to James Monroe, March 18, 1813; April 29, 1823, in "Correspondence," p. 344, 348–53.

8. Letter from John Taylor to James Monroe, January 31, 1811, in "Correspondence," p. 316. Also see letter to John Breckinridge, December 22, 1801, *ibid.*, pp. 284–88; letter to Monroe, November 8, 1809, ibid., pp. 301–3; *Tyranny*, p. 6.

9. *Inquiry*, p. 2.

10. *Ibid.*, pp. 166, 228, 432, 458, 462; *Tyranny*, pp. 141, 253; *Enquiry*, pp. 23, 30; letter from Taylor to James Monroe, March 12, 1812, in "Correspondence," pp. 232–36; Taylor, *Arator*, pp. 69, 189; *Construction*, p. 212; *New Views*, p. 240; letter to Major William Popham, January 27, 1823, Morris Family Papers, Library of Congress; letter to Lucy P. Taylor, February 2, 1823, Virginia Historical Society, Richmond. Unlike Jefferson, Taylor seems to have believed in an afterlife, one achieved through good works. This made the stealing of moral choices an even more serious problem for him than it would be for those who affirm justification by faith or no afterlife at all.

11. Letter from James Mercer Garnett to John Randolph of Roanoke, January 3, 1820, Letters of John Randolph of Roanoke to James Mercer Garnett, Library of Congress.

12. Letter from Thomas Jefferson to Thomas Ritchie, December 25, 1820, *The Writings of Thomas Jefferson* (Washington, D.C.: Thomas Jefferson Memorial Association, 1905), 15:295.

13. Ibid.

14. Letters from Thomas Jefferson to Archibald Thweat, January 19, 1821, ibid., 15:307; and to John Taylor, February 14, 1821, ibid., 18:313.

15. Letters from John Adams to Thomas Jefferson, September 15, 1813; November 12, 1813; March 14, 1814, in *Works of John Adams*, Charles Francis Adams, ed. (Boston: Little, Brown and Company, 1850–56), 10:69, 80, 90.

16. Letter from Thomas Jefferson to Spencer Roane, June 27, 1821, Thomas Jefferson Papers, University of Virginia, Charlottesville, Virginia.

17. Letter from Thomas Jefferson to John Taylor, March 14, 1821, New York Historical Society.

18. Letter from Thomas Jefferson to John Taylor, June 1, 1798, *The Works of Thomas Jefferson* (New York: Paul Leicester Ford, 1892–99), 8:430. Taylor had written a letter to Anthony New in which he said it was not "unusual" in his area to hear of Virginia and North Carolina seceding. By the time Jefferson saw a copy of the letter, it was so smudged that he read "unwise" for "unusual." The effect of this misreading was to completely alter Taylor's role from reporter to advocate. This letter is also reprinted in *The Writings of Thomas Jefferson*, 10:44–45; the letter in reply from Taylor to Jefferson is the June 25, 1798, letter included in "Correspondence," pp. 271–76.

19. Adrienne Koch, *The Philosophy of Thomas Jefferson* (Chicago: Quadrangle Books, 1964); Daniel Boorstin, *The Lost World of Thomas Jefferson* (Boston: Beacon Press, 1963). For Jefferson's views on newspapers see Noble E. Cunningham, *The Jeffersonian Republicans in Power* (Chapel Hill, N. C.: University of North Carolina Press, 1963), pp. 255–58.

20. Koch, pp. 100–10; Boorstin, pp. 112–27; letter from John Taylor to Thomas Jefferson, June 25, 1798.

21. Letters from Thomas Jefferson to John Taylor, November 26, 1798, *The Writings of Thomas Jefferson*, Vol. 10:64; January 26, 1808, ibid., 11:414; May 28, 1816, ibid., 15:17–22; February 14, 1821, ibid., 18–312. Also Koch, pp. 140–41; Carl L. Becker, *The Heavenly City of the Eighteenth-Century Philosophers* (New Haven, Conn.: Yale University Press, 1932), p. 70; Bray Hammond, *Banks and Politics in America* (Princeton, N.J.: Princeton University Press, 1957), p. 221; William D. Grampp, "John Taylor: Economist of Southern Agrarians," *Southern Economic Journal* 11 (January 1944): 255–68; "A Re-examination of Jeffersonian Economics," *Southern Economic Journal* 12 (January 1946): 263–85.

22. Letter from Thomas Jefferson to Thomas Ritchie, December 25, 1820. Also see letters from Jefferson to John Taylor, January 6, 1805, and to Archibald Thweat, February 14, 1824, in *The Writings of Thomas Jefferson*, 11:56 and 16:14.

23. Letters from Thomas Jefferson to Thomas Ritchie, December 25, 1820; Archibald Thweat, January 19, 1821.

24. Letter from Thomas Jefferson to Spencer Roane, June 27, 1821.

25. Letter from Thomas Jefferson to John Taylor, July 16, 1816, *The Writings of Thomas Jefferson*, 15:45. Also see letter from Jefferson to Taylor, May 28, 1816, ibid., 15:21.

26. Grampp, "John Taylor: Economist of Southern Agrarians," p. 260; "A Reexamination of Jeffersonian Economics," p. 272; letter from Thomas Jefferson to John Taylor, December 29, 1794, *The Writings of Thomas Jefferson*, 18:192–93.

27. Of course, if Fawn Brodie's thesis is correct, much less can be made of Jefferson's generosity on this point, since the five slaves freed were either relatives of his mistress or their own sons; see Fawn M. Brodie, *Thomas Jefferson: an Intimate History* (Toronto: Bantam Books, 1975), pp. 630–31.

28. Joseph Charles discussed this attitude of Jefferson's in regard to the party system

emerging in the late 1790s, see Charles, *The Origins of the American Party System* (New York: Harper and Brothers, 1956), pp. 76, 84.

29. Noble E. Cunningham, *The Jeffersonian Republicans: The Formation of Party Organization, 1789–1801* (Chapel Hill, N.C.: University of North Carolina Press, 1957), chap. 4.

30. Letters from John Taylor to James Madison, May 11, 1793; June 20, 1793; August 5, 1793, in "Correspondence," pp. 253–59; letters from Madison to Edmund Pendleton, December 6, 1792, and February 23, 1793, *Letters and Other Writings of James Madison* (Philadelphia: J. B. Lippincott, 1865), 1:573–74; John Taylor notes to Madison, [1799?], included in Madison Papers, Library of Congress.

31. Letter from John Taylor to Henry Tazewell, June 13, 1797, Tazewell Papers, Virginia State Library, Richmond; letter from Taylor to Wilson Cary Nicholas, May 14, 1806, Edgehill-Randolph Papers, University of Virginia; *New Views*, p. 83.

32. *New Views*, pp. 32, 50–56, 90–97.

33. Taylor's notes to Madison (1799); Neal Riemer, *James Madison* (New York: Washington Square Press, 1968), p. 83.

34. *New Views*, pp. 26, 119, 167–68.

35. Letter from James Madison to N. P. Trist, December 1831, *Letters and Other Writings of James Madison*, 4:207.

36. Letter from James Madison to Joseph C. Cabell, December 27, 1832; ibid., 4:230; to Thomas Jefferson, June 27, 1823, ibid., 3:326; to W. C. Rives, ibid., 4:4, 313. Beveridge pointed out that Madison was a strong supporter of the Judiciary Act of 1789, Section 25, which allowed review of state court decisions on writ of error. *Life of John Marshall* (Boston: Houghton, Mifflin Company, 1919), 3:129. Madison's interpretation of Taylor's advocacy of the power of the judiciary to review state court decisions was warranted, for *Argument* talks of the possibility of state aristocracies (perhaps to frighten Chase into attacking the carriage tax) and the danger of disunion.

37. Letter from James Madison to Thomas Jefferson, June 27, 1823.

38. Letter from John Taylor to James Monroe, April 29, 1823, in "Correspondence," p. 352.

39. *Definition*, p. 2. Also see Riemer, pp. 126–27.

40. The Taylor-Nicholas correspondence has been referred to frequently throughout this study. Taylor's criticism of Nicholas's banking opinions was contained in a letter to Nicholas, June 14, 1805, Edgehill-Randolph Papers. A convenient small anthology of Randolph's speeches is reprinted as an appendix to Russell Kirk's study, *John Randolph of Roanoke*. See especially pp. 384–87, 431–57. Also see letter from John Randolph to James Mercer Garnett, April 26, 1824, Letters of John Randolph of Roanoke to James Mercer Garnett, Library of Congress.

41. The study by Norman K. Risjord, *The Old Republicans* (New York: Columbia University Press, 1965) has been referred to frequently in previous chapters and is an excellent study of the voting behavior of Old Republican statesmen. The revival of Old Republicanism after 1820 is best described in James Mercer Garnett's letter to John Randolph, January 3, 1820, Letters of John Randolph of Roanoke to James Mercer Garnett, in which Garnett said:

> *You* were actually toasted lately at a Public meeting in Prince Georges where there were some men present who, but a few short years before, would probably have seen you *roasted,* almost as soon as drink your health. Old Trismegistus [John Taylor] too is now eulogised to the skies by many who not long since would have thought it a national blessing for him to be hanged.

The role of Spencer Roane in this revival is described by Harry Ammon, "The Richmond

Junto, 1800–1824," *Virginia Magazine of History and Biography*, 61 (October 1953): 407–8. Taylor's disavowal of influence on Randolph was contained in a letter to Thomas Ritchie published in the *Enquirer*, March 14, 1809, in which Taylor said that up to that time he had never spent over three hours at one time with Randolph. Taylor criticized the latter's voting inconsistencies in a letter to Nicholas, November 30, 1807, Edgehill-Randolph Papers. Also see *McCulloch* v. *Maryland*, 4 Wheaton 316; *Martin* v. *Hunter's Lessee*, 1 Wheaton 304; *Cohens* v. *Virginia*, 6 Wheaton 264.

42. Letters from John Adams to Thomas Jefferson, September 15, 1813; November 12, 1813; March 14, 1814, all in *The Writings of Thomas Jefferson*, 20:69, 80, 90; letters from Adams to John Taylor, March 12, 1819 and April 12, 1824 in *Works of John Adams*, 10:375, 413. Also letter to Taylor, April 9, 1814, Duke University. One of Taylor's last projects in the Senate was working with Monroe and John Quincy Adams to get a convention between Britain and the United States declaring the slave trade piracy, through the Senate. See *Memoirs of John Quincy Adams*, Charles Francis Adams, ed., (Philadelphia: J. B. Lippincott, 1875), 6:344–45. Taylor's final evaluation of the Adams family was included in a letter to James Monroe, April 29, 1823, in "Correspondence," pp. 348–53. Taylor was ready to start a campaign in Virginia for Adams and Calhoun if Monroe could get Jefferson to join.

43. The collection of thirty-two letters is in *Works of John Adams*, 6:443f. Page references related to this discussion are 447–48, 450, 452, 456–57, 460, 461–62, 471, 493–94, 504, 506, 509–20.

44. Ibid., pp. 451, 456, 457, 461, 506. Adams's clearest definition of aristocracy was "all those men who can command, influence, or procure more than an average of votes; by an aristocrat every man who can and will influence one man to vote besides himself." Adams assumed that such men existed in Caroline County: "These are every one of them aristocrats, and you, who are the first of them, are the most eminent aristocrat of them all" (p. 506).

45. Thornton Anderson, *Jacobson's Development of American Political Thought* (New York: Appleton-Century-Crofts, Inc., 1961), p. 299; Albert J. Beveridge, 4:313–17.

46. John P. Frank, *Justice Daniel Dissenting* (Cambridge, Mass.: Harvard University Press, 1964), pp. 213–26.

47. Charles G. Haines and Foster H. Sherwood, *The Role of the Supreme Court in American Government and Politics 1835–1864* (Berkeley and Los Angeles: University of California Press, 1957) pp. 17–20; Alpheus T. Mason and Richard H. Leach, *In Quest of Freedom* (Englewood Cliffs, N. J.: Prentice-Hall, Inc., 1960), pp. 243–45.

48. Louis Hartz, *The Liberal Tradition in America* (New York: Harcourt, Brace and World, Inc., 1955), chaps. 6 and 7; Clement Eaton, *The Freedom-of-Thought Struggle in the Old South* (New York: Harper and Row, Publishers, 1964), chap. 1; Richard Current, *John C. Calhoun* (New York: Washington Square Press, 1963), pp. 134–35. The last source discusses the fact that the Confederate Government found it necessary to act with such vigor to fight the war that Jefferson Davis was attacked by Alexander Stephens as a consolidationist Southern nationalism was a consequence of Southern separatism.

49. Letter from John Taylor to James Monroe, April 29, 1823.

50. John C. Calhoun, *A Disquisition on Government and Selections from the Discourse* (Indianapolis, Inc.: The Bobbs-Merrill Company, Inc., 1953).

51. Ibid., pp. 3–22.

52. Ibid., p. 29.

53. Ibid., pp. 13–14; 30–33; 41–44. For the thesis that Calhoun put his whole system on the basis of group interests to the exclusion of the public interest, see Ralph Lerner, "Calhoun's New Science of Politics," *The American Political Science Review* 57 (December 1963): 918–32.

54. Hartz, pp. 158–62; Schlesinger, *The Age of Jackson* (Boston: Little, Brown and Company, 1946), pp. 308–9.

55. Jacksonian rhetoric as quoted in Marvin Myers, *The Jacksonian Persuasion* (New York: Vintage Books, 1957), chap. 5, 199; and Joseph L. Blau, ed., *Social Theories of Jacksonian Democracy* (New York: The Liberal Arts Press, 1954), pp. 69, 89.

56. Myers, pp. 30–32; Jackson's "Farewell Address" in Blau, pp. 3–5.

57. Haines and Sherwood, pp. 12–17, 393–435, 505–22; Felix Frankfurter, *The Commerce Clause Under Marshall, Taney, and Waite* (Chapel Hill, The University of North Caroline Press, 1937), pp. 49–58; *Bank of Augusta* v. *Earle*, 13 Peters 519; Cooley v. Board of Wardens, 12 Howard 299; *Charles River Bridge* v. *Warren Bridge*, 11 Peters 420; *West River Bridge Company* v. *Dix*, 6 Howard 507; *Dred Scott* v. *Sanford*, 19 Howard 393 *The License Cases*, 5 Howard 504. Daniel's view of the commerce power is often associated with Taney's, but the former accepted Marshall's doctrine of a separation between commerce and police powers in *Willson* v. *Black Bird Creek Marsh Company*, 2 Peters 245, and then expanded the definition of police power to include everything of importance. Daniel's refusal to accept the *Louisville Railway* v. *Letson* ruling, 2 Howard 497, prevented him from agreeing to view corporations as anything other than private citizens organized into a group, thus making it very difficult for any corporation to achieve complete diversity of citizenship. Consequently, Daniel used his interpretation of the Commerce and diversity of citizenship clauses to protect state ability to regulate and to prevent the federal judiciary from reviewing those regulations. See Frank, chap. 8.

58. Myers, p. 186. Also see Schlesinger, p. 308.

59. Myers, pp. 183–205; Blau, pp. 66–88; Lee Benson, *The Concept of Jacksonian Democracy* (New York: Atheneum, 1964), pp. 94–7. The Locofocos began as a faction in Tammany Hall, but broke away in 1835 and formed the Equal Rights Party, which polled 12 percent of the vote in the 1837 New York City mayoralty election. The Locofocos wanted no charters, exclusive privileges, monopolies, or any sort of governmental control except over actions that trespassed on their interpretation of natural rights. Following the panic of 1837, the Democratic Party and Martin Van Buren accepted the Locofoco logic and the faction returned to the Democratic fold.

60. Merle Curti, *The Growth of American Thought* (New York: Harper and Row, Publishers, 1964), pp. 564–70.

61. Henry George, *The Science of Political Economy* (New York: Robert Schalkenbach Foundation, 1941), pp. 152–53; 228; *Progress and Poverty* (New York: The Modern Library, 1938), p. 367; Charles M. Wiltse, *The Jeffersonian Tradition in American Democracy* (New York: Hill and Wang, Inc., 1960), pp. 246–50; Daniel Aaron, *Men of Good Hope* (New York: Oxford University Press, 1961), pp. 80–88.

62. Aaron, pp. 216–42. Veblen's phrase *force and fraud* was one often used by Taylor to refer to the techniques used by the aristocracies of medieval and modern times, respectively. See Douglas Dowd, *Thorstein Veblen* (New York: Washington Square Press, 1964), pp. xii, 10, 14, 120. Although no Jeffersonian writers seem to have had an influence on Veblen, he was sympathetic to Henry George, whose debt to Jefferson was great. See David Riseman, *Thorstein Veblen: A Critical Interpretation* (New York: Charles Scribner's Sons, 1953), p. 49.

63. Richard Hofstader, *The Age of Reform* (New York: Vintage Books, 1955), p. 70. Also see Peter Viereck, *The Unadjusted Man* (New York: Capricorn Books, 1956), chaps. 20–21; essays by Hofstadter and Viereck in *The Radical Right* (New York: Doubleday and Company, Inc., 1963), pp. 63–80, 135–54.

64. V. O. Key, Jr. and Alexander Heard, *Southern Politics* (New York: Vintage Books, 1949), pp. 668–70.

65. "Correspondence," p. 217. Dodd said that Taylor wrote under assumed names.

66. Lerner, p. 922. The devices mentioned by Calhoun were superstition, ceremonies, education, religion, and organic arrangements. The concurrent majority was one type of organic arrangement. As is evident, all the other devices mentioned by Calhoun other than organic arrangements involved the use of values and beliefs, as did Taylor's *divided powers*.

BIBLIOGRAPHY

Primary Sources

Books and Pamphlets

Adams, John. *Works of John Adams.* Edited by Charles Francis Adams. 10 vols. Boston: Little, Brown and Company, 1850–56.

Adams, John Quincy. *Memoirs of John Quincy Adams.* Edited by Charles Francis Adams. 12 vols. Philadelphia: J. B. Lippincott and Company, 1875.

Annals of the Congress of the United States. 43 vols. Washington, D.C.: Gales and Seaton, 1834–56.

Baritz, Loren, ed. *An Inquiry into the Principles and Policy of the Government of the United States.* Indianapolis, Ind.: Bobbs-Merrill, 1969.

Blau, Joseph L., ed. *Social Theories of Jacksonian Democracy.* New York: The Liberal Arts Press, 1954.

Burke, Edmund. *The Works of Edmund Burke.* 12 vols. 6th edition. Boston: Little, Brown and Company, 1880.

Calhoun, John C. *A Disquisition on Government and Selections from the Discourse.* Edited by C. Gordon Post. Indianapolis, Ind.: Bobbs-Merrill Company, Inc., 1953.

Columbus [John Taylor?] *Cautionary Hints to Congress.* Philadelphia: William H. Woodward, 1795.

Davis, Matthew L., ed. *Memoirs of Aaron Burr.* 2 vols. New York: Harper and Brothers, 1837.

Debates in the House of Delegates of Virginia, Upon Certain Resolutions Before the House. Richmond, Va.: Thomas Nicholson, 1818.

George, Henry. *Progress and Poverty*. New York: The Modern Library, 1938.

————. *The Science of Political Economy*. New York: Robert Schalkenbach Foundation, 1941.

Hobbes, Thomas. *Leviathan*. Edited by Herbert W. Schneider. Indianapolis, Ind.: Bobbs-Merrill Company, Inc., 1958.

Jefferson, Thomas. *The Writings of Thomas Jefferson*. Edited by Paul Leicester Ford. 10 vols. New York: G. P. Putnam's Sons, 1892–99.

————. *The Writings of Thomas Jefferson*. Edited by Andrew A. Lipscomb and Albert Ellery Bergh. 20 vols. Washington, D.C.: The Thomas Jefferson Memorial Association, 1903–04.

Locke, John. *Of Civil Government*. Edited by Peter Laslett. New York: the New American Library, 1960.

Madison, James. *Letters and Other Writings*. Edited by William Cabell Rives. 4 vols. Philadelphia: J. B. Lippincott and Company, 1865.

————; Hamilton, Alexander; and Jay, John. *The Federalist*. New York: The Modern Library, 1937.

Pocion [John Taylor?]. "To the Freeholders of Essex, Caroline, King and Queen, and King William." Fredericksburg, Va., 1803.

Rousseau, Jean Jacques. *The Social Contract*. Translated by Willmoore Kendall. Chicago: Henry Regnery Company, 1954.

Taylor, John. *Arator*. Petersburg, Virginia: John M. Carter, 1818.

————. *An Argument Respecting the Constitutionality of the Carriage Tax*. Richmond, Va.: Augustine Davis, 1795.

————. *Construction Construed and Constitutions Vindicated*. Richmond, Va.: Shepherd and Pollard, 1820.

————. *A Defence of the Measures of the Administration of Thomas Jefferson*. Washington, D. C.: Samuel H. Smith, 1804.

————. *Definition of Parties*. Philadelphia: Francis Bailey, 1794.

————. *An Enquiry into the Principles and Tendencies of Certain Public Measures*. Philadelphia: Thomas Dobson, 1794.

————. *An Inquiry into the Principles and Policy of the Government of the United States*. Fredericksburg, Va.: Green and Cady, 1814.

————. *New Views of the Constitution of the United States*. Washington, D. C.: Way and Gideon, 1823.

————. *Tyranny Unmasked*. Washington, D.C.: Davis and Force, 1822.

Veblen, Thorstein. *The Theory of the Leisure Class*. New York: The Modern Library, 1934.

"We the People" [John Taylor?]. "To the Freeholders of Essex, Caroline, King and Queen, and King William." Fredericksburg, Va. 1803.

Articles and Published Letters

McIlwaine, H. R., ed. "Journal of the House of Delegates for the Session Beginning the First of March, 1781." *Bulletin of the Virginia State Library* 17 (January 1928): 3–61.

Taylor, John. "Artificial Grasses." *American Farmer* 1 (November 12, 1819): 259–62.

———. "John Taylor Correspondence." Edited by William E. Dodd. *The John P. Branch Historical Papers of Randolph-Macon College* 2 (June 1908):253–353.

———. "Letters of John Taylor of Caroline." Edited by Hans Hammond. *The Virginia Magazine of History and Biography* 52 (January 1944): 1–14, and (April 1944): 121–34.

———. "A Letter on the Necessity of Defending the Rights and Interests of Agriculture, Addressed to the Delegation of the United Agricultural Societies of Virginia." *American Farmer* 3 (July 20, 1821): 431–33.

———. Letter from John Taylor to Timothy Dwight, September 1805, in "A Sheaf of Old Letters." Edited by David R. Barbee. *Tyler's Quarterly Historical and Genealogical Magazine* 32 (October 1950): 82–84.

———. Letters from John Taylor to George W. Jeffreys in *American Farmer* 2 (February 16, 1818): 374; (February 23, 1818): 380; (April 20, 1820): 31; (June 16, 1820): 93; (September 29, 1820): 212; (October 13, 1820): 229–30; (January 26, 1821): 348–49; (February 2, 1821): 357; (February 9, 1821): 366; (March 9, 1821): 397; (March 23, 1821): 415.

———. Letter from John Taylor to James Madison, May 11, 1794 in *Disunion Sentiment in Congress in 1794.* Edited by Gaillard Hunt. Washington, D.C. W. H. Lowdermilk and Company, 1905.

———. Letters from John Taylor to Thomas Ritchie in *A Pamphlet Containing a Series of Letters Written by Colonel John Taylor, of Caroline, to Thomas Ritchie, Editor of the "Enquirer" . . . Richmond in Consequence of an Unwarrantable Attack Made by that Editor upon Colonel Taylor.* Edited by E. C. Stanard. Richmond, Va., 1809.

———. "The Memorial of the Merchants, Agriculturalists, and Others, of the Town of Fredericksburgh and Adjacent County." *American Farmer* 2 (September 22, 1820): 201–2.

———. "The Necessities, Competency, and Profit of Agriculture." *Niles' Weekly Register,* Supplement to no. 2, 3 and 15 n.s. (November 7, 1818): 178–80.

———. "Original Letters: Col. John Taylor to Edmund Pendleton." *William and Mary Quarterly* (October 1895), p. 103.

———. "Remonstrance to Congress Regarding the Indifference to the South's Plight." *Tyler's Quarterly Historical and Genealogical Magazine* 12 (1930): 39–41.

Manuscript Collections

The Ayres Family Papers, 1741–1892. Virginia Historical Society, Richmond.

Baylor Family Papers. University of Virginia Library, Charlottesville.

Carter Family-Sabine Hall Papers. University of Virginia Library, Charlottesville.

William Garnett Chisholm Papers. Virginia Historical Society, Richmond.

Edgehill-Randolph Papers. Univeristy of Virginia Library, Charlottesville.

Jefferson Papers. University of Virginia Library, Charlottesville.

Lieper Family Letters. University of Virginia Library, Charlottesville.

Madison Papers. Library of Congress, Washington, D.C.

Miscellaneous Manuscripts. Virginia State Library, Richmond.

Wilson Cary Nicholas Papers. Library of Congress, Washington, D.C.

Gabriella Page Papers. Virginia Historical Society, Richmond.

Preston Papers. Virginia Historical Society, Richmond.

Letters of John Randolph of Roanoke to James Mercer Garnett. Transcripts. Library of Congress, Washington, D.C.

Letters from John Randolph of Roanoke to John Taylor. Massachusetts Historical Society, Boston.

The Stuart Family Papers, 1785–1888. Virginia Historical Society, Richmond.

Correspondence of Chancellor Creed Taylor, 1766–1836. University of Virginia Library, Charlottesville.

John Taylor Letters and Papers. Virginia State Library, Richmond.

John Taylor Papers. Duke University Library, Durham, North Carolina.

Letter from John Taylor to Wilson Cary Nicholas. Massachusetts Historical Society, Boston.

Letter from John Taylor to Wilson Cary Nicholas. New York Historical Society, New York City.

John Taylor letters to Edmund Pendleton. New York Historical Society, New York City.

John Taylor letter to Timothy Pickering. Massachusetts Historical Society, Boston.

Pendleton, Edmund, Jr. Third Census of the United States (Year 1810) for the County of Caroline, State of Virginia. Washington, D.C.: Library of Congress, 1934.

The State Records of North Carolina. Edited by Walter Clark. 26 vols. Raleigh, N. C.: P. M. Hale, 1886–1907, vol. 16, 1899; vol. 19, 1901; vol. 24, 1905.

United States Bureau of the Census. *Heads of Families at the First Census of the United States Taken in the Year 1790: Records of the State Enumerations: 1782 to 1785; Virginia.* Baltimore, Md. Genealogical Publishing Company, 1966.

————. *Historical Statistics of the United States: Colonial Times to 1957.* Washington, D.C.: United States Government Printing Office, 1960.

United States Congress, House of Representatives. *Biographical Directory of the American Congress, 1774–1927.* Washington, D.C.: United States Government Printing Office, 1928.

United States Congress, House of Representatives, Committee on the Judiciary. *The Constitution of the United States.* Washington, D.C.: United States Government Printing Office, 1967.

Virginia State Legislature. *Journal of the House of Delegates, 1798.* Richmond, Va.: Meriwether Jones and John Dixon, Printers, 1798.

John Taylor letters to Lucy Penn Taylor. Virginia Historical Society, Richmond.

Letters from John Taylor to Prominent Men, microfilm. University of Virginia Library, Charlottesville.

John Taylor letter to unknown. Massachusetts Historical Society, Boston.

Manuscripts Relating to John Taylor. University of Virginia Library, Charlottesville.

Deed Made Between John and Lucy Taylor and Their Son, Edmund, September 12, 1809. Caroline County, Va. Duke University Library, Durham, N. C.

Tazewell Papers. Virginia State Library, Richmond.

Government Publications

Calendar of Virginia State Papers and Other Manuscripts Preserved in the Capitol at Richmond. 11 vols. Edited by William B. Palmer and Sherwin McRae. Richmond, Va., Rush U. Deer, Superintendent of Public Printing, 1875–93.

Caroline County Legislative Petition, no. 634, June 1, 1781. Virginia State Library, Richmond.

Caroline County Legislative Petition, December 9, 1816. Virginia State Library, Richmond.

Court Decisions

Bank of Augusta v. *Earle,* 13 Peters 519.

The Reverend John Bracken v. *The Visitors of William and Mary College,* 3 Call (7 Va.) 583 (1790).

Charles River Bridge v. *Warren Bridge,* 11 Peters 420.

Cohens v. *Virginia,* 6 Wheaton 264.

Cooley v. *Board of Wardens,* 12 Howard 299.

Dartmouth College v. *Woodward,* 4 Wheaton 518.

Dred Scott v. *Sanford,* 19 Howard 393.

Fletcher v. *Peck,* 6 Cranch 87.

Hamilton v. *Maze,* 4 Call (8 Va.) 197 (1791).

Hylton v. *United States,* 3 Dallas 171.

The License Cases, 5 Howard 504.

Louisville Railway v. *Letson,* 2 Howard 497.

McCulloch v. *Maryland,* 4 Wheaton 316.

Martin v. *Hunter's Lessee,* 1 Wheaton 304.

National Labor Relations Board v. *Jones and Laughlin Steel Corporation,* 301 U.S. 1.

Sturges v. *Crowninshield,* 4 Wheaton 122.

Willson v. *Black-Bird Creek Marsh Company,* 2 Peters 245.

Secondary Sources

Books

Aaron, Daniel. *Men of Good Hope.* New York: Oxford University Press, 1961.

Adams, Randolph G. *Political Ideas of the American Revolution.* New York: Barnes and Noble, Inc., 1958.

Anderson, Thornton, ed. *Jacobson's Development of American Political Thought.* New York: Appleton-Century-Crofts, Inc., 1961.

Aptheker, Herbert. *Nat Turner's Slave Rebellion.* New York: Grove Press, 1966.

Arieli, Yehoshua. *Individualism and Nationalism in American Ideology.* Cambridge, Mass.: Harvard University Press, 1964.

Bailyn, Bernard. *The Ideological Origins of the American Revolution.* Cambridge, Mass.: Harvard University Press, 1967.

———. *The Origins of American Politics.* New York: Vintage Books, 1968.

Baritz, Loren. *City on a Hill.* New York: John Wiley and Sons, Inc., 1964.

Barnes, Harry Elmer. *A History of Historical Writing.* New York: Dover Publications, 1962.

Beard, Charles A. *An Economic Interpretation of the Constitution of the United States.* New York: The MacMillan Company, 1961.

————. *Economic Origins of Jeffersonian Democracy.* New York: The Free Press, 1965.

Becker, Carl L. *The Declaration of Independence.* New York: Vintage Books, 1942.

————. *The Heavenly City of the Eighteenth-Century Philosophers.* New Haven, Conn.: Yale University Press, 1932.

Bell, John Fred. *A History of Economic Thought.* New York: The Ronald Press Company, 1953.

Benson, Lee. *The Concept of Jacksonian Democracy.* New York: Atheneum Press, 1964.

Beveridge, Albert J. *The Life of John Marshall.* 4 vols. Boston: Houghton, Mifflin Company, 1919.

Binkley, Wilfred E. *American Political Parties.* New York: Alfred A. Knopf, 1959.

Bone, Hugh A. *American Politics and the Party System.* New York: McGraw-Hill Book Company, 1965.

Boorstin, Daniel J. *The Lost World of Thomas Jefferson.* Boston: Beacon Press, 1963.

Bridenbaugh, Carl. *Myths & Realities: Societies of the Colonial South.* New York: Atheneum, 1974.

Brodie, Fawn M. *Thomas Jefferson: an Intimate History.* Toronto: Bantam Books, Inc., 1974.

Brown, Robert, and Brown, Katherine. *Virginia, 1705–1786: Democracy or Aristocracy?* East Lansing, Mich.: Michigan State University Press, 1964.

Cambell, T.E. *Colonial Caroline: A History of Caroline County, Virginia.* Richmond, Va.: The Dietz Press, Inc., 1954.

Carpenter, Jesse Thomas. *The South as a Conscious Minority, 1789–1861.* New York: New York University Press, 1930.

Cash, Wilbur J. *The Mind of the South.* New York: Vintage Books, 1941.

Cassirer, Ernst. *The Philosophy of the Enlightenment.* Princeton, N.J.: Princeton University Press, 1951.

Charles, Joseph. *The Origins of the American Party System.* New York: Harper and Brothers, 1961.

Colbourn, H. Trevor. *The Lamp of Experience.* New York: W. W. Norton & Company, Inc., 1965.

Craven, Avery O. *Soil Exhaustion as a Factor in the Agricultural History of Virginia and Maryland, 1606–1860.* Urbana, Ill.: University of Illinois Press, 1926.

Cunningham, Noble E., Jr. *The Jeffersonian Republicans: The Formation of Party Organization, 1789–1801.* Chapel Hill, N. C.: The University of North Carolina Press, 1957.

———. *The Jeffersonian Republicans in Power: Party Operations, 1801–1809.* Chapel Hill, N.C.: The University of North Carolina Press, 1963.

Current, Richard N. *John C. Calhoun.* New York: Washington Square Press, Inc., 1963.

Curti, Merle. *The Growth of American Thought.* New York: Harper and Row, Publishers, 1964.

Dangerfield, George. *The Era of Good Feelings.* New York: Harcourt, Brace and World, Inc., 1963.

Dowd, Douglas. *Thorstein Veblen.* New York: Washington Square Press, Inc., 1964.

Eaton, Clement. *The Freedom-of-Thought Struggle in the Old South.* New York: Harper and Row, Publishers, 1964.

———. *Growth of Southern Civilization, 1790–1860.* New York: Harper and Brothers, 1961.

Frank, John P. *Justice Daniel Dissenting.* Cambridge, Mass.: Harvard University Press, 1964.

Frankfurter, Felix. *The Commerce Clause under Marshall, Taney, and Waite.* Chapel Hill, N.C.: The University of North Carolina Press, 1937.

Gay, Peter. *The Enlightenment: an Interpretation, the Rise of Modern Paganism.* New York: Vintage Books, 1968.

Grimes, Alan P. *American Political Thought.* New York: Henry Holt and Company, 1955.

Hacker, Louis M. *The Triumph of American Capitalism.* New York: McGraw-Hill Book Company, 1965.

Haines, Charles G., and Sherwood, Foster H. *The Role of the Supreme Court in American Government and Politics, 1835–1864.* Berkeley and Los Angeles, Calif.: University of California Press, 1957.

Hammond, Bray. *Banks and Politics in America.* Princeton, N. J.: Princeton University Press, 1957.

Hartz, Louis. *The Liberal Tradition in America.* New York: Harcourt, Brace and World, Inc., 1955.

Hofstadter, Richard. *The Age of Reform.* New York: Vintage Books, 1955.

Hunt, Gaillard. *Disunion Sentiment in Congress in 1794.* Washington, D.C.: W. H. Lowdermilk and Company, 1905.

Hunter, Floyd. *Community Power Structure.* Garden City, N. Y.: Doubleday and Company, Inc., 1953.

Huntington, Samuel P. *The Soldier and the State.* Cambridge, Mass.: Harvard University Press, 1959.

Jenkin, Thomas P. *The Study of Political Theory.* Garden City, N. Y.: Doubleday and Company, Inc., 1955.

Jensen, Merrill. *The New Nation.* New York: Vintage Books, 1965.

Key, V. O., and Heard, Alexander. *Southern Politics.* New York: Vintage Books, 1949.

Kirk, Russell. *John Randolph of Roanoke.* Chicago: Henry Regnery Company, 1964.

Koch, Adrienne. *The Philosophy of Thomas Jefferson.* Chicago: Quadrangle Books, 1964.

Kurtz, Stephen G. *The Presidency of John Adams: The Collapse of Federalism, 1795–1800.* New York: A. S. Barnes and Company, 1957.

Labaree, Leonard Woods. *Conservatism in Early American History.* Ithaca, N. Y.: Cornell University Press, 1959.

Littell, Franklin Hamlin. *From State Church to Pluralism.* Garden City, N. Y.: Doubleday and Company, Inc., 1962.

Lynd, Staughton. *Intellectual Origins of American Radicalism.* New York: Vintage Books, 1968.

McDonald, Forrest. *We the People.* Chicago: The University of Chicago Press, 1958.

Maier, Pauline. *From Resistance to Revolution.* New York: Vintage Books, 1972.

Main, Jackson Turner. *Political Parties Before the Constitution.* New York: W. W. Norton & Company, Inc., 1973.

Martin, Joseph. *A New and Comprehensive Gazetteer of Virginia and the District of Columbia.* Charlottesville, Va.: Joseph Martin, 1836.

Martin, Kingsley. *French Liberal Thought in the Eighteenth Century.* New York: Harper and Row, Publishers, 1962.

Mason, Alpheus Thomas, and Leach, Richard H. *In Quest of Freedom.* Englewood Cliffs, N. J.: Prentice-Hall, Inc., 1959.

Mays, David John. *Edmund Pendleton.* 2 vols. Cambridge, Mass.: Harvard University, 1952.

Meade, Bishop William. *Old Churches, Ministers, and Families of Virginia.* Philadelphia: J. B. Lippincott Company, 1897.

Miller, John C. *Crisis in Freedom: The Alien and Sedition Acts.* Boston: Little, Brown and Company, 1951.

Mudge, Eugene. *The Social Philosophy of John Taylor of Caroline.* New York: Columbia University Press, 1939.

Myers, Marvin. *The Jacksonian Persuasion.* New York: Vintage Books, 1957.

Niebuhr, H. Richard. *The Social Sources of Denominationalism.* New York: Meridian Books, 1957.

Padover, Saul K. *The Genius of America.* New York: McGraw-Hill Book Company, Inc., 1960.

Palmer, R. R. *The Age of the Democratic Revolution: The Challenge.* Princeton, N. J.: Princeton University Press, 1959.

Parrington, Vernon L. *Main Currents in American Thought.* 3 vols. New York: Harcourt, Brace and Company, 1930.

Peterson, Merrill D. *The Jefferson Image in the American Mind.* New York: Oxford University Press, 1962.

Phillips, Ulrich B. *American Negro Slavery.* New York: D. Appleton and Company, 1918.

Polsby, Nelson W. *Community Power and Political Theory.* New Haven, Conn.: Yale University Press, 1963.

Ranney, Austin. *The Doctrine of Responsible Party Government.* Urbana, Ill.: University of Illinois Press, 1962.

Riemer, Neal. *James Madison.* New York: Washington Square Press, Inc., 1968.

Riesman, David. *Thorstein Veblen: A Critical Interpretation.* New York: Charles Scribner's Sons, 1953.

Risjord, Norman K. *The Old Republicans.* New York: Columbia University Press, 1965.

Schlesinger, Arthur M., Jr. *The Age of Jackson.* Boston: Little, Brown and Company, 1946.

Simms, Henry H. *Life of John Taylor.* Richmond, Va.: The William Byrd Press, Inc., 1932.

Sorauf, Frank J. *Political Parties in the American System.* Boston: Little, Brown and Company, 1964.

Spain, August O. *The Political Theory of John C. Calhoun.* New York: Bookman Associates, 1951.

Stampp, Kenneth. *The Peculiar Institution.* New York: Vintage Books, 1956.

Strauss, Leo. *Natural Right and History.* Chicago: The University of Chicago Press, 1953.

Viereck, Peter. *The Unadjusted Man.* New York: Capricorn Books, 1956.

White, Leonard, D. *The Jeffersonians.* New York: The Free Press, 1965.

Wiltse, Charles M. *The Jeffersonian Tradition in American Democracy.* New York: Hill and Wang, Inc., 1960.

Vile, M.J.C. *Constitutionalism and the Separation of Powers.* Oxford: Clarendon Press, 1967.

Wingfield, Marshall. *A History of Caroline County, Virginia.* Richmond, Va.: Press of Trevvett, Christian, and Company, 1924.

Wish, Harvey. *George Fitzhugh: Propagandist of the Old South.* Baton Rouge, La.: Louisiana State University Press, 1943.

Wood, Gordon S. *The Creation of the American Republic, 1776–1787.* New York: W. W. Norton & Company, Inc., 1969.

Wright, Louis B. *The First Gentlemen of Virginia.* Charlottesville, Va.: The University Press of Virginia, 1964.

Articles

Ammon, Harry. "The Richmond Junto, 1800–1824." *Virginia Magazine of History and Biography* 61 (October 1953): 395–418.

Bailor, Keith M. "John Taylor of Caroline: Continuity, Change, and Discontinuity in Virginia's Sentiments toward Slavery, 1790–1820." *Virginia Magazine of History and Biography* 75 (July 1967): 290–304.

Beach, Rex. "Spencer Roane and the Richmond Junto." *William and Mary College Quarterly,* n.s. 22 (January 1942): 1–17.

Chandler, J.A.C., and Swen, E. G. "Notes Relating to Some of the Students Who Attended the College of William and Mary, 1753–1770." *William and Mary College Quarterly,* n.s. 1 (January 1921): 40.

————. "Notes Relative to Some of the Students Who Attended the College of William and Mary, 1770–1778." *William and Mary College Quarterly,* n.s. 1 (April 1921): 116, 128.

Craven, Avery O. "The Agricultural Reformers of the Ante-Bellum South." *American Historical Review* 33 (January 1928): 302–14.

————. "John Taylor and Southern Agriculture." *Journal of Southern History* 4 (1938): 137–47.

Current, Richard N. "John C. Calhoun, Philosopher of Reaction." *Antioch Review* 3 (June 1943): 223–34.

Dauer, Manning, and Hammond, Hans. "John Taylor: Democrat or Aristocrat?" *Journal of Politics* 6 (November 1944): 381–403.

Drell, Bernard. "John Taylor and the Preservation of an Old Social Order." *Virginia Magazine of History and Biography* 46 (1938): 285–98.

Dodd, William E. "John Taylor of Caroline, Prophet of Secession." *The John P. Branch Historical Papers of Randolph-Macon College* 2 (June 1908): 214–52.

Dorfman, Joseph. "The Economic Philosophy of Thomas Jefferson." *Political Science Quarterly* 55 (March 1940): 98–121.

Grampp, William D. "John Taylor: Economist of Southern Agrarians." *Southern Economic Journal* 11 (January 1944): 255–68.

———. "A Reexamination of Jeffersonian Economics." *Southern Economic Journal* 12 (January 1946): 263–82.

Lerner, Ralph. "Calhoun's New Science of Politics." *The American Political Science Review* 57 (December 1963): 918–32.

McConnell, Grant. "John Taylor and the Democratic Tradition." *Western Political Quarterly* 4 (March 1951): 17–31.

Randolph, Sarah Nicholas. "The Kentucky Resolutions in a New Light." *The Nation* 44 (1887): 382–84.

Stanard, William G., ed. "The Beverley Family." *Virginia Magazine of History and Biography* 22 (January 1914): 102.

Taylor, Joe W. "The Taylor Family." *William and Mary College Quarterly* 12 (October 1903): 129–34.

Wright, Benjamin F. "The Philosopher of Jeffersonian Democracy." *The American Political Science Review* 22 (November 1928): 870–92.

INDEX